Statistics for Social Science and Public Policy

Advisors:
S.E. Fienberg D. Lievesley J. Rolph

Springer
New York
Berlin
Heidelberg
Hong Kong
London
Milan
Paris
Tokyo

Statistics for Social Science and Public Policy

Brennan: Generalizability Theory.
Devlin/Fienberg/Resnick/Roeder (Eds.): Intelligence, Genes, and Success: Scientists Respond to *The Bell Curve.*
Finkelstein/Levin: Statistics for Lawyers, Second Edition.
Gastwirth (Ed.): Statistical Science in the Courtroom.
Handcock/Morris: Relative Distribution Methods in the Social Sciences.
Johnson/Albert: Ordinal Data Modeling.
Morton/Rolph: Public Policy and Statistics: Case Studies from RAND.
von Davier/Holland/Thayer: The Kernel Method of Test Equating.
Zeisel/Kaye: Prove It with Figures: Empirical Methods in Law and Litigation.

Alina A. von Davier
Paul W. Holland
Dorothy T. Thayer

The Kernel Method of Test Equating

With 63 Illustrations

Springer

Alina A. von Davier
Paul W. Holland
Dorothy T. Thayer
Educational Testing Service
Rosedale Road 12-T
Princeton, NJ 08541
USA

avondavier@ets.org
pholland@ets.org
dthayer@ets.org

Advisors:

Stephen E. Fienberg
Department of Statistics
Carnegie Mellon University
Pittsburgh, PA 15213
USA

Denise Lievesley
Institute for Statistics
Room H.113
UNESCO
7 Place de Fontenoy SP
75352 Paris 07
France

John Rolph
Department of Information and
Operations Management
Graduate School of Business
University of Southern California
Los Angeles, CA 90089
USA

Library of Congress Cataloging-in-Publication Data
Davier, Alina von.
The Kernel method of test equating / Alina von Davier, Paul Holland, Dorothy Thayer.
p. cm. — (Statistics for social science and public policy)
Includes bibliographical references and index.
ISBN 0-387-01985-5 (alk. paper)
1. Examinations—Scoring. 2. Examinations—Interpretation. 3. Examinations—Design and Construction. 4. Educational tests and measurements—Standards. I. Holland, Paul W. II. Thayer, Dorothy T. III. Title. IV. Series.
LB3060.77.D38 2003
371.26′01′3—dc21 2003050494

ISBN 0-387-01985-5 Printed on acid-free paper.

Printed in the United States of America.

9 8 7 6 5 4 3 2 1 SPIN 10925911

Typesetting: Pages created by the authors using a Springer LaTeX macro package.

www.springer-ny.com

Springer-Verlag New York Berlin Heidelberg
A member of BertelsmannSpringer Science+Business Media GmbH

To Matthias and Thomas
—A.A.v.D.

To John, Dawn, and Frank
—P.W.H.

To Richard
—D.T.T.

Preface

The antecedents of this book begin with the Program Statistics Research Project at Educational Testing Service (ETS). This was an initiative started in 1978 by Donald Rubin (in the Research Division) and Robert Solomon (the Executive Vice President of ETS at that time). Its purpose was to focus the statistical research interests of the newly formed Research Statistics Group on problems relevant to the work of the testing programs at ETS. Paul Holland was given the responsibility for test equating research while Rubin primarily worked on problems related to predictive validity (Rubin, 1980). These two topics are reoccurring themes for the testing programs. Of course, research on test equating has had a long history at ETS; the most notable early work was that of Lord (1950, 1955a) and Wilks (1961). In addition, Ledyard Tucker was renown for his many theoretical and practical developments in this area.

The work on test equating of the Program Statistics Research Project led to a conference on test equating in 1980 reported in Holland and Rubin (1982). A new equating method, Section Pre-Equating (Holland and Thayer, 1981), was invented as a direct consequence of the basic equating research of the project and the need for a technical response to the New York test disclosure legislation of the early 1980's (McAllister, 1993).

Kernel Equating (KE) was developed in a series of ETS technical reports as a natural next step in this program of research on test equating. The starting point was the development of useful probability models for fitting the score distributions that arise in test equating (Holland and Thayer, 1987). The log-linear models for score distributions discussed there were uniquely able to fit the real data of many practical testing situations. Prior to that work there were only a few models available for fitting score distributions and these did not deal with many of the complexities of actual test data. The next step was to develop a new equating method that could fully exploit the log-linear models for score distributions. This was quick to follow. The result was Kernel Equating. KE was developed during the late 1980's and documented in two ETS technical reports, (Holland and Thayer, 1989; Holland et al., 1989). Liou and Cheng (1995) also contributed to the development of KE by connecting it to problems of estimation when there is missing data.

After the initial flurry of this half-decade of development, further work on Kernel Equating stalled. While it remained a specialized method of some theoretical interest, during this period it was used in only one practical circumstance of which we are aware, reported in Dorans (2002). Other research and practical issues, such as DIF (Holland and Wainer, 1993), took attention away from further developments of KE at ETS. Work was done by others that showed the utility of log-linear smoothing of score distributions in test equating applications (Livingston, 1993a; Hanson, 1996). However, except for a brief evaluation study (Livingston, 1993b) nothing was done to widen the applicability of KE beyond the initial two designs discussed in the earlier technical reports—the Equivalent Groups and the Non-Equivalent groups with Anchor Test Designs.

In the summer of 2000, Holland returned to ETS after a seven-year period at the UC Berkeley Graduate School of Education and resumed his long-standing research collaboration with Dorothy Thayer. In the spring of 2001, he met Alina von Davier, a mathematical statistician who was looking for interesting research questions. Their conversations led her to join the research staff at ETS in the summer of 2001 and to the subsequent decision for the three authors to write this book. It was realized early on that to be useful, the book would need to include ways to apply KE to all of the usual equating designs. This required a good deal of new research that was carried out as the book was written and supported by the ETS Research Allocation.

Not only were we able to apply KE to all of the usual designs, but our research also led us to new ideas including the Standard Error of Equating Difference (SEED), a measure of the accuracy of the estimated difference between two equating functions.

By the winter of 2002, we had a good working draft of *The Kernel Method of Test Equating*, and began to try it out on those of our colleagues in R&D at ETS who have operational responsibilities for equating tests on a regular basis. We ran a workshop on KE at ETS and used it to improve the material in our initial draft of the book. This book is the final result.

However, we believe that serious further research on Kernel Equating is not only possible, but is a program likely to bear fruit. Throughout this book we indicate topics that can further illuminate and improve upon what we present here. We hope that researchers and graduate students in statistics, psychometrics, and educational measurement, looking for useful research topics, will consider some of the possibilities we indicate here, and push the work reported in this book in new directions.

It is important to remember that test equating is about 100 years old, and was used as early as the Army Alpha tests of the early part of the 20th century. By now some think that modern test theory has removed the need to equate tests, but we think this is a dream yet unrealized, and perhaps unrealizable. The equivalence of scores from different tests, no matter how carefully constructed to be parallel, is always an empirical question. The methods and models of test equating have been, for nearly a century, the way that data and theory have come to grips with this hoped-for equivalence. We do not expect it to be any different in the near future, or, perhaps, ever.

How this book is organized. The book is divided into two parts. In the first we develop the theory of Kernel Equating, and in the second, we apply it to real examples of the most important equating designs. Chapter 1 is an introduction in which we give a little history of equating, some general discussion about test linking and test equating in particular, and develop the basic notation that we use throughout the rest of the book. In addition, we review the linear and equipercentile equating functions and the standard error of equating (SEE). Chapter 2 reviews the four basic test-equating designs as well as the application of both the chain and the post-stratification approaches to the Non-Equivalent groups with Anchor Test Design. Our development of the equating designs is aimed at our later discussion of them within the context of KE. Chapters 3, 4, and 5 all deal with the mathematical basis of KE. These are technical chapters that spell out, in detail, the theory of KE. Chapter 6 compares KE to both the linear method and percentile rank method of equipercentile equating and addresses what we believe are its advantages over both.

Part II of the book begins with Chapter 7. Each of the five chapters in Part II addresses a different equating design and shows how to apply KE to it. In these chapters we use real data to show how KE can be applied in each situation. We have attempted to give enough information in each of these application chapters that practitioners can see how the new tools that KE provides work, as well as how the actual use of KE can proceed in practice. Furthermore, to aid in the use of this book as a reference for KE, we tried to make each of the chapters in Part II as similar as we could. The result is a certain amount of repetition in Chapters 7—11. We also make continual references to the appropriate parts of Part I in Chapters 7—11, as well.

Our application of KE to the Counterbalanced Design gives a new approach to equating using this design. Our treatment of both Chain and Post-Stratification Equating in the Non-Equivalent groups with Anchor Test Design is, to our knowledge, the first to give parallel developments of these two approaches from a common point of view. Finally, our development of the standard error of equating (SEE) for all of the common equating designs, including Chain Equating for the Non-Equivalent groups with Anchor Test Design, is probably the most comprehensive comparison of the SEE's since the early work of Lord (1950, 1955a).

Acknowledgements. We are indebted to ETS and to many ETSers for their assistance and encouragement in the production of this book: Drew Gitomer for financial support; John Mazzeo, Neil Dorans, Skip Livingston, Krishna Tateneni, Wen-Ling Yang, Cathy Wendler, and Miao-Hsiang Lin for encouragement, review, and valuable suggestions; Kristen Huff and Miriam Feigenbaum for their support in the process of gathering the data; and Diane Rein, Elizabeth Brophy, and Martha Thompson for their assistance in the production of the book.

This work is a collaboration in every respect and the order of the authorship is alphabetical.

Princeton, NJ

September, 2003

Alina A. von Davier

Paul W. Holland

Dorothy T. Thayer

Contents

List of Notation

The list of notation is ordered, approximately, by first appearance in the book.

TABLE 1:

Symbol	Explanation	First appearance
X, Y :	The names of two tests to be equated.	1.2
A :	The name of the anchor test in the Non-Equivalent groups with Anchor Test (NEAT) Design.	1.2
$\boldsymbol{X}$, $\boldsymbol{Y}$:	The scores from X and Y, respectively, regarded as random variables.	1.2
$\boldsymbol{A}$:	The score on the anchor test, $\boldsymbol{A}$, regarded as a random variable.	1.2
J, K, L :	Number of possible $\boldsymbol{X}$-, $\boldsymbol{Y}$-, or $\boldsymbol{A}$-scores, respectively.	1.2
x_j :	A possible score value for $\boldsymbol{X}$, $j = 1$ to J.	1.2
y_k :	A possible score value for $\boldsymbol{Y}$, $k = 1$ to K.	1.2
a_l :	A possible score value for $\boldsymbol{A}$, $l = 1$ to L.	1.2

continued on the next page

TABLE 1: *continued*

Symbol	Explanation	First appearance
T :	The target population of examinees on which the equating of $\boldsymbol{X}$ and $\boldsymbol{Y}$ takes place.	1.2
$\sum_j$:	Sum over the full range of j.	1.2
$G^{-1}(u)$:	Inverse function of G. The solution to $u = G(y)$, for a specified u.	1.4
r_j :	$\text{Prob}\{\boldsymbol{X} = x_j \mid T\}$ = the score probability of $\boldsymbol{X} = x_j$ over the target population, T.	1.2
s_k :	$\text{Prob}\{\boldsymbol{Y} = y_k \mid T\}$= the score probability of $\boldsymbol{Y} = y_k$ over the target population, T.	1.2
t_l :	$\text{Prob}\{\boldsymbol{A} = a_l \mid T\}$ = the score probability of $\boldsymbol{A} = a_l$ over the target population, T.	1.2
$F(x)$:	$\text{Prob}\{\boldsymbol{X} \leq x \mid T\}$ = cumulative distribution function (cdf) of $\boldsymbol{X}$ over T.	1.2
$G(y)$:	$\text{Prob}\{\boldsymbol{Y} \leq y \mid T\}$ = cdf of $\boldsymbol{Y}$ over T.	1.2
$H(a)$:	$\text{Prob}\{\boldsymbol{A} \leq a \mid T\}$ = cdf of $\boldsymbol{A}$ over T. Subscripts on F, G, and H indicate that the cdf's refer to other populations, i.e., P or Q.	1.2
μ_X, σ_X :	The mean and standard deviation of $\boldsymbol{X}$ over the target population, T.	1.2
μ_Y, σ_Y :	The mean and standard deviation of $\boldsymbol{Y}$ over the target population, T.	1.2
Lin_Y :	The linear equating function for equating $\boldsymbol{X}$ to $\boldsymbol{Y}$ over T.	1.3
Equi_Y :	Any version of the equipercentile equating function for equating $\boldsymbol{X}$ to $\boldsymbol{Y}$ over T.	1.4
e_Y :	Usually, the Kernel Equating function for equating $\boldsymbol{X}$ to $\boldsymbol{Y}$ over T. It is used in Chapter 1 to refer to any equating function that equates $\boldsymbol{X}$ to $\boldsymbol{Y}$ over T.	1.7

continued on the next page

TABLE 1: *continued*

Symbol	Explanation	First appearance
KE :	The Kernel Method of Equating.	1.1
EG :	The Equivalent-Groups Design.	1.6
SG :	The Single-Group Design.	1.6
CB :	The Counterbalanced Design.	1.6
NEAT :	The Non-Equivalent groups with Anchor Test Design.	1.6
SEE_Y :	The Standard Error of Equating for an equating function that equates $\boldsymbol{X}$ to $\boldsymbol{Y}$ on T.	1.7
P and Q :	Populations of examinees.	2
r_{Pj}, s_{Qk}, t_{Pl}, t_{Ql}:	Score probabilities for $\boldsymbol{X}$, $\boldsymbol{Y}$, and $\boldsymbol{A}$ over the populations P and Q (the NEAT Design).	2.4.1
$\boldsymbol{r}$:	The (column) vector of score probabilities, r_j.	2.1
$\boldsymbol{s}$:	The (column) vector of score probabilities, s_k.	2.1
$\boldsymbol{t}$:	The (column) vector of score probabilities, t_l.	2.4.1
$\boldsymbol{r}_P$, $\boldsymbol{s}_Q$, $\boldsymbol{t}_P$, $\boldsymbol{t}_Q$:	The (column) vectors of score probabilities for $\boldsymbol{X}$, $\boldsymbol{Y}$, and $\boldsymbol{A}$ over the populations P and Q (the NEAT Design).	2.4.1
DF :	Design Function.	2
df :	Degrees of freedom.	9
$\mathbb{R}^J$:	Euclidean J-dimensional space.	2.1
Ω_J:	The set of all J-dimensional score probability vectors, $\boldsymbol{r}$.	2.1
p_{jk} :	$\text{Prob}\{\boldsymbol{X} = x_j, \boldsymbol{Y} = y_k \mid T\}$ = the bivariate score probability of $\boldsymbol{X} = x_j$ and $\boldsymbol{Y} = y_k$ over the target population, T.	2.2

continued on the next page

TABLE 1: *continued*

Symbol	Explanation	First appearance
$\mathbf{P}$:	For the SG Design, the J by K matrix of bivariate score probabilities for $(\boldsymbol{X}, \boldsymbol{Y})$. For the NEAT Design, the J by L matrix of bivariate score probabilities, p_{jl}, for $(\boldsymbol{X}, \boldsymbol{A})$.	2.2
$\boldsymbol{p}_k$:	The kth column vector of $\mathbf{P}$.	2.2, 2.4
$v(\mathbf{P})$:	The vectorization of the matrix, $\mathbf{P}$. In the SG Design, $v(\mathbf{P})$ is a JK-dimensional column vector.	2.2
q_{kl} :	$\text{Prob}\{\boldsymbol{Y} = y_k, \boldsymbol{A} = a_l \mid Q\}$ = the bivariate score probability of $\boldsymbol{Y} = y_k$ and $\boldsymbol{A} = a_l$ over the population, Q.	2.4
$\mathbf{Q}$:	For the NEAT Design, the K by L matrix of bivariate score probabilities for $(\boldsymbol{Y}, \boldsymbol{A})$ on Q.	2.4
$\boldsymbol{q}_l$:	The lth column of $\mathbf{Q}$.	2.4
$v(\mathbf{Q})$:	The vectorization of $\mathbf{Q}$. In the NEAT Design, $v(\mathbf{Q})$ is a KL-dimensional column vector.	2.4
$\mathbf{I}_J$:	The J by J identity matrix.	2.1
$\mathbf{0}$:	A matrix or vector of all zeros of appropriate dimension.	2.1
$\mathbf{M}$:	A matrix of zeros and ones used to compute the column vector of the row sums of a bivariate score probability matrix, $\mathbf{P}$, from its vectorized version, $v(\mathbf{P})$. $\mathbf{M}$ is defined in equations (2.9) and (2.11). $\mathbf{M}$ with subscripts denotes versions of $\mathbf{M}$ that arise in various equating designs throughout this book.	2.2
$\mathbf{N}$:	A matrix of zeros and ones used to compute the column vector of the column sums of a bivariate score probability matrix, $\mathbf{P}$, from its vectorized version, $v(\mathbf{P})$. $\mathbf{N}$ is defined in equation (2.10) and (2.12). $\mathbf{N}$ with subscripts denotes versions of $\mathbf{N}$ that arise in various equating designs throughout this book.	2.2

continued on the next page

TABLE 1: *continued*

Symbol	Explanation	First appearance
$\mathbf{1}_J$:	A column vector of all ones.	2.2
$\boldsymbol{X}_1$:	In the CB Design, the $\boldsymbol{X}$-score that is obtain when examinees are tested first by X and second by Y. Likewise, $\boldsymbol{X}_2$, $\boldsymbol{Y}_1$, and $\boldsymbol{Y}_2$ are defined analogously.	2.3
$\mathbf{P}_{(12)}$:	The version of the bivariate score probability matrix that arises in the CB design when X is taken first and Y second. $P_{(21)}$ is defined analogously.	2.3
$p_{(12)jk}$:	The entries in the matrix, $\mathbf{P}_{(12)}$. $p_{(21)jk}$ are the entries in $\mathbf{P}_{(21)}$.	2.3
w_X, w_Y :	In the CB Design, the weight given to the data that are not subject to order effects.	2.3
$\boldsymbol{r}_1$, $\boldsymbol{s}_1$, $\boldsymbol{r}_2$, $\boldsymbol{s}_2$:	In the CB Design, the score probability vectors for $\boldsymbol{X}_1$, $\boldsymbol{Y}_1$, $\boldsymbol{X}_2$, and $\boldsymbol{Y}_2$, respectively.	2.3
w :	In the NEAT Design, the weight given to population P in the definition of the Target Population, $T = wP + (1 - w)Q$.	2.4
$e_{Y(CE)}$:	Chain Equating function equating $\boldsymbol{X}$ to $\boldsymbol{Y}$.	2.4.1
$e_{Y(PSE)}$:	Post-Stratification Equating function equating $\boldsymbol{X}$ to $\boldsymbol{Y}$.	2.4.2
$\hat{e}_{Yh_Xh_Y}$:	KE function equating $\boldsymbol{X}$ to $\boldsymbol{Y}$ using bandwidths, h_X and h_Y, in the continuization step.	3.1
$\hat{F}_{h_X}$:	The KE continuized version of $F(x)$ using a bandwidth of h_X. Defined in (4.5).	4.1
$\hat{G}_{h_Y}$:	The KE continuized version of $G(y)$ using a bandwidth of h_Y. Defined in (4.8).	4.1
$\boldsymbol{u}$:	The vector used to specify a log-linear model for score probabilities, whose dimension equals the number of score values. In our examples, $\boldsymbol{u} = \mathbf{0}$.	3.2.1

continued on the next page

TABLE 1: *continued*

Symbol	Explanation	First appearance
$\mathbf{B}$:	The **B**-matrix used to specify a log-linear model for score probabilities. Row dimension of $\mathbf{B} =$ the number of parameters in the model and the Column dimension of $\mathbf{B} =$ the number of score values.	3.2.1
$I_S(x_j)$:	The subset indicator variable, which has the value 1 if $x_j \in S$, and 0 otherwise.	3.2.1
$\mathbf{\Sigma}_{\hat{r},\,\hat{s}}$:	The cross-covariance matrix of the estimated score probability vectors, $\hat{\boldsymbol{r}}$ and $\hat{\boldsymbol{s}}$.	3.2.1
$\mathbf{\Sigma}_{\hat{r}}$:	The covariance matrix of the estimated score probability vector, $\hat{\boldsymbol{r}}$.	3.2.1
$\mathbf{C}_r$:	The **C**-matrix factor of $\mathbf{\Sigma}_{\hat{r}}$. **C**-matrices occur throughout this book, with and without subscripts, to make them appropriate to specific equating designs.	3.2.1
$\mathbf{D}_r$:	The diagonal matrix with the vector $\boldsymbol{r}$ along its main diagonal.	3.2.1
$\sqrt{\boldsymbol{r}}$:	The vector whose entries are the (positive) square roots of the vector $\boldsymbol{r}$.	3.2.1
a_X :	The value defined in equation (4.4), that is part of the definition of the KE continuization process using Gaussian Kernel smoothing.	4.1.1
h_X, h_Y :	The two bandwidths that are used to define the KE continuizations of $F(x)$ and $G(y)$. They are positive numbers. Large values of the bandwidths lead to linear equating, while smaller values give more "equipercentile-like" equating functions.	4.1.1
$\mathcal{N}(\mu,\, \sigma^2)$:	The Normal or Gaussian distribution with mean μ and variance, σ^2.	4.1.1
Φ :	The Normal or Gaussian cdf.	4.1.1

continued on the next page

TABLE 1: *continued*

Symbol	Explanation	First appearance
PEN_1 :	A penalty function used to chose an "optimal" bandwidth in the continuization process. Defined in equation (4.27).	4.1.2
PEN_2 :	A penalty function used to chose an "optimal" bandwidth in the continuization process. Defined in equation (4.29).	4.1.2
$\text{PRE}(p)$:	The "Percent Relative Error" in the pth moments. A tool to compare the distribution of $\boldsymbol{Y}$ with the equated values, $e_Y(\boldsymbol{X})$.	4.2
$\boldsymbol{R}$, $\boldsymbol{S}$:	A general notation to denote the pre-smoothed data that arises in any equating design. Values of $\boldsymbol{R}$ and $\boldsymbol{S}$ are specified in Table 5.1 for each equating design in this book. The related notation for the number of score values, parameter estimates and $\mathbf{C}$-matrices are given in Table 5.2.	5.2
$\mathbf{J}_{e_Y}$:	The Jacobian matrix of the KE function with respect to the score probabilities, $\boldsymbol{r}$ and $\boldsymbol{s}$. Defined in equations (5.9) and (5.19).	5.2
$\mathbf{J}_{DF}$:	The Jacobian matrix of the Design Function with respect to the score probabilities of the pre-smoothed data in each equating design. Defined in Tables 5.3 and 5.4 for the designs used in this book.	5.2
$\|\| \boldsymbol{v} \|\|$:	The Euclidean length (norm) of the vector, $\boldsymbol{v}$. The square-root of the sum of squares of its coordinates.	5.2
$\frac{\partial F}{\partial \boldsymbol{r}}$:	The row vector of partial derivatives of the KE continuized cdf, $F(x; \boldsymbol{r})$ with respect to each coordinate of $\boldsymbol{r}$. Analogously for $\frac{\partial G}{\partial \boldsymbol{s}}$.	5.3.1
F', G' :	The density functions of the continuized cdf's F and G.	5.3.1
$\mathbf{U}$, $\mathbf{V}$:	Matrices, with and without various subscripts, that are all similar and defined in the discussion of Tables 5.5 and 5.6.	5.3.2

continued on the next page

TABLE 1: *continued*

Symbol	Explanation	First appearance
SE-vector:	A vector, of the general form, $\mathbf{J}_{e_Y}\mathbf{J}_{DF}\mathbf{C}$, whose length is the value of $\text{SEE}_Y(x)$. An important computational tool for KE.	5.2
SEED_Y :	The Standard Error of Equating Difference for the difference between two equating functions that both equate $\boldsymbol{X}$ to $\boldsymbol{Y}$ on T.	5.3.3
PRM_Y :	The percentile rank method of equipercentile equating $\boldsymbol{X}$ to $\boldsymbol{Y}$.	6.2
N, M:	The samples sizes for various designs. Subscripts are added as necessary to deal with individual equating designs.	7
LR :	Likelihood ratio Chi-square statistic.	9.1

1
Introduction and Notation

> "The comparability of measurements made in differing circumstances by different methods and investigators is a fundamental pre-condition for all of science. Psychological and educational measurement is no exception to this rule. Test equating techniques are those statistical and psychometric methods used to adjust scores obtained on different tests measuring the same construct so that they are comparable."
>
> Dorans and Holland (2000)

1.1 Introduction

The assertion above follows a long line of similar claims about what test equating is, and what it is supposed to accomplish. Related observations may be found in Lord (1950, 1955a), Wilks (1961), Angoff (1971), Holland and Rubin (1982), Petersen et al. (1989), Kolen and Brennan (1995), and Dorans (2000).

The need for *test equating* arises when there are two or more tests of the same construct or subject that can yield different scores for the same examinee. The most common example is a testing *program*, as opposed to a single testing *instrument*. A testing program is a system that regularly produces different *test forms* that are similar in content and format, but may contain completely different test questions. Because the tests may contain different questions, they can vary in difficulty depending on the degree of control available in the test development process. Examinees tested with the more difficult test forms will get lower scores than they would get had they been tested with the easier forms. Because testing programs often require comparability of the scores produced on these different forms, test-equating techniques were developed to adjust for these differences in test difficulty. The goal of test equating is to allow the scores on different forms of the same tests to be used and interpreted interchangeably.

Test equating, as it is currently practiced, requires some type of control for differential examinee ability, or proficiency, in the assessment of, and adjustment for, differential test difficulty. An early reference to test equating is Kelley (1923) in a chapter entitled "Comparable Measures." Kelley uses the phrase "method of equating scores" and illustrates two common methods that continue to be used today—the linear and equipercentile equating functions. He is vague about the need to control for differential examinee ability, but seems to be aware of the problem as the following quotation suggests.

> "It is frequently desired to compare the performances of pupils receiving marks in different subjects. If the pupils have no subjects and no teacher in common this can only be done by making some assumption. If there are three teachers each with 50 pupils, it is more reasonable to assume that the mean abilities of the three groups are equal than that similar literal or percentage grades of the three teachers are equivalent." (page 120)

If we substitute "tests" for "teachers" in Kelley's remarks, then the possibility that differential examinee ability can *confound* an assessment of differential test difficulty (or teacher grading severity), and *vice versa*, is a plausible part of Kelley's thinking at that early date.

By the time the large-scale testing programs came into existence in the 1930's, 1940's and 1950's, with the need for the continual development of new test forms (the ACT and SAT being easily identified examples), test equating had become a specialized need, and regular activity of, the organizations responsible for these programs.

From the 1920's to the 1970's various test-equating methods were developed and applied to the specific circumstances of different testing programs. Gulliksen (1950) describes several methods that were developed from the 1920's to the late 1940's. Angoff (1971) codified the procedures used throughout the testing industry in a reference that is still up-to-date in many respects. In the 1980's a mathematical theory for test equating was seen to be a desirable enterprise and Lord (1980), Braun and Holland (1982), and Morris (1982) proposed different first attempts at such mathematical theories. However, it is probably fair to say that past and current discussions of test equating are less about mathematical theories of equating and more about *methods* of test equating. The scholarly work of Kolen and Brennan (1995) discusses many issues that are involved in actually doing test equating, and is an important reference for the many methods used to equate tests.

The advent of modern statistical models for test data, in particular, Item Response Theory (Lord, 1980; Hambleton et al., 1991; Thissen and Wainer, 2001; and many others), has provided new ways to think about and to carry out procedures that attempt to solve some of the problems addressed by the older test equating methods.

The focus in this book is on *observed-score test equating* (Braun and Holland, 1982), and we develop extensively one particular method called Kernel Equating (KE). Observed-score test equating is just one of several topics that fall within the general area of linking together scores from different tests. But observed-score test equating is widely applicable, is used in many diverse situations, and is a useful framework for discussing other aspects of test-score linking.

We may briefly describe observed-score equating in the following general terms. The raw scores on a new test, say test X, are to be transformed to be "equivalent" to the raw scores on an old test, say test Y. For example, it might be that a 5 on X gets "equated to" or transformed to a 6.3 on Y. The job of equating is accomplished by finding a suitable transformation, called an *equating function*, that is applied to each raw-score from test X and results in the *equivalent* Y-score for each X-score. The term "observed-score test equating" is used to distinguish it from methods that are more appropriate for transforming the "true scores" of Classical Test Theory rather than transforming the observed scores that examinees obtain on real tests (Lord and Novick, 1968; Feldt and Brennan, 1989). We give a more precise definition of observed-score equating in Section 1.4.

We shall use the term "test linking" to refer to the general problem of linking or in some way connecting the scores on two different tests. We will reserve "test equating" to mean something special within the general area of test linking. Ideally, when the scores on two tests are equated they may be used interchangeably for any purpose.

While there is no unified perspective on test equating, over the last century, practitioners and theoreticians have identified five guidelines or "requirements" as a core of ideas that are important for understanding the issues involved in test *equating*, as opposed to weaker (i.e., more general) forms of test *linking*. We summarize these guidelines using the words of Dorans and Holland (2000), but these ideas were explicitly stated in similar, if not, identical, terms, by Angoff (1971), Lord (1980), Petersen et al. (1989), Kolen and Brennan (1995) and probably by many others as well.

> "In addition to the many techniques for actually doing test linking, there are five 'requirements' that are often regarded as basic to all of test equating.
>
> (a) **The Equal Construct Requirement**: tests that measure different constructs should not be equated.

(b) **The Equal Reliability Requirement**: tests that measure the same construct but which differ in reliability should not be equated.

(c) **The Symmetry Requirement**: the equating function for equating the scores of Y to those of X should be the *inverse* of the equating function for equating the scores of X to those of Y.

(d) **The Equity Requirement**: it ought to be a matter of indifference for an examinee to be tested by either one of two tests that have been equated.

(e) **Population Invariance Requirement**: the choice of (sub) population used to compute the equating function between the scores of tests X and Y should not matter, i.e., the equating function used to link the scores of X and Y should be *population invariant.*"

Dorans and Holland (2000) comment on these five requirements and indicate how they are, at best, rough guidelines rather than easily verified conditions. In addition, (a)–(e) refer to different levels of analysis. For example, Equity is stated in terms of individual examinees, while Equal Reliability and Population Invariance are stated in terms of population quantities. Symmetry is about a mathematical property and Equal Construct is about the nature and possible uses of the tests.

The requirements of test equating are often regarded as the most stringent of the various methods for linking test scores (Linn, 1993; Mislevy, 1992; Angoff, 1971). We will not discuss other linking methods in this book, but for the sake of completeness we will now indicate how one might think of some of the other methods in terms of *weakening* the above five requirements.

If we ignore the Population Invariance requirement, (e), then the linking relationship is sometimes called a *concordance.* A concordance between the scores of two tests is a transformation between the scores of Y and X that is designed to hold for a *specific* population of examinees, and there is no claim that it holds for any other. The methods used to form concordances are often the very same as those used to carry out observed-score test equating. Moreover, some of the other five requirements may fail to hold sufficiently well in situations that are called concordances. For example, the Constructs the tests measure may not be the same, but may be similar; or they may not be Equally Reliable; or there may be some other sense in which the Equity Requirement does not hold well enough. The Symmetry condition often *does* hold for concordances.

In other situations, we are only interested in *predicting* the scores or the distribution of scores on one test from those on another test. *Predicting* individual scores or *projecting* distributions of scores on one test from data from another test may not involve *any* of the five requirements of equating.

Certainly, prediction is an asymmetric relationship and it is well known that regression equations do not invert in the way that the Symmetry condition requires (discussions of this point arose at least as early as Thorndike, 1922, and Otis, 1922). Tests of any type can be used to predict scores on a given test, they need not measure the same construct nor be similar in reliability. The Equity Requirement has little to do with prediction. Predictions may vary with subpopulations and, indeed, subpopulation information may be included in predictions or projections, thereby explicitly violating the Population Invariance requirement.

The five requirements of test equating are intended to insure that scores on the two tests are interchangeable. While this is a difficult goal, it is what test equating is all about.

The five requirements are helpful in deciding when equating is appropriate or inappropriate. Feuer et al. (1999) use such an approach to address the question of the feasibility of creating a system of linking functions between several commonly used standardized tests and the scale of the National Assessment of Educational Progress (NAEP).

However, the five requirements do not address the question of whether or not test equating is *necessary* or not. Not every pair of tests or test forms actually needs to be equated. This decision depends on the use to which the test are to be put and the circumstances of this use. For example, some testing programs give one test a year, and students are ranked on that test for some purpose such as college admissions. If all that the test is used for is to find the top performing students on it for that year, and the scores from one year are not ever compared to those from previous years, then equating the forms given annually to a common scale may be an unnecessary and expensive exercise. It is rarely useful to equate course exams given in high school or college because teachers often either "grade on a curve" or use their judgement as to the adequacy of each individual's test performance relative to the course goals. On the other hand, if several test forms are used throughout the testing year for a common purpose and it is important that differences between the relative difficulties of the different test forms not affect the assessment of students taking different forms, then test equating is probably necessary.

1.2 The Notation Used in This Book

We adopt a notational scheme in this book that we will apply consistently across all of the chapters. In this section we develop some of this notation and then use it in the next two sections to discuss the linear and the equipercentile equating functions. In this and the next three sections our concern is with population level quantities rather than sample estimates. We will turn to estimating equating functions in Section 1.7.

We let X and Y denote two tests or two forms of the same test. In addition, we let T denote the target population on which the observed-score equating is to be done. Following Braun and Holland (1983) and Kolen and Brennan (1995), we explicitly include the target population T in the discussion for any observed-score test equating method.

Thus, we follow Dorans and Holland (2000), in regarding satisfaction of the Population Invariance requirement of Section 1.1 as an empirical question that can only be answered by varying the target population, T. If the resulting equating functions for different Ts are different enough to have practical consequences, then we would regard the Population Invariance requirement as being violated. However, the use of a common target population is the way that we "control for" differential examinee ability in observed-score test equating. The difference in observed test performance is due to test differences, not examinee differences because the tested population is the same.

We will denote the scores on X and Y by $\boldsymbol{X}$ and $\boldsymbol{Y}$, and regard $\boldsymbol{X}$ and $\boldsymbol{Y}$ as random variables with distributions. The motivation for this is to regard $\boldsymbol{X}$ or $\boldsymbol{Y}$ as the scores of randomly selected examinees from T.

As we shall see in Chapter 2, the target population is very clear for some data collection designs used in test equating, but for other designs it needs careful definition. We will give the details of the choice of T in our discussions of the different data collection designs in Chapter 2.

Score distributions are usually discrete so that to adequately describe them we need to specify both their possible values and the associated probabilities of these possible values. This level of detail, in the description of test score distributions, is necessary to adequately describe KE.

We will denote the possible values of $\boldsymbol{X}$ by

$$x_j \quad \text{for} \quad j = 1, \ldots, J, \tag{1.1}$$

and those of $\boldsymbol{Y}$ by

$$y_k \quad \text{for} \quad k = 1, \ldots, K. \tag{1.2}$$

We then denote the score probabilities of $\boldsymbol{X}$ and $\boldsymbol{Y}$ by

$$r_j = \text{Prob}\{\boldsymbol{X} = x_j \,|\, T\} \quad \text{and} \quad s_k = \text{Prob}\{\boldsymbol{Y} = y_k \,|\, T\}\,, \tag{1.3}$$

where the probability, Prob$\{\,|\,T\}$, in (1.3), is that associated with random sampling from (or conditional on) the target population, T. We will adopt the convention of suppressing T in our notation as much as possible, but it is always implied. This is why we do not subscript r_j and s_k with a T. However, when there are other populations that must be considered, as there are in the anchor test designs discussed in Chapters 2, 10 and 11, we will make them explicit in the notation, usually as subscripts.

To help clarify our notation so far, in the simple case of "number right scoring," the possible values for $\boldsymbol{X}$ are just the consecutive integers, $x_1 = 0$,

$x_2 = 1$, $x_3 = 2$, etc. In other cases, the possible values of $\boldsymbol{X}$ and $\boldsymbol{Y}$ need not be consecutive integers and can be negative or have fractional parts—unrounded formula scores are the most well known example of this, but "theta-hats" from models that use some form of Item Response Theory are another example of scores that need not be consecutive integers. However, in all of the examples used in this book the $\{x_j\}$ and $\{y_k\}$ *are* consecutive integers. We do not give any serious consideration to other possibilities in this book.

The score probabilities, $\{r_j\}$ and $\{s_k\}$, are positive numbers that sum to unity. While the *sample* frequencies corresponding to a given score for $\boldsymbol{X}$ or $\boldsymbol{Y}$ may be zero, in the *target population* we always assume that every score is possible, and simply delete from consideration any that are not logically possible. In this book we will assume that the values of $\{x_j\}$ and $\{y_k\}$ are specified and known.

In some settings we will need to refer to an "anchor test," $\boldsymbol{A}$, and will use the following similar notation for its distribution over T :

$$t_l = \text{Prob}\{\boldsymbol{A} = a_l \,|\, T\}\,, \quad \text{for} \quad l = 1, \ldots, L\,, \tag{1.4}$$

where a_l denotes a possible value of $\boldsymbol{A}$.

In Chapters 2, 10, and 11 we will define additional notation that arises when an anchor test is part of the data collection design, but in this chapter we are interested in more general considerations and the above level of notational detail is sufficient for our purposes.

In addition to the discrete score distributions described above, we will also need a notation for the cumulative distribution functions (cdf's) of $\boldsymbol{X}$, $\boldsymbol{Y}$ and $\boldsymbol{A}$, so we set up that notation now. The cdf's of $\boldsymbol{X}$, $\boldsymbol{Y}$ and $\boldsymbol{A}$ over T are denoted by:

$$\begin{aligned} F(x) &= \text{Prob}\{\boldsymbol{X} \leq x \,|\, T\}\,, \\ G(y) &= \text{Prob}\{\boldsymbol{Y} \leq y \,|\, T\}\,, \\ H(a) &= \text{Prob}\{\boldsymbol{A} \leq a \,|\, T\}\,. \end{aligned} \tag{1.5}$$

Again, we suppress the reference to T in F, G and H, but it is always implied when we refer to these cdf's, and when we need to indicate the population that is relevant to a cdf we will include it as a subscript. This will arise in the chapters that consider anchor test designs.

We will denote the moments of $\boldsymbol{X}$ and $\boldsymbol{Y}$ over T in a familiar way whenever possible. For example, the means and standard deviations of $\boldsymbol{X}$ and $\boldsymbol{Y}$ over T are denoted as

$$\mu_X = \text{E}(\boldsymbol{X} \,|\, T), \qquad \mu_Y = \text{E}(\boldsymbol{Y} \,|\, T),$$

$$\sigma_X = \text{SD}(\boldsymbol{X} \,|\, T), \qquad \sigma_Y = \text{SD}(\boldsymbol{Y} \,|\, T),$$

where $\text{E}(\boldsymbol{X} \,|\, T)$ denotes the expected value of $\boldsymbol{X}$ over (or conditional on) T and $\text{SD}(\boldsymbol{X} \,|\, T)$ denotes the standard deviation of $\boldsymbol{X}$ over T.

As an example of our use of this notation, the moments indicated above are calculated from the possible values and the score probabilities in the following, well known, manner:

$$\mu_X = \sum_j x_j r_j, \qquad \mu_Y = \sum_k y_k s_k,$$

$$\sigma_X^2 = \sum_j (x_j - \mu_X)^2 r_j, \qquad \sigma_Y^2 = \sum_k (y_k - \mu_Y)^2 s_k. \tag{1.6}$$

Throughout this book we will use the vector notation, $\boldsymbol{r}^t = (r_1, \ldots, r_J)$, where the superscript t always denote vector transpose. The J-dimensional (column) vector, $\boldsymbol{r}$, contains all of the $\boldsymbol{X}$-score probabilities over T. Similarly, $\boldsymbol{s}$ is the corresponding K-dimensional (column) vector of $\boldsymbol{Y}$-score probabilities over T. In Appendix D we review the ideas of vectors and matrices that we use throughout this book.

We emphasize here that, in our notation, the score distributions specified by $\boldsymbol{r}$ and $\boldsymbol{s}$ *always* refer to the target population, T, on which the observed-score equating function is being computed. There may be other populations that arise besides the target population, and there may be relevant score distributions for $\boldsymbol{X}$ and $\boldsymbol{Y}$ over them, but we will use different symbols to refer to score distributions that are not computed over T. However, in specifying an observed-score equating method it is important to clearly specify the target population. In observed-score test equating, the Population Invariance requirement is always an open question that should be empirically examined.

1.3 The Linear Equating Function

Perhaps the most familiar and widely computed, if not actually used, of all the equating functions is the *linear equating function*. We denote it by $\mathrm{Lin}_Y(x)$ to indicate that $\boldsymbol{X}$ is being linearly equated to $\boldsymbol{Y}$ on T. $\mathrm{Lin}_Y(x)$ is old and well known (Otis, 1922; Hull, 1922; Angoff, 1971) and given by the formula,

$$\mathrm{Lin}_Y(x) = \mu_Y + (\sigma_Y/\sigma_X)(x - \mu_X), \tag{1.7}$$

where the relevant moments of $\boldsymbol{X}$ and $\boldsymbol{Y}$ are specified in (1.6). As usual, in the notation of (1.7) we have suppressed any explicit reference to T, but it is there implicitly because the moments of $\boldsymbol{X}$ and $\boldsymbol{Y}$ are computed over T.

It is often noted that $\mathrm{Lin}_Y(x)$ has the form of a simple linear regression function of $\boldsymbol{Y}$ on $\boldsymbol{X}$ where the correlation is assumed to be unity. This observation is more confusing that helpful—a confusion that has been pointed out repeatedly (Otis, 1922; Hull, 1922; Flanagan, 1939; Lord, 1950, 1955a)—and we will not propagate this confusion here. $\mathrm{Lin}_Y(x)$ is also called the "mu and sigma line" as well. Its main property, for use in test equating, is that it is a *transformation* of $\boldsymbol{X}$-raw scores into $\boldsymbol{Y}$-raw scores that has the property that the distribution of $\boldsymbol{X}$ is changed so that it has the same mean and variance over T that $\boldsymbol{Y}$ has, that is,

$$\mathrm{E}(\mathrm{Lin}_Y(\boldsymbol{X})\,|\,T) = \mu_Y \quad \text{and} \quad \mathrm{Var}(\mathrm{Lin}_Y(\boldsymbol{X})\,|\,T) = \sigma_Y^2\,. \tag{1.8}$$

Note that the linear regression function of $\boldsymbol{Y}$ on $\boldsymbol{X}$ would *not* satisfy the second part of (1.8), because the squared correlation coefficient would multiply σ_Y^2.

The earliest uses of the linear equating function were based on a very old notion (going back to Galton according to Kelley, 1923) of the "equivalence" of "standard scores." $\boldsymbol{X}$-score x and $\boldsymbol{Y}$-score y are *equivalent* in this sense if they are the same numbers of standard deviation units away from their respective means in T, i.e., if they have the same "standard score" or "z-score",

$$(x - \mu_X)/\sigma_X = (y - \mu_Y)/\sigma_Y\,. \tag{1.9}$$

It is a simple exercise to derive (1.7) from (1.9). It is also easy to show that the linear equating function satisfies the Symmetry requirement listed in Section 1.1. This follows from the fact that if we solve the equation, $y = \mathrm{Lin}_Y(x)$, for x in terms of y we get $x = \mu_X + (\sigma_X/\sigma_Y)(y - \mu_Y) = \mathrm{Lin}_X(y)$.

1.4 The Equipercentile Equating Function

We now turn to the most important of the observed-score equating methods, the *equipercentile equating function.* We may think of it as arising from generalizations of either (1.8) or (1.9). To generalize (1.8), we might ask if an equating function can be found that forces *all of the moments* of the transformed $\boldsymbol{X}$ to match those of $\boldsymbol{Y}$ on T. To generalize (1.9) we could propose a notion of equivalence in which x and y are *equivalent* if they are at the same *quantile* of their respective distributions over T rather than merely having the same z-score. Both of these approaches, suitably interpreted, lead to the equipercentile equating function. We begin with generalizing (1.8).

It is well known (Kennedy and Gentle, 1980, page 176) that if $F(x)$ from (1.5) were a continuous and strictly increasing cdf, then the transformed random variable $\boldsymbol{U} = F(\boldsymbol{X})$ has the uniform distribution over $(0, 1)$. Similarly, if G from (1.5) has a (properly defined) inverse, $G^{-1}(u)$, for u in $(0, 1)$, then $\boldsymbol{V} = G^{-1}(\boldsymbol{U})$ has the distribution specified by G when $\boldsymbol{U}$ has the uniform distribution on $(0, 1)$. Hence, the composed transformation $\boldsymbol{V} = G^{-1}(F(\boldsymbol{X}))$ will have exactly the same distribution as $\boldsymbol{Y}$ over T. Thus, in the case where both of the cdf's involved are continuous and strictly increasing, the transformation of $\boldsymbol{X}$,

$$\mathrm{Equi}_Y(\boldsymbol{X}) = G^{-1}(F(\boldsymbol{X})), \tag{1.10}$$

is a generalization of $\text{Lin}_Y(x)$ in (1.8) in the sense that it matches *all* of the moments of $\boldsymbol{Y}$ over T.

However, score distributions are *discrete* in most cases and therefore the cdf's are not continuous and strictly increasing, instead, they are *jump functions*, with jumps at the possible values of the discrete distribution. Hence, in order to use formula (1.10), some way must be found to deal with the discreteness of the two score distributions.

The earliest motivation for equipercentile equating comes from generalizing the notion of equivalence in (1.9) as follows. Regard $\boldsymbol{X}$-score x and $\boldsymbol{Y}$-score y as *equivalent* if

$$F(x) = u = G(y)\,, \tag{1.11}$$

for u in $(0,\,1)$. This definition, that the quantiles of the two score distributions corresponding to u are "equivalent," occurs at least as early as Kelley (1923). However, for any given value of u in (0, 1), it is almost never the case that both of the equations in (1.11) can be satisfied exactly by x and y for the same value of u. This has the same root cause that we have mentioned earlier—the discreteness of the two score distributions. Ignoring this problem for the moment, and formally solving for x in terms of y in (1.11), we obtain the same function that arises in (1.10), i.e.,

$$y = \text{Equi}_Y(x) = G^{-1}(F(x))\,. \tag{1.12}$$

If a proper meaning can be given to the inverse function in $G^{-1}(F(x))$ then (1.12) defines the *equipercentile equating function* of $\boldsymbol{X}$ to $\boldsymbol{Y}$ on T, $\text{Equi}_Y(x)$. It is also a transformation of X-raw scores into Y-raw scores, and, if done carefully, will make the distribution of $\text{Equi}_Y(\boldsymbol{X})$ even closer to that of $\boldsymbol{Y}$ than $\text{Lin}_Y(\boldsymbol{X})$ is.

All methods of equipercentile equating must circumvent the discreteness that plagues the definition of $G^{-1}(F(x))$. The equipercentile method that is in wide use, which we will call the "percentile rank method," or the PRM, replaces the discrete cdf's, $F(x)$ and $G(y)$, by piecewise linear continuous cdf's (Holland and Thayer, 1989; Kolen and Brennan, 1995; and Chapter 6). The method of Kernel Equating that we discuss in this book replaces $F(x)$ and $G(y)$ with continuous approximations that are smoother than the approximation of the "percentile rank method." The Kernel Equating method uses Gaussian kernel smoothing rather than linear interpolation.

Angoff (1971) and Kolen and Brennan (1995) both discuss how to carry out versions of the PRM so we will not discuss it further here. For the rest of this chapter we will simply assume that, in some way or another, $F(x)$ and $G(y)$ have been approximated by continuous cdf's (i.e., that F and G have been *continuized*) so that (1.12) is a meaningful definition of the equipercentile equating function on T. We will compare KE to the percentile rank method in Chapter 6.

When F and G both have proper inverses, we can easily see that any equating function of the form given in (1.12) satisfies the Symmetry condition. This is done by solving (1.12) for y in terms of x. Using the standard properties of inverse functions we have $x = F^{-1}(G(y)) = Equi_X(y)$.

We will say that a mapping from the raw scores of X to those of Y, $e(x)$, is an *observed score equating function* if it can be written in the form (1.12) where F and G can be interpreted as the (continuized) cdf's of $\boldsymbol{X}$ and $\boldsymbol{Y}$, respectively, on a common target population, T. In some cases, this is quite straightforward, as, for example, in the Equivalent-Groups and Single-Group Designs. In other cases, in particular the Non-Equivalent groups with Anchor Test Design, additional assumptions need to be made before $e(x)$ can be so interpreted. The crucial condition, in order to show that $e(x)$ *is* an observed score equating function, is that $e(x)$ has the form of the right-hand side of (1.12) over a common population of examinees.

1.5 The Relationship Between $\text{Lin}_Y(x)$ and $\text{Equi}_Y(x)$

In this section we will show that there is a close relationship between the linear and equipercentile equating functions. They are sometimes viewed as very different, but as we shall show, if $\text{Equi}_Y(x)$ is constructed carefully, then $\text{Lin}_Y(x)$ is the "linear part" or "first term" in an expansion of $\text{Equi}_Y(x)$.

We suppose that $F(x)$ and $G(y)$ have been made into continuous cdf's and that this has been done in such a way as to preserve the first two moments of $\boldsymbol{X}$ and $\boldsymbol{Y}$, respectively. This requires that means and variances that are computed from $F(x)$ and $G(y)$ are exactly the same as the means and variances computed in (1.6) using the original discrete score distributions of $\boldsymbol{X}$ and $\boldsymbol{Y}$. (We should point out that while Kernel Equating is designed to achieve this equality, the percentile rank method of making F and G continuous does not exactly reproduce the second moments of the original score distributions, though it is usually close. We discuss this point more carefully in Chapter 6.) In view of the fact that KE *does* match the appropriate moments, the results of this section, i.e., Theorem 1.1, apply to it exactly. However, in this book we will denote the KE function by $e_Y(x)$ and let $\text{Equi}_Y(x)$ denote any solution to (1.10), where F and G have been appropriately continuized.

When $F(x)$ and $G(y)$ do reproduce the first two moments of the discrete score distributions, they can be expressed in a convenient way in terms of two other continuous cdf's, $F_0(x)$ and $G_0(y)$, both of which are standardized to have mean 0 and variance 1. Thus,

$$F(x) = F_0((x - \mu_X)/\sigma_X) \quad \text{and} \quad G(y) = G_0((y - \mu_Y)/\sigma_Y). \qquad (1.13)$$

The equations in (1.13) are analogous to the way the general $\mathcal{N}(\mu, \sigma)$ cdf is expressed in terms of the $\mathcal{N}(0, 1)$ cdf, i.e., as $\Phi((x-\mu)/\sigma)$.

Once we have introduced $F_0(x)$ and $G_0(y)$, we can compute $G^{-1}(F(x))$ in terms of the standardized cdf's, $F_0(x)$ and $G_0(y)$, plus the means and standard deviations of $\boldsymbol{X}$ and $\boldsymbol{Y}$ over T. We show this next.

If $G(y) = u$, then

$$(y - \mu_Y)/\sigma_Y = G_0^{-1}(u),$$

or

$$G^{-1}(u) = \mu_Y + \sigma_Y G_0^{-1}(u). \tag{1.14}$$

In addition to showing how the inverse of G is related to that of G_0, we also need to define the "shape difference function," $\epsilon(z)$, given by

$$\epsilon(z) = G_0^{-1}(F_0(z)) - z. \tag{1.15}$$

The function $\epsilon(z)$ is a measure of how different the shapes of $F(x)$ and $G(y)$ are. If $F(x)$ and $G(y)$ only differ by location and/or scale, then they have the same shape. $F_0(x)$ and $G_0(y)$ are then identical so that $\epsilon(z)$ is identically zero. Whenever the shapes of F and G differ, $\epsilon(z)$ is *not* identically zero.

Theorem 1.1 summarizes the connection between $\mathrm{Lin}_Y(x)$ and $\mathrm{Equi}_Y(x)$ using the shape difference function to express the difference between these two basic observed-score equating functions.

Theorem 1.1. *For any target population T, $\mathrm{Lin}_Y(x)$ and $\mathrm{Equi}_Y(x)$ satisfy the following equation:*

$$\mathrm{Equi}_Y(x) = \mathrm{Lin}_Y(x) + R(x). \tag{1.16}$$

The "remainder" $R(x)$ is $\sigma_Y\,\epsilon((x-\mu_X)/\sigma_X)$ where $\epsilon(z)$ is the shape difference function defined in (1.15).

Proof. To prove Theorem 1.1, apply (1.14) and (1.13) to $G^{-1}(F(x))$ and obtain

$$\begin{aligned} G^{-1}(F(x)) &= \mu_Y + \sigma_Y G_0^{-1}(F(x)) \\ &= \mu_Y + \sigma_Y G_0^{-1}(F_0((x-\mu_X)/\sigma_X)) \\ &= \mu_Y + \sigma_Y[G_0^{-1}(F_0((x-\mu_X)/\sigma_X)) - (x-\mu_X)/\sigma_X] \\ &\quad + \sigma_Y[(x-\mu_X)/\sigma_X]. \end{aligned} \tag{1.17}$$

Then (1.17) simplifies to

$$G^{-1}(F(x)) = \mu_Y + \sigma_Y[(x-\mu_X)/\sigma_X] + \sigma_Y\epsilon((x-\mu_X)/\sigma_X), \tag{1.18}$$

which is equivalent to the assertion in (1.16). □

The remainder term, $R(x)$, in (1.16) is the difference between the two equating functions and is useful in its own right. Because $F_0(x)$ and $G_0(y)$ both have mean 0 and variance 1, the shape difference function must fluctuate around 0. This means that $\text{Equi}_Y(x)$ should wind around $\text{Lin}_Y(x)$ and they should be reasonably close to each other as functions.

Figure 1.1 shows the remainder function, $R(x)$, for an equating of two tests where the linear and equipercentile equating functions give very similar results. It is based on the data given in Chapter 7. We can see the general pattern. $R(x)$ winds around the zero line, and, in this example, is small in terms of the range of $\boldsymbol{X}$ and $\boldsymbol{Y}$ scores.

It is often of interest to discover whether or not a given equating problem is simple enough that the linear equating function is a sufficiently good solution. If the remainder term in (1.16) is small relative to the accuracy of estimating it, i.e., the *Standard Error of Equating Difference* (the SEED), discussed in Chapter 5, then the linear equating function may be an acceptable alternative to the curvilinear solution produced by the equipercentile method.

Theorem 1.1 is a slight generalization and a more precise statement of the well known fact that, when the two score distributions have the same shape, the equipercentile and the linear equating functions are the same (Angoff, 1971).

1.6 Data Collection Designs

We devote an entire chapter to the issues surrounding the way data are collected for carrying out test equating. Here we simply indicate some of the basic issues. As mentioned in Section 1.1, current test equating practice requires explicit methods for separating the effects of examinee ability from the assessment of the differences in the difficulty of the two tests. The primary way that this is accomplished is through the use of special ways of collecting the data used in the test equating process. Every test equating includes a data collection design and one or more methods of using the data to estimate the equating function. There are two basic ways that the data collection design can control for, or take account of, examinee ability in test equating. The first is by the use of "common examinees," i.e., by having the same (or similar) examinees take both tests. The data collection designs that use this approach are called here "The Equivalent-Groups (EG)," "The Single-Group (SG)," and "The Counterbalanced (CB)"Designs. These are probably the oldest designs.

The other approach to controlling for examinee ability is to use "common items" rather than common examinees. The data collection designs that use this method are called here "The Non-Equivalent groups with Anchor Test

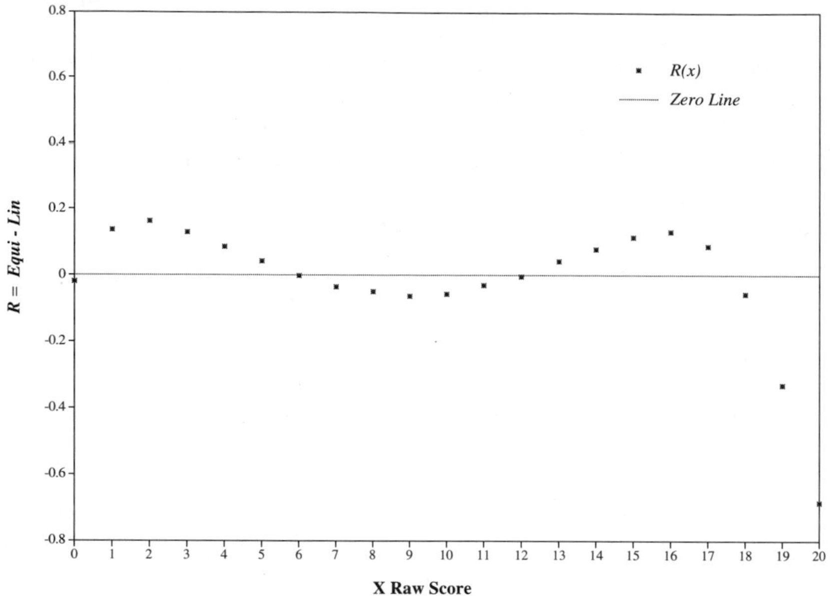

FIGURE 1.1. The difference between the equipercentile and linear equating functions from $\boldsymbol{X}$ to $\boldsymbol{Y}$.

(NEAT)" Designs and can have both internal and external anchor tests. They have been used since at least the 1940s.

The use of a particular data collection design is usually the result of many different factors, including available sample sizes, the time available for testing, test security issues, the possibility of practice or other order effects and costs. The methods that we include in this book are the most commonly used in practice.

1.7 Sample Estimates of the Equating Functions and the Standard Error of Equating

All of our development so far in this chapter has been at the population level, but in practice equating functions must be estimated using data from samples. Estimated equating functions are sample estimates of population quantities and are, therefore, subject to sampling variability. The way that the sampling variability of equating functions is measured is by the *Standard Error of Equating*, or the SEE. In this section we briefly outline some of the issues that arise in the estimation of equating functions and the computation of the SEE.

Suppose we consider an equating function that equates $\boldsymbol{X}$ to $\boldsymbol{Y}$ on T. As we can see clearly in the definition of $\mathrm{Lin}_Y(x)$ in (1.7), such population-level equating functions will depend on various parameters of the population T. In (1.7) these parameters are the means and standard deviations of $\boldsymbol{X}$ and $\boldsymbol{Y}$ over T. For other equating functions other parameters are involved. To reflect this, we denote a generic population equating function in a way that specifically includes its dependence on population parameters, i.e.,

$$e_Y(x;\, \boldsymbol{\pi}_T) = \text{ a generic population equating function,} \tag{1.19}$$

where $\boldsymbol{\pi}_T$ denotes a vector of population parameters. If we wish to reverse the direction of the equating function, and go from $\boldsymbol{Y}$ to $\boldsymbol{X}$, then we can denote this by $e_X(y;\, \boldsymbol{\pi}_T)$.

Typically, equating functions are estimated by substituting estimates of the population parameters into (1.19), i.e.,

$$\hat{e}_Y(x) = e_Y(x;\, \hat{\boldsymbol{\pi}}_T)\,, \tag{1.20}$$

where $\hat{\boldsymbol{\pi}}_T$ denotes a sample estimate of $\boldsymbol{\pi}_T$.

Hence, the uncertainty in $\hat{e}_Y(x)$ derives from the uncertainty in the estimate, $\hat{\boldsymbol{\pi}}_T$. A standard way that this uncertainty is captured is through the *delta method* (Rao, 1973; Bishop et al., 1975; Lehmann, 1999; von Davier, 2001; and Appendix A). In this approach, the limiting or asymptotic distribution of $\hat{\boldsymbol{\pi}}_T$ is first found from the Central Limit Theorem and then the Taylor expansion of $e_Y(x;\, \boldsymbol{\pi}_T)$ in $\boldsymbol{\pi}_T$ is used to find the asymptotic distribution of $e_Y(x;\, \hat{\boldsymbol{\pi}}_T)$. The standard deviation of the asymptotic distribution of $e_Y(x;\, \hat{\boldsymbol{\pi}}_T)$ is used as the Standard Error of Equating, i.e.,

$$\mathrm{SEE}_Y(x) = \text{asymptotic SD}(e_Y(x;\, \hat{\boldsymbol{\pi}}_T))\,. \tag{1.21}$$

The method of Kernel Equating discussed in this book includes an elegant and consistent system for deriving the SEE's for all of the standard data collection designs used in test equating, and we use it to develop the useful computing formulas for the SEE for Kernel Equating that are reported in this book.

In addition, in Chapter 5, we introduce the concept of the *Standard Error of Equating Difference* (the SEED). The SEED is the standard error of the difference between two equating functions. In KE it can be computed using methods similar to those for computing the SEE. In this book we give several different uses for SEED's.

1.8 A Summary of the New Material in This Book

While we were writing this book we found that we had to extend Kernel Equating in several ways beyond what had been done before. We can now treat all the standard equating designs. In addition to the Equivalent Groups (EG) and the Non-Equivalent groups with Anchor Test (NEAT) Designs, the book now includes the Single-Group (SG) Design, the Counterbalanced (CB) Design and gives a through treatment of Chain Equating in the NEAT Design.

In addition to applying KE to more designs, three new theoretical breakthroughs arose as we developed material for the applied half of the book. First, we extended the notion of the standard error of equating (the SEE) for a single equating function, to the standard error of the difference between two equating functions—the standard error of equating difference (the SEED). The SEED is a new tool, previously not available to users of any test equating method. We apply the SEED to several problem areas: (a) linear versus nonlinear equating function decisions, (b) to give an evenhanded discussion of Chain versus Post-Stratification Equating methods for the NEAT Design, and (c) to operationalize our new proposal for the CB Design. We think the SEED will have wide applicability to other equating problems.

Our second breakthrough is a new treatment of the CB Design in which the decision to use part or all of the data collected in that design is given a firmer statistical basis than ever before. Our third breakthrough is the Design Function. This function characterizes each equating design and is used to calculate both the SEE and the SEED's. The Design Function was a crucial ingredient that was missing from earlier work on KE. Finally, we have made systematic use of matrix notation in the analysis of the SEE and SEED's for each design. We use this notation to generalize the computational formulas that incorporate matrix factorizations developed earlier for the SEE's of KE. This approach has made several complicated calculations more easily analyzed than they would be otherwise and indicates the value of using this more general approach to the analysis of equating methods. In particular, the notion of the SE-vector unifies all of our calculations of SEE's and SEED's throughout this book.

Part I

The Kernel Method of Test Equating: Theory

2

Data Collection Designs

Observed score test equating has two basic components, (*i*) the data collection design and (*ii*) the equating method used. This chapter is concerned solely with (*i*), while Chapters 3, 4 and 5 are concerned with several aspects of (*ii*). Petersen et al. (1989) use the term *data collection design* and we follow this usage rather than the older, *equating experiment* (Braun and Holland, 1982). We will also use *equating design* (Kolen and Brennan, 1995) or simply *design* synonymously with data collection design.

In this book we concentrate on a single, unified approach to observed-score test equating, Kernel Equating (KE), and we show how it can be applied to each of the commonly used data collection designs. In this chapter we review the basic structure of each of these designs in a way that we can exploit in the later chapters.

Our purpose is to develop a common framework to describe each of the important equating designs in similar terms. This will allow the general description of Kernel Equating, given in the next three chapters, to be more easily connected to each of the designs discussed in Part II of the book.

In order to control for differences in examinee ability or proficiency, each data collection design must be able to provide estimates of the score probabilities, $\boldsymbol{r}$ and $\boldsymbol{s}$, of the two tests on a common target population, T (see Chapter 1, Section 1.4). For some designs these estimates are straightforward, but for others they are indirect and depend on additional assumptions. The transformation between the score data for the two tests and the pair of discrete score distributions on T, i.e., $\boldsymbol{r}$ and $\boldsymbol{s}$ defined in (1.3) in Chapter 1, will be called the *Design Function* throughout this book. The

Design Function is denoted by DF and maps the population score distributions (estimated from the raw data) into $\boldsymbol{r}$ and $\boldsymbol{s}$. As such, the DF maps the (often higher dimensional) data into the $(J+K)$-dimensional vector of score frequencies

$$\begin{pmatrix} \boldsymbol{r} \\ \boldsymbol{s} \end{pmatrix}. \tag{2.1}$$

In the Equivalent-Groups Design, the DF is simply the identity function. In other designs, i.e., the Single-Group and Counterbalanced Designs, the DF is a linear transformation; and in the Non-Equivalent groups with Anchor Test Design (NEAT), the DF for the Post-Stratification approach is a non-linear function of score probabilities. The DF for Chain Equating (CE), in the NEAT Design, is slightly different from the others we discuss. In CE, $\boldsymbol{r}$ and $\boldsymbol{s}$ are not actually estimated. Instead, there are intermediate DF's that apply to each link in the chain. We will develop the needed expressions in our discussion of CE.

The standard error of equating, the SEE, also varies with the data collection design, as well as other factors. The effect of the equating design on the SEE can be quite large. The SEE is also significantly affected by the way that the score data are pre-smoothed prior to their transformation by the DF into $\hat{\boldsymbol{r}}$ and $\hat{\boldsymbol{s}}$. In this book, we follow Holland and Thayer (1987, 2000), Livingston (1993a) and others by advocating the use of log-linear models for score distributions to estimate the univariate and bivariate score distributions that arise from the different data collection designs. As we will show in Chapter 5, the SEE for Kernel Equating has three parts, (*i*) one that depends on Kernel Equating itself (i.e., on the use of the Kernel Equating function), (*ii*) one that depends on the data collection design (through the Design Function), and (*iii*) one that depends on the method of pre-smoothing the raw data.

For each data collection design discussed in this chapter, we will (a) describe the structure of the resulting data set, (b) identify the assumptions that underlie our analysis, (c) identify the target population on which the observed score equating is being computed, (d) discuss the score probabilities , $\{r_j\}$ and $\{s_k\}$, that describe the score distributions of the two tests on the target population and the Design Function through which they are obtained from the data, and (e) mention any other material that is of special relevance to the use of the equating design.

We will focus on these important designs: the Equivalent-Groups Design (EG), the Single-Group Design (SG), the Counterbalanced Design (CB), and several versions of the Non-Equivalent groups with Anchor Test (NEAT) Design, with internal and external anchor tests.

In our discussion of the NEAT Design in this chapter we cover both "Chain Equating" and "Post-Stratification Equating" methods (the latter includes the KE version of both "Tucker's method" and "frequency estimation").

TABLE 2.1. Equivalent-Groups Design.

Population	Sample	X	Y
P	1	$\surd$	
P	2		$\surd$

2.1 The Equivalent-Groups Design (EG)

In the Equivalent-Groups (EG) Design, two independent random samples are drawn from a common population of examinees, P, the test X is administered to one sample while test Y is administered to the other. Table 2.1 is the way that we will indicate that two different samples are drawn from P with X administered to one and Y to the other, and no one taking both X and Y. We will use similar figures as a short hand for describing all of the other designs. A similar schematic notation for data collection designs is used in Braun and Holland (1982), and Petersen et al. (1989).

The EG Design is attractive because of its simplicity. The population, P, is usually easy to identify, and is the target population T. The two samples provide data that can be used to estimate $\boldsymbol{r}$ and $\boldsymbol{s}$ directly. Moreover, there are no additional assumptions to consider besides 2.1 and 2.2, below. Nor are there issues of "practice, fatigue, learning" or other "order effects" between the data for $\boldsymbol{X}$ and $\boldsymbol{Y}$ that must be considered in the use of other designs. However, this simplicity comes with a price. The EG design usually demands the largest sample sizes to achieve a given level of precision as measured by the standard error of equating. In addition, the design is not practical in those circumstances in which a test can not be reused for reasons of test security. Assumption 2.1 says that the examinees can take either test and if test security is a serious issue then it is usually not feasible for an examinee to take a test that has already been given at an earlier test administration.

The following assumptions underlie our analysis of the EG Design:

Assumption 2.1. *There is a single population P of examinees who could take either test.*

Assumption 2.2. *The two samples are independently and randomly drawn from the common population of examinees, P.*

If the test administration conditions (e.g., section time limits) are the same for the two tests, spiraled sampling can be used to create the groups. (A discussion of random vs. spiraled sampling is given in the last section of this chapter). If Assumption 2.2 does not hold and the samples are not similar with respect to the ability being measured, an unknown degree of bias will be introduced in the equating process. This violates the basic requirement of controlling for differences in examinee ability between the samples of examinees taking each test. In order to minimize the *random* differences between the samples, the sample sizes need to be large.

As indicated earlier, because the two samples are drawn from a single population, it follows that the target population, T, on which the observed-score equating will be done, is exactly the population P, from which the examinees are sampled.

Reiterating the notation introduced in Chapter 1, Section 1.2, we denote the possible raw-score values of $\boldsymbol{X}$ and $\boldsymbol{Y}$, by $x_1, \ldots, x_J$ and $y_1, \ldots, y_K$, respectively, and denote the score probabilities for $\boldsymbol{X}$ and $\boldsymbol{Y}$ by

$$r_j = \text{Prob}\{\boldsymbol{X} = x_j \,|\, T\} \quad \text{and} \quad s_k = \text{Prob}\{\boldsymbol{Y} = y_k \,|\, T\} \tag{2.2}$$

where $j = 1, \ldots, J$ and $k = 1, \ldots, K$.

Finally, denote by $\boldsymbol{r}$ the (column) vector given by $(r_1, \ldots, r_J)^t$ and by $\boldsymbol{s}$ the (column) vector given by $(s_1, \ldots, s_K)^t$.

The Design Function is, in this case, very simple because in the EG Design there is no further transformation of the data to obtain $\boldsymbol{r}$ and $\boldsymbol{s}$, i.e., they are estimated directly.

In the EG Design, the Design Function is given by

$$\begin{pmatrix} \boldsymbol{r} \\ \boldsymbol{s} \end{pmatrix} = \text{DF}(\boldsymbol{r}, \boldsymbol{s}) = \begin{pmatrix} \mathbf{I}_J & \mathbf{0} \\ \mathbf{0} & \mathbf{I}_K \end{pmatrix} \begin{pmatrix} \boldsymbol{r} \\ \boldsymbol{s} \end{pmatrix}, \tag{2.3}$$

where $\mathbf{I}_J$ is a $J \times J$ identity matrix. Thus, the DF is the identity mapping between $\Omega_J \times \Omega_K$ and itself, where

$$\Omega_J = \left\{ \boldsymbol{r} \in \mathrm{I\!R}^J : r_j > 0 \text{ and } \sum_j r_j = 1 \right\}, \tag{2.4}$$

i.e., Ω_J is the collection of all J-vectors with positive coordinates that sum to 1. Ω_K is defined analogously for K-vectors.

The Design Function is more complicated in the other equating designs.

2.2 The Single-Group Design (SG)

In the Single-Group (SG) Design, the two tests to be equated are administered to the same group of examinees drawn from a single population P. Hence, a single random sample of examinees from P takes both tests X and Y. This was probably the first type of equating design ever used and addresses the need to control for examinee ability by testing the *same examinees* with *both tests*. Table 2.2 denotes this data structure in a manner similar to Table 2.1 for the EG Design.

One of the advantages of the SG Design is that because each examinee produces data for both tests, the groups taking both tests are identical,

TABLE 2.2. The Single-Group Design.

Population	Sample	X	Y
P	1	$\surd$	$\surd$

whereas, in the EG Design in Section 2.1, the groups are only as similar as two random samples from P can be. This pairing of $\boldsymbol{X}$- and $\boldsymbol{Y}$-scores in the SG Design can create a strong correlation between $\boldsymbol{X}$ and $\boldsymbol{Y}$ and can result in smaller standard errors for the resulting equating functions that arise in the SG Design. We will discuss this in more detail in Chapter 8.

Our analysis of the SG Design makes these two assumptions:

Assumption 2.3. *There is a single population P of examinees who can take both tests.*

Assumption 2.4. *A random sample from P is tested with both $\boldsymbol{X}$ and $\boldsymbol{Y}$.*

The SG Design is also simple, like the EG Design, but it introduces stronger assumptions (i.e., Assumption 2.3). In practice, Assumption 2.4 is rarely more than a convenient fiction. The population P is usually not clearly stated and, often, all that is really available is a sample of data from examinees who took both tests. The SG design is rarely used to equate two distinct parallel forms of the same test because it requires twice as much testing time. It is usually applied to special situations that arise when there are examinees who have two scores. Typical examples are when a part of a test is equated to the whole test. This can arise when an item is deleted from the score after equating has taken place. Another part/whole example occurs when a subscore is equated to the total score of the test. In this situation, the total score is equated to a previous test through some other equating design. A different type of example arises when an essay or other type of "free response" is regraded using a different scoring rubric than the one used initially. Finally, it can occur that examinees have taken two different tests at two different administrations and their data for both tests can be linked up. This type of situation often arises when a *concordance* between two different tests is being constructed. In addition, the SG Design can play a role in more complicated designs such as in Chain Equating for the NEAT Design.

Since the examinees are drawn from a single population, the target population, T, is again P, as it was for the EG Design.

As before, we denote the possible raw scores for $\boldsymbol{X}$ by x_j, with $j = 1, \ldots, J$, and those for $\boldsymbol{Y}$ by y_k, with $k = 1, \ldots, K$.

We define the joint probability distribution of $\boldsymbol{X}$ and $\boldsymbol{Y}$ over T (i.e., P) as

$$p_{jk} = \text{Prob}\{\boldsymbol{X} = x_j,\, \boldsymbol{Y} = y_k \,|\, T\}, \qquad (2.5)$$
$$j = 1, \ldots, J, \quad k = 1, \ldots, K.$$

Then the marginal probabilities for $\boldsymbol{X}$ and $\boldsymbol{Y}$ are given by:

$$\begin{aligned} r_j &= \text{Prob}\{\boldsymbol{X} = x_j \mid T\} = \sum_k p_{jk} \\ s_k &= \text{Prob}\{\boldsymbol{Y} = y_k \mid T\} = \sum_j p_{jk}. \end{aligned} \tag{2.6}$$

We let $\mathbf{P}$ denote the J by K matrix whose $(j,\, k)$-entry is p_{jk}. Then from (2.5) and (2.6) we see that the row sums of $\mathbf{P}$ are the r_j's and the column sums are the s_k's. As before, let $\boldsymbol{r}$ and $\boldsymbol{s}$ denote the (column) vectors of the r_j's and s_k's, respectively.

In order to estimate the equating function for the SG Design it is only necessary to estimate the two vector parameters, $\boldsymbol{r}$ and $\boldsymbol{s}$. In this respect the SG Design is similar to the EG Design in that $\boldsymbol{r}$ and $\boldsymbol{s}$ can be estimated directly without further assumptions. However, in order to properly estimate the SEE for this case, we require an estimate of the full joint distribution, $\mathbf{P}$. For this reason, we will base our analysis on an estimate of $\mathbf{P}$ using the sample of examinees for whom we have scores for both $\boldsymbol{X}$ and $\boldsymbol{Y}$.

It is convenient at this point to introduce a notation that will arise in other data collection designs, *vectorizing the matrix* $\mathbf{P}$. We will use this notation repeatedly. First, let

$$\mathbf{P} = (\boldsymbol{p}_1,\, \boldsymbol{p}_2,\, \ldots,\, \boldsymbol{p}_K), \tag{2.7}$$

where $\boldsymbol{p}_k$ denotes the kth column of $\mathbf{P}$. Then define the JK-dimensional *vectorized* version of $\mathbf{P}$ by:

$$v(\mathbf{P}) = \begin{pmatrix} \boldsymbol{p}_1 \\ \vdots \\ \boldsymbol{p}_K \end{pmatrix}. \tag{2.8}$$

In (2.8), $v(\mathbf{P})$ is created by stacking the columns of $\mathbf{P}$, one on the top of the other. We shall use the vectorized version of a matrix so often throughout this book that it is important to be clear about how it is related to the matrix being vectorized. $\mathbf{P}$ is a $(J \times K)$-matrix and $v(\mathbf{P})$ is a JK-dimensional column vector whose elements are the same as those of $\mathbf{P}$. Equations (2.7) and (2.8) show how this is done.

Here is a small example that illustrates what happens when we vectorize a matrix. Suppose $\mathbf{P}$ is the following 3 by 2 matrix:

$$\mathbf{P} = \begin{pmatrix} 0.2 & 0.1 \\ 0.2 & 0.2 \\ 0.1 & 0.2 \end{pmatrix},$$

then $v(\mathbf{P})$ is the following 6-dimensional column vector:

$$v(\mathbf{P}) = \begin{pmatrix} 0.2 \\ 0.2 \\ 0.1 \\ --- \\ 0.1 \\ 0.2 \\ 0.2 \end{pmatrix}.$$

The Design Function for the SG Design is the transformation of $v(\mathbf{P})$ into $\boldsymbol{r}$ and $\boldsymbol{s}$. To express it as a linear function of $v(\mathbf{P})$ we will define two matrices of 0's and 1's, $\mathbf{M}$ and $\mathbf{N}$, as follows.

$\mathbf{M}$ is the $(J \times KJ)$-matrix

$$\mathbf{M} = \begin{pmatrix} \overbrace{\mathbf{I}_J \quad \ldots \quad \mathbf{I}_J}^{K\ times} \end{pmatrix}, \tag{2.9}$$

where $\mathbf{I}_J$ is a $J \times J$-identity matrix. $\mathbf{N}$ is the $(K \times KJ)$-matrix

$$\mathbf{N} = \begin{pmatrix} \overbrace{\begin{matrix} \mathbf{1}_J^t & \mathbf{0}_J^t & \ldots & & \mathbf{0}_J^t \\ & & \vdots & & \\ \mathbf{0}_J^t & & \ldots & \mathbf{0}_J^t & \mathbf{1}_J^t \end{matrix}}^{K\ times} \end{pmatrix}, \tag{2.10}$$

where $\mathbf{1}_J$ is a (column) J-vector of 1's and $\mathbf{1}_J^t$ is its transpose. $\mathbf{0}_J$ is a (column) J-vector of 0's and $\mathbf{0}_J^t$ is its transpose. It is a straightforward calculation to show that

$$\boldsymbol{r} = \mathbf{M}\, v(\mathbf{P}) = \sum_k \boldsymbol{p}_k = \text{the row sums} \tag{2.11}$$

and

$$\boldsymbol{s} = \mathbf{N}\, v(\mathbf{P}) = \begin{pmatrix} \mathbf{1}_J^t \boldsymbol{p}_1 \\ \vdots \\ \mathbf{1}_J^t \boldsymbol{p}_K \end{pmatrix} = \text{the column sums.} \tag{2.12}$$

In the 2 by 3 illustration given above, $\mathbf{M}$ and $\mathbf{N}$ have the following form:

$$\mathbf{M} = \begin{pmatrix} 1 & 0 & 0 & 1 & 0 & 0 \\ 0 & 1 & 0 & 0 & 1 & 0 \\ 0 & 0 & 1 & 0 & 0 & 1 \end{pmatrix},$$

$$\mathbf{N} = \begin{pmatrix} 1 & 1 & 1 & 0 & 0 & 0 \\ 0 & 0 & 0 & 1 & 1 & 1 \end{pmatrix},$$

so that

$$\boldsymbol{r} = \mathbf{M}v(\mathbf{P}) = \begin{pmatrix} 0.3 \\ 0.4 \\ 0.3 \end{pmatrix}$$

and

$$\boldsymbol{s} = \mathbf{N}v(\mathbf{P}) = \begin{pmatrix} 0.5 \\ 0.5 \end{pmatrix}.$$

Hence, for the SG Design, the Design Function, DF, is given by

$$\begin{pmatrix} \boldsymbol{r} \\ \boldsymbol{s} \end{pmatrix} = \mathrm{DF}\,(\mathbf{P}) = \begin{pmatrix} \mathbf{M}\,v(\mathbf{P}) \\ \mathbf{N}\,v(\mathbf{P}) \end{pmatrix} = \begin{pmatrix} \mathbf{M} \\ \mathbf{N} \end{pmatrix} v(\mathbf{P}). \qquad (2.13)$$

In the 3 by 2 illustration given above the DF is given by

$$\begin{pmatrix} \boldsymbol{r} \\ \boldsymbol{s} \end{pmatrix} = \begin{pmatrix} 0.3 \\ 0.4 \\ 0.3 \\ --- \\ 0.5 \\ 0.5 \end{pmatrix} = \mathrm{DF}\left(\begin{pmatrix} 0.2 & 0.1 \\ 0.2 & 0.2 \\ 0.1 & 0.2 \end{pmatrix}\right).$$

In the SG case, the DF is a mapping of Ω_{JK} into $\Omega_J \times \Omega_K$ where Ω_J and Ω_K are described in (2.4) and

$$\Omega_{JK} = \left\{ \mathbf{P} \in \mathbb{R}^{JK} : p_{jk} > 0 \text{ and } \sum_{jk} p_{jk} = 1 \right\}. \qquad (2.14)$$

For the SG Design the estimates of $\boldsymbol{r}$ and $\boldsymbol{s}$ come from estimates of the bivariate distribution $\mathbf{P}$, via (2.13).

The Single-Group Design is potentially affected by order effects because one of the tests must be given first, and the other given second, to each examinee. The EG Design avoids the possibility of order effects by giving each examinee only one test. In our discussion of the SG Design we have not mentioned or assumed anything about the effect of the order of taking tests X and Y. In this book we assume one of two possibilities for the SG Design. In the first case, we assume there is no effect of order. This is possible in special circumstances. In the second case, we assume that each examinee gets both tests in the same order, say X then Y. This situation arises in Chain-Equating in the NEAT Design discussed later. In the second case, the order is fixed for all examinees and "test Y" means "test Y after taking test X." The next design we consider here explicitly counterbalances the order of testing with X and Y.

TABLE 2.3. The Counterbalanced Design.

Population	Sample	X_1	Y_1	X_2	Y_2
P	1	$\surd$			$\surd$
P	2		$\surd$	$\surd$	

2.3 The Counterbalanced Design (CB)

In the Counterbalanced (CB) Design, two independent, random samples of examinees from a single population P take both tests, X and Y, in different orders. The first sample takes test X first (denoted in the following as X_1) and test Y second (denoted Y_2), as in a Single-Group Design. The other sample takes test Y first (denoted Y_1) and test X second (denoted X_2).

The intent of counterbalancing the order of testing is to insure that any order effects are present equally in the scores obtained for both X and Y. For this reason, if possible, the samples are of equal size, or nearly so. Table 2.3 describes the data in the CB Design using the type of notation we used in Tables 2.1 and 2.2. Comparing Tables 2.1, 2.2 and 2.3 we see that the CB Design actually contains both of the two previously considered designs, EG and SG. This implies that there are several ways to use the data from a CB Design to equate X and Y. We will return to this point shortly. The assumptions that underlie our analysis are given below.

Assumption 2.5. *There is a single population P of examinees who can take both tests, in either order.*

Assumption 2.6. *The two samples are independently and randomly drawn from the common population of examinees, P.*

Again, because the examinees are drawn from a single population, the target population, T, is P, as in both the EG and the SG Designs discussed earlier.

As mentioned earlier, the CB Design contains the EG and the SG Designs within it. For example, comparing Tables 2.1 and 2.3 we see that there are two (dependent) EG Designs, one for X_1 and Y_1, and another for X_2 and Y_2. In addition, comparing Tables 2.2 and 2.3 we see that there are two (independent) SG Designs, one for X_1 and Y_2, and another for X_2 and Y_1. These four possible equatings are illustrate by Figure 2.1.

We may also ignore the two orders and pool the data from X_1 and X_2 (calling it simply X) and the data from Y_1 and Y_2 (calling it Y), and regard the data for X and Y as a SG Design in which order effects have been "counterbalanced."

Because of these different ways of regarding the CB Design, there are several approaches to using the data from this design to equate tests. The utility of each of these approaches depends on the nature and size of the

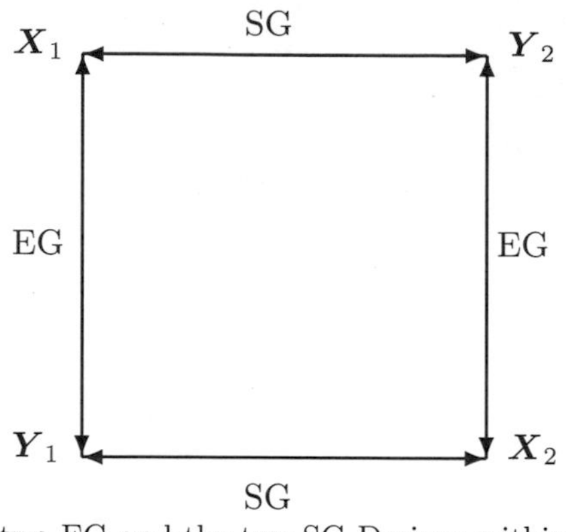

FIGURE 2.1. The two EG and the two SG Designs within the CB Design.

order effects that may be present. Our prefered treatment of the CB Design is new and somewhat different from prior methods. We will discuss four possible approaches, the last of which is our suggestion for integrating the others in a way that makes full use of the data in Table 2.3, when appropriate.

1. *The EG Design for X_1 and Y_1 only.* This approach is really a last resort. We mention it here for completeness because it throws away half of the data and makes no use of the correlation between $\boldsymbol{X}$ and $\boldsymbol{Y}$ that is implicit in the SG aspects of the CB Design. There are circumstances where the counterbalancing is not effective and this approach may be the only one that makes any sense. The data for X_1 and Y_1 are used rather than those for X_2 and Y_2 because in actual use we would not expect both tests to be given and the ones in the CB Design that are affected by order (i.e., $\boldsymbol{X}_2$ and $\boldsymbol{Y}_2$) are therefore irrelevant to the equating problem. Because it introduces no new ideas we will not consider this approach further here, but it will arise in Chapter 9.

2. *The EG pooling method.* There are two EG Designs within a CB Design, X_1 to Y_1 and X_2 to Y_2. If the two equating functions appear similar we may be inclined to average them rather than to use only the data from the X_1 to Y_1 equating. Averaging two equating functions involves some subtlety if the condition of symmetry is to be maintained. In addition, the X_1 to Y_1 and the X_2 to Y_2 EG Designs are not independent of each other in the CB Design so the two equating functions will be correlated to some degree. This correlation will have an impact on the SEE for the average of the two equating functions. We do not examine this effect in this book and it might be a useful area for future research.

3. *The pooled SG method.* This is the approach mentioned above where the order of the tests is ignored and the result is treated as an SG Design. There is some subtlety to this approach, which is often ignored. One naive

view is that by pooling together the "before and after" data for each test any order effect is counterbalanced and can be ignored. This assumes that a "canceling out" will occur. If there are order effects, then we expect that the distribution of $\boldsymbol{X}_1$ and $\boldsymbol{X}_2$ will be different in some way (similarly for $\boldsymbol{Y}_1$ and $\boldsymbol{Y}_2$). Hence, when we pool these two distributions and call the result $\boldsymbol{X}$ we create a new distribution that belongs to no *real* test, some of the time "$\boldsymbol{X}$" is from $\boldsymbol{X}_1$ and some of the time $\boldsymbol{X}$ is from $\boldsymbol{X}_2$, similarly for "$\boldsymbol{Y}$." We discuss a more careful version of this as our fourth, and preferred, approach.

4. *The two independent SG method.* We regard this approach as the most accurate in that it reflects the details of the sampling more faithfully, and uses the data more completely, than the three other approaches. It consists of separately pre-smoothing the data from the two SG Designs, for $(\boldsymbol{X}_1, \boldsymbol{Y}_2)$ and $(\boldsymbol{X}_2, \boldsymbol{Y}_1)$, and then combining them by regarding $\boldsymbol{X}$ as a stochastic mixture of $\boldsymbol{X}_1$ and $\boldsymbol{X}_2$, and $\boldsymbol{Y}$ as a stochastic mixture of $\boldsymbol{Y}_1$ and $\boldsymbol{Y}_2$. The target population, T, is the common one, P, from which the two samples are drawn. We prefer this approach and now give more details that show how it is closely related to the other three methods.

More on the two independent SG method. The two SG Designs within the CB Design result in data for two joint distributions. The first is denoted $\mathbf{P}_{(12)}$ for $(\boldsymbol{X}_1, \boldsymbol{Y}_2)$ from the first sample, and the second is $\mathbf{P}_{(21)}$ for $(\boldsymbol{X}_2, \boldsymbol{Y}_1)$, from the second sample. Both $\mathbf{P}_{(12)}$ and $\mathbf{P}_{(21)}$ are J by K matrices (analogous to $\mathbf{P}$ in the SG Design) of the joint probabilities for $\boldsymbol{X}$ and $\boldsymbol{Y}$. Both $\boldsymbol{X}_1$ and $\boldsymbol{X}_2$ have the same set of possible raw-score values, $\{x_j\}$; similarly, $\boldsymbol{Y}_1$ and $\boldsymbol{Y}_2$ have the same set of possible raw-score values, $\{y_k\}$. In view of this, we use the following notation to denote the entries in $\mathbf{P}_{(12)}$ and $\mathbf{P}_{(21)}$:

$$\begin{aligned} p_{(12)jk} &= \text{Prob}\{\boldsymbol{X}_1 = x_j, \boldsymbol{Y}_2 = y_k \,|\, T\}, \\ p_{(21)jk} &= \text{Prob}\{\boldsymbol{X}_2 = x_j, \boldsymbol{Y}_1 = y_k \,|\, T\}. \end{aligned} \tag{2.15}$$

By analogy with r_j and s_k from (2.2) and (2.6) we define

$$r_{1j} = \text{Prob}\{\boldsymbol{X}_1 = x_j \,|\, T\} = \sum_k p_{(12)jk}, \tag{2.16}$$

$$s_{2k} = \text{Prob}\{\boldsymbol{Y}_2 = y_k \,|\, T\} = \sum_j p_{(12)jk}, \tag{2.17}$$

$$r_{2j} = \text{Prob}\{\boldsymbol{X}_2 = x_j \,|\, T\} = \sum_k p_{(21)jk}, \tag{2.18}$$

$$s_{1k} = \text{Prob}\{\boldsymbol{Y}_1 = y_k \,|\, T\} = \sum_j p_{(21)jk}, \tag{2.19}$$

where $j = 1, \ldots, J$ and $k = 1, \ldots, K$. We denote the corresponding vectors of score probabilities by $\boldsymbol{r}_1$, $\boldsymbol{s}_2$, $\boldsymbol{r}_2$, and $\boldsymbol{s}_1$.

Now we define the *synthetic* $\boldsymbol{X}$-score probabilities r_j by

$$\begin{aligned} r_j &= \text{Prob}\{\boldsymbol{X} = x_j \,|\, T\} \\ &= w_X \text{Prob}\{\boldsymbol{X}_1 = x_j \,|\, T\} + (1 - w_X)\text{Prob}\{\boldsymbol{X}_2 = x_j \,|\, T\}. \quad (2.20) \end{aligned}$$

The weight, w_X, satisfies $0 \leq w_X \leq 1$, and needs to be specified. Similarly, define the synthetic $\boldsymbol{Y}$-score probabilities s_k by

$$\begin{aligned} s_k &= \text{Prob}\{\boldsymbol{Y} = y_k \,|\, T\} \\ &= w_Y \text{Prob}\{\boldsymbol{Y}_1 = y_k \,|\, T\} + (1 - w_Y)\text{Prob}\{\boldsymbol{Y}_2 = y_k \,|\, T\}, \quad (2.21) \end{aligned}$$

where $0 \leq w_Y \leq 1$, is a second weight that needs to be specified. In both cases, w_X and w_Y indicate the weight put on the data that is *not* subject to order effects. Recall that the target population, T, is P in the CB Design. T also has this interpretation in (2.20) and (2.21).

We may express (2.20) and (2.21) in vector form as

$$\boldsymbol{r} = w_X \boldsymbol{r}_1 + (1 - w_X)\boldsymbol{r}_2, \quad (2.22)$$

$$\boldsymbol{s} = w_Y \boldsymbol{s}_1 + (1 - w_Y)\boldsymbol{s}_2. \quad (2.23)$$

The use of the weights, w_X and w_Y, allow us to tailor this approach to equal or, at least, to be similar to the other three approaches discussed above. For example, if $w_X = 1$ and $w_Y = 1$, we get exactly approach 1, where $\boldsymbol{X}_2$ and $\boldsymbol{Y}_2$ are completely ignored. To obtain an approach that is similar to approaches 2 and 3, set $w_X = w_Y = \frac{1}{2}$. This gives equal weight to both sets of data. Setting $w_X = 1$ and $w_Y = 0$ correspond to the SG Design $\boldsymbol{X}_1 \longrightarrow \boldsymbol{Y}_2$. There are other possibilities as well. Our preferred approach to the CB Design is to vary the weights w_X and w_Y, over the range $[\frac{1}{2}, 1]$ to see how sensitive to them are the resulting equating functions and their SEE's.

It is natural to regard $(w_X, w_Y) = (1, 1)$ as the default case, because it is the most conservative use of the data in the CB Design. The case, $(w_X, w_Y) = (\frac{1}{2}, \frac{1}{2})$, is probably the most generous in the use of the $(\boldsymbol{X}_2, \boldsymbol{Y}_2)$-data because it weights the two versions of $\boldsymbol{X}$ and $\boldsymbol{Y}$ equally. We can also consider intermediate cases of interest, i.e., $(w_X, w_Y) = (\frac{3}{4}, \frac{3}{4})$, where only one-fourth of the weight is put on the $(\boldsymbol{X}_2, \boldsymbol{Y}_2)$-data that is possibly subject to order effects.

In Chapter 9 we illustrate a tool, a type of SEED, that measures the standard error of the difference between the equating function obtained for $(w_X, w_Y) = (1, 1)$ and any other choice of (w_X, w_Y). This version of the SEED can be used to give a basis for choosing w_X and w_Y.

As in Section 2.2, define the vectorized $\mathbf{P}_{(12)}$ by

$$v(\mathbf{P}_{(12)}) = \begin{pmatrix} \boldsymbol{p}_{(12)1} \\ \vdots \\ \boldsymbol{p}_{(12)K} \end{pmatrix}, \quad (2.24)$$

where $\boldsymbol{p}_{(12)k}$ is the kth column of $\mathbf{P}_{(12)}$. Define $v(\mathbf{P}_{(21)})$ in a similar manner.

Then, $\boldsymbol{r}_1$ and $\boldsymbol{s}_2$ are computed from the first SG Design as in (2.11) and (2.12), i.e.,

$$\boldsymbol{r}_1 = \mathbf{M}\, v(\mathbf{P}_{(12)}) \quad \text{and} \quad \boldsymbol{s}_2 = \mathbf{N}\, v(\mathbf{P}_{(12)}), \tag{2.25}$$

where $\mathbf{M}$ and $\mathbf{N}$ are defined in (2.9) and (2.10), respectively.

Analogously, $\boldsymbol{r}_2$ and $\boldsymbol{s}_1$ are computed from the second SG Design as in (2.25), i.e.,

$$\boldsymbol{r}_2 = \mathbf{M}\, v(\mathbf{P}_{(21)}) \quad \text{and} \quad \boldsymbol{s}_1 = \mathbf{N}\, v(\mathbf{P}_{(21)}). \tag{2.26}$$

Hence, the Design Function, DF, for the CB Design using the two independent SG approach is

$$\begin{aligned} \begin{pmatrix} \boldsymbol{r} \\ \boldsymbol{s} \end{pmatrix} &= \mathrm{DF}\left(\mathbf{P}_{(12)}, \mathbf{P}_{(21)}\right) \\ &= \begin{pmatrix} w_X \mathbf{M} & (1-w_X)\mathbf{M} \\ (1-w_Y)\mathbf{N} & w_Y \mathbf{N} \end{pmatrix} \begin{pmatrix} v(\mathbf{P}_{(12)}) \\ v(\mathbf{P}_{(21)}) \end{pmatrix}. \end{aligned} \tag{2.27}$$

In this approach, DF is a mapping from $\Omega_{JK} \times \Omega_{JK}$ into $\Omega_J \times \Omega_K$ where Ω_{JK} was defined in (2.14), and Ω_J was defined in (2.4).

In summary, the sequence for deriving estimates of $\boldsymbol{r}$ and $\boldsymbol{s}$ in this approach to the CB Design is as follows. First, we pre-smooth the joint distributions, $\mathbf{P}_{(12)}$ and $\mathbf{P}_{(21)}$, using log-linear models. Next, we compute the implied estimates of $\boldsymbol{r}_1$, $\boldsymbol{s}_2$, $\boldsymbol{r}_2$, and $\boldsymbol{s}_1$ that come from the pre-smoothed matrices, $\mathbf{P}_{(12)}$ and $\mathbf{P}_{(12)}$. Finally, we use the Design Function described in (2.27) to obtain estimates of $\boldsymbol{r}$ and $\boldsymbol{s}$. The choices of w_X and w_Y were discussed above and reflect how much weight we put on each source of data.

Our preference for the *two independent SG method* for the CB Design is based on both its flexibility and its use of all the data, when this is appropriate. By varying the weights, w_X and w_Y, over a range we can examine the sensitivity of the final equating function and its SEE to the choice of weights. We illustrate this in Chapter 9, where we set $w_X = w_Y = w$.

It is appropriate here to compare our preferred approach to the linear method described in Lord (1950) for use in the CB Design. Lord's approach is to use the data from $\boldsymbol{X}_2$ and $\boldsymbol{Y}_2$, which are subject to order effects, but to adjust them to be more comparable to $\boldsymbol{X}_1$ and $\boldsymbol{Y}_1$. He does this by introducing a strong model that assumes that each person's value of $\boldsymbol{X}_2$ (or $\boldsymbol{Y}_2$) is a constant "order effect" K_X (or K_Y) added to the $\boldsymbol{X}_1$ (or $\boldsymbol{Y}_1$) score they would have obtained had they been tested with $\boldsymbol{X}$ (or $\boldsymbol{Y}$) first. Lord assumes that the order effects are the same for all examinees and are proportional to the relevant standard deviations, that is

$$K_X = C\sigma_{X_1} = C\sigma_{X_2} = C\sigma_X, \tag{2.28}$$

and

$$K_Y = C\sigma_{Y_1} = C\sigma_{Y_2} = C\sigma_Y. \tag{2.29}$$

The equality of σ_{X_1} and σ_{X_2} or of σ_{Y_1} and σ_{Y_2} follows from his constant order-effect assumption.

Lord suggests simple method-of-moment estimates of all the relevant parameters and applies them to the linear equating function.

Our mixture approach would produce almost the same estimated linear equating function as the one that Lord proposed (when $w_X = w_Y = \frac{1}{2}$) except for the standard deviation estimates, $\hat{\sigma}_X$ and $\hat{\sigma}_Y$. His are based on $\hat{\sigma}_X^2 = \frac{1}{2}(s_{X_1}^2 + s_{X_2}^2)$ and $\hat{\sigma}_Y^2 = \frac{1}{2}(s_{Y_1}^2 + s_{Y_2}^2)$. Ours would be larger and would add terms of $\frac{1}{4}(\bar{\boldsymbol{X}}_1 - \bar{\boldsymbol{X}}_2)^2$ and $\frac{1}{4}(\bar{\boldsymbol{Y}}_1 - \bar{\boldsymbol{Y}}_2)^2$ to each of $\hat{\sigma}_X^2$ and $\hat{\sigma}_Y^2$, above. When the order effects are small relative to $\hat{\sigma}_{X_i}^2$ and $\hat{\sigma}_{Y_j}^2$ our and Lord's approach to the linear equating function in the CB design are very close.

Lord (1950) indicates that without making a strong model there is little hope of using $\boldsymbol{X}_2$ and $\boldsymbol{Y}_2$ in the equating, and that corresponding equipercentile methods that adjust for the effects of order are not available. We believe that our proposal of the two independent SG method given above does provide an equipercentile-type of approach to the CB Design. Furthermore, it does not assume a strong model for the effect of order on individual level test scores. In addition, it uses all of the data collected in the CB Design to the extent that this is appropriate.

In Chapter 9 we discuss the "two independent SG method" for the CB Design in more detail in a real example.

2.4 Non-Equivalent groups with Anchor Test Design (NEAT)

As mentioned at the beginning of this chapter, in order to control for differences in examinee ability, we need either equivalent groups of examinees, who take both tests, or we need data on common items that are given along with the two tests. The designs we have addressed in Sections 2.1–2.3 all use "common examinees." We now turn to designs that involve "common items."

In the Non-Equivalent groups with Anchor Test (NEAT) Design there are two populations, P and Q, of test-takers and a sample of examinees from each. The sample from P takes test X, the sample from Q takes test Y, and both samples take a set of common items, the anchor test, A. This design often is used when only one test form can be administered at one test administration because of test security or other practical concerns. P and Q are used to indicate that the two populations may not be "equivalent" (i.e., the two samples are not from a common population).

TABLE 2.4. Non-Equivalent groups with Anchor Test Design.

Population	Sample	X	Y	A
P	1	√		√
Q	2		√	√

It is usually advised that the anchor test be administered in the same order to both samples, so that scores on the anchor test and on the other tests are affected in the same way if there are order effects. The anchor test is usually composed of items similar to those in X and Y in terms of content and difficulty. The higher the correlation between scores on $\boldsymbol{A}$ and scores on the tests to be equated, $\boldsymbol{X}$ and $\boldsymbol{Y}$, the better the anchor test is for equating. Angoff (1971) gives additional advice on designing anchor tests. For a comparison of a variety of methods for treating the NEAT Design, see Petersen et al. (1982) and Marco et al. (1983).

The data structure for the NEAT Design is described in Table 2.4, using the notation we have developed in Tables 2.1–2.3.

From Tables 2.2 and 2.4 we see that NEAT Design also contains two independent SG Designs. The two SG Designs within the NEAT Design result in data for two joint distributions. The first is denoted by $\mathbf{P}$ for $(\boldsymbol{X}, \boldsymbol{A})$ for the first sample drawn from P, and the second is denoted by $\mathbf{Q}$ for $(\boldsymbol{Y}, \boldsymbol{A})$ for the second sample drawn from Q. $\mathbf{P}$ is a J by L matrix and $\mathbf{Q}$ is a K by L matrix, whose entries are given by

$$p_{jl} = \text{Prob}\{\boldsymbol{X} = x_j, \boldsymbol{A} = a_l \mid P\}, \tag{2.30}$$

$$q_{kl} = \text{Prob}\{\boldsymbol{Y} = y_k, \boldsymbol{A} = a_l \mid Q\}, \tag{2.31}$$

where $\mathbf{P} = (p_{jl})$ and $\mathbf{Q} = (q_{kl})$.

We have tried to use a consistent notation to refer to the two populations, P and Q, as well as to the two joint distributions and their individual score probabilities. $\mathbf{P}$ and p_{jl} both refer to quantities from population P. $\mathbf{Q}$ and q_{kl} both refer to quantities from population Q. We hope there is no confusion about this. It is important to keep the distinction between P and Q in mind as well as the distinction between them and the target population, T, which we will describe shortly in (2.32). We hope that by using p's for "P-things" and q's for "Q-things" that we can make the necessary distinctions without burdening the notation with extra subscripts.

It should be pointed out that, while there are formally two SG Designs within one NEAT Design, these involve two tests $\boldsymbol{X}$ and $\boldsymbol{A}$, and $\boldsymbol{Y}$ and $\boldsymbol{A}$ that are, in general, not *parallel*. The anchor test, $\boldsymbol{A}$, is usually shorter and less reliable than are either $\boldsymbol{X}$ or $\boldsymbol{Y}$. In some applications certain item types used in $\boldsymbol{X}$ and $\boldsymbol{Y}$ are not feasible to include in $\boldsymbol{A}$.

The NEAT Designs are of two kinds, depending on whether the set of common items is *external* or *internal* to the two tests, $\boldsymbol{X}$ and $\boldsymbol{Y}$. An external anchor test is a separately timed test or test section that each examinee takes in addition to taking one or the other of the tests to be equated. Usually, scores on the external anchor test are not used in computing scores on the tests to be equated. An internal anchor test is a subset of items contained in both tests to be equated. Scores on this set of common items are usually used in computing scores on the total tests, $\boldsymbol{X}$ and $\boldsymbol{Y}$.

In our analysis of the NEAT Design we make the following assumptions:

Assumption 2.7. *There are two populations of examinees P and Q who can take one of the tests and the anchor.*

Assumption 2.8. *The two samples are independently and randomly drawn from P and Q, respectively.*

From Table 2.4 it can be seen that in the NEAT Design $\boldsymbol{X}$ is not observed in the population Q, and $\boldsymbol{Y}$ is not observed in the population P. To overcome this feature, all equating methods developed for the NEAT Design must make additional assumptions of a type that does not arise in the other equating designs.

In this book we examine two competing methods used in the NEAT Design to equate X and Y. The first method is called Chain Equating (CE) and we call the second method Post-Stratification Equating (PSE) in this book. PSE is a version of the method called "frequency estimation" (Angoff, 1971; Kolen and Brennan, 1995). It is closely related to the "Tucker Method" of linear equating (Kolen and Brennan, 1995). Each of these methods, CE or PSE, makes different assumptions to make up for the fact that $\boldsymbol{X}$ is "missing" for Q, and $\boldsymbol{Y}$ is missing for P. Post-Stratification Equating explicitly estimates $\{r_j\}$ and $\{s_k\}$ on a target population T that is a mixture of P and Q. Chain Equating directly exploits the two SG Designs within the NEAT Design and produces the equating function directly without first estimating $\{r_j\}$ and $\{s_k\}$. However, the cdf's, F_T *and* G_T, for CE, are implicitly defined through the assumptions that justify CE as an observed score equating method.

In this book we will investigate both CE and PSE methods. In this section we will discuss the assumptions that underlie each of them and the parameters of the final equating functions for both. In Chapters 3, 4, and 5 we show how to apply Kernel Equating to both of these methods. Finally, in Chapters 10 and 11 we will show how to implement CE and PSE in practice.

The rest of this section is structured as follows: first, we identify the aspects of the NEAT Design that are common to both CE and PSE. Then, in two separate subsections, we discuss how CE and PSE make use of the data.

The target population, T, for the NEAT Design is a mixture of both P and Q. We may think of T as a larger population that has P and Q as two mutually exclusive and exhaustive strata. We will denote this mixture of

P and Q as

$$T = wP + (1 - w)Q, \tag{2.32}$$

where $0 \leq w \leq 1$ is the weight given to P. When $w = 1$ then $T = P$ and when $w = 0$ then $T = Q$. This definition of the target population coincides with what Braun and Holland (1982) called the *synthetic population.*[1]

As we indicated earlier, we denote the possible raw scores for $\boldsymbol{X}$ by x_j, for $j = 1, \ldots, J$, those for $\boldsymbol{Y}$ by y_k, for $k = 1, \ldots, K$, and those of $\boldsymbol{A}$ by a_l, for $l = 1, \ldots, L$. The joint probabilities, p_{jl} and q_{kl}, are defined in (2.30) and (2.31).

As we did before, for both the SG and CB Designs, we will vectorize $\mathbf{P}$ and $\mathbf{Q}$. Hence, we define the JL-vector $v(\mathbf{P})$ and the KL-vector $v(\mathbf{Q})$ as

$$v(\mathbf{P}) = \begin{pmatrix} \boldsymbol{p}_1 \\ \vdots \\ \boldsymbol{p}_L \end{pmatrix} \quad \text{and} \quad v(\mathbf{Q}) = \begin{pmatrix} \boldsymbol{q}_1 \\ \vdots \\ \boldsymbol{q}_L \end{pmatrix}, \tag{2.33}$$

by stacking the columns of the matrix $\mathbf{P} = (p_{jl})$ and of the matrix $\mathbf{Q} = (q_{kl})$ into two column vectors as before. Here the lth-columns of $\mathbf{P}$ and $\mathbf{Q}$ are given by

$$\boldsymbol{p}_l = \begin{pmatrix} p_{1l} \\ \vdots \\ p_{Jl} \end{pmatrix} \quad \text{and} \quad \boldsymbol{q}_l = \begin{pmatrix} q_{1l} \\ \vdots \\ q_{Kl} \end{pmatrix}, \tag{2.34}$$

for $l = 1, \ldots, L$.

The rest of this section is structured into subsections as follows: Section 2.4.1 describes Chain Equating; Section 2.4.2 describes the Post-Stratification Equating; and Section 2.4.3 describes the issues that arise with an internal anchor test. We finish with a section on the special case of an EG Design that also has an anchor test. This is a special case of the NEAT Design where the groups are, in fact, equivalent, i.e., $P = Q$.

2.4.1 Chain Equating (CE)

Chain Equating may be the oldest method used for the NEAT Design. It is a simple extension of the ideas already present in the SG Design. In Livingston et al. (1990), CE was shown to give reasonable results compared to the other standard methods of treating the NEAT Design.

Chain Equating (CE) uses a two-stage transformation of $\boldsymbol{X}$ scores into $\boldsymbol{Y}$ scores. First, it links $\boldsymbol{X}$ to $\boldsymbol{A}$ on P and then links $\boldsymbol{A}$ to $\boldsymbol{Y}$ on Q. We call these maps "linking" because the test(s) and the anchor are not equally reliable,

---

[1] For a discussion of the relative merits of different choices of w see Kolen and Brennan (1987), Angoff's (1987) discussion, and their rejoiner, Brennan and Kolen (1987b).

and therefore, violate requirement 2 mentioned in Chapter 1. These two linking functions are then functionally composed to link $\boldsymbol{X}$ to $\boldsymbol{Y}$ through $\boldsymbol{A}$. In order for CE to make sense as an observed score equating method we must identify T, the target population, and see what assumptions are made in order for the score distributions of $\boldsymbol{X}$ and $\boldsymbol{Y}$ on T to be determined. The target population, T, turns out to be irrelevant for CE. Any T of the form (2.32) will result in exactly the same CE function.

Two assumptions, CE1 and CE2 below, make CE a valid observed-score equating method in the sense specified at the end of Section 1.4. They concern the linking functions between $\boldsymbol{X}$ and $\boldsymbol{Y}$ and the anchor, $\boldsymbol{A}$. These two assumptions do not directly provide information about the parameters $\{r_j\}$ and $\{s_k\}$; however, they are important for understanding the way CE makes use of the data from the NEAT Design, and for comparing it to the PSE method. The cumulative distribution functions that appear in the two assumptions, (CE1) and (CE2), were defined in Chapter 1. We repeat them here:

$$
\begin{aligned}
F(x) &= \text{Prob}(\boldsymbol{X} \leq x \,|\, T), & F_P(x) &= \text{Prob}(\boldsymbol{X} \leq x \,|\, P),\\
G(y) &= \text{Prob}(\boldsymbol{Y} \leq y \,|\, T), & G_Q(y) &= \text{Prob}(\boldsymbol{Y} \leq y \,|\, Q),\\
H(a) &= \text{Prob}(\boldsymbol{A} \leq a \,|\, T), & H_P(a) &= \text{Prob}(\boldsymbol{A} \leq A \,|\, P),\\
& & H_Q(a) &= \text{Prob}(\boldsymbol{A} \leq A \,|\, Q).
\end{aligned}
$$

We assume that F, G, and H (with and without subscripts) have all been continuized (i.e., made continuous and strictly increasing as discussed in Section 1.4 and operationalized for KE in Chapter 4). We use subscripts "P" and "Q" to indicate that the cdf's F, G, and H are computed on them, except that we do not use the subscript T when referring to the target population (see Chapter 1 for details on the notation used throughout the book).

Assumption 2.9. (CE1): *Given any target population T, the link from $\boldsymbol{X}$ to $\boldsymbol{A}$ is population invariant, i.e.,*

$$H_P^{-1}\left(F_P(x)\right) = H^{-1}\left(F(x)\right). \tag{2.35}$$

In (2.35), $H^{-1}\left(F(x)\right)$ denotes the equipercentile function linking $\boldsymbol{X}$ to $\boldsymbol{A}$ on the population T, while $H_P^{-1}\left(F_P(x)\right)$ denotes this linking on P.

In this subsection we will use the composition of functions repeatedly. To simplify the notation we will use "$\circ$" to denote this.

Equation (2.35) implicitly defines the cdf of $\boldsymbol{X}$ on T as

$$F(x) = H\left(H_P^{-1}\left(F_P(x)\right)\right), \tag{2.36}$$

or

$$F(x) = H \circ H_P^{-1} \circ F_P(x). \tag{2.37}$$

Because we can, in principal, construct H, H_P, and F_P based on the data in the NEAT Design, equation (2.37) shows how to compute F from them.

Assumption 2.10. (CE2): *Given any target population T, the link from $\boldsymbol{A}$ to $\boldsymbol{Y}$ is population invariant, i.e.,*

$$G_Q^{-1}\left(H_Q(a)\right) = G^{-1}\left(H(a)\right), \tag{2.38}$$

or

$$G_Q^{-1} \circ H_Q = G^{-1} \circ H. \tag{2.39}$$

Again, (2.39) implicitly defines the cdf of $\boldsymbol{Y}$ on T as

$$G(y) = H \circ H_Q^{-1} \circ G_Q(y),$$

or, taking inverses,

$$G^{-1}(u) = G_Q^{-1} \circ H_Q \circ H^{-1}(u). \tag{2.40}$$

We *define* the Chain Equating function, $e_{Y(CE)}$, as follows:

$$e_{Y(CE)}(x) \quad = \quad G^{-1} \circ F(x). \tag{2.41}$$

Then we apply (2.40) and (2.37) to (2.41) to get

$$e_{Y(CE)}(x) \quad = \quad G_Q^{-1} \circ H_Q \circ H^{-1} \circ H \circ H_P^{-1} \circ F_P(x). \tag{2.42}$$

Because $H^{-1} \circ H = I$, the identity function, we have

$$e_{Y(CE)}(x) \quad = \quad G_Q^{-1}\left(H_Q\left(H_P^{-1}\left(F_P(x)\right)\right)\right), \tag{2.43}$$

which is the function obtained by functionally composing the "equipercentile link" from $\boldsymbol{X}$ to $\boldsymbol{A}$ on P with the equipercentile link from $\boldsymbol{A}$ to $\boldsymbol{Y}$ on Q. Because (2.41) defines the equipercentile equating function that equates $\boldsymbol{X}$ to $\boldsymbol{Y}$ on T, our analysis shows that under the additional assumptions, (CE1) and (CE2), $e_{Y(CE)}(x)$ *is an observed-score equating function defined on* T, and not merely an ad hoc, but plausible, chaining together of linking functions.

We note that H, which depends on the target population, T, cancels out in the formula (2.42). In a sense then, $e_{Y(CE)}(x)$ is assumed to apply to any T of the form (2.32). Through CE1 and CE2, CE is defined to be Population Invariant (which is one of the requirements of an equating procedure—see Chapter 1, Section 1.1). However, this is only strictly true for populations that are mixtures of P and Q in the sense of (2.32), and not for subpopulations of P or Q which cannot be represented by (2.32)(see von Davier et al., 2003, for a discussion about the population invariance of equating functions applied to CE).

Chain equating does not involve any new ideas beyond those used in the Single-Group (SG) Design. It simply functionally composes or "chains together" the results from the two SG Designs.

The cdf's in (2.43), F_P, H_P, H_Q, and G_Q require estimates of four sets of score probabilities: $\boldsymbol{r}_P = (r_{Pj})$, $\boldsymbol{t}_P = (t_{Pl})$, $\boldsymbol{t}_Q = (t_{Ql})$, and $\boldsymbol{s}_Q = (s_{Qk})$, for $j = 1, \ldots, J$, $k = 1, \ldots, K$, and $l = 1, \ldots, L$. These marginal probabilities for $\boldsymbol{X}$ and $\boldsymbol{A}$ in P, and $\boldsymbol{Y}$ and $\boldsymbol{A}$ in Q are given by

$$\begin{aligned} r_{Pj} &= \text{Prob}\{\boldsymbol{X} = x_j \mid P\} = \sum_l p_{jl}, \\ t_{Pl} &= \text{Prob}\{\boldsymbol{A} = a_l \mid P\} = \sum_j p_{jl}, \\ t_{Ql} &= \text{Prob}\{\boldsymbol{A} = a_l \mid Q\} = \sum_k q_{kl}, \\ s_{Qk} &= \text{Prob}\{\boldsymbol{Y} = y_k \mid Q\} = \sum_l q_{kl}. \end{aligned} \tag{2.44}$$

As in the case of SG Design, in order to formally write the marginal probabilities of $\boldsymbol{X}$ and $\boldsymbol{Y}$ in terms of the vectorized arrays, $v(\mathbf{P})$ and $v(\mathbf{Q})$, we will make use of the two matrices, $\mathbf{M}$ and $\mathbf{N}$, of 0's and 1's defined in (2.9) and (2.10).

$$\boldsymbol{r}_P = \mathbf{M}_P\, v(\mathbf{P}) \quad \text{and} \quad \boldsymbol{t}_P = \mathbf{N}_P\, v(\mathbf{P}), \tag{2.45}$$

where $\mathbf{M}_P$ is a $(J \times JL)$-matrix similar to the one in (2.9) and $\mathbf{N}_P$ is a $(L \times JL)$-matrix, with rows that contain $\mathbf{1}_J^t$ as in (2.10). Analogously, $\boldsymbol{s}_Q$ and $\boldsymbol{t}_Q$ can be computed as linear functions of $v(\mathbf{Q})$:

$$\boldsymbol{s}_Q = \mathbf{M}_Q\, v(\mathbf{Q}) \quad \text{and} \quad \boldsymbol{t}_Q = \mathbf{N}_Q\, v(\mathbf{Q}), \tag{2.46}$$

where $\mathbf{M}_Q$, a $(K \times KL)$-matrix, and $\mathbf{N}_Q$, a $(L \times KL)$-matrix, are defined analogously to $\mathbf{M}_P$ and $\mathbf{N}_P$.

The linear transformations in (2.45) and (2.46) describe the two Design Functions that arise when the equating is carried out through Chain Equating. Hence, the first Design Function, DF_P is defined by

$$\begin{pmatrix} \boldsymbol{r}_P \\ \boldsymbol{t}_P \end{pmatrix} = \text{DF}_P\,(\mathbf{P}) = \begin{pmatrix} \mathbf{M}_P \\ \mathbf{N}_P \end{pmatrix} v(\mathbf{P}), \tag{2.47}$$

and the second Design Function, DF_Q is defined by

$$\begin{pmatrix} \boldsymbol{t}_Q \\ \boldsymbol{s}_Q \end{pmatrix} = \text{DF}_Q\,(\mathbf{Q}) = \begin{pmatrix} \mathbf{N}_Q \\ \mathbf{M}_Q \end{pmatrix} v(\mathbf{Q}). \tag{2.48}$$

The Design Function DF_P maps Ω_{JL} into $\Omega_J \times \Omega_L$ and the Design Function DF_Q transforms Ω_{KL} into $\Omega_L \times \Omega_K$, where the Ω's have been defined in (2.4) and (2.14).

In (2.43) we see that $e_{Y(CE)}(x)$ depends on all four sets of score probabilities, $\boldsymbol{r}_P$, $\boldsymbol{t}_P$, $\boldsymbol{t}_Q$, and $\boldsymbol{s}_Q$. Hence the "full" Design Function is the mapping from

$$(\mathbf{P},\,\mathbf{Q}) \quad \text{to} \quad \begin{pmatrix} \boldsymbol{r}_P \\ \boldsymbol{t}_P \\ \boldsymbol{t}_Q \\ \boldsymbol{s}_Q \end{pmatrix}.$$

It is given by

$$\begin{aligned} \begin{pmatrix} \boldsymbol{r}_P \\ \boldsymbol{t}_P \\ \boldsymbol{t}_Q \\ \boldsymbol{s}_Q \end{pmatrix} &= \mathrm{DF}\,(\mathbf{P},\,\mathbf{Q}) = \begin{pmatrix} \mathrm{DF}_P\,(\mathbf{P})) \\ \mathrm{DF}_Q\,(\mathbf{Q}) \end{pmatrix} \\ &= \begin{pmatrix} \begin{pmatrix} \mathbf{M}_P \\ \mathbf{N}_P \end{pmatrix} & \mathbf{0} \\ \mathbf{0} & \begin{pmatrix} \mathbf{N}_Q \\ \mathbf{M}_Q \end{pmatrix} \end{pmatrix} \begin{pmatrix} v(\mathbf{P}) \\ v(\mathbf{Q}) \end{pmatrix}. \end{aligned} \tag{2.49}$$

2.4.2 Post-Stratification Equating (PSE)

In Post-Stratification Equating (PSE), we first estimate the marginal distributions, $\boldsymbol{r}$ and $\boldsymbol{s}$, of both $\boldsymbol{X}$ and $\boldsymbol{Y}$ on the target population T, which is a specific mixture of P and Q in the form of (2.32), and then compute the equating function from $\boldsymbol{r}$ and $\boldsymbol{s}$.

As mentioned earlier in this section, the target population in the NEAT Design is defined in (2.32), i.e.,

$$T = wP + (1-w)Q,$$

where $0 \leq w \leq 1$ is the weight that defines T. Unlike Chain Equating, in PSE the choice of w *can* affect the resulting equating function.

The probabilities r_j and s_k on T are computed based on the conditional probabilities in the two strata (i.e., P and Q) of T, i.e.,

$$r_j = \mathrm{Prob}\{\boldsymbol{X} = x_j \,|\, T\} = w r_{Pj} + (1-w) r_{Qj}, \tag{2.50}$$

$$s_k = \mathrm{Prob}\{\boldsymbol{Y} = y_k \,|\, T\} = w s_{Pk} + (1-w) s_{Qk}, \tag{2.51}$$

$$t_l = \mathrm{Prob}\{\boldsymbol{A} = a_l \,|\, T\} = w t_{Pl} + (1-w) t_{Ql}. \tag{2.52}$$

In (2.50) through (2.52), the probabilities r_{Pj}, s_{Qk}, t_{Pl}, and t_{Ql}, may be computed via (2.44). The other two probabilities,

$$r_{Qj} = \mathrm{Prob}\{\boldsymbol{X} = x_j \,|\, Q\} \tag{2.53}$$

and

$$s_{Pk} = \mathrm{Prob}\{\boldsymbol{Y} = y_k \,|\, P\}\,, \tag{2.54}$$

are not directly estimable from the data collected in the NEAT Design. However, they are needed in order to use PSE. They are obtained, in PSE, by conditioning on the anchor-test scores and using the assumptions PSE1 and PSE2, below. We denote the conditional distributions of $\boldsymbol{X}$ given $\boldsymbol{A}$ in P, and of $\boldsymbol{Y}$ given $\boldsymbol{A}$ in Q, by

$$r_P(x_j \mid a_l) = \text{Prob}\{\boldsymbol{X} = x_j \mid \boldsymbol{A} = a_l,\, P\} \tag{2.55}$$

$$s_Q(y_k \mid a_l) = \text{Prob}\{\boldsymbol{Y} = y_k \mid \boldsymbol{A} = a_l,\, Q\}. \tag{2.56}$$

Likewise we define $r_Q(x_j \mid a_l)$ and $s_P(y_k \mid a_l)$ analogously to (2.55) and (2.56). The assumptions made by PSE will allow estimation of r_j and s_k. These two assumptions are stated next.

Assumption 2.11. (PSE1): *$r_Q(x_j \,|a_l) = r_P(x_j \,|a_l)$ so that for any target population, T, the conditional distribution of $\boldsymbol{X}$ given $\boldsymbol{A}$ is population invariant, and therefore*

$$r_j = \sum_l r_P(x_j \mid a_l) t_l. \tag{2.57}$$

In (2.57) t_l is defined on T by equation (2.52) where its dependence on w is explicit.

Assumption 2.12. (PSE2): *$s_P(y_k \,|a_l) = s_Q(y_k \,|a_l)$ so that for any target population, T, the conditional distribution of $\boldsymbol{Y}$ given $\boldsymbol{A}$ is population invariant, and therefore*

$$s_k = \sum_l s_Q(y_k \mid a_l) t_l. \tag{2.58}$$

Once the score probabilities, r_j and s_k, are computed on T by reweighting by $\boldsymbol{t}$, as indicated in (2.57) and (2.58), the rest of PSE is easy. Simply continuize the resulting F and G, and compute the equating function. This will be discussed more carefully in Chapter 11.

Note that the equating function for PSE, $e_{Y(PSE)}(x)$, can depend on the choice of T, unlike the equating function for chain equating, $e_{Y(CE)}(x)$. Therefore, PSE can be different from CE. As von Davier et al. (2003) show, CE and PSE can also be identical in particular circumstances that are interesting from a practical point of view.

The Design Function for Post-Stratification Equating is more complicated than those for the other designs because it involves conditional distributions. We summarize this in Theorem 2.1

Theorem 2.1. *Under the Assumptions 2.11 and 2.12, the Design Function for PSE is given by*

$$\begin{pmatrix} \boldsymbol{r} \\ \boldsymbol{s} \end{pmatrix} = \text{DF}\,(\mathbf{P},\, \mathbf{Q}) \tag{2.59}$$

where

$$\boldsymbol{r} = \boldsymbol{r}(\mathbf{P}, \mathbf{Q}, w) = \sum_l \left[w + \frac{(1-w)(t_{Ql})}{t_{Pl}} \right] \boldsymbol{p}_l, \tag{2.60}$$

and

$$\boldsymbol{s} = \boldsymbol{s}(\mathbf{P}, \mathbf{Q}, w) = \sum_l \left[(1-w) + \frac{w(t_{Pl})}{t_{Ql}} \right] \boldsymbol{q}_l. \tag{2.61}$$

In (2.60) and (2.61) t_{Pl} and t_{Ql} are column sums of $\mathbf{P}$ *and* $\mathbf{Q}$*, respectively, while $\boldsymbol{p}_l$ is the lth column of* $\mathbf{P}$ *and $\boldsymbol{q}_l$ is the lth column of* $\mathbf{Q}$*.*

Proof. Start from the assumptions about r_j and s_k in (2.57) and (2.58), express the conditional probabilities as ratios of joint and marginal probabilities and simplify the result. □

As before, p_{jl} and q_{kl} are population parameters that must be estimated from the data. $\hat{\boldsymbol{r}}$ and $\hat{\boldsymbol{s}}$ will be computed from (2.60) and (2.61), respectively. These estimates will be used to compute the equating functions, and their covariance matrix will be used for computing the SEE (see Chapter 11).

2.4.3 Internal Anchor Tests and Structural Zeros

The anchor test in a NEAT Design can be either external or internal to the scores, $\boldsymbol{X}$ and $\boldsymbol{Y}$. From the point of view of Kernel Equating, the two cases are identical in every respect but one. Both involve two populations, P and Q (Assumption 2.7), and the samples from the two populations are assumed to be independent and drawn randomly from them (Assumption 2.8). The data collection design described in Table 2.4 applies to either an internal or an external anchor test.

When the score, $\boldsymbol{A}$, is *external* to $\boldsymbol{X}$, it come from a separate test or separate test section and because of this the value of $\boldsymbol{A}$ does not deterministically restrict the value of $\boldsymbol{X}$ in any way. Of course, if an examinee gets a high score on $\boldsymbol{A}$, we would also expect him or her to get a high score on $\boldsymbol{X}$ as well, but the relationship is not deterministic or forced. An *internal anchor* test is different in this respect. Suppose for example that $\boldsymbol{X}$, $\boldsymbol{Y}$ and $\boldsymbol{A}$ are all "number-right" scores and that $\boldsymbol{X} = \boldsymbol{X}^* + \boldsymbol{A}$, while $\boldsymbol{Y} = \boldsymbol{Y}^* + \boldsymbol{A}$. Then, the "common part" of $\boldsymbol{X}$ and $\boldsymbol{Y}$, $\boldsymbol{A}$, is the internal anchor test score, while $\boldsymbol{X}^*$ and $\boldsymbol{Y}^*$ are the "unique parts" of $\boldsymbol{X}$ and $\boldsymbol{Y}$, respectively. Because $\boldsymbol{A}$ is a part of $\boldsymbol{X}$, the score on $\boldsymbol{A}$ can directly force the score on $\boldsymbol{X}$ to *avoid* certain values. For number-right scores this is easy to see. If $\boldsymbol{A} = 5$, then because $\boldsymbol{X}^*$ can not be negative we must have $\boldsymbol{X} \geq 5$. In this example, $\boldsymbol{X}$ must always equal or exceed $\boldsymbol{A}$, it can never be less than $\boldsymbol{A}$. This deterministic relationship between $\boldsymbol{X}$ and $\boldsymbol{A}$ results in "structural zeros" in the system of joint probabilities, $\{p_{jl}\}$. A structural zero is a value of p_{jl} that must be zero because the combination of $\boldsymbol{X} = x_j$ and $\boldsymbol{A} = a_l$ is impossible. This is very different from a sample frequency that just happens to be zero due to sampling variability (i.e. sampling zeros). Structural zeros arise in a variety of ways in joint distributions (Bishop et al., 1975), and a "part-whole" relationship between two variables, as illustrated by internal anchor tests, is one of these.

While we have demonstrated how structural zeros can arise with number-right scores, they can arise with any type of internal anchor test and any of the usual scoring systems. In number-right scoring the effect of the internal anchor on the structural zeros is easy to see, and Holland et al. (1989) show how to locate where they are in the matrix, $\mathbf{P} = (p_{jl})$. In "rounded formula scores" it is harder to give a simple algorithm for locating the structural zeros, but they are always there when the anchor test is internal.

The reason for mentioning structural zeros at all is that when they are present, a proper pre-smoothing will not make any of them nonzero. In the univariate case impossible cells (i.e., structural zeros) are just eliminated and ignored, but in the bivariate case it is the combination of two values, one for $\boldsymbol{X}$ and one for $\boldsymbol{A}$, that is impossible, and so special procedures and models are used to deal with them.

In the examples of Part II of this book we do not include the case of an internal anchor test even though they often arise in practice. Our excuse for this incompleteness is that the only special issue that an internal anchor test would raise for us is the technique for properly pre-smoothing the resulting two-way arrays of frequencies. Examples of fitting distributions and frequency tables with structural zeros is discussed in many places including Holland and Thayer (2000), Bishop et al. (1975), Haberman (1979), Fienberg (1980), and Agresti (1990), among others. With such thorough attention to structural zeros elsewhere, we did not feel we needed to give a detailed example of an internal anchor test in this book.

We should mention in closing this subsection that the Single-Group Design is another place where structural zeros can occur in special applications. The cases we are referring to also arise when there is a part-whole relationship between $\boldsymbol{X}$ and $\boldsymbol{Y}$. A common example is when one or a few items have been deleted from a test after it has been equated. In this case, $\boldsymbol{Y}$ is the score on the whole test and $\boldsymbol{X}$ is the score on the part that is remaining after the items have been deleted. In such a situation, it is clear that the joint distribution of $\boldsymbol{X}$ and $\boldsymbol{Y}$ can have many structural zeros, and this may need to be taken into account when pre-smoothing their joint distribution. In such situations, linear equating is often used, and this avoids pre-smoothing with structural zeros.

In many settings, it is usually unwise to ignore structural zeros, but for applications to Kernel Equating it is possible that there are important cases where attention to them makes little difference either to the estimated equating function or to estimates of its standard error. We have not examined this issue and believe that it may be an interesting topic for future research with practical consequences.

2.4.4 The EG Design with an Anchor Test

It sometimes happens that an EG Design also includes an anchor test. This is formally like a NEAT Design except that $P = Q$. When $P = Q$ and if T is defined by (2.32), then $T = P = Q$ and both sets of assumptions, CE1 & CE2 and PSE1 & PSE2, are automatically true. In addition, the two approaches, CE and PSE, will lead to identical equating functions. What will be different between these two approaches will be the SEE. PSE makes use of the correlation between $\boldsymbol{X}$ and $\boldsymbol{A}$ and between $\boldsymbol{Y}$ and $\boldsymbol{A}$, in a way that is different from CE. Our comparison of CE and PSE in Chapter 11 suggests, however, that the SEE's for CE and PSE can be very similar.

2.5 Random versus Spiraled Samples

In all of our analyses, we assume that all samples are drawn randomly from the relevant population(s). In actual practice this is rarely done. Instead, when equivalent groups are needed to take different tests, forms for the various tests are alternated in bundles for distribution to examinees (i.e., "spiraled"). The spiraled sampling method results, ideally, in adjacent-sitting examinees getting different tests. It often produces samples that are "more equivalent" than simple random sampling would yield because it is more like proportionate stratified random sampling where the strata are the rooms used for testing. For this reason we use the term "Equivalent Groups" rather than earlier "Random Groups" (Angoff, 1971) to refer to the EG Design.

The use of spiraled sampling has wider applicability than the case of the EG Design. Our repeatedly used assumption that the samples are random is an approximation, but one that is widely used. To our knowledge, no tractable analysis of the results of spiraled sampling exists. In addition, as far as its implications for the SEE is concerned, the use of the random sampling approximation is conservative in the sense that the actual standard errors are smaller under spiraled sampling than they are computed to be under simple random sampling. How much smaller is not known and depends on factors that are usually not available to the analyst. However, we believe that approximating spiraled samples by random sampling assumptions does not lead to substantial overestimates in the resulting SEE's. This is, of course, an interesting topic for further research.

TABLE 2.5. Classification of Equating Designs Based on the Number of Testing Populations Involved and the Number of Samples Used.

	1 sample	2 samples
One population	SG	EG CB EG with anchor
Two populations		CE in NEAT PSE in NEAT

2.6 Summary

This chapter classifies the Equating Designs in order to show the similarities and differences between them. For example, the NEAT Design can be viewed as containing the EG Design as a special case when $P = Q$ and $\boldsymbol{A}$ has only a single score value. Similarly the CB Design contains both EG and SG Designs in it.

Another approach to classifying the designs is based on the estimation of the parameters in the pre-smoothing step, i.e., the numbers and type of the distributions to be estimated—univariate (EG) and bivariate (SG, CB, and NEAT).

We can also classify the designs by the number of populations and samples that are involved. Table 2.5 identifies some of the various ways Equating Designs may be classified.

Some designs are simple, i.e., involve a single population of examinees, have less assumptions, but need either larger sample sizes (EG), or require the same people to take two test forms at the same time (SG and CB). Other designs are more complicated, i.e., involve two populations of test takers, make use of an anchor test, and require that additional assumptions be fulfilled (i.e., NEAT). These complexities are often compensated by their increased versatility.

3

Kernel Equating: Overview, Pre-smoothing, and Estimation of $\boldsymbol{r}$ and $\boldsymbol{s}$

This and the next two chapters describe the kernel method of test equating, Kernel Equating (KE). KE is a unified approach to test equating based on a flexible family of equipercentile-like equating functions that contains the linear equating function as a special case. The name "Kernel Equating" arises because of its use of the well-studied methods of nonparametric density estimation using a Gaussian kernel (Tapia and Thompson, 1978; Silverman, 1986). Kernel Equating is "equipercentile-like" because it generalizes certain features of the equipercentile method described by Angoff (1971), Kolen and Brennan (1995), and Chapter 1, Section 1.4.

We view KE as having five separate steps or parts, each of which involves distinct ideas. We will briefly describe each step and then discuss each one more thoroughly in this and the next two chapters. In this chapter our goal is to give a clear account of pre-smoothing by log-linear models and the basic estimation phase of the equating process. Chapters 4 and 5 continue our description of KE.

In Chapter 7 through Chapter 11 we apply KE to each of the specific data collection designs in common use, using real data to illustrate our methods.

3.1 The Five Steps of Kernel Equating: Overview

Step 1: Pre-smoothing. In this step, estimates of the relevant univariate and/or bivariate score probabilities are obtained by fitting appropriate statistical models to the raw data obtained by the data collection design. This is a purely statistical phase in which various models for the data are tried out and one is selected to give an adequate fit to the data. In Section 3.2 we illustrate this approach and focus on the use of log-linear models (Holland and Thayer, 2000). In Part II of this book we describe the model-fitting aspects of pre-smoothing for all important equating designs.

Step 2: Estimation of the score probabilities. Here, the score probabilities on the target population, T, are obtained from the score distributions estimated in Step 1. In Step 2, a crucial role is played by the Design Function that characterizes each design.

The Design Function, DF, is a linear or nonlinear transformation of the estimated score distributions from *Step 1* into the estimated score probabilities, $\hat{\boldsymbol{r}}$ and $\hat{\boldsymbol{s}}$, for test $\boldsymbol{X}$ and $\boldsymbol{Y}$ on the target population, T (using the notation introduced in Chapter 1). The Design Functions for the data collection designs used in this book are given explicitly in Chapter 2 and summarized in Chapter 5. The Design Function for Chain Equating in the NEAT Design is somewhat different from those of the other methods and designs. In Chain Equating, $\boldsymbol{r}$ and $\boldsymbol{s}$ are not computed directly. However, Design Functions do play an intermediate role in Chain Equating. This will be discussed in more detail in Section 3.3.

Step 3: Continuization. In this step, we determine continuous approximations, $\hat{F}_{h_X}(x)$ and $\hat{G}_{h_Y}(y)$, to the estimated discrete cdf's, $\hat{F}(x)$ and $\hat{G}(y)$. Here we need to choose the *bandwidth parameters*, h_X and h_Y. It should be emphasized that continuization is not a statistical estimation procedure. Rather, in continuization we are attempting to decide which *continuous* cdf, $\hat{F}_{h_X}(x)$, is "closest," in some appropriate sense, to the estimated *discrete* cdf, $\hat{F}(x)$. In Section 4.1 we describe two criteria for automatically selecting h_X and h_Y that we have found useful in practice. Continuization is closely related to "post-smoothing" (Kolen and Brennan, 1995).

Step 4: Equating. In this phase, the estimated equating function is formed from the two continuized cdf's, $\hat{F}_{h_X}(x)$ and $\hat{G}_{h_Y}(y)$, using formulas (1.12) that describes the "general" equipercentile equating function, i.e.,

$$\hat{e}_{Yh_Xh_Y}(x) = \hat{G}_{h_Y}^{-1}(\hat{F}_{h_X}(x)).$$

Once Steps 1 to 3 are completed, Step 4 is an automatic calculation that requires no additional judgment or input. It is in Step 4 that the data on both tests, X and Y, are finally combined into the equating function. Chapter 4 is concerned with Steps 3 and 4 of Kernel Equating. In addition to computing $\hat{e}_{Yh_Xh_Y}(x)$ in the Equating Step, we also investigate or *diagnose* how well $\hat{e}_{Yh_Xh_Y}(\boldsymbol{X})$ transforms the discrete distribution of $\boldsymbol{X}$ into the discrete distribution of $\boldsymbol{Y}$.

Step 5: Calculating the Standard Error of Equating. The explicitness of KE results in an elegant formula for the standard error of equating (the SEE) for any equating design. We give a method for the computation of the SEE that is based on the estimated standard errors for the score probabilities that are available if they are obtained using log-linear models as described in Section 3.2. In addition, we give a general formula for the standard error of the difference (the SEED) between the equating functions that corresponds to two different choices of the bandwidth parameters, h_X and h_Y. This can be used to aid in the decision of whether the estimated equating function is sufficiently close to a straight line that the linear equating function can be used instead of a curvilinear one. The SEED can also be used in the CB Design to decide on how to use the data that is possibly subject to order effects. Chapter 5 is concerned with the issues of statistical accuracy measured by the SEE and the SEED.

3.2 Pre-smoothing Using Log-Linear Models

The raw score data obtained in each of the data collection designs described in Chapter 2 can be used to estimate the appropriate score probabilities for that design.

The estimation of score probabilities is a purely statistical problem in the sense that the appropriate score probabilities are well-defined parameters and hence their estimates should have desirable statistical properties. Fairbank (1987), refer to this as "pre-smoothing" and we adopt this terminology. While it is true that the estimates of the score probabilities ought to exhibit appropriate degrees of smoothness, this can be achieved in various ways. We regard pre-smoothing as a problem of statistical estimation of the relevant score probabilities. There are at least four statistical properties that might be considered in the choice of the estimated score probabilities. We list them below.

- **Consistency**: As sample sizes increase, the estimates ought to converge, in an appropriate sense, to the population values.
- **Efficiency**: Given the sample sizes involved, the deviations of the estimated score probabilities from the population values ought to be as small as possible. Of course these deviations always involve a random element, and the problem is to keep it to a minimum in an appropriate average sense.
- **Positivity**: For each possible score the estimated score probabilities ought to be positive. For most tests, estimating a score probability to be zero is unreasonable. (There are exceptions that occur in special problems that arise in the NEAT Design with an internal anchor test and in some applications of the SG Design. This is discussed in Chapters 8, 10, and 11.)

- **Integrity**: When possible, the integrity of the sample mean, variance, and possibly other sample moments ought to be preserved in the estimated score distributions. This property is closely related to the mean and variance matching property of linear equating and which is desirable for equipercentile methods as well.

The approach to score probability estimation that we will use in this book is to fit a sequence of parametric, log-linear models to the data and to make appropriate diagnoses of these fitted models until one is found that describes the data "well enough" with as few parameters as possible. The log-linear models described in Rosenbaum and Thayer (1987) and in Holland and Thayer (1987, 2000) are especially useful because they are flexible enough to fit the types of univariate and bivariate score distributions that arise in practice and to smooth them in reasonable ways. More specialized models such as the negative hypergeometric (Keats and Lord, 1962) or those based on item response theory (Lord, 1955b, 1980) are more restrictive and do not adequately describe many data sets. Log-linear models are well-behaved and relatively easy to estimate because they are exponential families of discrete distribution and may be estimated by maximum likelihood using efficient iterative techniques. Because these models are exponential families, maximum likelihood estimation forces the equality of certain sample and estimated moments.

Bivariate distributions, useful for SG, CB, and NEAT Designs, are also easily estimated using the class of log-linear models. Holland and Thayer (2000) discuss these models in detail.

The models for estimating univariate or bivariate score distributions usually fit various power moments of the distributions. The power moments are useful because of the wide familiarity of distributional measures based on the first four power moments—i.e., mean, variance, skewness and kurtosis. In our experience, it is often necessary to include power moments as high as five or six to obtain good fits to univariate data distributions, although this clearly depends on several factors including the sample size, N. Log-linear models that use the power moments are also called polynomial log-linear models (Hanson, 1996). However, the power moments are not the only ones that have utility in fitting (univariate) distributions. A very useful class of alternative moments is the class of "subset moments" which is described in Appendix C. Such moments are useful when some of the cells frequencies are different in systematic ways from the others. This happens when the frequencies exhibit nonrandom features such as "teeth" or "gaps" spaced at regular intervals along the score scale (a phenomena that often arise for formula scored tests). We give a detailed example of such a case in Chapter 10. Finally, these models automatically satisfy the positivity and integrity conditions listed above. Careful data analysis using these models also leads to the consistency and efficiency conditions being satisfied as well.

The data that arise in the designs described in Chapter 2 are either univariate or bivariate frequency distributions. In the rest of this section we will briefly outline the estimation procedure for a univariate distribution. This estimation problem arises in the Equivalent-Groups Design. In Appendix B we will briefly outline the estimation of bivariate score distributions. This estimation problem arises in the SG Design, CB Design, and in the NEAT Designs. For more extensive discussions of these models and how to use them to fit univariate and bivariate distributions we refer the reader to Holland and Thayer (2000). Fitting both univariate and bivariate score distributions to real data is illustrated in each of Chapters 7—10.

3.2.1 Estimating a Univariate Score Distribution

In this subsection we briefly indicate the relevant aspects of estimating a univariate score distribution using log-linear models. Our discussion is based on Holland and Thayer (2000), and to be both concrete and simple we will assume the data come from an EG Design, described in Chapter 2.

Samples. The raw data obtained from an EG Design can be summarized as two sets of univariate frequencies:

$$n_j = \text{number of examinees in the sample with } \boldsymbol{X} = x_j,$$
$$m_k = \text{number of examinees in the sample with } \boldsymbol{Y} = y_k.$$

We denote the two sample sizes by $N = \sum_j n_j$ and $M = \sum_k m_k$.

If we regard the data $\{n_j\}$ and $\{m_k\}$ as coming from two independent random samples from very large populations, then we may make the following distributional assumption.

Assumption 3.1. *The vectors* $\boldsymbol{n} = (n_1, \ldots, n_J)^t$ *and* $\boldsymbol{m} = (m_1, \ldots, m_K)^t$ *are independent and they each have multinomial distributions, i.e.,*

$$\text{Prob}(\boldsymbol{n}) = \frac{N!}{n_1! \ldots n_J!} \prod r_j^{n_j}, \tag{3.1}$$

$$\text{Prob}(\boldsymbol{m}) = \frac{M!}{m_1! \ldots m_K!} \prod s_k^{m_k}. \tag{3.2}$$

We use $\{r_j\}$ and $\{s_k\}$ as the score probabilities in Assumption 3.1 because in the EG Design the samples are, by definition, from the target population, T. In the EG Design $\boldsymbol{r}$ and $\boldsymbol{s}$ are estimated directly from $\boldsymbol{n}$ and $\boldsymbol{m}$, respectively.

Assumption 3.1 will be approximately satisfied in those cases where it is reasonable to regard the data as a random sample without replacement from a larger population for which each possible value is, indeed, “possible” if not actually observed. Sometimes the data represent the entire population of test takers of a given test. In such cases it may still be useful to use Assumption 3.1 to smooth out inessential irregularities in the pattern of the frequencies in order to focus on their main features. In many testing applications the actual population is not well specified, and instead of random samples, the samples are obtained by spiraling, as described in Section 2.5.

Under the assumption of a multinomial distribution, the log-likelihood function for $\boldsymbol{r}$ is

$$L_r = \sum_j n_j \log(r_j). \tag{3.3}$$

A similar formula hold for L_s.

Log-linear models. To estimate the population parameters, $\boldsymbol{r}$, using a log-linear model we make this assumption:

Assumption 3.2. *The vector $\boldsymbol{r}$ satisfies a log-linear model*

$$\log(r_j) = \alpha + u_j + \boldsymbol{b}_j^t \boldsymbol{\beta}, \tag{3.4}$$

where $\boldsymbol{\beta}$ is a T_r-vector of free parameters, u_j is a known constant, α is the normalizing constant selected to make the sum of r_j equal to one, and $\boldsymbol{b}_j^t$ is the transpose of $\boldsymbol{b}_j$. $\boldsymbol{b}_j$ a T_r-vector of known constants, where T_r is the number of free parameters used to estimate $\boldsymbol{r}$.

The model in (3.4) may be written in matrix form as:

$$\log(\boldsymbol{r}) = \alpha + \boldsymbol{u} + \mathbf{B}^t \boldsymbol{\beta}, \tag{3.5}$$

where $\boldsymbol{u}$ is a known J-vector, $\mathbf{B} = (\boldsymbol{b}_1, \ldots, \boldsymbol{b}_J)$ is a $T_r \times J$-matrix (a "design matrix") of known constants, and $\boldsymbol{\beta}$ is a T_r-dimensional vector of parameters. Hence, in this book, the columns of the matrix $\mathbf{B}$, are denoted by $\boldsymbol{b}_j$ with $j = 1, \ldots, J$, while the entries of the matrix $\mathbf{B}$ are denoted by b_{ij}, with $i = 1, \ldots, T_r$. The same type of model assumptions are made for $\boldsymbol{s}$.

The role of $\boldsymbol{u}$ is to specify a "null" distribution for the exponential family that holds when the parameter $\boldsymbol{\beta} = \mathbf{0}$. In practice $\boldsymbol{u} = \mathbf{0}$ is often a useful choice (Holland and Thayer, 2000, discuss other possibilities for $\boldsymbol{u}$.). Log-linear models based on power moments have $b_{ij} = (x_j)^i$, for $i = 1, \ldots, T_r$, where $(x_j)^i$ is the ith-power of the scores x_j, $j = 1, \ldots, J$. Other examples of choices of b_{ij} include those of the form $b_{ij} = I_S(x_j)$, where $I_S(x_j)$ is a 0/1-indicator variable of the form

$$I_S(x_j) = \begin{cases} 1 & \text{if} \quad x_j \text{ in } S, \\ 0 & \text{if} \quad \textit{otherwise}. \end{cases} \tag{3.6}$$

A fundamental restriction is that $T_r \leq J - 1$ and $T_s \leq K - 1$, i.e., that the number of the parameter is less than the number of the possible scores values. In our examples in Part II of this book, T_r and T_s are much smaller than $J - 1$ and $K - 1$.

Estimation of $\boldsymbol{r}$ and $\boldsymbol{s}$. The models specified by (3.5) are well-behaved exponential families of discrete distributions and the vector parameter, $\boldsymbol{\beta}$, may be estimated by maximum likelihood. Maximum likelihood estimation proceeds by maximizing the log-likelihood function given in (3.3). When a log-linear model of the form (3.4) is substituted for $\log r_j$ in (3.3), L_r becomes a well-behaved function of $\boldsymbol{\beta}$, $L_r(\boldsymbol{\beta})$, and can be maximized by differentiating L_r and solving the resulting likelihood equations, i.e., by solving

$$\frac{\partial L_r}{\partial \boldsymbol{\beta}} = 0 \tag{3.7}$$

for $\boldsymbol{\beta}$. The solution, $\hat{\boldsymbol{\beta}}$, is the maximum likelihood estimate (mle) of $\boldsymbol{\beta}$. The estimator of r_j is $\hat{r}_j = r_j(\hat{\boldsymbol{\beta}})$, and is also called the mle (or mle fitted value) of the cell probability, r_j.

Denote the mles of $\boldsymbol{r}$ and $\boldsymbol{s}$ based on $\boldsymbol{n}$ and $\boldsymbol{m}$, by $\hat{\boldsymbol{r}}$ and $\hat{\boldsymbol{s}}$. Equation (3.7) implies the well-known "moment matching" property of log-linear models, i.e., that the mle $\hat{\boldsymbol{r}}$ satisfies the condition that the sample and fitted moments (specified by the rows of $\mathbf{B}$) are matched perfectly, i.e.,

$$\sum_j b_{ij}(n_j/N) = \sum_j b_{ij}\hat{r}_j, \tag{3.8}$$

for $i = 1, \ldots, T_r$.

Analogous moment matching holds for s_k. This property is very useful. It allows users to choose $\mathbf{B}$ to fit the moments of $\boldsymbol{n}$ that describe the important features of its shape. Holland and Thayer (1987, 2000) show that with 2 to 6 parameters, i.e., fitting 2 to 6 moments, these models can adequately describe a wide variety of univariate score distributions.

Assessing model fit. In order to be a useful summary of the data, a model must obviously fit the data. Holland and Thayer (2000) describe several tools for assessing the fit of log-linear models for score distributions. In the examples used in Chapters 7—11 we will illustrate some of them. One of the important reasons for obtaining a model that fits well in the pre-smoothing step is that the results from this model will be carried through to the estimation of the standard error of equating (SEE). A model that does not fit adequately may not produce an accurate SEE.

Covariance matrix of $\hat{\boldsymbol{r}}$. This special topic is included here because we will regularly exploit a computationally useful matrix factorization of the covariance matrix of $\hat{\boldsymbol{r}}$ and $\hat{\boldsymbol{s}}$ that was derived in Holland and Thayer (1987).

We are assuming (Assumption 3.1) that $\boldsymbol{n}$ and $\boldsymbol{m}$ are independent and we further assume here that $\hat{\boldsymbol{r}}$ and $\hat{\boldsymbol{s}}$ are *estimated separately* (i.e., that the models for $\boldsymbol{r}$ and $\boldsymbol{s}$ do not share any common parameters across the two independent samples so that $\boldsymbol{r}$ depends only on $\boldsymbol{n}$ and $\boldsymbol{s}$ depends only on $\boldsymbol{m}$). This is summarized in

Assumption 3.3. *The estimates, $\hat{\boldsymbol{r}}$ and $\hat{\boldsymbol{s}}$, are obtained separately, so that*

$$\text{Cov}(\hat{\boldsymbol{r}},\, \hat{\boldsymbol{s}}) = \boldsymbol{\Sigma}_{\hat{r},\,\hat{s}} = \mathbf{0}. \tag{3.9}$$

Under Assumption 3.3 we only need to compute estimates of the asymptotic covariance matrix of $\hat{\boldsymbol{r}}$, $\boldsymbol{\Sigma}_{\hat{r}}$, and of $\hat{\boldsymbol{s}}$, $\boldsymbol{\Sigma}_{\hat{s}}$.

Applying well-known results from Lehmann (1983) and Barndorff-Nielsen (1978), Holland and Thayer (1987) derived the result summarized in Theorem 3.1.

Theorem 3.1. *When $\hat{\boldsymbol{r}}$ is the mle of a log-linear model for $\boldsymbol{r}$, the estimated covariance matrix $\boldsymbol{\Sigma}_{\hat{r}} = \text{Cov}(\boldsymbol{r})$ can be computed as*

$$\boldsymbol{\Sigma}_{\hat{r}} = \mathbf{C}_r \mathbf{C}_r^t \tag{3.10}$$

where $\mathbf{C}_r$ is the J by T_r matrix

$$\mathbf{C}_r = N^{-\frac{1}{2}} \mathbf{D}_{\sqrt{\hat{r}}} \mathbf{Q}.$$

The diagonal matrix, $\mathbf{D}_{\sqrt{\hat{r}}}$, has the diagonal entries $\sqrt{\hat{r}_j}$, and $\mathbf{Q}$ is the $J \times T_r$ orthogonal matrix that comes from the following $\mathbf{QR}$-factorization

$$[\mathbf{D}_{\sqrt{\hat{r}}} - \sqrt{\hat{\boldsymbol{r}}}\,\hat{\boldsymbol{r}}^t]\mathbf{B}^t = \mathbf{QR}.$$

$\mathbf{Q}$ is a $J \times T_r$-matrix with orthogonal columns, $\mathbf{R}$ is a $T_r \times T_r$ upper triangular matrix, and $\mathbf{B}$ is the $\mathbf{B}$-matrix from (3.5).

The details of the proof of Theorem 3.1 can be found in Holland and Thayer (1987, p. 18). A discussion of the $\mathbf{QR}$ factorization of a rectangular matrix can be found in Dongarra et al. (1979) and Epperson (2002).

Hence, if the model used for estimating $\boldsymbol{r}$ has T_r parameters and the model used for estimating $\boldsymbol{s}$ has T_s parameters, then two matrices, a $J \times T_r$-matrix, $\mathbf{C}_r$, and a $K \times T_s$-matrix, $\mathbf{C}_s$, may be derived so that

$$\boldsymbol{\Sigma}_{\hat{r}} = \mathbf{C}_r \mathbf{C}_r^t \quad \text{and} \quad \boldsymbol{\Sigma}_{\hat{s}} = \mathbf{C}_s \mathbf{C}_s^t. \tag{3.11}$$

Formula (3.10) expresses the potentially large $(J \times J)$ estimated covariance matrix, $\boldsymbol{\Sigma}_{\hat{\boldsymbol{r}}}$, in terms of the much smaller $(J \times T_r)$ matrix $\mathbf{C}_r$. For all of the standard error calculations in this book the factors, $\mathbf{C}_r$ and $\mathbf{C}_s$, give simple computational formulas that substantially reduce the size of the arrays that must be manipulated. These matrix factors, and others like them, are used throughout this book in the computation of standard errors.

The estimation procedure for a bivariate distribution is described in the Appendix B.

3.3 Estimation of the Score Probabilities

In Chapter 2 we give the Design Functions (DF) for the data collection designs that are discussed in this book. We repeat them here for summary purposes and refer to Chapter 2 for the details and notation. The DF maps the population scores probabilities relevant to the data collected in a design into $\boldsymbol{r}$ and $\boldsymbol{s}$, the score probabilities for $\boldsymbol{X}$ and $\boldsymbol{Y}$ on the target population, T.

EG Design. In the EG Design, the DF is given by

$$\begin{pmatrix} \boldsymbol{r} \\ \boldsymbol{s} \end{pmatrix} = \mathrm{DF}\,(\boldsymbol{r},\, \boldsymbol{s}) = \begin{pmatrix} \mathbf{I}_J & \mathbf{0} \\ \mathbf{0} & \mathbf{I}_K \end{pmatrix} \begin{pmatrix} \boldsymbol{r} \\ \boldsymbol{s} \end{pmatrix}.$$

SG Design. For the SG Design the DF is given by

$$\begin{pmatrix} \boldsymbol{r} \\ \boldsymbol{s} \end{pmatrix} = \mathrm{DF}\,(\mathbf{P}) = \begin{pmatrix} \mathbf{M} \\ \mathbf{N} \end{pmatrix} v(\mathbf{P}).$$

CB Design. The Design Function, for the CB Design using the two independent SG approach, is

$$\begin{aligned} \begin{pmatrix} \boldsymbol{r} \\ \boldsymbol{s} \end{pmatrix} &= \mathrm{DF}\left(\mathbf{P}_{(12)},\, \mathbf{P}_{(21)}\right) \\ &= \begin{pmatrix} w_X\mathbf{M} & (1-w_X)\mathbf{M} \\ (1-w_Y)\mathbf{N} & w_Y\mathbf{N} \end{pmatrix} \begin{pmatrix} v(\mathbf{P}_{(12)}) \\ v(\mathbf{P}_{(21)}) \end{pmatrix}. \end{aligned}$$

NEAT Design—CE. There are two levels of Design Functions that arise when the equating is carried out through Chain Equating in a NEAT Design. At the first level, there are two Design Functions that are from the two SG Designs inside the NEAT Design, denoted DF_P and DF_Q. DF_P is defined by

$$\begin{pmatrix} \boldsymbol{r}_P \\ \boldsymbol{t}_P \end{pmatrix} = \mathrm{DF}_P\,(\mathbf{P}) = \begin{pmatrix} \mathbf{M}_P \\ \mathbf{N}_P \end{pmatrix} v(\mathbf{P}),$$

and DF_Q is defined by

$$\begin{pmatrix} \boldsymbol{t}_Q \\ \boldsymbol{s}_Q \end{pmatrix} = \mathrm{DF}_Q\,(\mathbf{Q}) = \begin{pmatrix} \mathbf{N}_Q \\ \mathbf{M}_Q \end{pmatrix} v(\mathbf{Q}).$$

At the second level, these two Design Functions are combined into a single function

$$\begin{aligned} \begin{pmatrix} \boldsymbol{r}_P \\ \boldsymbol{t}_P \\ \boldsymbol{t}_Q \\ \boldsymbol{s}_Q \end{pmatrix} &= \mathrm{DF}\,(\mathbf{P},\, \mathbf{Q}) = \begin{pmatrix} \mathrm{DF}_P(\mathbf{P}) \\ \mathrm{DF}_Q(\mathbf{Q}) \end{pmatrix} \\ &= \begin{pmatrix} \begin{pmatrix} \mathbf{M}_P \\ \mathbf{N}_P \end{pmatrix} & \mathbf{0} \\ \mathbf{0} & \begin{pmatrix} \mathbf{N}_Q \\ \mathbf{M}_Q \end{pmatrix} \end{pmatrix} \begin{pmatrix} v(\mathbf{P}) \\ v(\mathbf{Q}) \end{pmatrix}. \end{aligned}$$

NEAT Design—PSE. The Design Function for PSE in a NEAT Design is given by

$$\begin{pmatrix} \boldsymbol{r} \\ \boldsymbol{s} \end{pmatrix} = \mathrm{DF}\left(\mathbf{P},\, \mathbf{Q};\, w\right) = \begin{pmatrix} \boldsymbol{r}(\mathbf{P},\, \mathbf{Q},\, w) \\ \boldsymbol{s}(\mathbf{P},\, \mathbf{Q},\, w) \end{pmatrix}$$

where

$$\boldsymbol{r}\left(\mathbf{P},\, \mathbf{Q},\, w\right) = \sum_{l} \left[w + \frac{(1-w)(t_{Ql})}{t_{Pl}} \right] \boldsymbol{p}_{l},$$

and

$$\boldsymbol{s}\left(\mathbf{P},\, \mathbf{Q},\, w\right) = \sum_{l} \left[(1-w) + \frac{w(t_{Pl})}{t_{Ql}} \right] \boldsymbol{q}_{l} \;.$$

The most important aspect of the DF in this book is its Jacobian, i.e., the matrix of the first derivatives of the Design Function with respect to the parameters $\boldsymbol{r}$ and $\boldsymbol{s}$. In the case of Chain Equating in a NEAT Design the derivatives are with respect to the parameters $\boldsymbol{r}_{P}$, $\boldsymbol{t}_{P}$, $\boldsymbol{t}_{Q}$, and $\boldsymbol{s}_{Q}$. These Jacobians are given in detail in Chapter 5.

4

Kernel Equating: Continuization and Equating

In this chapter, we discuss that part of Kernel Equating from which its name derives, i.e., continuization by use of Gaussian kernel smoothing. In addition, we will briefly cover how to compute the final KE function once the continuization step is finished and how to assess the ability of this equating function to match the discrete distributions of $\hat{e}_Y(\boldsymbol{X})$ and $\boldsymbol{Y}$. In this book, we will reserve the notation, $e_Y(x)$ and $e_X(y)$ for the KE functions for equating $\boldsymbol{X}$ to $\boldsymbol{Y}$ and $\boldsymbol{Y}$ to $\boldsymbol{X}$, respectively, on the target population, T. Even though the KE function is a type of equipercentile equating function, we will reserve the notation, $\mathrm{Equi}_Y(x)$, to refer to any version of the equipercentile equating function. The previous chapter covered the issues involved in pre-smoothing and the estimation of $\boldsymbol{r}$ and $\boldsymbol{s}$ from the pre-smoothed data. In the next chapter we will discuss the statistical accuracy of the estimated $e_Y(x)$ using the SEE and the SEED.

4.1 Continuization

A distinctive feature of Kernel Equating is its explicit consideration of the need to change the step-function cdf's of $\boldsymbol{X}$ and $\boldsymbol{Y}$ on T into approximating continuous cdf's in order to solve the basic equations (1.11) or to compute the inverse function in $G^{-1}(F(x))$. The traditional "percentile rank" approach to equipercentile equating treats this as a problem of linear interpolation, but in KE we identify it as an explicit step in the equating process.

The cumulative distribution functions (cdf's) of the score distributions for $\boldsymbol{X}$ and $\boldsymbol{Y}$ in (2.2) are defined as

$$F(x) = \text{Prob}(X \leq x) = \sum_{j,\, x_j \leq x} r_j, \tag{4.1}$$

$$G(y) = \text{Prob}(Y \leq y) = \sum_{k,\, y_k \leq y} s_k, \tag{4.2}$$

where $x, y \in \mathbb{R}$. These discrete cdf's have jumps at each score value, x_j or y_k.

Because $\boldsymbol{X}$ has a discrete distribution, the graph of $F(x)$ is flat for any $x \in [x_j, x_{j+1})$ and has a jump of size r_j at x_j. Similarly the graph of $G(y)$ is flat for any $y \in [y_k, y_{k+1})$ and has a jump of size s_k at y_k. In the cases that arise in practice the discrete set of values that $F(x)$ and $G(y)$ take on only rarely coincide. This means that in practice it never occurs that $F(x) = u$ and $G(y) = u$ for the same value of u in $(0, 1)$. This problem was mentioned earlier in Section 1.4. If $F(x)$ and $G(y)$ are continuous and strictly increasing for all x and $y \in \mathbb{R}$ this problem does not arise, and $F(x) = u = G(y)$ can always be solved for y, i.e.,

$$y = G^{-1}(F(x)), \tag{4.3}$$

where G^{-1} denote the inverse of G defined by: $y = G^{-1}(u)$ if and only if $u = G(y)$.

All methods of equipercentile-type equating, including KE, must address this problem of discreteness. In this section we first give the formulas used to continuize F and G and then provide some motivating discussion for this approach.

4.1.1 Gaussian Kernel Smoothing of Discrete Distributions

Let $\Phi(z)$ denote the cdf of the standard Normal (mean zero, variance one) or Gaussian distribution and let h_X be a positive number. μ_X and σ_X^2 denote the mean and variance, respectively, of $\boldsymbol{X}$ over T. Define a_X by

$$a_X^2 = \frac{\sigma_X^2}{\sigma_X^2 + h_X^2}. \tag{4.4}$$

Then the Gaussian kernel smoothing of the distribution of $\boldsymbol{X}$ has a cdf given by

$$F_{h_X}(x) = \sum_j r_j \Phi(R_{jX}(x)), \tag{4.5}$$

where

$$R_{jX}(x) = \frac{x - a_X x_j - (1 - a_X)\mu_X}{a_X h_X}, \tag{4.6}$$

and the constant, h_X, is the "bandwidth" of F_{h_X}. It is evident that $F_{h_X}(x)$ is a continuous cdf for any $h_X > 0$ because it is a weighted average of Normal cdf's, and it has a density function, $f_{h_X}(x)$, found by differentiating $F_{h_X}(x)$ in x, i.e.

$$f_{h_X}(x) = \sum_j r_j \phi\left(R_{jX}(x)\right) \frac{1}{a_X h_X}, \tag{4.7}$$

where $\phi(\cdot)$ is the standard Normal (or Gaussian) density function.

While formulas (4.5), (4.6), and (4.7) may appear somewhat strange at first, they are reasonably tractable for computations using a computer. In a similar manner, G may be continuized using G_{h_Y} defined as

$$G_{h_Y}(y) = \sum_k s_k \Phi\left(R_{kY}(y)\right), \tag{4.8}$$

where

$$R_{kY}(y) = \frac{y - a_Y y_k - (1 - a_Y)\mu_Y}{a_Y h_Y}, \tag{4.9}$$

and $G_{h_Y}(y)$ has the density function

$$g_{h_Y}(y) = \sum_k s_k \phi\left(R_{kY}(y)\right) \frac{1}{a_Y h_Y}. \tag{4.10}$$

Next we motivate these definitions of $F_{h_X}(x)$ and $G_{h_Y}(y)$ and show some of the senses in which they "approximate" F and G, respectively.

In this book we reserve the term "continuous distribution" to refer to one that has a density function (with respect to Lebesgue measure) that is positive over all of $\mathbb{R}$. A reoccurring example is any Normal distribution $\mathcal{N}(\mu, \sigma^2)$ with $\sigma^2 > 0$. If $\boldsymbol{X}$ is a discrete random variable, $\boldsymbol{V}$ is independent of $\boldsymbol{X}$ and has the Normal $\mathcal{N}(0, 1)$ distribution then $\boldsymbol{X} + h_X\boldsymbol{V}$ is an approximation to $\boldsymbol{X}$ that approaches $\boldsymbol{X}$ when h_X is small. However, because $\boldsymbol{V}$ has a continuous distribution it is intuitively evident that $\boldsymbol{X} + h_X\boldsymbol{V}$ is continuously distributed as well. A clearer argument why $\boldsymbol{X} + h_X\boldsymbol{V}$ has a continuous distribution is evident from the proof of Theorem 4.1, below. The new random variable $\boldsymbol{X} + h_X\boldsymbol{V}$ has the same mean or expected value as $\boldsymbol{X}$ because $\boldsymbol{V}$ has mean 0, so it "approximates" $\boldsymbol{X}$ in this sense (same mean) for any h_X. However, $\mathrm{Var}(\boldsymbol{X} + h_X\boldsymbol{V}) = \sigma_X^2 + h_X^2 > \sigma_X^2$ so that $\boldsymbol{X} + h_X\boldsymbol{V}$ does not have the same variance as $\boldsymbol{X}$ for any $h_X > 0$. It is easy to linearly transform $\boldsymbol{X} + h_X\boldsymbol{V}$ so that both the mean and the variance of the transformed approximation to $\boldsymbol{X}$ are the same as those for $\boldsymbol{X}$ for any h_X. This transformation is given by

$$\boldsymbol{X}(h_X) \quad = \quad a_X(\boldsymbol{X} + h_X\boldsymbol{V}) + (1 - a_X)\mu_X, \tag{4.11}$$

where a_X was defined in (4.4). It is a useful exercise for the reader to show that $\mathrm{E}(\boldsymbol{X}(h_X)) = \mathrm{E}(\boldsymbol{X})$ and that $\mathrm{Var}(\boldsymbol{X}(h_X)) = \mathrm{Var}(\boldsymbol{X})$, for any $h_X > 0$.

Analogously, we define the random variable, $\boldsymbol{Y}(h_Y)$,

$$\boldsymbol{Y}(h_Y) = a_Y(\boldsymbol{Y} + h_Y\boldsymbol{W}) + (1 - a_Y)\mu_Y, \tag{4.12}$$

where $\boldsymbol{W}$ is independent of $\boldsymbol{Y}$ and has the $\mathcal{N}(0, 1)$ distribution. $\boldsymbol{Y}(h_Y)$ is an approximation to $\boldsymbol{Y}$ in the same way that $\boldsymbol{X}(h_X)$ approximates $\boldsymbol{X}$. In (4.12), a_Y is defined similarly to a_X in (4.4) using μ_Y and σ_Y.

The bandwidths, h_X or h_Y, are positive constants that we are free to select to achieve some useful purpose. We use Theorem 4.1 to summarize the behavior of $\boldsymbol{X}(h_X)$ as $h_X \to 0$ and $h_X \to \infty$. As h_X varies over $(0, \infty)$, $\boldsymbol{X}(h_X)$ ranges from $\boldsymbol{X}$ to the $\mathcal{N}(\mu_X, \sigma_X^2)$ distribution so that, for large h_X, $\boldsymbol{X}(h_X)$ is a "Normal approximation" to $\boldsymbol{X}$.

Theorem 4.1. *Given the above notation, the following statements hold:*

$$(a) \quad \lim_{h_X \to 0} a_X = 1, \tag{4.13}$$

$$(b) \quad \lim_{h_X \to \infty} a_X = 0, \tag{4.14}$$

$$(c) \quad \lim_{h_X \to \infty} h_X a_X = \sigma_X, \tag{4.15}$$

$$(d) \quad \lim_{h_X \to 0} \boldsymbol{X}(h_X) = \boldsymbol{X}, \tag{4.16}$$

$$(e) \quad \lim_{h_X \to \infty} \boldsymbol{X}(h_X) = \sigma_X \boldsymbol{V} + \mu_X. \tag{4.17}$$

When $h_X > 0$, then $\boldsymbol{X}(h_X)$ has a continuous distribution with a cdf that we denote by

$$F_{h_X}(x) = \mathrm{Prob}\{\boldsymbol{X}(h_X) \leq x\}. \tag{4.18}$$

We will regard

$$\{F_{h_X}(x), \text{ for } h_X > 0\},$$

as a family of continuous approximations to the discrete cdf $F(x)$.

Theorem 4.2, below, shows that the cdf of $\boldsymbol{X}(h_X)$ is exactly the continuized version of F given earlier in (4.5) and (4.6). The proof of Theorem 4.2 is simple but instructive so we include it.

Theorem 4.2. *If $\boldsymbol{X}(h_X)$ is defined by (4.11) and $F_{h_X}(x)$ is the cdf in (4.18) then*

$$F_{h_X}(x) = \sum_j r_j \Phi\left(R_{jX}(x)\right),$$

where

$$R_{jX}(x) = \frac{x - a_X x_j - (1 - a_X)\mu_X}{a_X h_X}.$$

Thus, the Gaussian kernel continuization of F defined in (4.5) is exactly the cdf of $\boldsymbol{X}(h_X)$.

Proof.

$$\begin{aligned}
F_{h_X}(x) &= \text{Prob}\{\boldsymbol{X}(h_X) \le x\} \\
&= \text{Prob}\{a_X(\boldsymbol{X} + h_X\mathbf{V}) + (1 - a_X)\mu_X \le x\} \\
&= \text{Prob}\{a_X h_X \mathbf{V} \le x - a_X\boldsymbol{X} - (1 - a_X)\mu_X\} \\
&= \sum_j \text{Prob}\{a_X h_X \mathbf{V} \le x - a_X x_j - (1 - a_X)\mu_X \mid \boldsymbol{X} = x_j\} r_j \\
&= \sum_j \text{Prob}\{\mathbf{V} \le \frac{x - a_X x_j - (1 - a_X)\mu_X}{a_X h_X}\} r_j \\
&= \sum_j r_j \Phi\left(\frac{x - a_X x_j - (1 - a_X)\mu_X}{a_X h_X}\right).
\end{aligned}$$

□

Theorem 4.3. *Using the notation of Theorem 4.2, $R_{jX}(x)$, defined in (4.6), has the following approximate forms when h_X is either very small or very large:*

$$(a) \quad R_{jX}(x) = \frac{x - x_j}{h_X} + o(h_X) \quad as \quad h_X \to 0, \tag{4.19}$$

$$(b) \quad R_{jX}(x) = \frac{x - \mu_X}{\sigma_X} - \frac{\sigma_X}{h_X}\frac{x_j - \mu_X}{\sigma_X} + o\left(\frac{\sigma_X}{h_X}\right) \quad as \quad h_X \to \infty. \tag{4.20}$$

In (a) the remainder term, $o(h_X)$, is small compared to h_X as $h_X \to 0$, and in (b) the remainder term, $o(\sigma_X/h_X)$, is small compared to σ_X/h_X as $h_X \to \infty$.

The proof of 4.3 is straightforward and we omit it.

The results in Theorem 4.3 combined with those of Theorem 4.2 show that the analytical expression for $F_{h_X}(x)$ given in (4.5) and in Theorem 4.2 behaves in the same manner as suggested in Theorem 4.1, parts (d) and (e). As $h_X \to 0$, $R_{jX}(x)$ has a rapid change from large negative to large positive at $x = x_j$ so that $F_{h_X}(x)$ is nearly a discrete step function with a jump of r_j at x_j. On the other hand, as $h_X \to \infty$, $R_{jX}(x) = [(x - \mu_X)/\sigma_X]$ plus an error that is small if σ_X/h_X is small. In the latter case, $F_{h_X}(x)$ is nearly the Normal cdf, $\Phi((x - \mu_X)/\sigma_X)$. Theorem 4.3 part (b) suggests that the proper measure of "h_X is large" is when σ_X/h_X is small. We will make use of this observation and regard h_X as large whenever σ_X/h_X is less than 0.1, i.e., $h_X > 10\sigma_X$.

As mentioned earlier it is easy to show that the mean and variance of $\boldsymbol{X}(h_X)$ exactly match those of the original discrete random variable $\boldsymbol{X}$. To study the sense in which the family of cdf's, $\{F_{h_X}(x), \text{for } h_X > 0\}$, approximates F it is of some interest to know how the higher moments of $\boldsymbol{X}(h_X)$ differ from those of $\boldsymbol{X}$. It is, however, the *cumulants* of $\boldsymbol{X}(h_X)$ rather than its moments that have the simplest relationship to those of $\boldsymbol{X}$. The j-th cumulant of a distribution is the coefficient of $(t)^j/j!$ in the Taylor expansion (about zero) of the natural logarithm of its moment generating function. See Kendall and Stuart (1977) for a thorough discussion of cumulants. It is well-known that the first and second cumulants are the mean and variance respectively, of the distribution. Furthermore, the third and fourth cumulants are related to the usual measure of skewness and kurtosis by

$$k_{3X} = 3^{\text{rd}} \text{ cumulant of } \boldsymbol{X} = \sigma_X^3 \operatorname{skew}(\boldsymbol{X}); \tag{4.21}$$

$$k_{4X} = 4^{\text{rd}} \text{ cumulant of } \boldsymbol{X} = \sigma_X^4 \operatorname{kurt}(\boldsymbol{X}); \tag{4.22}$$

where

$$\operatorname{skew}(\boldsymbol{X}) = \mathrm{E}\left(\frac{\boldsymbol{X} - \mu_X}{\sigma_X}\right)^3; \tag{4.23}$$

$$\operatorname{kurt}(\boldsymbol{X}) = \mathrm{E}\left(\frac{\boldsymbol{X} - \mu_X}{\sigma_X}\right)^4 - 3. \tag{4.24}$$

The third and higher cumulants of any Normal distribution are all zero. In addition, cumulants have the property that the cumulants of the sum of two *independent* random variables is the sum of their respective cumulants. Thus, the cumulants share the summation property of variances for moments higher than the second. Cumulants beyond the first are not affected by adding a constant to the random variable, and multiplication by a constant merely changes the cumulants by multiplying them by the corresponding power of the constant—the pth power for the pth cumulant.

Theorem 4.4 shows the relationship between the cumulants of $\boldsymbol{X}(h_X)$ and those of $\boldsymbol{X}$. The proof can be found in Holland and Thayer (1989, p. 47).

Theorem 4.4. *If $k_j(h_X)$ denotes the j-th cumulant of $\boldsymbol{X}(h_X)$, and k_{jX} denotes the j-th cumulant of $\boldsymbol{X}$, then for $j \geq 3$ we have*

$$k_j(h_X) = (a_X)^j k_{jX}, \tag{4.25}$$

where a_X is defined in (4.4).

We may interpret Theorem 4.4 as saying that the higher cumulants of $\boldsymbol{X}(h_X)$ are all smaller in absolute size (i.e., more like those of the Normal distribution) than the corresponding cumulants of the original distribution of $\boldsymbol{X}$. This is because

$$(a_X)^j < 1 \quad \text{if} \quad h_X > 0.$$

Thus, $\boldsymbol{X}(h_X)$ has cumulants that are more like those of $\boldsymbol{X}$ when h_X is small and more like those of the $\mathcal{N}(\mu_X, \sigma_X^2)$ when h_X is large.

4.1.2 Choice of the Bandwidth

There is a variety of ways to select the "bandwidth," h_X. Perhaps the easiest is to always use a specific fixed value. Two useful examples are $h_X = \infty$ and $h_X = 0.33$. When h_X is large (i.e., $h_X > 10\sigma_X$), F_{h_X} is a "Normal approximation" to F, that is

$$F_{h_X}(x) \approx \Phi\left(\frac{x - \mu_X}{\sigma_X}\right). \tag{4.26}$$

When both h_X and h_Y are large, the resulting Kernel Equating function is the linear equating function (this is discussed more in Section 4.2). The choice of $h_X = 0.33$ was originally motivated to simulate the traditional percentile rank method of equipercentile equating. When h_X is this small (i.e., $h_X = 0.33$) $F_{h_X}(x)$ is a close continuous approximation to F which is a discontinuous jump function. This has both positive and negative consequences. For example, as mentioned in the previous subsection, the smaller h_X is, the closer the distribution of $\boldsymbol{X}(h_X)$ is to that of $\boldsymbol{X}$. On the other hand, the smaller h_X is, the less the density function $f_{h_X}(x)$ in (4.7) tracks the shape of the score probabilities of $\boldsymbol{X}$, $\{r_j\}$. Figures 4.1 and 4.2 illustrate this well. In Figure 4.2 we show two different KE density functions that approximate the discrete distribution described by the histogram in Figure 4.1. In Figure 4.2 the smaller bandwidth, $h_X = 0.33$, results in a very "spikey" density function that looks less like Figure 4.1 than the smoothed density ($h_X = 0.622$) does.

While a fixed choice of h_X is convenient, it ignores the idea that the distribution that $F_{h_X}(x)$ specifies should *approximate* the distribution that F specifies. To do this we have developed two automatic ways of choosing h_X that do attend to the shape of the resulting approximating density function. Our approaches both use the density function, $f_{h_X}(x)$, to approximate the score probabilities, $\{r_j\}$. It is easiest to motivate this in the case when the scores are consecutive integers such as "number right scoring" where, $x_1 = 0$, $x_2 = 1$, $\ldots$, $x_J = J - 1$. We will make that assumption here, as we do in our examples in Part II. We create a histogram from $\{(r_j, x_j)\}$ in the following way. There are series of J class intervals of width 1 with x_j at the midpoint of its interval. The height of histogram for the jth class interval is r_j. The area of the histogram-bar for the jth class interval is r_j times the interval's width, which is just 1 in this simplest case. On the other hand, $f_{h_X}(x_j)$ is the height of the density function at the score x_j.

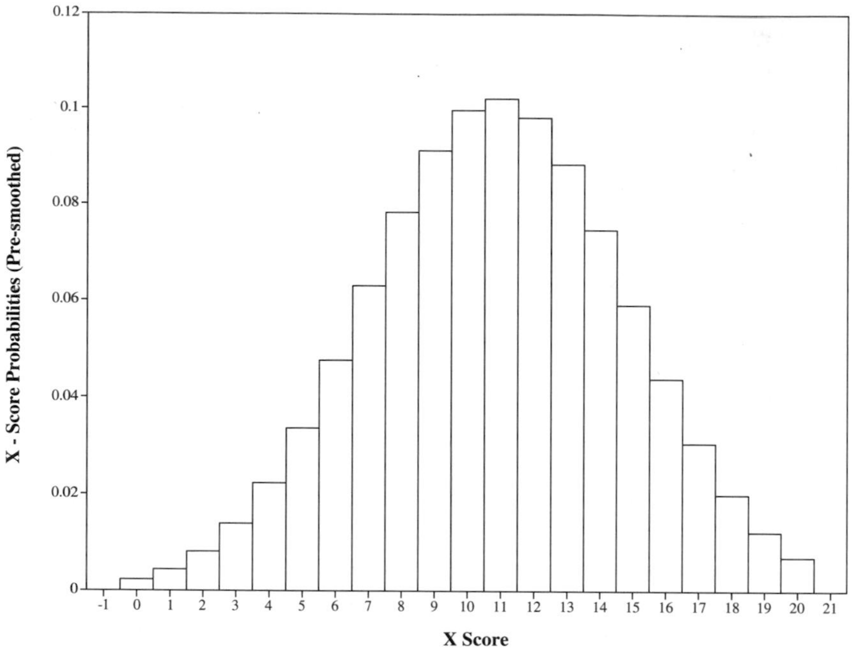

FIGURE 4.1. Histogram from the pre-smoothed $\{(\hat{r}_j,\, x_j)\}$.

The product of the interval width times the height of the density, $f_{h_X}(x_j)$, should be similar to r_j times the interval width if $f_{h_X}(x)$ mirrors the shape of the frequencies, r_j. To choose h_X automatically, we propose selecting it to minimize

$$\mathrm{PEN}_1(h_X) = \sum_j \left(\hat{r}_j - \hat{f}_{h_X}(x_j)\right)^2 . \tag{4.27}$$

Our experience suggests that use of PEN_1 leads to values of h_X that are two or three times as big as $h_X = 0.33$. Figure 4.2 illustrates this well. In Figure 4.2 we have graphed the density, $f_{h_X}(x)$, for $h_X = 0.33$ and for the h_X that minimizes (4.27) in a particular example (0.622). As we mentioned earlier, the spikey look of $f_{0.33}(x)$ compared to $f_{0.622}(x)$ shows that the latter better approximates the histogram in Figure 4.1 than the former. $\mathrm{PEN}_1(h_X)$ can be minimized using a variety of different algorithms, but we will not discuss them here.

In certain cases, in particular when the r_j exhibit "teeth," "gaps," or other nonrandom nonsmoothness, it is necessary to smooth $f_{h_X}(x)$ more than PEN_1 will accomplish. Our approach is to prevent the density $f_{h_X}(x)$ from having more than a few modes. We do this by penalizing choices of h_X that allow the derivative of $f_{h_X}(x)$, which we denote by $f'_{h_X}(x)$, to have a sign change near several score values, x_j. The function $f'_{h_X}(x)$, is given

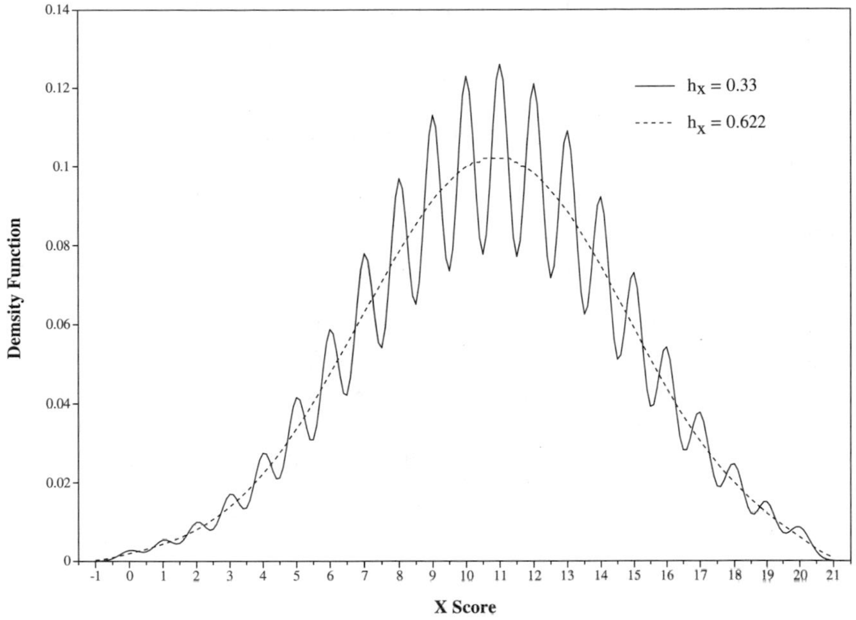

FIGURE 4.2. Density $f_{h_X}(x_j)$ for two h_X values, $h_X = 0.33$ and the optimal h_X, which in this case is 0.622.

by

$$
\begin{aligned}
f'_{h_X}(x) &= \frac{\partial f_{h_X}}{\partial x} \\
&= -\sum_j r_j \phi\left(R_{jX}(x)\right) \frac{1}{(a_X h_X)^2} \left(R_{jX}(x)\right), \qquad (4.28)
\end{aligned}
$$

where $R_{jX}(x)$ was defined in (4.6).

We use the penalty function

$$
\mathrm{PEN}_2(h_X) = \sum_j A_j(1 - B_j), \tag{4.29}
$$

where $A_j = 1$ if $f'_{h_X}(x) < 0$ a little to the left of x_j, and $B_j = 0$ if $f'_{h_X}(x) > 0$ a little to the right of x_j. Thus we get a penalty of 1 for every score point where $f_{h_X}(x)$ is "U-shaped" around it. What "near" means is a parameter of $\mathrm{PEN}_2(h_X)$. In our own work we set "near" to mean $\pm\frac{1}{4}$ of a score point and evaluate f'_{h_X} at $x_j \pm \frac{1}{4}$ in computing A_j and B_j, above. We may combine the two penalties with a weight such as

$$
\mathrm{PEN}_1(h_X) + K \times \mathrm{PEN}_2(h_X). \tag{4.30}
$$

This will force the histogram and the density to be near each other but will keep the density from having too many zero derivatives. We have used $K = 1$ in our examples. The bigger K is, the fewer modes the resulting density function will have.

The combined penalty function in (4.30) provides a useful solution to the problem of "grinding down teeth" in an estimated score distribution. "Teeth" or "gaps" in the raw score distribution can arise in the estimation or pre-smoothing phase of the equating process. (See Chapter 10 for an example that has "gaps" in the score probabilities.) Our recommendation is to preserve these features of the data during pre-smoothing so that the models that are fit to the raw data actually do fit it, rather than "grinding down the teeth" at the pre-smoothing stage. Our rationale for this recommendation is that in order for the standard errors that come out of the pre-smoothing phase to be valid, the model has to fit the data. However, it is rarely plausible to keep the teeth in $f_{h_X}(x)$ and $F_{h_X}(x)$ and so we recommend that they be removed in the continuization step. The penalty function in (4.30) will do this.

4.2 Equating

Once $\hat{F}_{h_X}$ and $\hat{G}_{h_Y}$ are in hand, it is a relatively straightforward process to compute the Kernel Equating functions via the KE analog of the definition of $\mathrm{Equi}_Y(x)$ in Chapter 1, i.e.,

$$\begin{aligned} \hat{e}_Y(x) = e_Y(x; \hat{\boldsymbol{r}}, \hat{\boldsymbol{s}}) &= G_{h_Y}^{-1}(F_{h_X}(x; \hat{\boldsymbol{r}}); \hat{\boldsymbol{s}}) \\ &= \hat{G}_{h_Y}^{-1}(\hat{F}_{h_X}(x)). \end{aligned} \tag{4.31}$$

Analogously, the KE equating function for equating $\boldsymbol{Y}$ to $\boldsymbol{X}$ on T is given by

$$\begin{aligned} \hat{e}_X(y) = e_X(y; \hat{\boldsymbol{r}}, \hat{\boldsymbol{s}}) &= F_{h_X}^{-1}(G_{h_Y}(y; \hat{\boldsymbol{s}}); \hat{\boldsymbol{r}}) \\ &= \hat{F}_{h_X}^{-1}(\hat{G}_{h_Y}(y)). \end{aligned} \tag{4.32}$$

The computational issue for (4.31) and (4.32) is the accuracy with which the inverse functions $\hat{F}_{h_X}^{-1}(\cdot)$ and $\hat{G}_{h_Y}^{-1}(\cdot)$ need to be computed. However, due to the smooth form of both $\hat{F}_{h_X}$ and $\hat{G}_{h_Y}$ Newton's method can be used effectively to solve this problem.

The next theorem (see also Holland and Thayer, 1989) demonstrates that when h_X and h_Y are both large, the KE functions closely approximate the standard linear equating function.

Theorem 4.5. *If $e_Y(x)$ is defined by (4.3) then*

$$\lim_{h_X, h_Y \to \infty} e_Y(x) = \mu_Y + \frac{\sigma_Y}{\sigma_X}(x - \mu_X) = \mathrm{Lin}_Y(x).$$

Proof. From (4.14), as h_X and $h_Y \to \infty$, $F_{h_X}(x)$ and $G_{h_Y}(y)$ approach these Normal cdf's

$$F_{h_X}(x) \to \Phi\left(\frac{x-\mu_X}{\sigma_X}\right),$$
$$G_{h_Y}(y) \to \Phi\left(\frac{y-\mu_Y}{\sigma_Y}\right).$$

Hence

$$G_{h_Y}^{-1}(u) \to \mu_Y + \sigma_Y \Phi^{-1}(u),$$

where $\Phi^{-1}(u)$ is the inverse of the standard Normal cdf, therefore

$$\begin{aligned} e_Y(x) &\to \mu_Y + \sigma_Y \Phi^{-1}\left(\Phi\left(\frac{x-\mu_X}{\sigma_X}\right)\right), \\ &= \mu_Y + \sigma_Y\left(\frac{x-\mu_X}{\sigma_X}\right). \end{aligned}$$

□

Thus, the KE functions estimated in (4.31) and (4.32) provide equipercentile-type equating functions that can be linear or nonlinear depending on the actual form of the score distributions. In addition, because $\mathrm{Lin}_Y(x)$ is a limiting form of a KE function, we are able, in the next chapter, to find a standard error for the difference between $\hat{e}_Y(x)$ and $\widehat{\mathrm{Lin}}_Y(x)$. This can assist in choosing between a linear and equipercentile equating function. Due to Theorem 4.5, whenever we refer to a KE function as linear we always mean choosing the bandwidths, h_X and h_Y, to exceed 10 times their respective standard deviations, σ_X and σ_Y.

Diagnosing the effectiveness of $e_Y(x)$. Once we have computed $e_Y(x)$, we can ask how well does it work when applied to $\boldsymbol{X}$ and $\boldsymbol{Y}$ rather than to $\boldsymbol{X}(h_X)$ and $\boldsymbol{Y}(h_Y)$ The equating function, $e_Y(x)$, is designed to perfectly transform the entire *continuous* distribution of $\boldsymbol{X}(h_X)$ into the *continuous* distribution of $\boldsymbol{Y}(h_Y)$. But, of course, we should really only care about what this transformation does to the *discrete* distribution of $\boldsymbol{X}$. Equating $\boldsymbol{X}$ to $\boldsymbol{Y}$ is the problem, $\boldsymbol{X}(h_X)$ and $\boldsymbol{Y}(h_Y)$ are just tools to facilitate this.

Thus, we need to compare these two discrete distributions, $\{(e_Y(x_j), r_j)\}$ and $\{(y_k, s_k)\}$. We note that the equating process cannot alter the score probabilities, r_j. All that is altered is the location of the possible values of $\boldsymbol{X}$, from x_j to $e_Y(x_j)$. In addition, it is unlikely that the sets of possible values of $e_Y(\boldsymbol{X})$ and $\boldsymbol{Y}$ will coincide to any appreciable degree.

There are at least two different ways that could be used to compare the distribution of $e_Y(\boldsymbol{X})$ to that of $\boldsymbol{Y}$. The first is to compare the moments of these two distributions. The second is to compare their discrete cdf's.

These two cdf's are

$$F_{e(X)}(y) = \sum_{j:\, e_Y(x_j) \leq y} r_j \quad \text{and} \quad G(y) = \sum_{k:\, y_k \leq y} s_k. \tag{4.33}$$

The difference $F_{e(X)}(y) - G(y)$ gives the amount by which $F_{e(X)}(y)$ misses $G(y)$ for each value, y. In our work, we have not used these cdf's for comparing the two discrete distributions, but they are certainly worth considering. In our work we have concentrated on the first approach using moments.

To compare the moments of $\boldsymbol{Y}$ and $e_Y(\boldsymbol{X})$ we use the Percent Relative Error in the pth moments, the PRE(p), which we now define. First, let the moments of $\boldsymbol{Y}$ and $e_Y(\boldsymbol{X})$ be denoted by

$$\mu_p(\boldsymbol{Y}) = \sum_k (y_k)^p s_k \quad \text{and} \quad \mu_p(e_Y(\boldsymbol{X})) = \sum_j (e_Y(x_j))^p r_j, \tag{4.34}$$

then the PRE(p) is

$$\text{PRE}(p) = 100 \frac{\mu_p(e_Y(\boldsymbol{X})) - \mu_p(\boldsymbol{Y})}{\mu_p(\boldsymbol{Y})}. \tag{4.35}$$

Our experience shows that for $p = 1$ and 2 the PRE(p) is quite small, but not zero. This is due to the fact that the first two moments of $\boldsymbol{X}$ and $\boldsymbol{Y}$ are preserved by $\boldsymbol{X}(h_X)$ and $\boldsymbol{Y}(h_Y)$. In our work we have routinely examined the first 10 moments of $\boldsymbol{Y}$ and $e_Y(\boldsymbol{X})$. As p increases, the PRE(p) usually increases as well, but, as will be seen in the detailed examples of the chapters in Part II of the book, they are often remarkably small when the continuization step has been done carefully (for example, see Table 7.5 in Chapter 7). Thus, while it is impossible to turn the discrete distribution of $\boldsymbol{X}$ exactly into that of $\boldsymbol{Y}$, via an observed score equating function, it can be done well enough to make the first ten moments of these two distributions almost indistinguishable.

5

Kernel Equating: The SEE and the SEED

In this chapter, we discuss the last step of the equating process, computing the Standard Error of Equating, the SEE. We derive general results that can be applied to all of the equating designs discussed in this book. Our goal here is to develop our way of computing the SEE for KE as generally as we can, so that the features of the SEE for the several equating designs can be put on a common footing and compared. Except for the early work of Lord (1950, 1955a), which was done under the assumption that all of the test scores were Normally distributed, we do not believe that such a comprehensive analytic discussion of the SEE has been done before. Liou et al. (1997) discuss the standard error of equating for KE in the NEAT Design. They take a different point of view from the approach we follow in this chapter.

We also include the special features needed to discuss the SEE for Chain Equating in the NEAT Design. In addition, we will discuss a new concept, the SEED, or the Standard Error of Equating Difference, which can be used in many designs to compare two KE functions, (e.g., to compare the KE function obtained using a penalty function to determine h_X and h_Y to the linear KE function obtained using large values of h_X and h_Y.) The SEED can assist the analyst in making decisions about equating functions.

In the previous two chapters we covered the issues involved in presmoothing, and the estimation of $\boldsymbol{r}$ and $\boldsymbol{s}$ (Chapter 3) as well as continuization and the computation and assessment of the Kernel Equating functions (Chapter 4).

5.1 Introduction

As outlined in Section 1.7, estimated equating functions are estimates of population quantities and are, therefore, subject to sampling variability that arises from the fact that the estimate of the equating function would have been different had different random samples of examinees been selected in the data collection design. The standard error of equating, the SEE, measures this uncertainty in the estimated equating function.

As we indicated in (4.31), the KE function depends on both $\boldsymbol{r}$ and $\boldsymbol{s}$, the estimated score probabilities for $\boldsymbol{X}$ and $\boldsymbol{Y}$ over T. (The slight modifications for Chain Equating in the NEAT Design is discussed in Section 5.3.4 and Chapter 10.) These two vectors of score probabilities, in turn, depend on the data collection design and the sample data collected with it, as explained in Chapter 2.

As indicated in Section 1.7, the SEE is based on the large sample distribution of $\hat{e}_Y(x)$, and it is the variance of this large sample (or asymptotic) distribution of $\hat{e}_Y(x)$ that is used in the computation of the SEE. Strictly speaking the formulas that we develop for the SEE in this book are more valid for larger sample sizes, and their utility for smaller sample sizes is a useful topic for further research.

Finally, in our calculation of the SEE for a KE function, we will assume that the bandwidths, h_X and h_Y, are fixed values and are not functions of $\boldsymbol{r}$ and $\boldsymbol{s}$. This is only an approximation when h_X and h_Y are obtained by minimizing a penalty function, as discussed in Section 4.1.2. It is a useful approximation, we think, but further research is necessary to investigate the degree to which the minimization affects estimates of the SEE. Such an investigation is beyond the scope of this book, but it is worth further research.

With this understanding, we denote the SEE for equating $\boldsymbol{X}$ to $\boldsymbol{Y}$ by

$$\text{SEE}_Y(x) = \hat{\sigma}_Y(x) = \sqrt{\text{Var}(\hat{e}_Y(x))}, \tag{5.1}$$

and the SEE for equating $\boldsymbol{Y}$ to $\boldsymbol{X}$ by

$$\text{SEE}_X(y) = \hat{\sigma}_X(y) = \sqrt{\text{Var}(\hat{e}_X(y))}, \tag{5.2}$$

where the equating functions are given by (4.31) and (4.32).

Formula (1.20) is useful to recall because it emphasizes that for fixed choices of h_X and h_Y, all of the randomness or uncertainty in $\hat{e}_X(y)$ or $\hat{e}_Y(x)$ comes from the estimation of $\boldsymbol{r}$ and $\boldsymbol{s}$.

Lord (1950) gives formulas for the SEE in the case of linear equating for several equating designs. Strictly speaking, Lord's formulas are valid only under the assumption that the scores are Normally distributed. Braun and Holland (1982) give the general asymptotic formula for the SEE for the linear equating function for the EG Design. Kolen (1985) derives formulas of similar generality for the SEE for linear equating in the NEAT Designs with both internal and external anchor tests. Lord (1982) gives the SEE for the equipercentile equating function in the case of the EG Design. He assumes no pre- or post-smoothing in his derivations. Jarjoura and Kolen (1985) give formulas for the SEE for equipercentile equating in the case of an anchor test (also called the frequency estimation method). Their formulas also assume no pre- or post-smoothing. Thus, the currently available formulas for the SEE for equipercentile equating are not flexible enough to take into account the variance reduction implicit in pre- and post-smoothing. Studies of the usefulness of pre- and post-smoothing are given in Fairbank (1987), Kolen (1984) and Kolen and Jarjoura (1987), and few practitioners would now leave out pre-smoothing (see, e.g., Livingston, 1993a), except when dealing with the enormous samples that can arise in large testing programs.

Our approach to computing the SEE for KE uses the explicit formulas for the equating functions given in (4.3), and (4.31) and the estimated covariance matrices, $\boldsymbol{\Sigma}_{\hat{r}}$, $\boldsymbol{\Sigma}_{\hat{s}}$, and $\boldsymbol{\Sigma}_{\hat{r},\hat{s}}$. We derive formulas that are valid approximations for all of the types of equating designs described in Chapter 2. In all of our analyses, we assume that the **C**-matrices (see Theorem 3.1) for computing $\boldsymbol{\Sigma}_{\hat{r}}$, $\boldsymbol{\Sigma}_{\hat{s}}$, and $\boldsymbol{\Sigma}_{\hat{r},\hat{s}}$ are available. Thus our SEE's reflect the data collection design (through the Design Function), the method of estimating the population score probabilities, i.e., pre-smoothing (through the **C**-matrices), and the formula used for the equating function. In this regard, our formulas for the SEE for the Kernel Equating are more satisfactory than the earlier derivations of the SEE for equipercentile equating. As mentioned earlier, being based on large sample approximations, all of these SEE's, both ours and those referenced, are strictly valid for large samples of examinees, but in small samples they may often be the only measure of uncertainity available. The usefulness of the SEE for small samples is a good topic for future research.

5.2 The δ-Method Divides the Problem in Three

At this point we believe it is useful to stand back and look at the transformation that starts with the (pre-smoothed) data and ends up with the estimated equating function, $\hat{e}_Y(x)$. The material in this section will be modified appropriately for the case of Chain Equating in Section 5.3.4.

We begin with the Design Function that transforms the pre-smoothed score distributions from the original equating design into $\boldsymbol{r}$ and $\boldsymbol{s}$, the distributions of $\boldsymbol{X}$ and $\boldsymbol{Y}$ on T, respectively. In order to have a general formulation we let $\boldsymbol{R}$ and $\boldsymbol{S}$ stand for the vectors of pre-smoothed score distributions. Table 5.1 indicates the interpretation of $\boldsymbol{R}$ and $\boldsymbol{S}$ for each equating design. For example, in the EG design, $\boldsymbol{R}$ is just the vector $\boldsymbol{r}$ and $\boldsymbol{S}$ is $\boldsymbol{s}$ (see (2.3)). However, in the CB design $\boldsymbol{R}$ is $v(\mathbf{P}_{(12)})$ and $\boldsymbol{S}$

TABLE 5.1. The Vectors $\boldsymbol{R}$ and $\boldsymbol{S}$ Across Four Data Collection Designs.

	EG	SG	CB	NEAT
$\hat{\boldsymbol{R}}$	$\hat{\boldsymbol{r}}$	$v(\hat{\mathbf{P}})$	$v(\hat{\mathbf{P}}_{(12)})$	$v(\hat{\mathbf{P}})$
$\hat{\boldsymbol{S}}$	$\hat{\boldsymbol{s}}$	—	$v(\hat{\mathbf{P}}_{(21)})$	$v(\hat{\mathbf{Q}})$

is $v(\mathbf{P}_{(21)})$, where $v(\mathbf{P}_{(12)})$ and $v(\mathbf{P}_{(21)})$ are defined in (2.24). In the SG design, $\boldsymbol{R}$ is $v(\mathbf{P})$ and there is no $\boldsymbol{S}$ (see (2.7) and (2.8) for the definition of $v(\mathbf{P})$ and (2.13) for the definition of the Design Function for the SG Design). In order to accommodate the SG Design in what follows we make the convention in the SG Design that $\boldsymbol{S}$ is an arbitrary vector that has no influence on either $\boldsymbol{r}$ or $\boldsymbol{s}$. This will give us the correct formulas for the Jacobian matrix that are the important consequence of this integration of the four designs into a common framework. The vectorized versions of $\mathbf{P}$ and $\mathbf{Q}$, $v(\mathbf{P})$ and $v(\mathbf{Q})$, for the NEAT Design, were defined in (2.33).

In this general framework we denote a general Design Function as

$$\begin{pmatrix} \hat{\boldsymbol{r}} \\ \hat{\boldsymbol{s}} \end{pmatrix} = \mathrm{DF}\left(\hat{\boldsymbol{R}}, \hat{\boldsymbol{S}}\right). \tag{5.3}$$

Furthermore, we assume that $\boldsymbol{R}$ and $\boldsymbol{S}$ are estimated independently so that $\mathrm{Cov}(\hat{\boldsymbol{R}}, \hat{\boldsymbol{S}}) = 0$. We also assume that the "**C**-matrices", $\mathbf{C}_R$ and $\mathbf{C}_S$, are available, so that

$$\boldsymbol{\Sigma}_{\hat{R}} = \mathrm{Cov}(\hat{\boldsymbol{R}}) = \mathbf{C}_R\mathbf{C}_R^t, \tag{5.4}$$

$$\boldsymbol{\Sigma}_{\hat{S}} = \mathrm{Cov}(\hat{\boldsymbol{S}}) = \mathbf{C}_S\mathbf{C}_S^t. \tag{5.5}$$

Thus,

$$\begin{aligned} \mathrm{Cov}\begin{pmatrix} \hat{\boldsymbol{R}} \\ \hat{\boldsymbol{S}} \end{pmatrix} &= \begin{pmatrix} \mathbf{C}_R\mathbf{C}_R^t & 0 \\ 0 & \mathbf{C}_S\mathbf{C}_S^t \end{pmatrix} \\ &= \begin{pmatrix} \mathbf{C}_R & 0 \\ 0 & \mathbf{C}_S \end{pmatrix}\begin{pmatrix} \mathbf{C}_R^t & 0 \\ 0 & \mathbf{C}_S^t \end{pmatrix} = \mathbf{C}\mathbf{C}^t, \end{aligned} \tag{5.6}$$

where

$$\mathbf{C} = \begin{pmatrix} \mathbf{C}_R & 0 \\ 0 & \mathbf{C}_S \end{pmatrix}. \tag{5.7}$$

Hence,

$$\mathrm{Cov}\begin{pmatrix} \hat{\boldsymbol{R}} \\ \hat{\boldsymbol{S}} \end{pmatrix} = \mathbf{C}\mathbf{C}^t. \tag{5.8}$$

TABLE 5.2. The **C**-Matrices, $\mathbf{C}_R$ and $\mathbf{C}_S$, and J_X, K_Y, T_X, and T_Y Across Four Data Collection Designs.

	EG	SG	CB	NEAT
$\mathbf{C}_R$	$\mathbf{C}_r$	$\mathbf{C}_P$	$\mathbf{C}_{(12)}$	$\mathbf{C}_P$
$\mathbf{C}_S$	$\mathbf{C}_s$	—	$\mathbf{C}_{(21)}$	$\mathbf{C}_Q$
J_X	J	JK	JK	JL
K_Y	K	—	JK	KL
T_X	T_r	T_P	$T_{(12)}$	T_P
T_Y	T_s	—	$T_{(21)}$	T_Q

The matrix **C** is (J_X+K_Y) by (T_X+T_Y)-matrix when J_X is the dimension of $\boldsymbol{R}$, K_Y the dimension of $\boldsymbol{S}$, T_X the number of parameters estimated in $\hat{\boldsymbol{R}}$ and T_Y the number of parameters estimated in $\hat{\boldsymbol{S}}$. We use this notation to include all the designs in Chapter 2. For example, in the EG Design $J_X = J$ while in the NEAT Design $J_X = JL$. For the SG Design $J_X = JK$ and K_Y is arbitrary because $\boldsymbol{S}$ is.

Table 5.2 identifies the interpretation of $\mathbf{C}_R$ and $\mathbf{C}_S$ in each of the designs using the notation from Chapters 2 and 3, as well as the values of J_X and K_Y, and of T_X and T_Y.

The matrices $\mathbf{C}_r$ and $\mathbf{C}_s$ are described in Theorem 3.1 and are part of the output of the univariate pre-smoothing procedure described in Section 3.2. The matrices $\mathbf{C}_P$, $\mathbf{C}_Q$, $\mathbf{C}_{(12)}$, and $\mathbf{C}_{(21)}$ are also described by Theorem 3.1 and they are part of the bivariate pre-smoothing procedure outlined in Appendix B.

We use the δ-method, described in Appendix A, to calculate the asymptotic variance, $\text{Var}(\hat{e}_Y(x))$, whose square root is the $\text{SEE}_Y(x)$. To use the δ-method we need three ingredients. The first is denoted by $\mathbf{J}_{e_Y}$, the Jacobian matrix of the equating function defined in (4.31).

The Jacobian, $\mathbf{J}_{e_Y}$, is a $(1 \times (J+K))$-row vector whose entries are the first derivatives of $e_Y(x; \boldsymbol{r}, \boldsymbol{s})$ with respect to each component of $\boldsymbol{r}$ and $\boldsymbol{s}$, i.e., $\partial e_Y/\partial r_j$ and $\partial e_Y/\partial s_k$. The array, $\mathbf{J}_{e_Y}$, does not depend on the data collection design, and has the same form for all KE equating functions.

The second ingredient needed to calculate $\text{Var}(\hat{e}_Y(x))$ is the Jacobian matrix of the Design Function, $\mathbf{J}_{\text{DF}}$. This Jacobian does depend on the data collection design. When the DF is a linear transformation, as it is for the EG, SG, and CB Designs, then the Jacobian is identical with the matrix that specifies the Design Function (see Table 5.3). In Post-Stratification Equating for the NEAT Design, the DF is a nonlinear function and its Jacobian requires the computation of the derivatives of $\boldsymbol{r}$ and $\boldsymbol{s}$ with respect to the elements of $v(\mathbf{P})$ and $v(\mathbf{Q})$, given in (2.60) and (2.61). This Jacobian is given in Table 5.4.

Note that $\mathbf{J}_{e_Y}$ is a vector, because $e_Y(x)$ is a real-valued function, while $\mathbf{J}_{\mathrm{DF}}$ is a matrix of dimension $(J+K) \times (J_X + K_Y)$. Using the notation for matrix derivatives (see Appendix D) we may express $\mathbf{J}_{e_Y}$ and $\mathbf{J}_{\mathrm{DF}}$ as

$$\mathbf{J}_{e_Y} = \left(\frac{\partial e_Y}{\partial \boldsymbol{r}}, \frac{\partial e_Y}{\partial \boldsymbol{s}} \right), \tag{5.9}$$

and

$$\mathbf{J}_{\mathrm{DF}} = \begin{pmatrix} \frac{\partial \boldsymbol{r}}{\partial \boldsymbol{R}} & \frac{\partial \boldsymbol{r}}{\partial \boldsymbol{S}} \\ \\ \frac{\partial \boldsymbol{s}}{\partial \boldsymbol{R}} & \frac{\partial \boldsymbol{s}}{\partial \boldsymbol{S}} \end{pmatrix}. \tag{5.10}$$

The matrix derivatives in (5.9) and (5.10) have the following dimensions: $\partial e_Y / \partial \boldsymbol{r}$ is 1 by J, and $\partial e_Y / \partial \boldsymbol{s}$ is 1 by K (so that $\mathbf{J}_{e_Y}$ is $1 \times (J+K)$); $\partial \boldsymbol{r} / \partial \boldsymbol{R}$ is J by J_X, and $\partial \boldsymbol{r} / \partial \boldsymbol{S}$ is J by K_Y; $\partial \boldsymbol{s} / \partial \boldsymbol{R}$ is K by J_X, and $\partial \boldsymbol{s} / \partial \boldsymbol{S}$ is K by K_Y. We will make use of (5.9) and (5.10) in Section 5.3.1, below.

The final ingredient in the calculation of $Var(\hat{e}_Y(x))$ is the asymptotic covariance matrix of the pre-smoothed score frequencies obtained by the data collection design. We have already mentioned this covariance matrix and the key matrix factorization given in (5.8). We shall exploit the $\mathbf{C}$-matrix factorization of the covariance matrix of the pre-smoothed score distributions in Theorem 5.1.

The next theorem gives the most general form of our results in order to include all of the designs used in this book.

Theorem 5.1. *If* $\begin{pmatrix} \hat{\boldsymbol{R}} \\ \hat{\boldsymbol{S}} \end{pmatrix}$ *is approximately Normally distributed as*

$$\mathcal{N}\left(\begin{pmatrix} \boldsymbol{R} \\ \boldsymbol{S} \end{pmatrix}, \boldsymbol{\Sigma}_{\hat{R}, \hat{S}} \right),$$

where

$$\boldsymbol{\Sigma}_{\hat{R}, \hat{S}} = \mathrm{Cov} \begin{pmatrix} \hat{\boldsymbol{R}} \\ \hat{\boldsymbol{S}} \end{pmatrix} = \mathbf{C}\mathbf{C}^t, \tag{5.11}$$

then for each x, $\hat{e}_Y(x) = e_Y(x; \hat{\boldsymbol{r}}, \hat{\boldsymbol{s}})$, *given by (4.31), is also approximately Normally distributed as*

$$\mathcal{N}\left(e_Y(x; \boldsymbol{r}, \boldsymbol{s}), \mathbf{J}_{e_Y} \mathbf{J}_{\mathrm{DF}} \mathbf{C}\mathbf{C}^t \mathbf{J}_{\mathrm{DF}}^t \mathbf{J}_{e_Y}^t \right), \tag{5.12}$$

where $\mathbf{J}_{e_Y}$ *and* $\mathbf{J}_{\mathrm{DF}}$ *are the Jacobian matrices described above and* $\mathbf{C}$ *is the factor of the covariance matrix of* $\hat{\boldsymbol{R}}$ *and* $\hat{\boldsymbol{S}}$ *given in (5.8).*

Moreover, the expression,

$$\mathbf{J}_{e_Y}\mathbf{J}_{\mathrm{DF}}\mathbf{C}, \tag{5.13}$$

in (5.12), is a row vector of dimension 1 by $(T_X + T_Y)$ *so that (5.12) can be simplified to*

$$\mathrm{Var}(\hat{e}_Y(x)) = ||\mathbf{J}_{e_Y}\mathbf{J}_{\mathrm{DF}}\mathbf{C}||^2, \tag{5.14}$$

where $||\boldsymbol{v}||^2 = \sum_j v_j^2$ *denotes the square of the Euclidian norm of the vector,* $\boldsymbol{v}$.

The vector, $\mathbf{J}_{e_Y}\mathbf{J}_{\mathrm{DF}}\mathbf{C}$, is usually considerably smaller than most of the others that have arisen in the discussion so far. It is only as long as the number of parameters used in fitting the data in the pre-smoothing step. Expression (5.14) is a key result. It expresses $\mathrm{Var}(\hat{e}_Y(x))$ in terms of $\mathbf{J}_{e_Y}$, $\mathbf{J}_{\mathrm{DF}}$ and $\mathbf{C}$. Two of these depend on the data collection design, $\mathbf{J}_{\mathrm{DF}}$ and $\mathbf{C}$, while $\mathbf{J}_{e_Y}$ does not. This is how the δ-method "divides the problem in three."

The vector, $\mathbf{J}_{e_Y}\mathbf{J}_{\mathrm{DF}}\mathbf{C}$, is so important in our analysis that we give it a special name, the SE-vector. The SE-vector is used to compute both the SEE's and the SEED's that arise in this book.

The product, $\mathbf{J}_{\mathrm{DF}}\mathbf{C}$, represents the contribution of the equating design to the variance, while $\mathbf{J}_{e_Y}$ represents the contribution of the choice of bandwidth h_X and h_Y and the final calculation of $\hat{e}_Y(x)$.

The standard error of equating of $\hat{e}_Y(x)$ is just the length of the SE-vector, i.e.,

$$\mathrm{SEE}_Y(x) = ||\hat{\mathbf{J}}_{e_Y}\hat{\mathbf{J}}_{\mathrm{DF}}\mathbf{C}\,||, \tag{5.15}$$

where $||\boldsymbol{v}|| = \sqrt{\sum_j v_j^2}$ denotes the Euclidian norm of the vector $\boldsymbol{v}$.

5.3 The SEE and the SEED for Kernel Equating

In this section we derive the SEE for the EG, SG, and CB Designs and for Post-Stratification Equating (PSE) in the NEAT Design. We do this by applying the general result (5.14) from Theorem 5.1 to each of these designs and methods. Subsections 5.3.1 and 5.3 2 are concerned with the SEE while subsection 5.3.3 modifies the results of those sections to the case of the SEED. The SEE and the SEED for Chain Equating in the NEAT Design are addressed in Section 5.4.

5.3.1 Computing $\mathbf{J}_{e_Y}$ *for Kernel Equating*

In this subsection we show how to compute $\mathbf{J}_{e_Y}$, and we do this in two steps: First, we compute the derivatives of the equipercentile equating function for any sufficiently smoothly continuized cdf's, F and G. Second, we will compute the derivatives for the specific F and G used in KE.

Derivatives for smooth cdf's, F and G. The formulas given in the next lemma can be used for any sufficiently smooth equipercentile equating function based on (1.10). However, we state it in a form that is convenient for our application to KE. Lemma 5.1 is proved using the chain rule and implicit differentiation, and so we omit the proof.

Lemma 5.1. *If* $e_Y(x;\, \boldsymbol{r},\, \boldsymbol{s}) = G^{-1}(F(x;\, \boldsymbol{r});\, \boldsymbol{s})$ *then*

$$\frac{\partial e_Y}{\partial r_j} = \frac{1}{G'}\frac{\partial F(x;\, \boldsymbol{r})}{\partial r_j}, \tag{5.16}$$

$$\frac{\partial e_Y}{\partial s_k} = -\frac{1}{G'}\frac{\partial G(e_Y(x);\, \boldsymbol{s})}{\partial s_k}, \tag{5.17}$$

where

$$G' = \frac{\partial G(e_Y(x);\, \boldsymbol{s})}{\partial y} \tag{5.18}$$

is the density of G evaluated at $e_Y(x)$.

The use of matrix notation is helpful when dealing with Jacobians (see Appendix D) . We use the notation $\partial F/\partial \boldsymbol{r}$ to denote the J-dimensional row vector whose entries are the J derivatives $\partial F(x;\, \boldsymbol{r})/\partial r_j$. Similarly, $\partial G/\partial \boldsymbol{s}$ is a K-dimensional row vector whose entries are $\partial G(e_Y(x);\, \boldsymbol{s})/\partial s_k$.

We may use this matrix notation to write (5.16) and (5.17) more compactly and show the relationship to $\mathbf{J}_{e_Y}$.

$$\mathbf{J}_{e_Y} = \left(\frac{\partial e_Y}{\partial \boldsymbol{r}}, \frac{\partial e_Y}{\partial \boldsymbol{s}}\right) = \frac{1}{G'}\left(\frac{\partial F}{\partial \boldsymbol{r}}, -\frac{\partial G}{\partial \boldsymbol{s}}\right). \tag{5.19}$$

Similar results hold for $e_X(y;\, \boldsymbol{r},\, \boldsymbol{s}) = F^{-1}(G(y;\, \boldsymbol{s});\, \boldsymbol{r})$, with the roles of F and G reversed, i.e., the Jacobian $\mathbf{J}_{e_X}$, for equating $\boldsymbol{Y}$ to $\boldsymbol{X}$, is,

$$\mathbf{J}_{e_X} = \left(\frac{\partial e_X}{\partial \boldsymbol{r}}, \frac{\partial e_X}{\partial \boldsymbol{s}}\right) = \frac{1}{F'}\left(-\frac{\partial F}{\partial \boldsymbol{r}}, \frac{\partial G}{\partial \boldsymbol{s}}\right). \tag{5.20}$$

Next we evaluate $\partial F/\partial \boldsymbol{r}$ and $\partial G/\partial \boldsymbol{s}$ for KE.

$\mathbf{J}_{e_Y}$ *for Kernel Equating.* Examining the formulas from Lemma 5.1 and making use of the fact that F and G are similar in form, there are really only two cases to consider, $\partial F/\partial x$ and $\partial F/\partial r_j$. $\partial F/\partial x$ is the density of F, $F' = f$, but $\partial F/\partial r_j$ is the derivative of F with respect to a score probability and is not a probability density function. All of the other derivatives can be found by substitution. Lemma 5.2 summarizes the results.

Lemma 5.2. *If* $F(x;\, \boldsymbol{r}) = F_{h_X}(x)$ *is given by (4.5) then*

$$\frac{\partial F(x;\, \boldsymbol{r})}{\partial r_j} = \Phi\left(R_{jX}(x;\, \boldsymbol{r})\right) - M_{jX}(x;\, \boldsymbol{r})\frac{\partial F(x;\, \boldsymbol{r})}{\partial x} \tag{5.21}$$

TABLE 5.3. The Entries in $\mathbf{J}_{\mathrm{DF}}$ for the EG, SG and CB Designs.

	EG	SG	CB
$\frac{\partial \boldsymbol{r}}{\partial \boldsymbol{R}}$	$\mathbf{I}_J$	$\mathbf{M}$	$w_X\mathbf{M}$
$\frac{\partial \boldsymbol{s}}{\partial \boldsymbol{R}}$	$\mathbf{0}$	$\mathbf{N}$	$(1-w_Y)\mathbf{N}$
$\frac{\partial \boldsymbol{r}}{\partial \boldsymbol{S}}$	$\mathbf{0}$	$\mathbf{0}$	$(1-w_X)\mathbf{M}$
$\frac{\partial \boldsymbol{s}}{\partial \boldsymbol{S}}$	$\mathbf{I}_K$	$\mathbf{0}$	$w_Y\mathbf{N}$

and

$$\begin{aligned}\frac{\partial F(x;\,\boldsymbol{r})}{\partial x} &= F'_{h_X}(x) = f_{h_X}(x) \\ &= \sum_j r_j\phi\left(R_{jX}(x;\,\boldsymbol{r})\right)\frac{1}{a_Xh_X}, \qquad (5.22)\end{aligned}$$

where

$$R_{jX}(x;\,\boldsymbol{r}) = \frac{x-a_Xx_j-(1-a_X)\mu_X}{a_Xh_X}, \qquad (5.23)$$

$$M_{jX}(x;\,\boldsymbol{r}) = \frac{1}{2}(x-\mu_X)(1-a_X^2)z_{jX}^2+(1-a_X)x_j, \qquad (5.24)$$

and

$$z_{jX} = \frac{x_j-\mu_X}{\sigma_X}. \qquad (5.25)$$

As usual, $\phi(z)$ *in (5.22) is the* $\mathcal{N}(0,\,1)$ *density,* $\Phi(z)$ *in (5.21) is the* $\mathcal{N}(0,\,1)$ *cumulative distribution function, and* $f_{h_X}(x)$ *is the density function given in (4.5).*

Only the details of the derivation of (5.21) are at all complicated and these are given in Holland and Thayer (1989, p. 34). The derivatives, $\partial G/\partial y$ and $\partial G/\partial s_k$, are analogous to the results in Lemma 5.2 with $\boldsymbol{X}$ replaced by $\boldsymbol{Y}$, F replaced by G, and $\boldsymbol{r}$ by $\boldsymbol{s}$.

To obtain $\mathbf{J}_{e_Y}$ for KE, substitute (5.21) and the appropriate modification of (5.21) for $\partial G/\partial \boldsymbol{s}$ into (5.19); G' is just the density of G and is analogous to the density of F given in (5.22).

TABLE 5.4. The Entries in $\mathbf{J}_{\mathrm{DF}}$ for the Case of the PSE for the NEAT Design.

	PSE for the NEAT Design
$\frac{\partial \boldsymbol{r}}{\partial \boldsymbol{p}_l}$	$w_{lP}\mathbf{I}_J - (1-w)(t_{Ql}/t_{Pl})[(t_{Pl})^{-1}\boldsymbol{p}_l]\mathbf{1}_J^t$
$\frac{\partial \boldsymbol{s}}{\partial \boldsymbol{p}_l}$	$w[(t_{Ql})^{-1}\boldsymbol{q}_l]\mathbf{1}_J^t$
$\frac{\partial \boldsymbol{r}}{\partial \boldsymbol{q}_l}$	$(1-w)[(t_{Pl})^{-1}\boldsymbol{p}_l]\mathbf{1}_K^t$
$\frac{\partial \boldsymbol{s}}{\partial \boldsymbol{q}_l}$	$w_{lQ}\mathbf{I}_K - w(t_{Pl}/t_{Ql})[(t_{Ql})^{-1}\boldsymbol{q}_l]\mathbf{1}_K^t$

5.3.2 Applying the General Formula for the SEE to Specific Equating Designs

In this section we develop a formula for the SEE that holds for any sufficiently smooth method of equipercentile equating in the equating designs that are considered in this book. Of course KE satisfies this requirement and we will apply these general results to KE in Chapters 7—11. In the NEAT Design, the Chain Equating (CE) approach requires the results of the SG Design plus a summation of the results from the two links in the chain. We discuss the CE case in more detail in Section 5.4.

To clarify this development we consider the product $\mathbf{J}_{\mathrm{DF}}\mathbf{C}$ in (5.15). Repeating (5.10) we have

$$\mathbf{J}_{\mathrm{DF}} = \begin{pmatrix} \frac{\partial \boldsymbol{r}}{\partial \boldsymbol{R}} & \frac{\partial \boldsymbol{r}}{\partial \boldsymbol{S}} \\ \frac{\partial \boldsymbol{s}}{\partial \boldsymbol{R}} & \frac{\partial \boldsymbol{s}}{\partial \boldsymbol{S}} \end{pmatrix}$$

Then the product $\mathbf{J}_{\mathrm{DF}}\mathbf{C}$ is

$$\begin{aligned} \mathbf{J}_{\mathrm{DF}}\mathbf{C} &= \begin{pmatrix} \frac{\partial \boldsymbol{r}}{\partial \boldsymbol{R}} & \frac{\partial \boldsymbol{r}}{\partial \boldsymbol{S}} \\ \frac{\partial \boldsymbol{s}}{\partial \boldsymbol{R}} & \frac{\partial \boldsymbol{s}}{\partial \boldsymbol{S}} \end{pmatrix} \begin{pmatrix} \mathbf{C}_R & \mathbf{0} \\ \mathbf{0} & \mathbf{C}_S \end{pmatrix} \\ &= \begin{pmatrix} \frac{\partial \boldsymbol{r}}{\partial \boldsymbol{R}}\mathbf{C}_R & \frac{\partial \boldsymbol{r}}{\partial \boldsymbol{S}}\mathbf{C}_S \\ \frac{\partial \boldsymbol{s}}{\partial \boldsymbol{R}}\mathbf{C}_R & \frac{\partial \boldsymbol{s}}{\partial \boldsymbol{S}}\mathbf{C}_S \end{pmatrix}, \end{aligned} \tag{5.26}$$

or

$$\mathbf{J}_{\mathrm{DF}}\mathbf{C} = \begin{pmatrix} \mathbf{U}_R & \mathbf{U}_S \\ \mathbf{V}_R & \mathbf{V}_S \end{pmatrix}, \tag{5.27}$$

TABLE 5.5. The Entries for $\mathbf{J}_{\mathrm{DF}}\mathbf{C}$ for EG, SG, and CB Designs.

	EG	SG	CB
$\mathbf{U}_R$	$\mathbf{C}_r$	$\mathbf{U}$	$w_X\mathbf{U}_{(12)}$
$\mathbf{V}_R$	$\mathbf{0}$	$\mathbf{V}$	$(1-w_Y)\mathbf{V}_{(12)}$
$\mathbf{U}_S$	$\mathbf{0}$	$\mathbf{0}$	$(1-w_X)\mathbf{U}_{(21)}$
$\mathbf{V}_S$	$\mathbf{C}_s$	$\mathbf{0}$	$w_Y\mathbf{V}_{(21)}$

where the **U**'s and **V**'s denote the corresponding entries in (5.26). The values of the **U**'s and **V**'s are given in Tables 5.5 and 5.6 for the EG, SG, CB, and for PSE in the NEAT Design.

If we combine (5.27) with (5.19) we obtain the following important formula for the SE-vector that applies to the EG, SG, and CB Designs and for PSE to the NEAT Design:

$$\mathbf{J}_{e_Y}\mathbf{J}_{\mathrm{DF}}\mathbf{C} = \frac{1}{G'}\left(\frac{\partial F}{\partial \boldsymbol{r}}\mathbf{U}_R - \frac{\partial G}{\partial \boldsymbol{s}}\mathbf{V}_R,\ \frac{\partial F}{\partial \boldsymbol{r}}\mathbf{U}_S - \frac{\partial G}{\partial \boldsymbol{s}}\mathbf{V}_S\right). \tag{5.28}$$

It is easy to see that the SE-vector in (5.28) is a 1 by $(T_X + T_Y)$ row vector, even though its component matrices are much larger, in general. Theorem 5.2 applies (5.28) to obtain a general formula for the SEE for KE in a variety of equating designs.

Theorem 5.2. *If* $e_Y(x;\, \boldsymbol{r},\, \boldsymbol{s}) = G^{-1}(F(x;\, \boldsymbol{r});\, \boldsymbol{s})$ *then the* $\mathrm{SEE}_Y(x)$ *for the data collection designs, EG, SG, CB and PSE for the NEAT Design, can be written as:*

$$\mathrm{SEE}_Y(x) = \frac{1}{G'}\left[\left\|\frac{\partial F}{\partial \boldsymbol{r}}\mathbf{U}_R - \frac{\partial G}{\partial \boldsymbol{s}}\mathbf{V}_R\right\|^2 + \left\|\frac{\partial F}{\partial \boldsymbol{r}}\mathbf{U}_S - \frac{\partial G}{\partial \boldsymbol{s}}\mathbf{V}_S\right\|^2\right]^{1/2} \tag{5.29}$$

where $||\boldsymbol{v}||^2 = \sum_i v_i^2$ *is the squared Euclidian norm of the vector* $\boldsymbol{v}$ *and* $\mathbf{U}_R$, $\mathbf{U}_S$, $\mathbf{V}_R$, *and* $\mathbf{V}_S$ *are the matrices in Tables 5.5 and 5.6.*

Equation (5.28) and Theorem 5.2 are general results. To apply them to a specific equating design we need to specify the entries in $\mathbf{J}_{\mathrm{DF}}$ and $\mathbf{J}_{\mathrm{DF}}\mathbf{C}$ for that design. Table 5.3 summarizes the values of $\mathbf{J}_{\mathrm{DF}}$ for the EG, SG and CB Designs. In these three designs, the Design Function is linear so that $\mathbf{J}_{\mathrm{DF}}$ is just its matrix. The entries in Table 5.3 come from (2.3), (2.13), and (2.27) from Chapter 2. For Post-Stratification Equating (PSE) in the NEAT Design, the Design Function is nonlinear and is given by (2.59),

(2.60), and (2.61). Its Jacobian is more complicated than for the other three cases.

To display the $\mathbf{J}_{\mathrm{DF}}$ for the NEAT/PSE case we need a little more preparation. The structure of the derivative matrix, $\partial \boldsymbol{r}/\partial \boldsymbol{R}$, is determined by the partitioning of $\boldsymbol{R} = v(\mathbf{P})$ by the L columns of $\mathbf{P}$. It has the form

$$\frac{\partial \boldsymbol{r}}{\partial \boldsymbol{R}} = \left(\frac{\partial \boldsymbol{r}}{\partial \boldsymbol{p}_1}, \ldots, \frac{\partial \boldsymbol{r}}{\partial \boldsymbol{p}_L} \right)$$

where $\partial \boldsymbol{r}/\partial \boldsymbol{p}_l$ is the J by L matrix of partial derivatives of $\boldsymbol{r}$ with respect to the elements of the lth column of $\mathbf{P}$, $\boldsymbol{p}_l$ (see Appendix D). It therefore suffices to display the following four partial derivative matrices of $\boldsymbol{r}$ and $\boldsymbol{s}$: $\partial \boldsymbol{r}/\partial \boldsymbol{p}_l$, $\partial \boldsymbol{s}/\partial \boldsymbol{p}_l$, $\partial \boldsymbol{r}/\partial \boldsymbol{q}_l$, and $\partial \boldsymbol{s}/\partial \boldsymbol{q}_l$. These are displayed in Table 5.4.

In Table 5.4 we use the notation

$$w_{lP} = w + (1-w)(t_{Ql}/t_{Pl}), \tag{5.30}$$

$$w_{lQ} = (1-w) + w(t_{Pl}/t_{Ql}), \tag{5.31}$$

where

$$t_{Pl} = \mathrm{Prob}\{\boldsymbol{A} = a_l \mid P\} = \sum_j p_{jl} \tag{5.32}$$

and

$$t_{Ql} = \mathrm{Prob}\{\boldsymbol{A} = a_l \mid Q\} = \sum_k q_{kl}. \tag{5.33}$$

In addition, in Table 5.4, $\boldsymbol{p}_l$ is the lth column of $\mathbf{P}$, $\boldsymbol{q}_l$ is the lth column of $\mathbf{Q}$, $\mathbf{I}$ is an identity matrix and $\mathbf{1}$ is a column vector of 1's.

While the Jacobian of the DF, $\mathbf{J}_{\mathrm{DF}}$, is of some independent interest, it is its product with the matrix $\mathbf{C}$ that has all the information relevant to the SEE (and the SEED) for each equating design.

Table 5.5 summarizes the matrix entries for $\mathbf{J}_{\mathrm{DF}}\mathbf{C}$, the $\mathbf{U}$'s and the $\mathbf{V}$'s indicated in (5.27), for the EG, SG, and CB Designs.

In Table 5.5, we use the following definitions. $\mathbf{C}_{Pk}$, $\mathbf{C}_{(12)k}$, and $\mathbf{C}_{(21)k}$ are matrix-blocks in $\mathbf{C}_P$, $\mathbf{C}_{(12)}$, and $\mathbf{C}_{(21)}$, respectively. $\mathbf{C}_{Pk}$ and $\mathbf{C}_{(12)k}$ are J by T_X dimensional, while $\mathbf{C}_{(21)k}$ is J by T_Y dimensional, using the definitions of T_X and T_Y in Table 5.2.

In addition, $\mathbf{U}$, $\mathbf{V}$, $\mathbf{U}_{(12)}$, $\mathbf{V}_{(12)}$, $\mathbf{U}_{(21)}$, and $\mathbf{V}_{(21)}$ are defined by:

$$\begin{aligned}
\mathbf{U} &= \mathbf{M}\mathbf{C}_P = \sum_k \mathbf{C}_{Pk}, \\
\mathbf{V} &= \mathbf{N}\mathbf{C}_P = \begin{pmatrix} \mathbf{1}_J^t\mathbf{C}_{P1} \\ \vdots \\ \mathbf{1}_J^t\mathbf{C}_{PK} \end{pmatrix}, \\
\mathbf{U}_{(12)} &= \mathbf{M}\mathbf{C}_{(12)} = \sum_k \mathbf{C}_{(12)k}, \\
\mathbf{V}_{(12)} &= \mathbf{N}\mathbf{C}_{(12)} = \begin{pmatrix} \mathbf{1}_J^t\mathbf{C}_{(12)1} \\ \vdots \\ \mathbf{1}_J^t\mathbf{C}_{(12)K} \end{pmatrix}, \\
\mathbf{U}_{(21)} &= \mathbf{M}\mathbf{C}_{(21)} = \sum_k \mathbf{C}_{(21)k}, \\
\mathbf{V}_{(21)} &= \mathbf{N}\mathbf{C}_{(21)} = \begin{pmatrix} \mathbf{1}_J^t\mathbf{C}_{(21)1} \\ \vdots \\ \mathbf{1}_J^t\mathbf{C}_{(21)K} \end{pmatrix}.
\end{aligned}$$

In Table 5.6 we use the following definitions:

$$\begin{aligned}
\mathbf{U}_P &= \mathbf{M}_P\mathbf{C}_P = \sum_l \mathbf{C}_{Pl}, \\
\mathbf{U}_P^* &= \sum_l (t_{Ql}/t_{Pl})\mathbf{C}_{Pl}, \\
\mathbf{U}_Q &= \mathbf{M}_Q\mathbf{C}_Q = \sum_l \mathbf{C}_{Ql}, \\
\mathbf{U}_Q^* &= \sum_l (t_{Pl}/t_{Ql})\mathbf{C}_{Ql},
\end{aligned}$$

$$\boldsymbol{v}_{Pl}^t = \mathbf{1}_J^t\mathbf{C}_{Pl} \quad \text{and} \quad \boldsymbol{v}_{Ql}^t = \mathbf{1}_K^t\mathbf{C}_{Ql}.$$

Furthermore, $\boldsymbol{t}_{Pl}$ and $\boldsymbol{t}_{Ql}$ are the score probabilities for $\boldsymbol{A}$ in P and Q given in (5.32) and (5.33), while $\boldsymbol{p}_l$ and $\boldsymbol{q}_l$ are the lth columns of the bivariate score probabilities, $\mathbf{P} = (p_{jl})$ and $\mathbf{Q} = (q_{kl})$, respectively. Finally, $\mathbf{C}_{Pl}$ and $\mathbf{C}_{Ql}$ are the matrix blocks of $\mathbf{C}_P$ and $\mathbf{C}_Q$. $\mathbf{C}_{Pl}$ is J by T_P dimensional, while $\mathbf{C}_{Ql}$ is K by T_Q dimensional.

5.3.3 The Standard Error of the Difference Between Two Kernel Equating Functions

In this subsection we state a result that is analogous to formula (5.14) and which allows us to compute a standard error for the difference between two

TABLE 5.6. The Entries for $\mathbf{J}_{\mathrm{DF}}\mathbf{C}$ for the Case of PSE for the NEAT Design.

$\mathbf{U}_R$	$w\mathbf{U}_P + (1-w)\mathbf{U}_P^* - (1-w)\sum_l (t_{Ql}/t_{Pl}) t_{Pl}^{-1} \boldsymbol{p}_l \boldsymbol{v}_{Pl}^t$
$\mathbf{V}_R$	$w \sum_l t_{Ql}^{-1} \boldsymbol{q}_l \boldsymbol{v}_{Pl}^t$
$\mathbf{U}_S$	$(1-w) \sum_l t_{Pl}^{-1} \boldsymbol{p}_l \boldsymbol{v}_{Ql}^t$
$\mathbf{V}_S$	$(1-w)\mathbf{U}_Q + w\mathbf{U}_Q^* - w\sum_l (t_{Pl}/t_{Ql}) t_{Ql}^{-1} \boldsymbol{q}_l \boldsymbol{v}_{Ql}^t$

Kernel Equating functions. This standard error can be used to inform decisions about the final form of an equating function. In particular, because the linear equating function, $\mathrm{Lin}_Y(x)$, defined in Section 1.3, is a limiting form of the KE functions, the standard error of the difference between it and another KE function can be computed using the results of Theorem 5.3, below. When the difference is small compared to this standard error then it may be reasonable to consider using the simpler $\mathrm{Lin}_Y(x)$ than $e_Y(x)$. Of course, in KE, $\mathrm{Lin}_Y(x)$ is computed using (4.31) with large bandwidths, rather than formula (1.7).

To set things up, suppose $e_1(X)$ and $e_2(X)$ denote two equating functions that have the KE form (4.31) but differ due to their values of h_X and h_Y. We are interested in

$$\mathrm{Var}\left(\hat{e}_1(x) - \hat{e}_2(x)\right). \tag{5.34}$$

Theorem 5.3, below, shows that if we have computed the SE-vectors for $\hat{e}_1$ and $\hat{e}_2$, i.e., the vectors $\mathbf{J}_{e_1}\mathbf{J}_{\mathrm{DF}}\mathbf{C}$ and $\mathbf{J}_{e_2}\mathbf{J}_{\mathrm{DF}}\mathbf{C}$ from (5.13), then we already have the ingredients for the SEED for the difference between $\hat{e}_1$ and $\hat{e}_2$.

Theorem 5.3. *If $\hat{e}_1(x)$ and $\hat{e}_2(x)$ are given by (4.31) but have different values for the bandwidths, h_X and h_Y, then*

$$\begin{aligned}\mathrm{Var}\left(\hat{e}_1(x) - \hat{e}_2(x)\right) &= ||\,(\mathbf{J}_{e_1} - \mathbf{J}_{e_2})\mathbf{J}_{\mathrm{DF}}\mathbf{C}\,||^2 \\ &= ||\,\mathbf{J}_{e_1}\mathbf{J}_{\mathrm{DF}}\mathbf{C} - \mathbf{J}_{e_2}\mathbf{J}_{\mathrm{DF}}\mathbf{C}\,||^2,\end{aligned} \tag{5.35}$$

where $\mathbf{J}_e$, $\mathbf{J}_{\mathrm{DF}}$, and $\mathbf{C}$ are as given in Theorem 5.1.

The proof of Theorem 5.3 is similar to that of Theorem 5.1 except that it exploits the relationship $\mathbf{J}_{e_1-e_2} = \mathbf{J}_{e_1} - \mathbf{J}_{e_2}$.

Using Theorem 5.3 we define the "standard error of equating difference," the SEED, as

$$\begin{aligned}\mathrm{SEED}_Y(x) &= \sqrt{\mathrm{Var}\left(\hat{e}_1(x) - \hat{e}_2(x)\right)} \\ &= ||\,\mathbf{J}_{e_1}\mathbf{J}_{\mathrm{DF}}\mathbf{C} - \mathbf{J}_{e_2}\mathbf{J}_{\mathrm{DF}}\mathbf{C}\,||.\end{aligned} \tag{5.36}$$

Hence, the SEED is the length of the difference between the two SE-vectors.

Our use of the **C**-matrices of Theorem 5.1 and elsewhere is motivated by the result in (5.15) and (5.28). These provide computationally efficient ways of computing the SEE and SEED using the SE-vectors. Theorem 5.3 can be generalized slightly to accommodate more complicated differences between $\hat{e}_1$ and $\hat{e}_2$ than the bandwidth differences from the continuization process. In the CB Design, the choice of w_X and w_Y affect the Jacobian of the DF as well as the final choices of the bandwidths. In this case, $\mathbf{J}_{e_1}\mathbf{J}_{\mathrm{DF}_1}\mathbf{C}$ and $\mathbf{J}_{e_2}\mathbf{J}_{\mathrm{DF}_2}\mathbf{C}$ need to be computed first, and then subtracted, i.e.,

$$\mathrm{Var}\,(\hat{e}_1 - \hat{e}_2) \quad = \quad ||\,\mathbf{J}_{e_1}\mathbf{J}_{\mathrm{DF1}}\mathbf{C} - \mathbf{J}_{e_2}\mathbf{J}_{\mathrm{DF2}}\mathbf{C}\,||^2. \qquad (5.37)$$

In Chapter 11, we will also consider a choice of e_1 and e_2 where e_1 is derived from Chain Equating assumptions, while e_2 is derived from Post-Stratification Equating assumptions. Formula (5.37) applies in that case as well, when we interpret the SE-vector for CE properly.

5.4 The SEE and SEED for Chain Equating

Chain equating is different in important ways from the other KE methods we have considered so far. It is a two-step procedure that combines the results of two SG linkings into an equating of X to Y. From the point of view of computing the SEE and the SEED, its most notable difference from the other designs is that $\boldsymbol{r}$ and $\boldsymbol{s}$, the vectors of score probabilities for $\boldsymbol{X}$ and $\boldsymbol{Y}$ on the target population, T, are never directly computed. Thus, the Design Function and its Jacobian, $\mathbf{J}_{\mathrm{DF}}$, which plays such an important role in computing the SEE and the SEED for the other designs, is of a different character in CE. In addition, the equating function, $e_{Y(CE)}(x)$, is a composition of two other linking functions, so that it does not directly have the form of (4.31), and, instead, involves the composition of four continuized cdf's and their inverses (see below), rather than just two, as the equating function does in the other KE cases we have discussed.

However, it is desirable to make as much use as we can of the fact that CE is constructed from two simpler SG linkings. Our approach to the SEE and SEED for CE exploits these connections to the simpler SG case, and makes use of results that we have established for the SG Design.

The equating function for CE has the form

$$e_{Y(CE)}(x;\, \boldsymbol{r}_P,\, \boldsymbol{t}_P,\, \boldsymbol{t}_Q,\, \boldsymbol{s}_Q) = e_Y(e_A(x;\, \boldsymbol{r}_P, \boldsymbol{t}_P);\, \boldsymbol{t}_Q,\, \boldsymbol{s}_Q), \qquad (5.38)$$

where $e_A(x) = e_A(x;\, \boldsymbol{r}_P,\, \boldsymbol{t}_P)$ is the SG link from X to A on P using the first SG Design, and $e_Y(a) = e_Y(a;\, \boldsymbol{t}_Q,\, \boldsymbol{s}_Q)$ is the SG link from A to Y on Q, using the second SG Design. The two links in the chain of CE each have the usual KE form:

$$e_A(x;\, \boldsymbol{r}_P,\, \boldsymbol{t}_P) = H^{-1}_{h_{AP}}(F_{h_{XP}}(x;\, \boldsymbol{r}_P);\, \boldsymbol{t}_P) \qquad (5.39)$$

and

$$e_Y(a;\, \boldsymbol{t}_Q,\, \boldsymbol{s}_Q) = G^{-1}_{h_{YQ}}(H_{h_{AQ}}(a;\, \boldsymbol{t}_Q);\, \boldsymbol{s}_Q). \tag{5.40}$$

The Jacobians of $e_A(x;\, \boldsymbol{r}_P,\, \boldsymbol{t}_P)$ and $e_Y(a;\, \boldsymbol{t}_Q,\, \boldsymbol{s}_Q)$ may be computed from formula (5.19) using suitable reinterpretations of F, G, $\boldsymbol{r}$, and $\boldsymbol{s}$. We denote them as $\mathbf{J}_{e_A}(x)$ and $\mathbf{J}_{e_Y}(a)$, respectively. The Jacobian of $e_{Y(CE)}$, $\mathbf{J}_{e_{Y(CE)}}(x)$, may be formed from $\mathbf{J}_{e_A}(x)$ and $\mathbf{J}_{e_Y}(a)$. To see this, we first note that the Jacobian of $e_{Y(CE)}$ is a row vector of the derivatives of $e_{Y(CE)}(x;\, \boldsymbol{r}_P,\, \boldsymbol{t}_P,\, \boldsymbol{t}_Q,\, \boldsymbol{s}_Q)$ with respect the four sets of score probabilities, $\boldsymbol{r}_P$, $\boldsymbol{t}_P$, $\boldsymbol{t}_Q$, and $\boldsymbol{s}_Q$, (in that order), rather than for just $\boldsymbol{r}$ and $\boldsymbol{s}$ as we had in the other designs. Next, let $e'_Y(a)$ denote the derivative of $e_Y(a)$ with respect to a, i.e.,

$$e'_Y(a) = \frac{\partial e_Y}{\partial a}(a). \tag{5.41}$$

Then, the chain rule for partial differentiation allows us to express $\mathbf{J}_{e_{Y(CE)}}$ as

$$\mathbf{J}_{e_{Y(CE)}}(x) = \left(e'_Y(a)\mathbf{J}_{e_A}(x),\ \mathbf{J}_{e_Y}(a)\right). \tag{5.42}$$

There is a slight complication in (5.42) concerning where the derivatives in it are to be evaluated. The rule is "set all a's to $e_A(x)$." If we do this, (5.42) becomes

$$\mathbf{J}_{e_{Y(CE)}}(x) = \left(e'_Y(e_A(x))\mathbf{J}_{e_A}(x),\ \mathbf{J}_{e_Y}(e_A(x))\right). \tag{5.43}$$

The left side of (5.43) is $[1 \times (J+L+L+K)]$-dimensional, and the right side has two components. The first, $e'_Y(a)\mathbf{J}_{e_A}(x)$, is $[1 \times (J+L)]$-dimensional, because $e'_Y(a)$ is a scalar and $\mathbf{J}_{e_A}(x)$ is $[1 \times (J+L)]$-dimensional, and the second, $\mathbf{J}_{e_Y}(a)$, is $[1 \times (L+K)]$-dimensional. Hence, both sides of (5.42) result in $[1 \times (J+2L+K)]$-dimensional row vectors.

In order to use the δ-method to evaluate the approximate variance of $e_{Y(CE)}$ we need the joint covariance matrix of the vector of score probability estimates,

$$\begin{pmatrix} \hat{\boldsymbol{r}}_P \\ \hat{\boldsymbol{t}}_P \\ \hat{\boldsymbol{t}}_Q \\ \hat{\boldsymbol{s}}_Q \end{pmatrix}. \tag{5.44}$$

The covariance matrix for the partitioned vector in (5.44) is easily obtained from the Design Function for the SG Design applied to the separate covariance matrices of $v(\hat{\mathbf{P}})$ and $v(\hat{\mathbf{Q}})$. First of all, because $v(\hat{\mathbf{P}})$ and $v(\hat{\mathbf{Q}})$ are independent we only need to find the covariance matrix

$$\mathrm{Cov}\begin{pmatrix} \hat{\boldsymbol{r}}_P \\ \hat{\boldsymbol{t}}_P \end{pmatrix} = \mathbf{D}_P\mathbf{D}_P^t \tag{5.45}$$

separately from the covariance matrix

$$\operatorname{Cov}\begin{pmatrix} \hat{\boldsymbol{t}}_Q \\ \hat{\boldsymbol{s}}_Q \end{pmatrix} = \mathbf{D}_Q \mathbf{D}_Q^t. \tag{5.46}$$

In (5.45) and (5.46) we adapt the notation from Table 5.5 for the SG Design and let

$$\mathbf{D}_P = \begin{pmatrix} \mathbf{U}_P \\ \mathbf{V}_P \end{pmatrix} = \begin{pmatrix} \mathbf{M}_P\mathbf{C}_P \\ \mathbf{N}_P\mathbf{C}_P \end{pmatrix} = \begin{pmatrix} \mathbf{M}_P \\ \mathbf{N}_P \end{pmatrix} \mathbf{C}_P \tag{5.47}$$

and

$$\mathbf{D}_Q = \begin{pmatrix} \mathbf{V}_Q \\ \mathbf{U}_Q \end{pmatrix} = \begin{pmatrix} \mathbf{N}_Q\mathbf{C}_Q \\ \mathbf{M}_Q\mathbf{C}_Q \end{pmatrix} = \begin{pmatrix} \mathbf{N}_Q \\ \mathbf{M}_Q \end{pmatrix} \mathbf{C}_Q. \tag{5.48}$$

The matrix factors, $\mathbf{D}_P$ and $\mathbf{D}_Q$, are $(J + L)$ by T_P dimensional and $(L + K)$ by T_Q dimensional, respectively. In (5.47) and (5.48) the **U**'s and **V**'s come from Table 5.5, but we add the subscripts P and Q to identify the population to which each refers.

$$\mathbf{U}_P = \mathbf{M}_P\mathbf{C}_P = \sum_l \mathbf{C}_{Pl} \quad \text{and} \quad \mathbf{U}_Q = \mathbf{M}_Q\mathbf{C}_Q = \sum_l \mathbf{C}_{Ql},$$

and

$$\mathbf{V}_P = \mathbf{N}_P\mathbf{C}_P = \begin{pmatrix} \mathbf{1}^t\mathbf{C}_{P1} \\ \vdots \\ \mathbf{1}^t\mathbf{C}_{PL} \end{pmatrix} \quad \text{and} \quad \mathbf{V}_Q = \mathbf{N}_Q\mathbf{C}_Q = \begin{pmatrix} \mathbf{1}^t\mathbf{C}_{Q1} \\ \vdots \\ \mathbf{1}^t\mathbf{C}_{QL} \end{pmatrix}.$$

Thus, the joint covariance matrix of the vector of score probabilities in (5.44) is $\mathbf{D}\mathbf{D}^t$, where

$$\mathbf{D} = \begin{pmatrix} \mathbf{D}_P & \mathbf{0} \\ \mathbf{0} & \mathbf{D}_Q \end{pmatrix}. \tag{5.49}$$

Now we can combine the Jacobian of $e_{Y(CE)}(x)$ with **D** to get the SEE for Chain Equating. In analogy with (5.14), the asymptotic variance of $\hat{e}_{Y(CE)}(x)$, is

$$\operatorname{Var}(\hat{e}_{Y(CE)}(x)) = ||\, \mathbf{J}_{e_{Y(CE)}}\mathbf{D}\, ||^2. \tag{5.50}$$

Hence, the SE-vector for the case of CE is $\mathbf{J}_{e_{Y(CE)}}\mathbf{D}$.

However,

$$\mathbf{J}_{e_{Y(CE)}}\mathbf{D} = (e'_Y\mathbf{J}_{e_A},\ \mathbf{J}_{e_Y})\,\mathbf{D} = (e'_Y\mathbf{J}_{e_A}\mathbf{D}_P,\ \mathbf{J}_{e_Y}\mathbf{D}_Q) \tag{5.51}$$

and each of the vector components of the right side of (5.51) is exactly of the form of (5.13) with $\mathbf{J}_{\mathrm{DF}}\mathbf{C}$ replaced by $\mathbf{D}_P$ or $\mathbf{D}_Q$. This observation allows us to use the methods already developed for the SG Design to compute the SEE for CE. The essential ingredient is the SE-vector, $\mathbf{J}_{e_{Y(CE)}}\mathbf{D}$. From (5.51) we have

$$\mathrm{Var}(\hat{e}_{Y(CE)}(x)) = ||\, e'_Y \mathbf{J}_{e_A} \mathbf{D}_P \,||^2 + ||\, \mathbf{J}_{e_Y} \mathbf{D}_Q \,||^2, \tag{5.52}$$

and each term of (5.52) is related to the asymptotic variance of one of the links in the CE chain. Thus,

$$||\, \mathbf{J}_{e_Y} \mathbf{D}_Q \,||^2 = \mathrm{Var}(\hat{e}_Y(a)) = \mathrm{SEE}_Y^2(a) \tag{5.53}$$

and

$$||e'_Y \mathbf{J}_{e_A} \mathbf{D}_P \,||^2 = [e'_Y(a)]^2 \mathrm{Var}(\hat{e}_A(x)) = [e'_Y(a)]^2 \mathrm{SEE}_A^2(x). \tag{5.54}$$

Evaluating a at $a = e_A(x)$ we get

Theorem 5.4. *The Standard Error of Equating for CE in the NEAT Design can be expresses in terms of the SEE's for each link in the chain as follows:*

$$\mathrm{SEE}_{Y(CE)}^2(x) = [e'_Y(e_A(x))]^2 \mathrm{SEE}_A^2(x) + \mathrm{SEE}_Y^2(e_A(x)). \tag{5.55}$$

In (5.55), for KE the value of $e'_Y(e_A(x))$ can be computed as

$$e'_Y(e_A(x)) = \frac{H'_Q(e_A(x))}{G'_Q(e_{Y(CE)}(x))}, \tag{5.56}$$

where $H'_Q(a)$ and $G'_Q(y)$ are the densities of $H_Q(a)$ and $G_Q(y)$, respectively.

Using the formulas for the SEE's of the SG links, we may express the SEE for CE in a form that is similar to the one given in Theorem 5.2 for the other designs. This is summarized in Theorem 5.5, below.

Theorem 5.5. *The* $\mathrm{SEE}_Y(x)$ *for Chain Equating used in the NEAT Design can be written as*

$$\mathrm{SEE}_Y(x)^2 = \left(\frac{1}{H'_P}\right)^2 \left\| \frac{\partial F_P}{\partial \boldsymbol{r}} \mathbf{U}_P - \frac{\partial H_P}{\partial \boldsymbol{t}} \mathbf{V}_P \right\|^2$$
$$+ \left(e'_Y(e_A(x))\right)^2 \left(\frac{1}{G'_Q}\right)^2 \left\| \frac{\partial H_Q}{\partial \boldsymbol{t}} \mathbf{V}_Q - \frac{\partial G_Q}{\partial \boldsymbol{s}} \mathbf{U}_Q \right\|^2. \tag{5.57}$$

In Theorem 5.5, F_P and H_P are the continuized cdf's of $\boldsymbol{X}$ and $\boldsymbol{A}$, respectively, on P; H_Q, G_Q are the continuized cdf's of $\boldsymbol{A}$ and $\boldsymbol{Y}$, respectively, on Q; and H'_P and G'_Q are the densities of H_P and G_Q. In addition, the matrices $\mathbf{U}_P$, $\mathbf{U}_Q$, $\mathbf{V}_P$ and $\mathbf{V}_Q$ correspond to the $\mathbf{U}$ and $\mathbf{V}$ matrices for the two SG Designs (see Table 5.5). $\mathbf{U}_P$ and $\mathbf{U}_Q$ also appear in Table 5.6 for the PSE for the NEAT Design. The vectors $\boldsymbol{v}_{Pl}^t$ and $\boldsymbol{v}_{Ql}^t$ in Table 5.6 are the rows of $\mathbf{V}_P$ and $\mathbf{V}_Q$, respectively.

What about the SEED for CE? The key ingredient is the SE-vector, $\mathbf{J}_{e_{Y(CE)}}\mathbf{D}$, given in (5.51). If $\hat{e}_{Y(CE)1}(x)$ and $\hat{e}_{Y(CE)2}(x)$ denote two CE functions obtained through (5.38) but using different sets of the four bandwidths, then

$$\mathrm{Var}(\hat{e}_{Y(CE)1}(x) - \hat{e}_{Y(CE)2}(x)) = ||\, \mathbf{J}_{e_{Y(CE)1}}\mathbf{D} - \mathbf{J}_{e_{Y(CE)2}}\mathbf{D}\, ||^2. \qquad (5.58)$$

As in the other designs, the SEED is the length of the difference between the SE-vectors.

Thus, once $\mathbf{J}_{e_{Y(CE)}}\mathbf{D}$ can be computed for a given set of bandwidths, the SEED is easy to obtain from it for two different choices of the h's. This also provides an alternative to (5.55) for computing the SEE for CE, i.e., formula (5.50).

6

Kernel Equating versus Other Equating Methods

In this chapter we compare Kernel Equating (KE) to the two other important methods of observed-score test equating—linear equating and the percentile rank method (PRM) of equipercentile equating. Our analysis is primarily a theoretical comparison rather than a comparison of numerical results in particular cases.

In general terms we believe that there are two major areas where KE can be viewed as an improvement on the older methods. First, because it makes consistent use of pre-smoothing as well as smooth transformations of the data, KE will often have smaller standard errors and be less subject to sampling variability than the other methods. Thus, it is well suited to applications where the sample sizes are small, but it can also intelligently handle any sample size.

Second, KE is a consistent system that develops equating functions and their estimated standard errors in a similar way across all of the commonly used data collection designs. The five steps of observed score test equating, outlined in Section 3.1, are common to all such methods, but they are sometimes not recognized as such. KE is built to attend clearly to each of these steps in a consistent and data-sensitive way. In the rest of this chapter, we will not dwell on these two claims in specific cases, but will discuss the differences between KE and the other two methods.

There is one area where KE is not as satisfactory as either linear or the PRM method. This is in the ease of computation. Both linear equating and PRM were created in the years before there were computers, and for this reason they can be graphed or calculated by hand once certain simple statistics are available. KE is a child of the computer age and reflects all of the tools that are implied by that status. We do not feel that this is a particularly important drawback. In the situations where test equating is a routine part of the work of psychometricians, hand calculations are not particularly useful. Computer programs are already processing the test data in many other ways prior to and after equating, so computer programs to implement KE can fit into many operational equating systems.

6.1 KE versus Linear Equating

The linear equating function, $\mathrm{Lin}_Y(x)$, defined in Section 1.3, i.e.,

$$\mathrm{Lin}_Y(x) = \mu_Y + (\sigma_Y/\sigma_X)(x - \mu_X), \tag{6.1}$$

is a general method that must be tailored to each equating design. Thus, there is no single linear equating method, but what is actually computed will vary from design to design. We briefly review these calculations next.

In the EG and SG Designs, the same formulas are used to estimate the parameters of (6.1), namely,

$$\begin{aligned}\hat{\mu}_X &= \bar{X},\\ \hat{\mu}_Y &= \bar{Y},\\ \hat{\sigma}_X &= s_X,\\ \hat{\sigma}_Y &= s_Y.\end{aligned}$$

For the CB Design, Lord's suggestion for linear equating is to estimate the parameters in (6.1) by

$$\begin{aligned}\hat{\mu}_X &= (\bar{X}_1 + \bar{X}_2)/2,\\ \hat{\mu}_Y &= (\bar{Y}_1 + \bar{Y}_2)/2,\\ \hat{\sigma}_X &= \sqrt{(s^2_{X_1} + s^2_{X_2})/2},\\ \hat{\sigma}_Y &= \sqrt{(s^2_{Y_1} + s^2_{Y_2})/2},\end{aligned}$$

where we use our notation from Chapter 2 for the data in the CB Design.

In the NEAT Design, Tucker's method of linear equating is an example of the Post-Stratification method of equating. It weakens the assumptions PSE1 and PSE2 (see Section 2.4.2) to the assumption that the regressions of $\boldsymbol{X}$ and $\boldsymbol{Y}$ on the anchor test are population invariant and then adds the further assumptions that they are linear and have constant residual variances. These assumptions are then used to derive estimates of the parameters of the linear equating function in (6.1) over a particular target population of the form $T = wP + (1 - w)Q$, from (2.32).

Finally, in the NEAT Design, Chain Linear Equating is a linear version of the Chain Equipercentile method described in Section 2.4.1. In this method, linear equating functions are computed for each of the two SG Designs and then functionally composed to get a final, linear, equating function. That this approach can be interpreted as an observed score equating method follows from the discussion in Section 2.4.1 where the equipercentile version of Chain Equating is emphasized. The assumptions, CE1 and CE2, of Section 2.4.1, are weakened so that only the linear equating functions on each population are assumed to be population invariant. The resulting linear equating function has the form

$$\begin{aligned}\mathrm{Lin}_{Y(CE)}(x) &= \mu_{YQ} + (\sigma_{YQ}/\sigma_{AQ})\mu_{AP} \\ &\quad + [(\sigma_{YQ}/\sigma_{XP})(\sigma_{AP}/\sigma_{AQ})](x - \mu_{XP}). \end{aligned} \tag{6.2}$$

Thus, linear equating is not a single method. It is shaped by the structure of the equating design. This is also true of KE as indicated in Chapter 2 and explained more fully in each of the chapters of Part II of this book.

However, there is one thing that is true of all uses of KE. If the bandwidth values, h_X and h_Y, used in the continuization step, are large (at least 10σ in many applications) then the KE equating function, $e_Y(x)$, will be a linear equating function because the continuizations will be Normal approximations to F and G. Theorem 1.1 insures this because F and G will have the same shape, i.e., Normal. Thus, in every equating design considered here, KE will be linear if the bandwidths used in the continuization step are large enough.

For this reason, for every design considered in this book KE contains the linear equating functions as the special case that arises when the bandwidths are taken to be large. (As we see in some of our examples in Part II, even relatively small bandwidths can lead to nearly linear KE equating functions.) In a sense then, KE *is* linear equating when the continuization is done in a particular way. On the other hand, the data may not support a continuization that leads to linear equating. In this sense, KE is more data sensitive than linear equating is. The SEED, discussed in Chapter 5, is a new tool, unique to KE, for evaluating the degree to which KE and linear equating agree.

However, KE can differ from ordinary linear equating even when large bandwidths are deemed acceptable. While the two equating functions will be identical in most case, their standard errors of equating (SEE's) may not be. Due to pre-smoothing the score distributions, it can arise (in the EG Design) that the SEE for KE will differ from the SEE for linear equating computed from the formulas in Braun and Holland (1982). This is due to the assumptions that are made in deriving these SEE formulas. Pre-smoothing can force the higher moments of the score distributions to be determined from the lower ones and this can result in different computed SEE's for KE and the usual SEE's for linear equating. We expect that if the models selected for the score distributions in the pre-smoothing step actually fit the data well, then this will result in more accurate and smaller

SEE's for the KE versions of linear equating compared to the usual formulas for these standard errors. While we have not explored this issue fully, we believe that these differences in SEE's are probably marginal in most cases. But examination of these possible differences are worthy of further investigation.

6.2 KE versus the Percentile Rank Method of Equipercentile Equating

The percentile rank method (PRM) is described in Angoff (1971) and Kolen and Brennan (1995) and it is often called "the equipercentile method." It is easiest to discuss this method when the possible scores of $\boldsymbol{X}$ and $\boldsymbol{Y}$ are both sets of consecutive integers, as will arise for "number right" scoring and for formula scores that are rounded to integer values. These are both common forms of raw scores and for that reason in this chapter we will restrict our attention to the case of raw scores that are consecutive integers. In this chapter, rather than the graphical procedure described by Angoff, we consider the "analytical procedure" for equipercentile equating described in Kolen and Brennan (1995, p. 42), but we will try to make our description of it as similar as possible to KE for comparison purposes.

Just as linear equating is not a single method, and must reflect the equating design, so too is *any* method of equipercentile equating, including KE and the percentile rank method (PRM). A properly executed version of any equipercentile equating method will involve attention to the presmoothing and estimation steps of observed score equating described in Section 3.1. Equipercentile methods must reflect the equating designs and will explicitly or implicitly use the Design Function appropriate to the design to estimate $\boldsymbol{r}$ and $\boldsymbol{s}$. Where PRM and KE differ is in the way that they continuize F and G.

6.2.1 *The Percentile Rank Method of Continuizing F and G*

The percentile rank method may be viewed as a way of continuizing the discrete distributions of $\boldsymbol{X}$ and $\boldsymbol{Y}$ in much the same way that formula (4.11) describes continuization for KE. We suppose that we add to $\boldsymbol{X}$ an independent random variable, U_X, that is uniformly distributed over the interval $[-\frac{1}{2}, \frac{1}{2}]$. Because the possible values of $\boldsymbol{X}$ are assumed here to be consecutive integers, the result will be a random variable,

$$\boldsymbol{X}^* = \boldsymbol{X} + U_X, \tag{6.3}$$

that has a continuous, strictly increasing cdf concentrated on the interval $[x_1 - \frac{1}{2}, x_J + \frac{1}{2}]$. We can do the same with $\boldsymbol{Y}$, i.e.,

$$\boldsymbol{Y}^* = \boldsymbol{Y} + U_Y, \tag{6.4}$$

where U_Y is independent of $\boldsymbol{Y}$. $\boldsymbol{Y}^*$ is a random variable with a continuous, strictly increasing cdf concentrated on the interval $[y_1 - \frac{1}{2}, y_K + \frac{1}{2}]$. It should be emphasized that we do not actually add U_X and U_Y to $\boldsymbol{X}$ and $\boldsymbol{Y}$, but rather the continuization process can be viewed as if this had been done. What U_X and U_Y do is spread out the discrete probability at each score point continuously over the unit interval around it, $[x_j - \frac{1}{2},\ x_j + \frac{1}{2}]$. We let F^* and G^* be the cdf's of $\boldsymbol{X}^*$ and $\boldsymbol{Y}^*$, respectively.

Using these continuized cdf's, the percentile rank method produces its version of the equipercentile equating function via the same type of formula used in KE, i.e.,

$$\mathrm{PRM}_Y(x) = {G^*}^{-1}(F^*(x)). \tag{6.5}$$

While F^* and G^* are continuous and strictly increasing over their ranges, they are piecewise-linear functions that are (usually) not differentiable at each half-integer in their range. Kolen and Brennan (1995, p. 41, Figure 2.4) graphically illustrate this phenomenon. The cdf, F^*, has a density function which is just the usual histogram that spreads the score probability r_j over the unit interval centered at the score point, x_j. Similarly for G^*.

$\mathrm{PRM}_Y(x)$ inherits its piecewise-linear character from those of F^* and G^*, which is also graphically illustrated in Kolen and Brennan (1995, p. 41, Figure 2.5). The need to further smooth $\mathrm{PRM}_Y(x)$ has been noticed from its earliest uses and graphical ways of doing this are suggested by Angoff (1971). Kolen and Brennan discuss various analytical methods that have been proposed to smooth $\mathrm{PRM}_Y(x)$. This type of "post-smoothing" differs from "pre-smoothing" (Chapter 3) in that it is not intended to remove sampling variability but is used, instead, to remove the inherent roughness (i.e., the piecewise-linear aspect) of $\mathrm{PRM}_Y(x)$. This roughness would exist even if all sampling variability had been removed by pre-smoothing the sample data.

6.2.2 Some Facts About PRM

The reader might first ask, why do we continually refer to (6.5) as the "percentile rank method" when, so far at least, there has been no mention of percentile ranks. The answer is that percentile ranks are implicit in formulas (4.1) and (4.2) applied to F^* and G^*. The cdf, F^*, for example, has the following value at x_j

$$F^*(x_j) = \sum_{i<j} r_i + \frac{1}{2} r_j, \tag{6.6}$$

where r_j is defined in (1.3).

This is discussed in Kolen and Brennan (1995) and shown analytically in Holland and Thayer (1989). Thus, the value $F^*(x_j)$ is exactly the usual definition of the percentile rank of a score, i.e., the "percent below" plus "one-half the percent at" the given score, i.e., x_j. The uniform distribution of U_X insures the linear interpolation of the scores between the integer scores.

So, the reason we call $\mathrm{PRM}_Y(x)$ in (6.5) the "percentile rank method" is that it linearly interpolates around each of the percentile ranks to compute the equated values.

6.2.3 *Distributional Characteristics of* PRM

Next, we might ask if there is any guarantee that $\boldsymbol{X}^*$ shares any distributional characteristics of $\boldsymbol{X}$? Here is what can be said. First of all, $\boldsymbol{X}$ and $\boldsymbol{X}^*$ do share the same mean value, μ_X, because U_X has mean zero. The same is true for $\boldsymbol{Y}$ and $\boldsymbol{Y}^*$. Second of all, we can not really say the same about the variances of $\boldsymbol{X}$ and $\boldsymbol{X}^*$ (or $\boldsymbol{Y}$ and $\boldsymbol{Y}^*$). In fact, we easily see from (6.3) and (6.4) that

$$\begin{aligned} \mathrm{Var}(\boldsymbol{X}^* \,|\, T) &= \mathrm{Var}(\boldsymbol{X} \,|\, T) + \frac{1}{12}, \\ \mathrm{Var}(\boldsymbol{Y}^* \,|\, T) &= \mathrm{Var}(\boldsymbol{Y} \,|\, T) + \frac{1}{12}. \end{aligned} \tag{6.7}$$

In practice, this discrepancy is easily observed, but it is also small, so that it is possible to confuse it with round-off error and similar numerical details of the computations.

Once we see that $\boldsymbol{X}^*$ is not guaranteed to match even the second moment of $\boldsymbol{X}$, it is evident that the sense in which $\boldsymbol{X}^*$ is supposed to approximate the distribution of $\boldsymbol{X}$ is vague (and similarly for $\boldsymbol{Y}$ and $\boldsymbol{Y}^*$).

However, it is the nearness of the distributions of $\boldsymbol{Y}$ and the transformed $\boldsymbol{X}$, $\mathrm{PRM}_Y(\boldsymbol{X})$, that is of chief importance. The failure of the percentile rank method of continuization to match even the *variances* of the distributions suggests that development of this procedure for equating was not driven by clear distribution-matching goals. In fact, the entire effort to post-smooth $\mathrm{PRM}_Y(x)$, in the usual ways that this is attempted, does not explicitly address the need to make the smoothed result more closely match the distribution of $\boldsymbol{Y}$ than $\mathrm{PRM}_Y(\boldsymbol{X})$ does. In fact, the discussion of Angoff suggests that post-smoothing is more esthetic than oriented toward the goal of matching the score distributions of $\mathrm{PRM}_Y(\boldsymbol{X})$ and $\boldsymbol{Y}$ in any sense.

6.2.4 *The Issue of the Finite Range*

Finally, we need to address the issue of the finite ranges of F^* and G^*. While there is an obvious sense in which F^* linearly interpolates between the scores from x_1 to x_J, what happens outside this range is settled by an arbitrary decision. The fact that $F^*(x)$ is zero below $x_1 - \frac{1}{2}$ is an artifact of how the continuization process is done in the percentile rank method. KE shows that it could be done in a different manner with different results. Be that as it may, the direct consequence of this finite range for F^* and G^* is that $\text{PRM}_Y(x)$ maps all x less than or equal to $x_1 - \frac{1}{2}$ into $y_1 - \frac{1}{2}$ and all x greater than or equal to $x_J + \frac{1}{2}$ into $y_K + \frac{1}{2}$. This fact is often stated more loosely as $\text{PRM}_Y(x)$ maps the top raw-score of $\boldsymbol{X}$ to the top raw-score of $\boldsymbol{Y}$, and the lowest raw-score of $\boldsymbol{X}$ to the lowest raw-score of $\boldsymbol{Y}$. If two tests differ sufficiently in difficulty, this property is usually not desirable. It is intuitively evident that the highest score on a much harder test ought to correspond to a score above *all* of the raw scores on an easier one. This last point is often made in support of linear equating rather than equipercentile equating. Linear equating is not subject to the restriction that the equating function must map the two raw-score ranges onto each other. For this reason, linear equating is often seen as something different from curvilinear or equipercentile equating. Our view is influenced by Theorem 1.1, which shows that linear equating is the linear approximation to any equipercentile method based on continuization and which matches the first two moments of the continuized $\boldsymbol{X}$ and $\boldsymbol{Y}$ distributions. For us, $\text{Lin}_Y(x)$ is just a special case of KE.

Other authors, such as Kolen and Brennan (1995), regard the fact the range of possible equated $\boldsymbol{X}$-scores lies within $[y_1 - \frac{1}{2}, y_K + \frac{1}{2}]$ as a virtue of PRM not always shared by linear equating, and, therefore, by KE. We respectfully disagree with such a position.

6.3 Viewing PRM from the KE Perspective

Using the approach described in Chapter 3 one might make the following suggestions regarding the percentile rank method. First of all, it is probably useful to add a linear transformation, in the spirit of (4.11), to $\boldsymbol{X}^* = \boldsymbol{X} + U_X$ and to $\boldsymbol{Y}^* = \boldsymbol{Y} + U_Y$, so that the new $\boldsymbol{X}^*$ and $\boldsymbol{Y}^*$ can actually match the first two moments of the $\boldsymbol{X}$ and $\boldsymbol{Y}$. These linear transformations will necessarily change the ranges of the $\boldsymbol{X}^*$ and $\boldsymbol{Y}^*$ from $[x_1 - \frac{1}{2}, x_J + \frac{1}{2}]$ and $[y_1 - \frac{1}{2}, y_K + \frac{1}{2}]$ to other intervals. Secondly, efforts to post-smooth $\text{PRM}_Y(x)$ ought to focus on changing $\text{PRM}_Y(x)$ in a way that makes the distribution of $\text{PRM}_Y(\boldsymbol{X})$ closer to that of $\boldsymbol{Y}$ in some well defined sense. In KE, post-smoothing of the equating function is unnecessary because whatever additional smoothing is necessary is carried out in the continuization phase. The choices of the bandwidths, and the penalty functions used to do this are the way that KE makes explicit the sense in which the continuous distributions approximate the original discrete ones. Once these approximations are chosen, the equating function automatically follows and is as smooth as necessary. Linear equating fits in as a limiting case that may be all that is needed. Finally, the finite range property of

$\text{PRM}_Y(x)$ can be changed if the continuization process is altered to use a distribution other than the uniform at the top and bottom scores. For example, the Normal distribution, $\mathcal{N}(0, h)$ could be used at these points where h is a bandwidth parameter that can be manipulated to achieve various goals. However, once we have gone this far, we have almost turned the percentile rank method into KE and our suggestion would be to go all the way to KE rather than to alter $\text{PRM}_Y(x)$ in a piecemeal way.

6.4 Some Desirable Features of KE Not Shared by PRM

Perhaps the nicest feature of KE is that it includes smooth mathematical functions for every aspect of the equating process. While it is true that one can give a formula for the piecewise-linear form of $\text{PRM}_Y(x)$, this is much less useful than the ones for KE simply because it needs to be defined for each segment of the domain of $\text{PRM}_Y(x)$.

We have exploited the formulas that come with KE to accomplish several goals. First, it allows us to produce something like a formula (i.e., (4.31)) for the equating function instead of reducing it to a table of correspondence between the raw scores of $\boldsymbol{X}$ and $\boldsymbol{Y}$. The advantage of this is that we do not need to interpolate the entries in the table when chaining together several equating functions. We call (4.31) "something like a formula" for the equating function because we still need to numerically invert $G_{h_Y}(y)$ to obtain $e_Y(x)$ from the formula for $G_{h_Y}(y)$. Because of the smooth nature of $G_{h_Y}(y)$, however, this is easily done using Newton's method for solving $u = G_{h_Y}(y)$ for y.

In order to store $e_Y(x)$, all we need to store are (a) the parameters of the log-linear models used to pre-smooth the raw score distributions, and (b) the values of the selected bandwidths, h_X and h_Y. From these quantities, F_{h_X} and G_{h_Y} can be computed, G_{h_Y} then inverted at the appropriate values and $e_Y(x)$ computed for any value x that is needed, including fractional ones.

Thus, KE reduces the problem of computing a sequence of equatings over a period of time to the storage of the parameters for each equating in the sequence along with specific computer programs to use these stored parameters to compute the values of the needed equating functions. Linear equating also allows this as well, but in a much simpler manner. All that needs to be updated at each new equating are the slope and intercept of $\text{Lin}_Y(x)$ if we use formula (1.7).

Another consequence of the nature of the mathematical formulas for KE is that it works easily with log-linear pre-smoothing to give useful standard errors in a consistent manner for all of the usual designs. It is known that using log-linear models to pre-smooth score data pays off handsomely in reducing the standard errors for equating functions, but KE allows us to quantify this reduction using well-established methods.

The analysis that we give regarding the SEE in Chapter 5 can be applied to other equating methods besides KE, and it is an interesting research question as to whether there are continuizations methods other than Gaussian kernel smoothing that result in smaller standard errors. We suspect this is not a topic that will lead to much of an improvement in KE.

Finally, we should mention that, because $\mathrm{Lin}_Y(x)$ is a limiting form for KE, we can use the formula for the SEED to give a standard error for the difference between the equating functions obtained using KE and $\mathrm{Lin}_Y(x)$. This gives a useful statistical tool to help make the "linear/curvilinear" equating decision. To do this using $\mathrm{PRM}_Y(x)$ is quite complicated, so that most equating decision processes in practice must rely solely on guesses, experience and intuition to choose between $\mathrm{PRM}_Y(x)$ and $\mathrm{Lin}_Y(x)$.

We point out that some of the objections to equipercentile equating do not apply to the kernel method of equating. By varying the choice of the bandwidths, h_X and h_Y, we may achieve a wide variety of equating functions that are "in between" the traditional linear and equipercentile functions.

Furthermore, depending on the choice of h_X and h_Y, the equating functions need not map the top and bottom scores on $\boldsymbol{X}$ onto the top and bottom scores of $\boldsymbol{Y}$. Moreover, the equating functions given by (4.31) and (4.32) are defined for all x and y and are not restricted to the raw score intervals, i.e., $[x_1, x_J]$ and $[y_1, y_K]$, (see Chapter 4 for details). Thus, they can be used in sequences of equatings that involve equated values outside of the raw score ranges.

Part II

The Kernel Method of Test Equating: Applications

7

The Equivalent-Groups Design

In Section 2.1, we introduced the Equivalent-Groups (EG) Design and we indicated which population parameters have to be estimated in order to compute the equating function. In the Equivalent-Groups Design, two independent random samples are drawn from a common population of examinees, P, the test X is administered to one sample while test Y is administered to the other. In Chapters 3, 4, and 5 we described the five steps of Kernel Equating (KE) that must take place for all equating designs: pre-smoothing, estimation of the score probabilities, continuization of the cumulative distribution functions (cdf's), computing the equating function, the standard error of equating (SEE) and the standard error of equating difference (SEED). In this chapter, we apply KE to the Equivalent-Groups Design.

We illustrate KE for the EG Design using an example described in Holland and Thayer (1989, p. 19). Using these data, we will go through the details of the five steps described in Chapters 3, 4, and 5.

Table 7.1 gives the raw sample frequencies of number-right scores for two parallel, 20-item-mathematics tests given to two samples from a national population of examinees.

The samples were obtained by spiraling the two forms together (see Section 2.5 for a discussion of spiraling).

The data in Table 7.1, are sample frequencies for two univariate distributions. We denote the two sets of sample frequencies by

$$n_j = \text{number of examinees with } \boldsymbol{X} = x_j,$$
$$m_k = \text{number of examinees with } \boldsymbol{Y} = y_k.$$

TABLE 7.1. Score Frequencies for $\boldsymbol{X}$ and $\boldsymbol{Y}$ for Two Equivalent Samples of Examinees. Example 1, EG Design.

Score	$\boldsymbol{X}$-frequencies	$\boldsymbol{Y}$-frequencies
0	1	0
1	3	4
2	8	11
3	25	16
4	30	18
5	64	34
6	67	63
7	95	89
8	116	87
9	124	129
10	156	124
11	147	154
12	120	125
13	129	131
14	110	109
15	86	98
16	66	89
17	51	66
18	29	54
19	15	37
20	11	17
Total	1453	1455
Mean	10.82	11.59
SD	3.81	3.94
Skewness	0.0026	−0.0626
Kurtosis	2.53	2.50

In this example, $x_1 = 0$, $x_2 = 1, \ldots, x_{21} = 20$; similarly, for y_k. The two sample sizes are given by

$$N = \sum_j n_j = 1453 \quad \text{and} \quad M = \sum_k m_k = 1455.$$

From Table 7.1 we can see that test Y, with a mean of 11.6 (± 0.1) is about one raw-score point easier than test X, which has a mean of 10.8 (± 0.1). Here and in Chapters 8, 9, and 10, when we report sample averages, we also indicate their accuracy by ($\pm$ one standard error). In this example, the single zero in the $\boldsymbol{Y}$-frequencies would prevent the raw sample proportions from satisfying the positivity condition described in Chapter 3.

The sample proportions, (n_j/N) and (m_k/M), are estimates of the population parameters, r_j and s_k, respectively. However, the raw sample proportions are rarely as satisfactory as smoothed proportions based on a good model for the data. They need not satisfy the positivity condition mentioned earlier. Of course, they always satisfy the consistency and integrity conditions, and, when M and N are very large, the raw sample proportions may be acceptable estimates of the population score probabilities. Even when M and N are very large, when there are many possible scores, i.e., when J and K are also large, smoothed sample proportions are usually preferable.

7.1 Pre-smoothing

In this section we illustrate how the method of pre-smoothing described in Section 3.2 applies to the data from an EG Design. We will indicate how to estimate two univariate distributions by fitting log-linear models having power moments of the sample distributions for their sufficient statistics.

Using the tools for assessing model fit for univariate score distributions (as described in Chapter 3 as well as in Holland & Thayer, 2000) we selected the following log-linear models for this example:

$$\log(r_j) = \alpha_r + \sum_{i=1}^{T_r} \beta_{ri}(x_j)^i \tag{7.1}$$

and

$$\log(s_k) = \alpha_s + \sum_{i=1}^{T_s} \beta_{si}(y_k)^i, \tag{7.2}$$

where $T_r = 2$, $T_s = 3$. The β's are the log-linear (or "natural") parameters, and α_r and α_s are the normalizing constants selected to make the sum of r_j and of s_k, respectively, equal to one.

In this case, the estimators of $\{r_j\}$ preserve two moments ($T_r = 2$) of the $\boldsymbol{X}$-distribution and the estimators of $\{s_k\}$ preserve three moments ($T_s = 3$) of the $\boldsymbol{Y}$-distribution. This reflects the differences in the skeweness for the two distributions as seen in the Table 7.1.

Table 7.2 shows the fitted frequencies and Freeman-Tukey residuals (Bishop et al., 1975) for the models described in (7.1) and (7.2). The likelihood ratio chi-square statistic for $\{r_j\}$ is 18.35 on 18 degrees of freedom while that for $\{s_k\}$ is 20.24 on 17 degrees of freedom. These values suggest that, overall, the fits of these two models are quite good. To get a more detailed look at these fits we examine the Freeman-Tukey residuals from Table 7.2. These residuals should behave roughly like independent standard Normal deviates if the models fit adequately. Since these residuals lie between -2 and $+2$, and show no pattern, we conclude that the fitted probabilities from these models are improved estimates of the population distributions in the sense of "consistency" and "stability" described in Chapter 3.

TABLE 7.2. Fitted Score Frequencies and Freeman-Tukey Residuals for $\boldsymbol{X}$ and $\boldsymbol{Y}$. Example 1, EG Design.

Score	$\boldsymbol{X}$-Fitted*	FT Residuals	$\boldsymbol{Y}$-Fitted**	FT Residuals
0	3.30	−1.35	1.71	−1.80
1	6.44	−1.44	3.77	0.22
2	11.77	−1.10	7.65	1.16
3	20.17	1.06	14.24	0.51
4	32.43	−0.39	24.44	−1.34
5	48.89	2.04	38.75	−0.74
6	69.10	−0.22	56.98	0.81
7	91.57	0.38	77.91	1.24
8	113.79	0.23	99.35	−1.25
9	132.58	−0.73	118.54	0.96
10	144.83	0.93	132.72	−0.75
11	148.36	−0.09	139.87	1.19
12	142.49	−1.94	139.15	−1.21
13	128.32	0.08	131.10	0.01
14	108.35	0.18	117.31	−0.76
15	85.79	0.05	100.00	−0.18
16	63.69	0.32	81.46	0.84
17	44.33	1.00	63.60	0.33
18	28.93	0.06	47.73	0.91
19	17.71	−0.60	34.54	0.45
20	10.16	0.33	24.18	−1.52
Total	1453		1455	
Mean	10.82		11.59	
SD	3.81		3.94	
Skewness	−0.0648		−0.0626	
Kurtosis	2.70		2.57	

Note: * 2-moment fit; ** 3-moment fit.

Comparing the summary statistics at the bottom of Tables 7.1 and 7.2 we see that the "two-moment fit" for the $\boldsymbol{X}$-score distribution preserves the mean and the standard deviation of the raw data but not the skewness or kurtosis. For the "three-moment fit" for the $\boldsymbol{Y}$-score distribution, the mean, standard deviation and the skewness are preserved but not the kurtosis.

The observed and the fitted distributions of $\boldsymbol{X}$ and $\boldsymbol{Y}$ are plotted in Figure 7.1 and Figure 7.2. In Figure 7.1 the largest discrepancies between the raw and fitted frequencies occur for $x_j = 5$ and $x_j = 12$, which have Freeman-Tukey (FT) residual values of 2.04 and −1.94, respectively—within the expected noise level for this sample size. The discrepancies in Figure 7.2 have even smaller FT residual values. These additional examinations of the data support the use of the two models we selected.

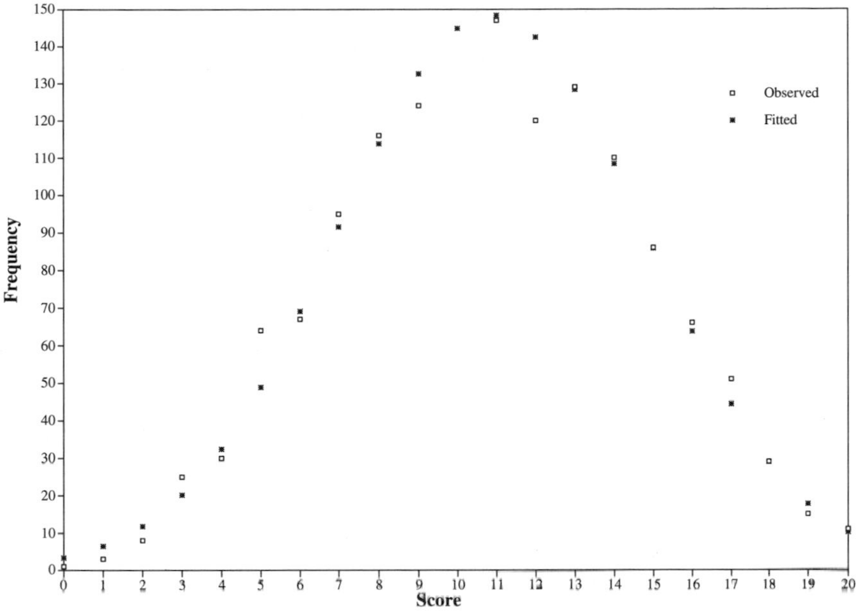

FIGURE 7.1. The observed and the fitted distributions of $\boldsymbol{X}$. Example 1, EG Design.

In addition to the estimated score probabilities, $\hat{r}_j$ and $\hat{s}_k$, the output of a satisfactory log-linear model program will include the "**C**-matrices" that are the essential information needed to compute the standard errors of $\hat{r}_j$ and $\hat{s}_k$ and which are used to compute the SEE and the SEED described in Chapter 5. In many of our examples the **C**-matrices are too large to be included in our discussion, but for this example the two **C** matrices are relatively small (i.e., 21×2 and 21×3, respectively). They are given (multiplied by 1000) in Table 7.3.

We denote the estimated covariance matrices of $\hat{\boldsymbol{r}}$ and $\hat{\boldsymbol{s}}$ by $\boldsymbol{\Sigma}_{\hat{r}}$ and $\boldsymbol{\Sigma}_{\hat{s}}$. Then, from (3.10), it follows that for the log-linear models fitted in this example there is a 21×2 matrix, $\mathbf{C}_r$, and a 21×3 matrix, $\mathbf{C}_s$, such that

$$\boldsymbol{\Sigma}_{\hat{r}} = \mathbf{C}_r\mathbf{C}_r^t \quad \text{and} \quad \boldsymbol{\Sigma}_{\hat{s}} = \mathbf{C}_s\mathbf{C}_s^t. \tag{7.3}$$

Because the two samples are independent, $\boldsymbol{\Sigma}_{\hat{r}\hat{s}} = 0$.

7.2 Estimation of the Score Probabilities

In the EG Design the estimated score probabilities $\{\hat{r}_j\}$ and $\{\hat{s}_k\}$ are obtained directly on the target population and there is no need to further

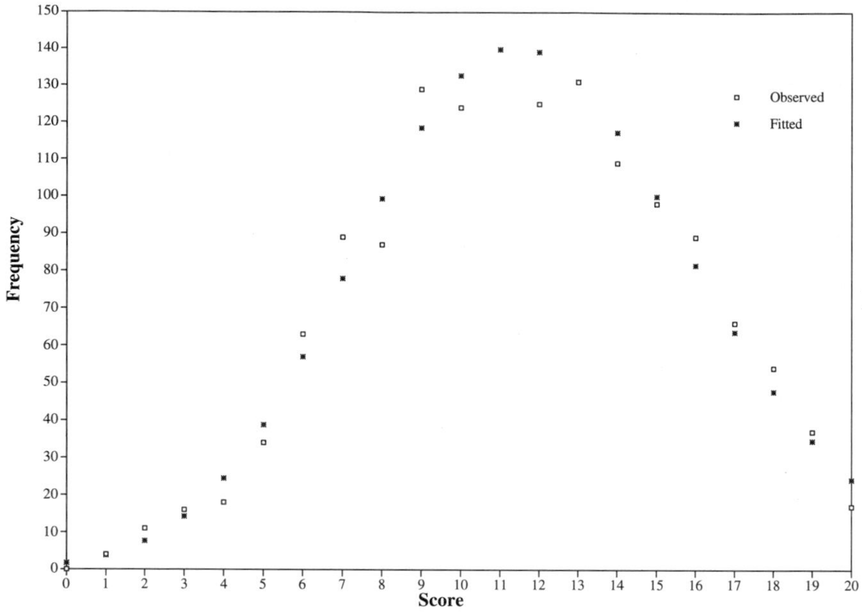

FIGURE 7.2. The observed and the fitted distributions of $\boldsymbol{Y}$. Example 1, EG Design.

transform the smoothed estimators that we already have. This is reflected by the fact that the Design Function in (2.3) is the identity transformation.

Table 7.4 gives the smoothed values of $\{\hat{r}_j\}$ and $\{\hat{s}_k\}$ to four significant digits; they are obtained by dividing the fitted frequencies in Table 7.2 by the respective sample sizes.

7.3 Continuization

The cdf's corresponding to the score probabilities, $\{r_j\}$ and $\{s_k\}$ in (2.2) are step functions with jumps at the possible values of $\boldsymbol{X}$ and $\boldsymbol{Y}$:

$$F(x) = \text{Prob}(\boldsymbol{X} \leq x) = \sum_{j,\, x_j \leq x} r_j,$$

$$G(y) = \text{Prob}(\boldsymbol{Y} \leq y) = \sum_{k,\, y_k \leq y} s_k. \tag{7.4}$$

In (7.4) x and y range over all real numbers, $\mathbb{R}$, whereas x_j and y_k are the possible values of $\boldsymbol{X}$ and $\boldsymbol{Y}$. We obtain $\hat{F}$ and $\hat{G}$ by substituting the estimates $\hat{r}_j$ and $\hat{s}_k$, for r_j and s_k in (7.4).

TABLE 7.3. The Matrices, $\mathbf{C}_r$ and $\mathbf{C}_s$ that Contribute to the Computation of $\hat{\mathbf{\Sigma}}_r$ and $\hat{\mathbf{\Sigma}}_s$. Example 1, EG Design. (Actual values have been multiplied by 1000.)

	$\mathbf{C}_r$		$\mathbf{C}_s$		
	1	2	1	2	3
0	−0.169	−0.316	−0.091	−0.184	−0.285
1	−0.300	−0.490	−0.183	−0.330	−0.429
2	−0.492	−0.688	−0.336	−0.527	−0.545
3	−0.748	−0.864	−0.560	−0.745	−0.546
4	−1.049	−0.942	−0.850	−0.915	−0.346
5	−1.349	−0.839	−1.170	−0.950	0.093
6	−1.579	−0.499	−1.460	−0.764	0.707
7	−1.659	0.074	−1.639	−0.325	1.319
8	−1.521	0.789	−1.635	0.319	1.690
9	−1.144	1.476	−1.408	1.035	1.629
10	−0.562	1.944	−0.968	1.645	1.084
11	0.128	2.047	−0.380	1.986	0.189
12	0.799	1.746	0.259	1.968	−0.785
13	1.328	1.129	0.845	1.603	−1.540
14	1.636	0.371	1.293	0.991	−1.865
15	1.702	−0.331	1.560	0.282	−1.704
16	1.566	−0.832	1.644	−0.381	−1.149
17	1.300	−1.072	1.575	−0.892	−0.383
18	0.986	−1.077	1.401	−1.205	0.394
19	0.687	−0.924	1.172	−1.323	1.029
20	0.443	−0.701	0.931	−1.287	1.443

TABLE 7.4. Estimated Score Probabilities for $\boldsymbol{X}$ and $\boldsymbol{Y}$ on the Target Population. Example 1, EG Design.

Score	$\hat{r}_j$	$\hat{s}_k$	Score	$\hat{r}_j$	$\hat{s}_k$
0	0.0023	0.0012	11	0.1021	0.0961
1	0.0044	0.0026	12	0.0981	0.0956
2	0.0081	0.0053	13	0.0883	0.0901
3	0.0139	0.0098	14	0.0746	0.0806
4	0.0223	0.0168	15	0.0590	0.0687
5	0.0336	0.0266	16	0.0438	0.0560
6	0.0476	0.0392	17	0.0305	0.0437
7	0.0630	0.0535	18	0.0199	0.0328
8	0.0783	0.0683	19	0.0122	0.0237
9	0.0912	0.0815	20	0.0070	0.0166
10	0.0997	0.0912			

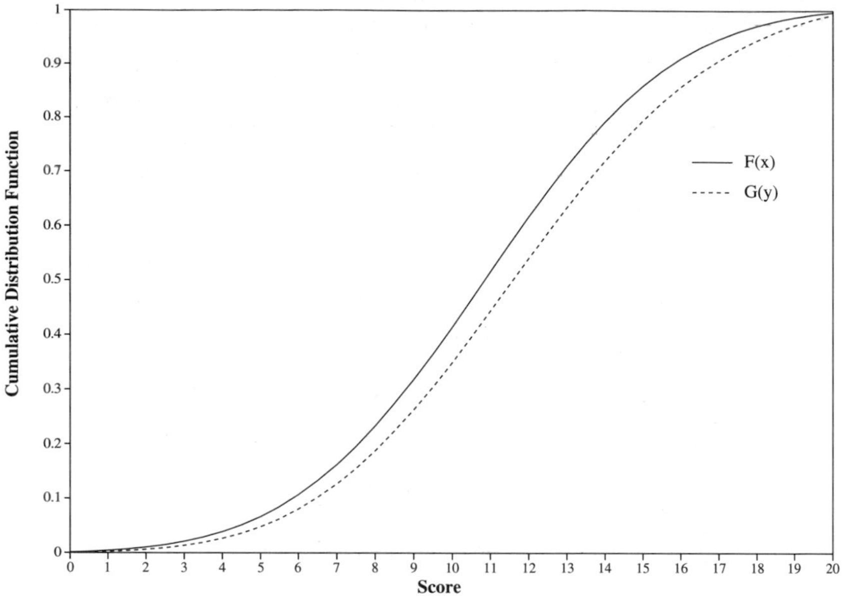

FIGURE 7.3. The continuized distributions $\hat{F}_{h_X}$ and $\hat{G}_{h_Y}$. Example 1, EG Design.

The cdf's, $\hat{F}$ and $\hat{G}$, are continuized using the technique in (4.5) and (4.8), and the continuized cdf's, $\hat{F}_{h_X}$ and $\hat{G}_{h_Y}$, are what we shall actually use to equate $\boldsymbol{X}$ to $\boldsymbol{Y}$.

Figure 7.3 shows the cdf's $\hat{F}_{h_X}$ and $\hat{G}_{h_Y}$ for this example.

As shown in Section 4.1.2, we choose h_X by minimizing the criterion from (4.30), i.e.,

$$\text{PEN}_1(h_X) + K \times \text{PEN}_2(h_X),$$

with PEN_1 and PEN_2 defined in (4.27) and (4.29), respectively. The weight K was set to 1. The value for for h_Y is obtained in a similar way. The smoothed score distributions displayed in Figures 7.1 and 7.2 are unimodal so that there was no effect of PEN_2 in this example. The resulting optimal values of h_X and h_Y were determined solely by PEN_1 and were 0.622 and 0.579, respectively.

7.4 Equating

Once the continuous approximations, $\hat{F}_{h_X}$ and $\hat{G}_{h_Y}$, are obtained, it is a straightforward process to compute the equating functions via (4.31) and

(4.32). The values of the inverse functions, $\hat{F}_{h_X}^{-1}(\cdot)$ and $\hat{G}_{h_Y}^{-1}(\cdot)$, need to be computed for the relevant values of their arguments.

The equating function for equating $\boldsymbol{X}$ to $\boldsymbol{Y}$ is

$$\hat{e}_Y(x) = \hat{G}_{h_Y}^{-1}(\hat{F}_{h_X}(x)),$$

and for equating $\boldsymbol{Y}$ to $\boldsymbol{X}$ is

$$\hat{e}_X(y) = \hat{F}_{h_X}^{-1}(\hat{G}_{h_Y}(y)).$$

We usually need the value of the equating function only for each raw score of $\boldsymbol{X}$. Hence, we need to compute

$$\hat{e}_Y(x_j) = \hat{G}_{h_Y}^{-1}(u_{Xj}),$$

where $u_{Xj} = \hat{F}_{h_X}(x_j)$ and

$$\hat{e}_X(y_k) = \hat{F}_{h_X}^{-1}(u_{Yk}),$$

where $u_{Yk} = \hat{G}_{h_Y}(y_k)$.

The two equating functions computed in the example are plotted in Figure 7.4. The differences between these two equating functions and their corresponding linear equating functions, for both $\boldsymbol{X}$ to $\boldsymbol{Y}$ and from $\boldsymbol{Y}$ to $\boldsymbol{X}$ are plotted in Figure 7.5.

As the graphs reveal, both $\hat{e}_Y(x)$ and $\hat{e}_X(y)$, are nearly linear in this example. The maximum difference between the equating functions obtained using KE and the linear equating function occurs (see Figure 7.5) at $x = y = 20$. This difference is less than a raw score point for either direction of the equating.

The equating function, $e_Y(x)$, is supposed to match the distribution of $e_Y(\boldsymbol{X})$ (i.e., the Kernel Equating function evaluated at the discrete values of $\boldsymbol{X}$) to that of $\boldsymbol{Y}$, but as we have indicated this is not completely possible because the two distributions are discrete. As we discuss in Section 4.2, we may investigate how well $\hat{e}_Y(\boldsymbol{X})$ approximates the distribution of $\boldsymbol{Y}$ by comparing the first several moments of $\hat{e}_Y(\boldsymbol{X})$ to the corresponding ones of $\boldsymbol{Y}$, using $\hat{\boldsymbol{r}}$ and $\hat{\boldsymbol{s}}$ to make the moment calculations.

Table 7.5 gives the differences between these moments expressed as a percent of the size of the moment of the score being "equated to" (i.e., PRE(p)) as discussed in Section 4.2. The moments range from the first to the tenth. Table 7.5 gives values for the equating in both directions, $\boldsymbol{X}$ to $\boldsymbol{Y}$ and $\boldsymbol{Y}$ to $\boldsymbol{X}$. As we can see, the discrepancy between these moments ranges from 0.01 to 0.67 percent for the $\boldsymbol{X}$ to $\boldsymbol{Y}$ equating and from -0.01 to -1.71 percent for the $\boldsymbol{Y}$ to $\boldsymbol{X}$ equating. These differences are very small and indicate how well KE achieves the matching of $e_Y(\boldsymbol{X})$ and $\boldsymbol{Y}$ and of $e_X(\boldsymbol{Y})$ and $\boldsymbol{X}$.

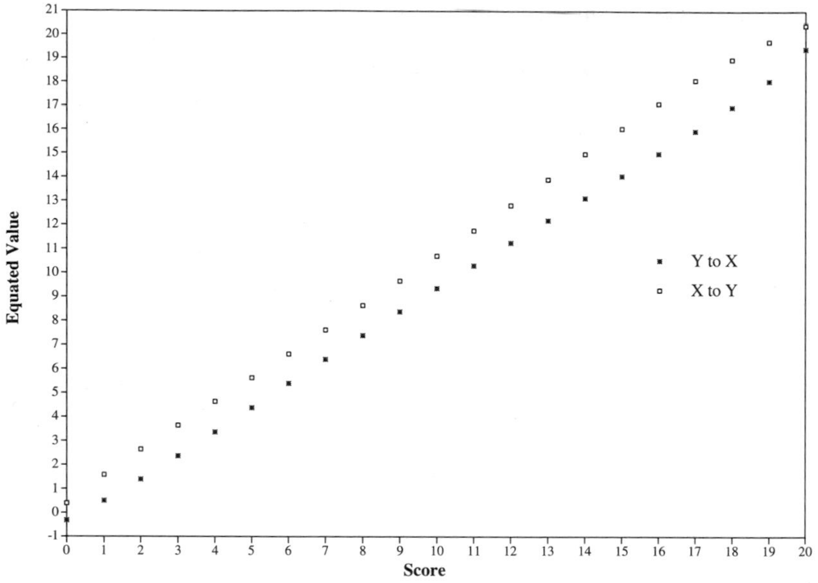

FIGURE 7.4. The equating functions $\hat{e}_X(y)$ and $\hat{e}_Y(x)$. Example 1, EG Design.

TABLE 7.5. Difference Between the Moments of the Equated Distribution and the Target Distribution Expressed as Percent Relative Error, PRE(p). Example 1, EG Design.

	Percent Relative Error	
Moments	(X to Y)	(Y to X)
1	0.01	−0.01
2	0.01	−0.02
3	0.02	−0.05
4	0.04	−0.11
5	0.07	−0.21
6	0.13	−0.37
7	0.22	−0.58
8	0.33	−0.88
9	0.48	−1.25
10	0.67	−1.71

7.5 Standard Error of Equating

In order to compute the SEE of the equating function computed above, we will apply Theorem 5.4 from Chapter 5.

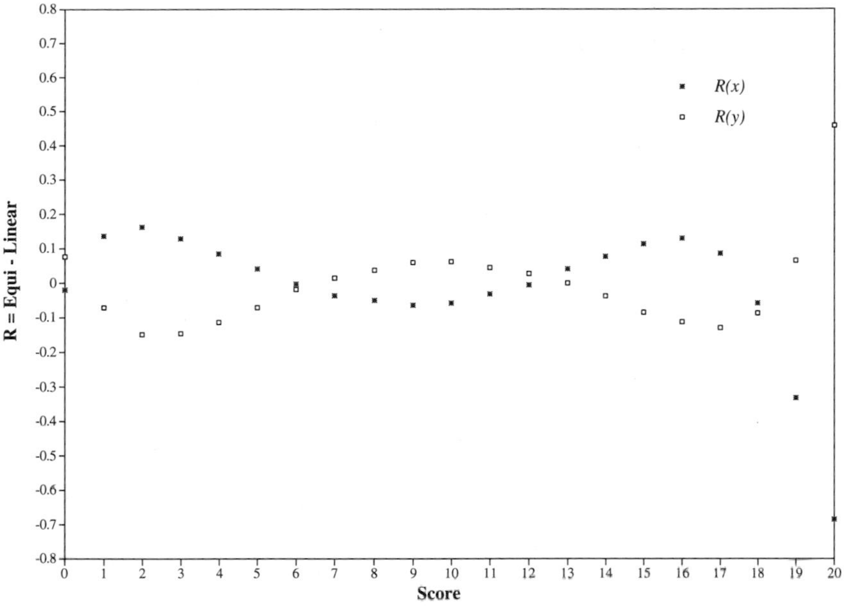

FIGURE 7.5. The differences between the KE ("Equi") and linear equating functions from $\boldsymbol{X}$ to $\boldsymbol{Y}$ and from $\boldsymbol{Y}$ to $\boldsymbol{X}$. Example 1, EG Design.

The main result is equation (5.29), which we repeat here,

$$\mathrm{SEE}_Y(x) = \frac{1}{G'}\left[\left\|\frac{\partial F}{\partial \boldsymbol{r}}\mathbf{U}_R - \frac{\partial G}{\partial \boldsymbol{s}}\mathbf{V}_R\right\|^2 + \left\|\frac{\partial F}{\partial \boldsymbol{r}}\mathbf{U}_S - \frac{\partial G}{\partial \boldsymbol{s}}\mathbf{V}_S\right\|^2\right]^{1/2}.$$

From Table 5.5 we see that in the EG Design $\mathbf{U}_R = \mathbf{C}_r$, $\mathbf{V}_S = \mathbf{C}_s$, and $\mathbf{U}_S = \mathbf{V}_R = \mathbf{0}$. Inserting these values into the expression above yields

$$\mathrm{SEE}_Y(x) \quad = \quad \frac{1}{G'}\left[\left\|\frac{\partial F}{\partial \boldsymbol{r}}\mathbf{C}_r\right\|^2 + \left\|\frac{\partial G}{\partial \boldsymbol{s}}\mathbf{C}_s\right\|^2\right]^{1/2}, \qquad (7.5)$$

where the matrices $\mathbf{C}_r$ and $\mathbf{C}_s$ were described in Section 3.2.1, in (3.10) and (3.11), and are given in this chapter's example, in Table 7.3.

Thus, in the EG Design, the computational ingredients of the SEE are G', $\| \frac{\partial F}{\partial \boldsymbol{r}}\mathbf{C}_r \|^2$, and $\| \frac{\partial G}{\partial \boldsymbol{s}}\mathbf{C}_s \|^2$. The vectors $\partial F/\partial \boldsymbol{r}\mathbf{C}_r$ and $\partial G/\partial \boldsymbol{s}\mathbf{C}_s$ are of dimension T_r and T_s, respectively, which in this example are 2 and 3. Formulas for $\partial F/\partial \boldsymbol{r}$ and $\partial G/\partial \boldsymbol{s}$ are given in Lemma 5.2 in Chapter 5.

Table 7.6 displays the standard error of equating for the two equating functions, equating both $\boldsymbol{X}$ to $\boldsymbol{Y}$ and $\boldsymbol{Y}$ to $\boldsymbol{X}$, evaluated at various score values. In this example, the SEE's range from 0.07 to 0.28 raw-score points. In Figure 7.6 we plot the SEE for the equating function form X to Y only.

TABLE 7.6. Standard Error of Equating for Equating $\boldsymbol{Y}$ to $\boldsymbol{X}$ and for Equating $\boldsymbol{X}$ to $\boldsymbol{Y}$. Example 1, EG Design.

$\boldsymbol{Y}$-Score	$\mathrm{SEE}_X(y)$	$\boldsymbol{X}$-Score	$\mathrm{SEE}_Y(x)$
0	0.145	0	0.220
1	0.225	1	0.289
2	0.275	2	0.287
3	0.279	3	0.266
4	0.261	4	0.241
5	0.235	5	0.217
6	0.210	6	0.197
7	0.190	7	0.181
8	0.174	8	0.171
9	0.164	9	0.165
10	0.157	10	0.162
11	0.154	11	0.162
12	0.153	12	0.165
13	0.155	13	0.172
14	0.161	14	0.183
15	0.171	15	0.195
16	0.184	16	0.204
17	0.199	17	0.199
18	0.210	18	0.170
19	0.205	19	0.119
20	0.144	20	0.070

7.6 Deciding Between $\hat{e}_Y(x)$ and $\widehat{\mathrm{Lin}}_Y(x)$

Combining (4.26) and the Theorem 1.1, when the bandwidths h_X and h_Y are both large, the KE equating function closely approximates the standard linear equating function because the shape difference function in Theorem 1.1 is then nearly identically zero. In this example, $\widehat{\mathrm{Lin}}_Y(x)$ was computed by choosing $h_X = h_Y = 20$.

In Figure 7.7 we plot $R(x)$, the difference

$$R(x) = e_Y(x) - \mathrm{Lin}_Y(x), \tag{7.6}$$

from (1.16). This shows how different the KE estimated equating function, $\hat{e}_Y(x)$, is from the KE estimated linear equating function, $\widehat{\mathrm{Lin}}_Y(x)$. In this case they are not far apart over the range of $\boldsymbol{X}$-raw score, 0 to 20.

To assess how this small difference compares to its uncertainty, we plot it along with $\pm 2\mathrm{SEED}(x)$, the standard error of equating difference defined

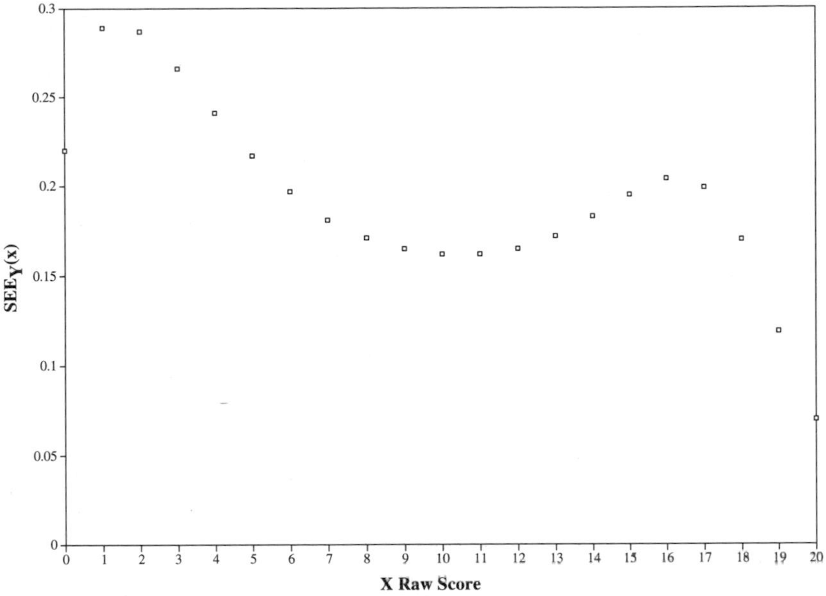

FIGURE 7.6. Standard error of equating for $\hat{e}_Y(x)$. Example 1, SG Design.

in Chapter 5 as

$$\begin{aligned} \text{SEED}^2(x) &= \text{Var}\left(\hat{e}_Y(x) - \widehat{\text{Lin}}_Y(x)\right) &\quad (7.7)\\ &= \|\, \mathbf{J}_{e_Y}\mathbf{J}_{\text{DF}}\mathbf{C} - \mathbf{J}_{\text{Lin}_Y}\mathbf{J}_{\text{DF}}\mathbf{C}\,\|^2, &\quad (7.8)\end{aligned}$$

where

$$\mathbf{J}_{e_Y}\mathbf{J}_{\text{DF}}\mathbf{C} = \frac{1}{G'}\left(\frac{\partial F}{\partial \boldsymbol{r}}\mathbf{C}_r,\ -\frac{\partial G}{\partial \boldsymbol{s}}\mathbf{C}_s\right). \quad (7.9)$$

The formula for $\mathbf{J}_{\text{Lin}_Y}$ is the same as for $\mathbf{J}_{e_Y}$, with the difference that $h_X = h_Y = 20$ in this example. Formula (7.8) can be simplified in exactly the same way that we derived (7.5) in order to produce a useful computing formula for the SEED.

This example shows that, for all but the highest two raw-scores, the linear equating function is an acceptable alternative to the curvilinear equating function. However, for $x = 19$ and 20 the difference exceeds two times the standard error of the difference between $\widehat{\text{Lin}}_Y(x)$ and $\hat{e}_Y(x)$. This could be used to support the choice of $\hat{e}_Y$ rather than $\widehat{\text{Lin}}_Y$ in this case.

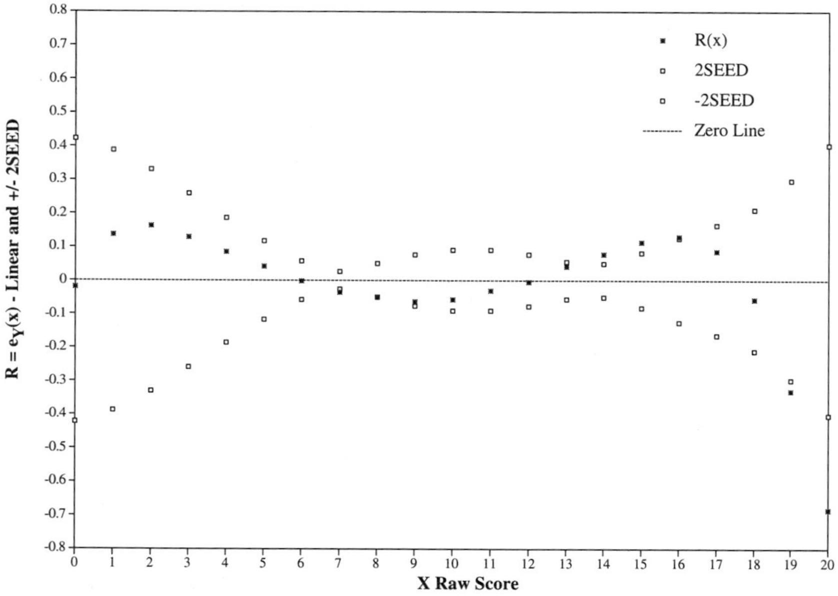

FIGURE 7.7. The difference between the KE and linear equating functions from $\boldsymbol{X}$ to $\boldsymbol{Y}$, and $\pm$2SEED. Example 1, EG Design.

8

The Single-Group Design

This chapter illustrates how to carry out the five steps of Kernel Equating (KE) for the Single-Group (SG) Design. In Section 2.12 we discussed the assumptions underlying this design and the population parameters that have to be estimated for computing the equating function.

We illustrate KE for the SG Design using an example from Holland et al. (1989). Using these data, we will go through the details of the steps described in Chapters 3, 4 and 5.

Table 8.1 gives the raw sample frequencies of number-right scores for two parallel, 20-item mathematics tests that were both given to a sample from a national population of examinees, at one administration. The data from Table 8.1 are the marginal frequencies from the bivariate frequencies given in Table 8.2.

Because each examinee in the sample has two test scores, the sample data consists of bivariate ($\boldsymbol{X}$, $\boldsymbol{Y}$)-frequencies, i.e.,

$$n_{jk} = \text{number of examinees with } \boldsymbol{X} = x_j \text{ and } \boldsymbol{Y} = y_k.$$

In this example, $x_1 = 0$, $x_2 = 1, \ldots, x_{21} = 20$; similarly, for y_k. The sample size is

$$N = \sum_{j,\,k} n_{jk} = 1453.$$

From the summary statistics at the bottom of Table 8.1 we can see that test Y, with a mean of 10.39 (± 0.1) is about half of a raw-score point harder than test X, which has a mean of 10.82 (± 0.1).

Table 8.2 shows the observed bivariate distribution. For this example, the sample correlation between $\boldsymbol{X}$ and $\boldsymbol{Y}$ is 0.775.

TABLE 8.1. Score Frequencies for $\boldsymbol{X}$ and $\boldsymbol{Y}$ for a Single Sample of Examinees. Example 2, SG Design.

Score	$\boldsymbol{X}$-Frequencies (Total)	$\boldsymbol{Y}$-Frequencies (Total)
0	1	0
1	3	0
2	8	12
3	25	24
4	30	41
5	64	57
6	67	92
7	95	100
8	116	119
9	124	143
10	156	149
11	147	153
12	120	146
13	129	127
14	110	92
15	86	76
16	66	56
17	51	38
18	29	19
19	15	9
20	11	0
Total	1453	1453
Mean	10.82	10.39
SD	3.81	3.59
Skewness	0.0026	−0.0056
Kurtosis	2.53	2.48

TABLE 8.2. Bivariate Score Frequencies for $\boldsymbol{X}$ (Rows) and $\boldsymbol{Y}$ (Columns) for a Single Sample of Examinees. Example 2, SG Design.

	0	1	2	3	4	5	6	7	8	9	10	11	12	13	14	15	16	17	18	19	20	Total
0	0	0	1	0	0	0	0	0	0	0	0	0	0	0	0	0	0	0	0	0	0	1
1	0	0	1	0	1	1	0	0	0	0	0	0	0	0	0	0	0	0	0	0	0	3
2	0	0	1	0	2	1	3	0	0	1	0	0	0	0	0	0	0	0	0	0	0	8
3	0	0	1	5	6	3	8	1	1	0	0	0	0	0	0	0	0	0	0	0	0	25
4	0	0	2	7	4	6	4	3	1	3	0	0	0	0	0	0	0	0	0	0	0	30
5	0	0	3	3	5	12	14	8	9	6	3	1	0	0	0	0	0	0	0	0	0	64
6	0	0	1	4	10	9	12	9	8	10	4	0	0	0	0	0	0	0	0	0	0	67
7	0	0	1	3	5	7	16	16	11	17	10	5	3	0	1	0	0	0	0	0	0	95
8	0	0	1	1	3	8	16	14	12	24	20	11	3	3	0	0	0	0	0	0	0	116
9	0	0	0	1	3	4	8	19	20	17	17	13	11	9	2	0	0	0	0	0	0	124
10	0	0	0	0	1	2	6	14	20	19	28	24	17	11	9	3	2	0	0	0	0	156
11	0	0	0	0	1	3	3	6	13	17	21	23	27	14	13	2	2	1	1	0	0	147
12	0	0	0	0	0	1	0	5	11	14	16	26	18	11	10	3	3	1	1	0	0	120
13	0	0	0	0	0	0	1	4	8	8	20	21	19	16	13	9	6	3	1	0	0	129
14	0	0	0	0	0	0	0	1	4	3	3	17	18	26	11	21	4	1	1	0	0	110
15	0	0	0	0	0	0	1	0	1	3	4	10	12	15	15	10	10	3	1	1	0	86
16	0	0	0	0	0	0	0	0	0	1	1	1	11	12	8	13	10	7	1	1	0	66
17	0	0	0	0	0	0	0	0	0	0	2	1	5	4	8	9	11	5	3	3	0	51
18	0	0	0	0	0	0	0	0	0	0	0	0	0	5	0	4	4	11	4	1	0	29
19	0	0	0	0	0	0	0	0	0	0	0	0	1	1	2	2	2	3	3	1	0	15
20	0	0	0	0	0	0	0	0	0	0	0	0	1	0	0	0	2	3	3	2	0	11
Total	0	0	12	24	41	57	92	100	119	143	149	153	146	127	92	76	56	38	19	9	0	1453

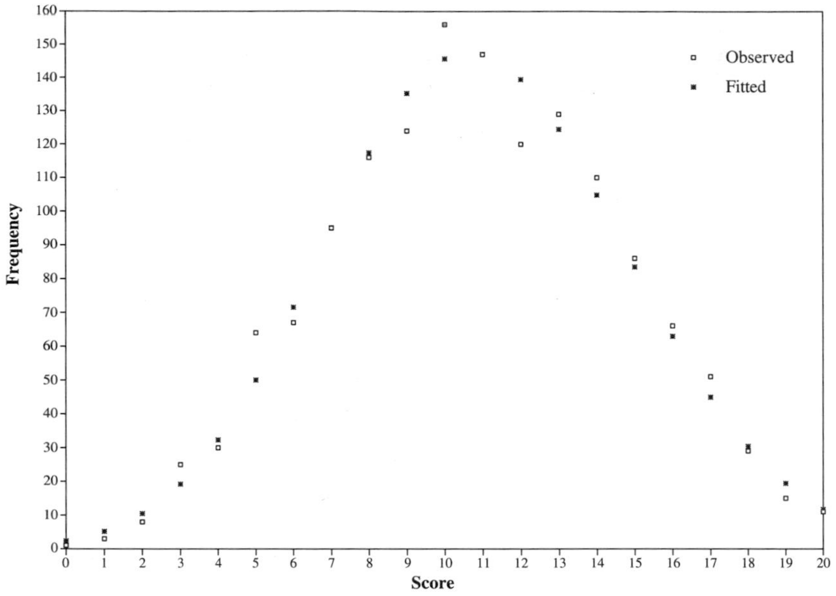

FIGURE 8.1. The observed and the fitted distributions of $\boldsymbol{X}$. Example 2, SG Design.

The raw sample proportions, (n_{jk}/N) are unsmoothed estimates of the population parameters, p_{jk}, of the joint distribution of $\boldsymbol{X}$ and $\boldsymbol{Y}$.

8.1 Pre-smoothing

The p_{jk} are assumed to follow a log-linear model. The log-linear model has the form

$$\log(p_{jk}) = \alpha + \sum_{i=1}^{T_X} \beta_{Xi}(x_j)^i + \sum_{i=1}^{T_Y} \beta_{Yi}(y_k)^i + \beta_{XY} x_j y_k, \qquad (8.1)$$

where p_{jk} are the probabilities from (2.5).

First, we fit the model from (8.1) setting β_{XY} to zero (i.e., assuming that the marginal distributions of $\boldsymbol{X}$ and $\boldsymbol{Y}$ are independent). This is equivalent to separately fitting models, similar to those from (7.1) and (7.2), to the *marginal distributions* of $\boldsymbol{X}$ and $\boldsymbol{Y}$.

This way, we first find the most suitable number of parameters, i.e., moments, to fit for each marginal distribution. In this example we decided to choose $T_X = T_Y = 3$ based on the size of the Freeman-Tukey residuals (see Table 8.3).

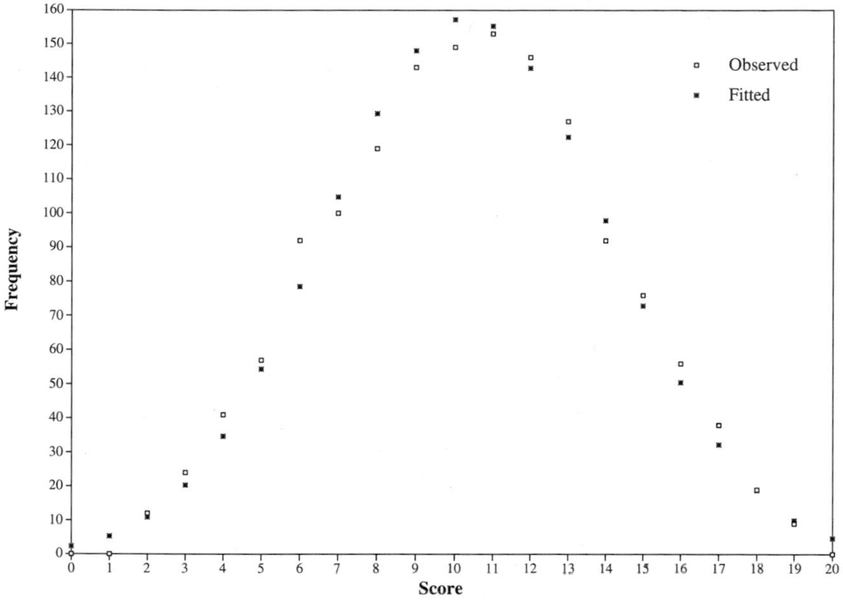

FIGURE 8.2. The observed and the fitted distributions of $\boldsymbol{Y}$. Example 2, SG Design.

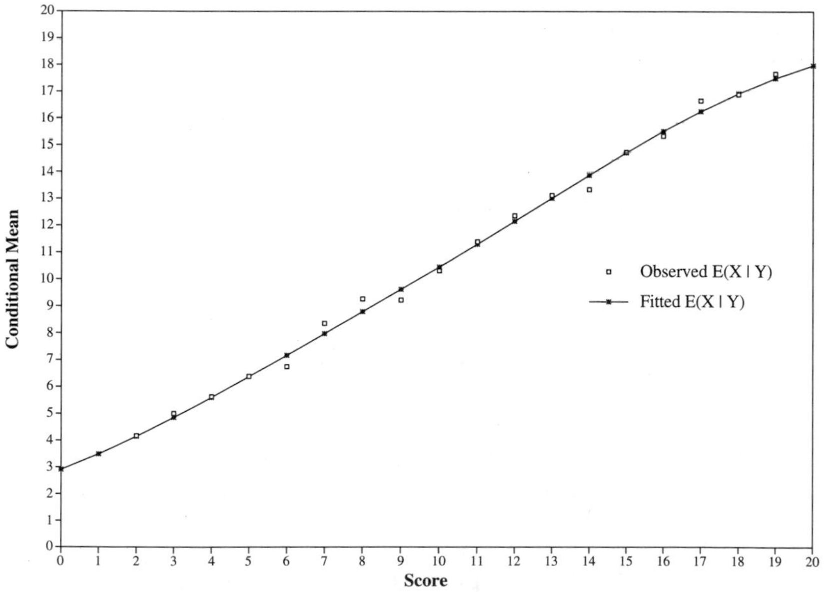

FIGURE 8.3. $\mathrm{E}(\boldsymbol{X} \mid \boldsymbol{Y})$: observed and fitted values. Example 2, SG Design.

TABLE 8.3. Fitted Score Frequencies for X and Y for a Single Sample of Examinees. Example 2, SG Design.

	$\boldsymbol{X}$-Fitted	FT Residuals	$\boldsymbol{Y}$-Fitted	FT Residuals
0	2.3	−0.78	2.29	−2.19
1	5.17	−0.93	5.27	−3.70
2	10.47	−0.72	10.86	0.40
3	19.22	1.27	20.31	0.83
4	32.32	−0.37	34.68	1.06
5	50.01	1 .88	54.38	0.38
6	71.57	−0.52	78.55	−1.48
7	95.03	0.02	104.78	−0.45
8	117.4	−0.11	129.34	−0.90
9	135.26	−0.97	147.99	−0.39
10	145.7	0.86	157.19	−0.64
11	147.07	0.01	155.24	−0.16
12	139.44	−1.68	142.76	0.29
13	124.46	0.42	122.39	0.43
14	104.81	0.52	97.87	−0.58
15	83.44	0.30	72.94	0.38
16	62.9	0.42	50.49	0.79
17	44.93	0.91	32.25	1.01
18	30.39	−0.21	18.83	0.09
19	19.42	−1.00	9.93	−0.22
20	11.67	−0.12	4.67	−3.44
Total	1453		1453	
Mean	10.82		10.39	
SD	3.81		3.59	
Skewness	0.0026		−0.0056	
Kurtosis	2.66		2.74	

Second, we fit the model from (8.1) with $T_X = T_Y = 3$ and one interaction term.

This model fits the first three moments (mean, variance, and skewness) for the two (univariate) marginal distributions and one moment for the interaction (i.e., the correlation between $\boldsymbol{X}$ and $\boldsymbol{Y}$).

Table 8.3 shows the fitted frequencies and Freeman-Tukey residuals for the two univariate (marginal) distributions. The likelihood ratio chi-square statistic for the model in (8.1) is 242.73 on 433 nominal degrees of freedom. The nominal degrees of freedom are not very helpful in this example because there are many very small fitted and observed values in an array as big as the one shown in Table 8.2. It is obvious that the observed value of the likelihood ratio chi-square statistic is much smaller than would be likely from the chi-square distribution with 433 degrees of freedom. To get a better look at the fit of the model, we examine the Freeman-Tukey (FT) residuals for the two marginal distributions, $\boldsymbol{X}$ and $\boldsymbol{Y}$, in Table 8.3. These residuals should behave roughly like independent standard Normal deviates if the models fit adequately. These residuals lie between -1.68 and $+1.88$ for the $\boldsymbol{X}$-fitted frequencies. For the $\boldsymbol{Y}$-fitted frequencies there are three larger FT residuals corresponding to the zero frequencies observed for $\boldsymbol{Y} = 0$, 1, and 20. The FT residuals for these $\boldsymbol{Y}$-values are -2.19, -3.70, and -3.44. We conclude that the fitted probabilities from these models are improved estimates of the population distributions in the sense of "consistency" and "stability" described in Chapter 3, but there may be some problems for the extreme values of $\boldsymbol{Y}$.

Comparing the summary statistics at the bottom of Tables 8.1 and 8.3 we see that the "three-moment fit" for the $\boldsymbol{X}$-score and the $\boldsymbol{Y}$-score distributions preserves the mean, the standard deviation and the skewness but not the kurtosis, as they are expected to do. In addition, the bivariate fitted distribution in Table 8.4 has the same correlation (0.775) as the raw frequencies in Table 8.2. The observed and the fitted marginal distributions of $\boldsymbol{X}$ and $\boldsymbol{Y}$ are plotted in Figure 8.1 and Figure 8.2.

For a more detailed examination of the fit of the bivariate distribution of $\boldsymbol{X}$ and $\boldsymbol{Y}$ we examine the two sets of conditional distributions ($\boldsymbol{X}$ given $\boldsymbol{Y}$ and $\boldsymbol{Y}$ given $\boldsymbol{X}$). We summarize the dependencies between $\boldsymbol{X}$ and $\boldsymbol{Y}$ by calculating the conditional means and standard deviations of the two fitted conditional distributions and comparing them to the corresponding values for the two observed conditional distributions. Figures 8.3–8.6 plot these. These four plots show that the two fitted conditional mean functions from the model accurately track the corresponding conditional averages in the data. There is poorer tracking of the conditional standard deviations in Figures 8.5 and 8.6, but this is to be expected and the trends are remarkably similar.

TABLE 8.4. Fitted Bivariate Score Frequencies for $\boldsymbol{X}$ (Rows) and $\boldsymbol{Y}$ (Columns) for a Single Sample of Examinees. Example 2, SG Design.

	0	1	2	3	4	5	6	7	8	9	10	11	12	13	14	15	16	17	18	19	20	Total
0	0.2	0.3	0.4	0.4	0.3	0.2	0.1	0.0	0.0	0.0	0.0	0.0	0.0	0.0	0.0	0.0	0.0	0.0	0.0	0.0	0.0	2.3
1	0.3	0.6	0.8	0.9	0.9	0.6	0.4	0.2	0.1	0.0	0.0	0.0	0.0	0.0	0.0	0.0	0.0	0.0	0.0	0.0	0.0	5.1
2	0.4	0.8	1.3	1.7	1.8	1.6	1.2	0.7	0.3	0.1	0.0	0.0	0.0	0.0	0.0	0.0	0.0	0.0	0.0	0.0	0.0	10.4
3	0.4	0.9	1.7	2.6	3.2	3.3	2.8	1.9	1.1	0.5	0.2	0.0	0.0	0.0	0.0	0.0	0.0	0.0	0.0	0.0	0.0	19.2
4	0.3	0.9	1.9	3.3	4.7	5.6	5.4	4.4	2.9	1.5	0.7	0.1	0.0	0.0	0.0	0.0	0.0	0.0	0.0	0.0	0.0	32.3
5	0.2	0.7	1.7	3.4	5.7	7.8	8.7	8.1	6.2	3.9	2.0	0.8	0.3	0.1	0.0	0.0	0.0	0.0	0.0	0.0	0.0	50.0
6	0.1	0.4	1.3	3.0	5.7	9.0	11.7	12.5	11.0	7.9	4.7	2.3	0.9	0.3	0.1	0.0	0.0	0.0	0.0	0.0	0.0	71.5
7	0.0	0.2	0.8	2.2	4.8	8.8	13.1	16.1	16.3	13.6	9.4	5.3	2.5	0.9	0.3	0.1	0.0	0.0	0.0	0.0	0.0	95.0
8	0.0	0.1	0.4	1.3	3.4	7.1	12.3	17.4	20.3	19.6	15.5	10.2	5.5	2.4	0.9	0.2	0.0	0.0	0.0	0.0	0.0	117.4
9	0.0	0.0	0.2	0.7	2.0	4.9	9.7	15.8	21.3	23.6	21.6	16.3	10.2	5.2	2.2	0.7	0.2	0.0	0.0	0.0	0.0	135.2
10	0.0	0.0	0.0	0.3	1.0	2.8	6.4	12.1	18.9	24.0	25.3	22.0	15.8	9.4	4.6	1.8	0.6	0.1	0.0	0.0	0.0	145.7
11	0.0	0.0	0.0	0.1	0.4	1.3	3.6	7.8	13.9	20.6	25.0	25.1	20.8	14.2	8.0	3.7	1.4	0.4	0.1	0.0	0.0	147.0
12	0.0	0.0	0.0	0.0	0.1	0.5	1.7	4.2	8.7	14.9	20.9	24.2	23.1	18.2	11.8	6.3	2.8	1.0	0.3	0.0	0.0	139.4
13	0.0	0.0	0.0	0.0	0.0	0.2	0.6	1.9	4.6	9.1	14.8	19.7	21.7	19.7	14.8	9.1	4.7	1.9	0.7	0.2	0.0	124.4
14	0.0	0.0	0.0	0.0	0.0	0.0	0.2	0.7	2.1	4.7	8.9	13.6	17.3	18.1	15.7	11.2	6.6	3.2	1.3	0.4	0.1	104.8
15	0.0	0.0	0.0	0.0	0.0	0.0	0.0	0.2	0.8	2.1	4.5	8.0	11.8	14.2	14.2	11.6	7.9	4.4	2.0	0.8	0.2	83.4
16	0.0	0.0	0.0	0.0	0.0	0.0	0.0	0.0	0.2	0.8	1.9	4.0	6.8	9.5	10.9	10.3	8.1	5.2	2.8	1.2	0.4	62.9
17	0.0	0.0	0.0	0.0	0.0	0.0	0.0	0.0	0.1	0.2	0.7	1.7	3.4	5.4	7.2	7.8	7.1	5.3	3.2	1.6	0.7	44.9
18	0.0	0.0	0.0	0.0	0.0	0.0	0.0	0.0	0.0	0.0	0.2	0.6	1.4	2.6	4.0	5.1	5.3	4.6	3.2	1.9	0.9	30.3
19	0.0	0.0	0.0	0.0	0.0	0.0	0.0	0.0	0.0	0.0	0.0	0.2	0.5	1.1	1.9	2.8	3.4	3.4	2.8	1.9	1.0	19.4
20	0.0	0.0	0.0	0.0	0.0	0.0	0.0	0.0	0.0	0.0	0.0	0.0	0.1	0.4	0.8	1.3	1.9	2.1	2.0	1.6	1.0	11.6
Total	2.2	5.2	10.8	20.3	34.6	54.3	78.5	104.7	129.3	147.9	157.1	155.2	142.7	122.3	97.8	72.9	50.4	32.2	18.8	9.9	4.6	1453

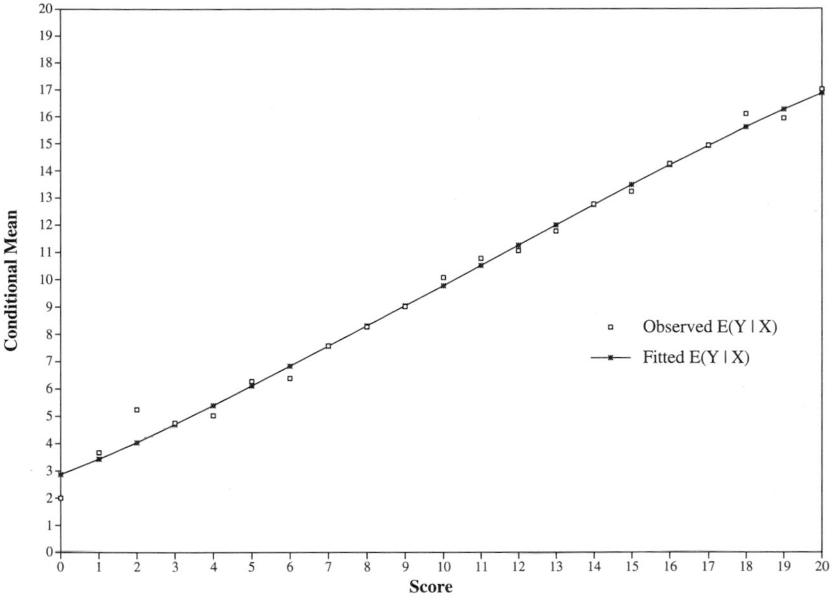

FIGURE 8.4. $\mathrm{E}(\boldsymbol{Y} \mid \boldsymbol{X})$: observed and fitted values. Example 2, SG Design.

In addition to the estimated joint probabilities, $\hat{p}_{jk}$, the output of a satisfactory log-linear model program will include the "**C**-matrices" that are the essential information needed to compute the standard errors of $\hat{p}_{jk}$, and which are used to compute the SEE described in Chapter 5.

In comparison with Example 1 from Chapter 7, in this example, there is only one **C**-matrix, $\mathbf{C}_P$, because the distribution to be estimated is bivariate and there is only one population, P, from which the sample is drawn. $\mathbf{C}_P$ is a very large array (441×7), and therefore it will not be reported here.

Hence, the estimated covariance matrix of $v(\hat{\mathbf{P}})$, $\boldsymbol{\Sigma}_{v(\hat{P})}$, is such that

$$\boldsymbol{\Sigma}_{v(P)} = \mathbf{C}_P \mathbf{C}_P^t,$$

where $\mathbf{C}_P$ is a $JK(=(21)(21)=441)$ by $T_P(=7)$ matrix defined as in Theorem 3.1.

8.2 Estimation of the Score Probabilities

In the SG Design the estimated joint probabilities $\{\hat{p}_{jk}\}$ are obtained directly on the target population, T which is P. However, in contrast to the EG Design, we need to further transform the smoothed $\{\hat{p}_{jk}\}$ to obtain $\hat{r}_j$

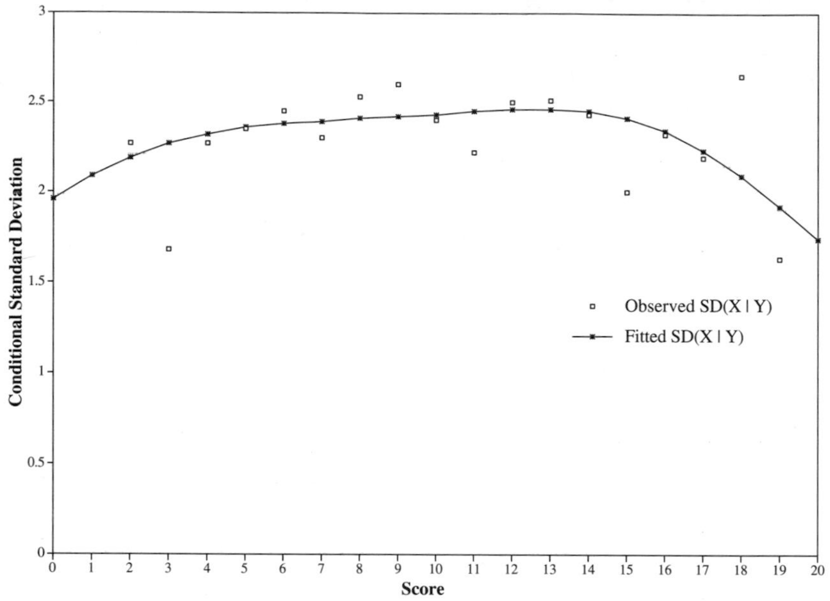

FIGURE 8.5. $SD(\boldsymbol{X} \mid \boldsymbol{Y})$: observed and fitted values. Example 2, SG Design.

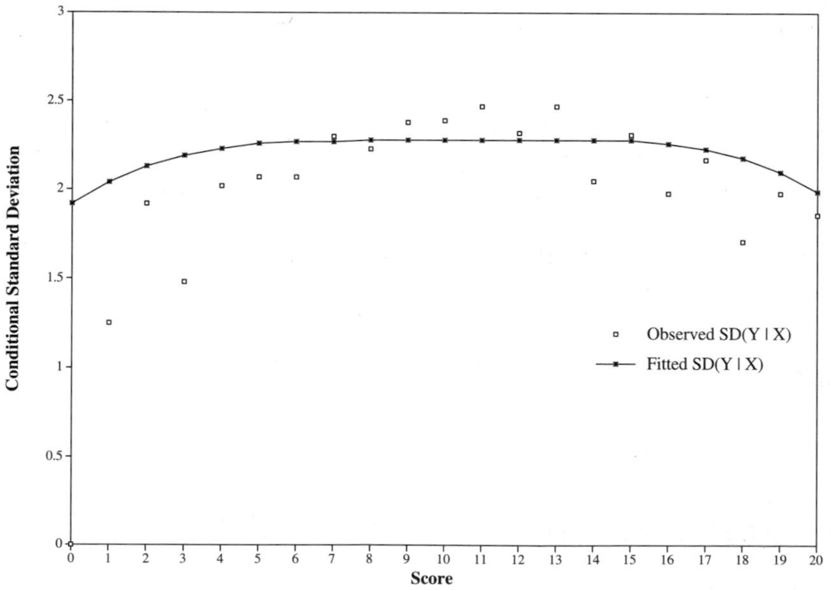

FIGURE 8.6. $SD(\boldsymbol{Y} \mid \boldsymbol{X})$: observed and fitted values. Example 2, SG Design.

TABLE 8.5. Estimated Score Probabilities for $\boldsymbol{X}$ and $\boldsymbol{Y}$ for one Sample of Examinees. Example 2, SG Design.

Score	$\hat{r}_j$	$\hat{s}_k$	Score	$\hat{r}_j$	$\hat{s}_k$
0	0.0016	0.0016	11	0.1012	0.1068
1	0.0036	0.0036	12	0.0960	0.0983
2	0.0072	0.0075	13	0.0857	0.0842
3	0.0132	0.0140	14	0.0721	0.0674
4	0.0222	0.0239	15	0.0574	0.0502
5	0.0344	0.0374	16	0.0433	0.0347
6	0.0493	0.0541	17	0.0309	0.0222
7	0.0654	0.0721	18	0.0209	0.0130
8	0.0808	0.0890	19	0.0134	0.0068
9	0.0931	0.1018	20	0.0080	0.0032
10	0.1003	0.1082			

and $\hat{s}_k$. This linear transformation is the Design Function, DF, we introduced in Chapter 2.

Let $\hat{p}_{jk}$ be the estimates of $\{p_{jk}\}$ based on the sample data $\{n_{jk}\}$. Then $\hat{\boldsymbol{r}}$ and $\hat{\boldsymbol{s}}$ are computed through SG Design Function described by (2.11) and (2.12), i.e.,

$$\hat{\boldsymbol{r}} = \mathbf{M}\, v(\hat{\mathbf{P}}) \quad \text{and} \quad \hat{\boldsymbol{s}} = \mathbf{N}\, v(\hat{\mathbf{P}}), \tag{8.2}$$

where $\mathbf{M}$ and $\mathbf{N}$ are the matrices described in (2.9) and (2.10).

Table 8.5 gives the smoothed values of $\{\hat{r}_j\}$ and $\{\hat{s}_k\}$ to four significant digits; they are obtained by applying the Design Function, DF, or in other words, they are the two fitted marginal distributions reported in Table 8.3 or 8.4 divided by the sample size.

8.3 Continuization

The cdf's associated with the score probabilities defined for the test scores $\boldsymbol{X}$ and $\boldsymbol{Y}$ in (2.2) are

$$F(x) = \text{Prob}(X \leq x) = \sum_{j,\, x_j \leq x} r_j,$$

and

$$G(y) = \text{Prob}(Y \leq y) = \sum_{k,\, y_k \leq y} s_k,$$

where $x,\ y\ \in \mathbb{R}$.

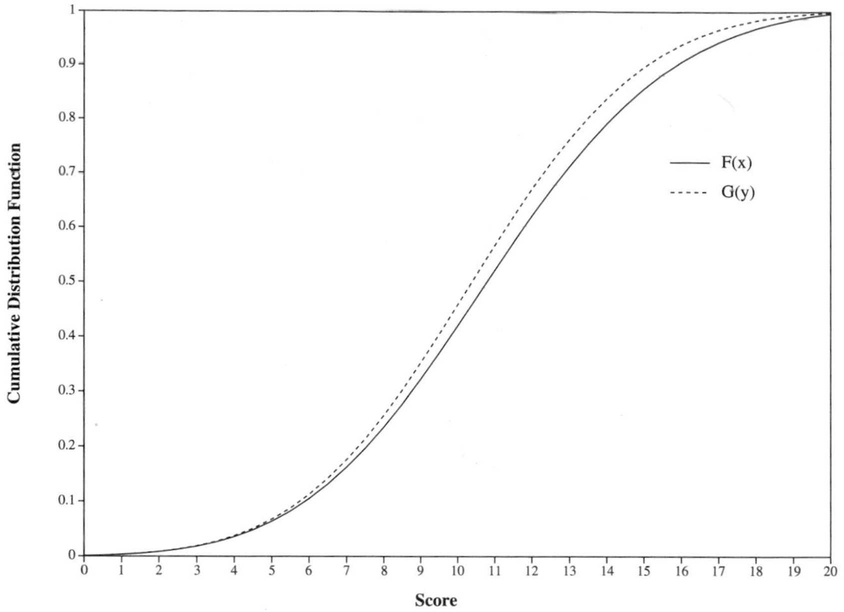

FIGURE 8.7. The continuized distributions, $\hat{F}_{h_X}$ and $\hat{G}_{h_Y}$. Example 2, SG Design.

$\hat{F}_{h_X}(x)$ and $\hat{G}_{h_Y}(y)$ are the continuous approximations to $\hat{F}(x)$ and $\hat{G}(y)$. The continuized cdf's are computed as described in (4.5) and (4.8), respectively.

As described in Section 4.2, h_X and h_Y are chosen to minimize the criterion given in (4.30), i.e.,

$$\text{PEN}_1(h_X) + K \times \text{PEN}_2(h_X),$$

with PEN_1 and PEN_2 defined in (4.27) and (4.29), respectively. The weight K was 1.

In this example there was no effect of PEN_2. The resulting optimal values of h_X and h_Y for this example were 0.61225 and 0.663940, respectively. Figure 8.7 shows the cdf's $\hat{F}_{h_X}$ and $\hat{G}_{h_Y}$ for this example.

8.4 Equating

Once the continuous approximations to $\hat{F}(x)$ and $\hat{G}(y)$ are available, we compute the equating functions via (4.31) and (4.32), i.e., the equating functions are

$$\hat{e}_Y(x) = \hat{G}_{h_Y}^{-1}(\hat{F}_{h_X}(x)),$$

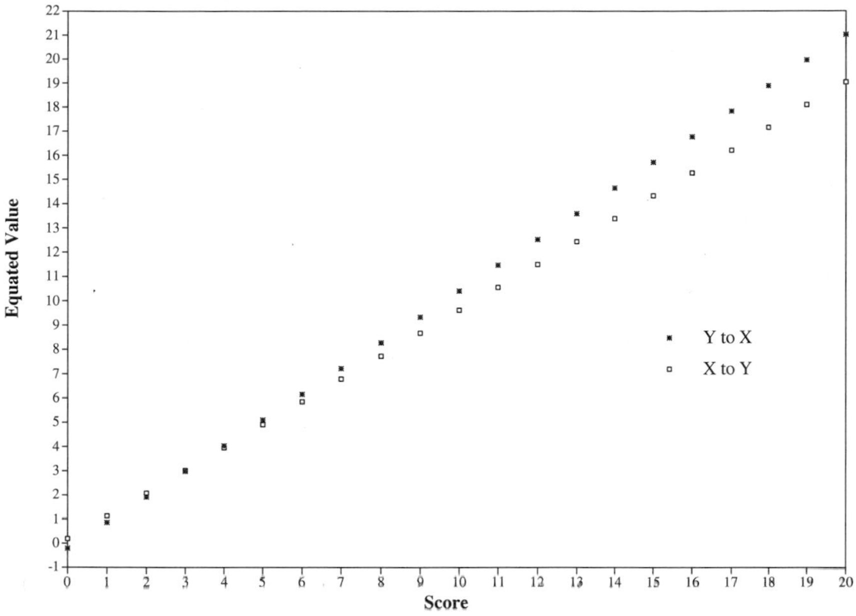

FIGURE 8.8. The equating functions, $\hat{e}_X(y)$ and $\hat{e}_Y(x)$. Example 2, SG Design.

and

$$\hat{e}_X(y) = \hat{F}_{h_X}^{-1}(\hat{G}_{h_Y}(y)).$$

As already explained in Chapter 7, we usually need the value of the equating function only for each raw score of $\boldsymbol{X}$. Hence, we need to compute

$$\hat{e}_Y(x_j) = \hat{G}_{h_Y}^{-1}(u_{Xj}),$$

where $u_{Xj} = \hat{F}_{h_X}(x_j)$ and

$$\hat{e}_X(y_k) = \hat{F}_{h_X}^{-1}(u_{Yk}),$$

where $u_{Yk} = \hat{G}_{h_Y}(y_k)$.

The two equating functions computed in this example are plotted in Figure 8.8. The differences between these two equating functions and their corresponding linear equating functions, for both $\boldsymbol{X}$ to $\boldsymbol{Y}$ and from $\boldsymbol{Y}$ to $\boldsymbol{X}$ are plotted in Figure 8.9.

As the graphs reveal, both $\hat{e}_Y(x)$ and $\hat{e}_X(y)$, are nearly linear in this example. The maximum difference between the equating functions obtained using KE and the linear equating function occurs (see Figure 8.9) at $x = y = 20$. This difference is less than a raw score point for either direction of the equating.

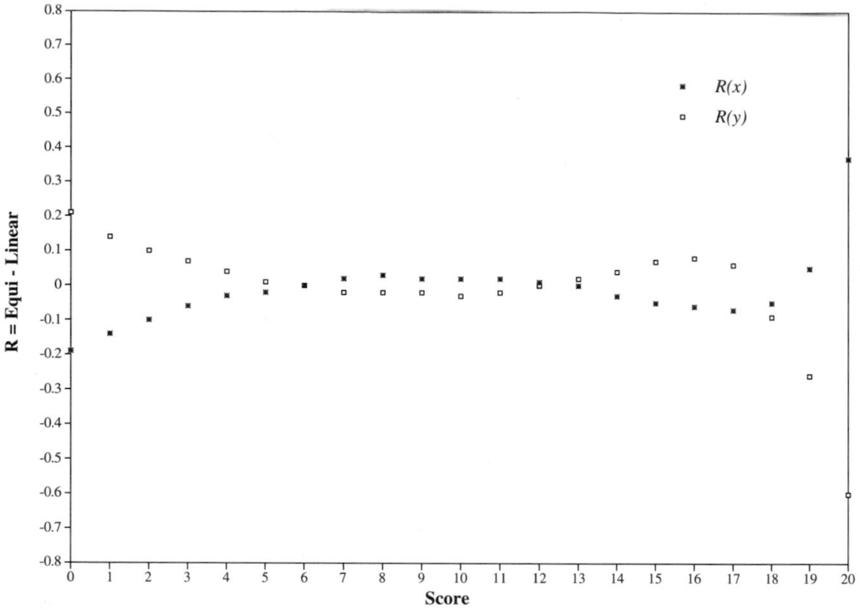

FIGURE 8.9. The differences between the KE ("Equi") and linear equating functions from $\boldsymbol{X}$ to $\boldsymbol{Y}$ and from $\boldsymbol{Y}$ to $\boldsymbol{X}$. Example 2, SG Design.

The equating function, $\hat{e}_Y(x)$, is supposed to match the distribution of $\hat{e}_Y(\boldsymbol{X})$ to that of $\boldsymbol{Y}$, but as we have indicated this is not completely possible because the two distributions are discrete. As we discuss in Section 4.2, we may investigate how well $\hat{e}_Y(\boldsymbol{X})$ approximates the distribution of $\boldsymbol{Y}$ by comparing the first several moments of $\hat{e}_Y(\boldsymbol{X})$ to the corresponding ones of $\boldsymbol{Y}$ using $\hat{\boldsymbol{r}}$ and $\hat{\boldsymbol{s}}$ to make the moment calculations.

Table 8.6 gives the differences between these moments as percents of the size of the moment of the score being "equated to" as discussed in Chapter 4. The moments range from the first to the tenth. Table 8.6 gives values for the equating in both directions, $\boldsymbol{X}$ to $\boldsymbol{Y}$ and $\boldsymbol{Y}$ to $\boldsymbol{X}$. As we can see, the discrepancy between these moments ranges from -0.0 to -1.2 percent for the $\boldsymbol{X}$ to $\boldsymbol{Y}$ equating and from 0.0 to 0.5 percent for the $\boldsymbol{Y}$ to $\boldsymbol{X}$ equating. These differences are very small and indicate how well KE achieves the matching of $e_Y(\boldsymbol{X})$ to $\boldsymbol{Y}$, and $e_X(\boldsymbol{Y})$ to $\boldsymbol{X}$.

8.5 Standard Error of Equating

In order to compute the SEE of the equating function given above, we will apply Theorem 5.4 from Chapter 5.

TABLE 8.6. Difference Between the Moments of the Equated Distribution and the Target Distribution Expressed as Percent Relative Error, PRE(p). Example 2, SG Design.

	Percent Relative Error	
Moments	(X to Y)	(Y to X)
1	−0.0031	0.0007
2	−0.0133	0.0059
3	−0.0332	0.0148
4	−0.0701	0.0309
5	−0.1333	0.0590
6	−0.2330	0.1042
7	−0.3793	0.1714
8	−0.5817	0.2654
9	−0.8481	0.3900
10	−1.1851	0.5485

The main result is equation (5.29), which we repeat here,

$$\mathrm{SEE}_Y(x) = \frac{1}{G'}\left[\left\|\frac{\partial F}{\partial \boldsymbol{r}}\mathbf{U}_R - \frac{\partial G}{\partial \boldsymbol{s}}\mathbf{V}_R\right\|^2 + \left\|\frac{\partial F}{\partial \boldsymbol{r}}\mathbf{U}_S - \frac{\partial G}{\partial \boldsymbol{s}}\mathbf{V}_S\right\|^2\right]^{1/2},$$

where $\mathbf{U}_R$, $\mathbf{U}_S$, $\mathbf{V}_R$, and $\mathbf{V}_S$ are the matrix-entries of $\mathbf{J}_{\mathrm{DF}}\mathbf{C}$ given in Table 5.5 and $||\boldsymbol{v}||^2 = \sum_i v_i^2$ is the squared Euclidian norm of the vector $\boldsymbol{v}$. From Table 5.5 it follows that, for the SG Design, $\mathbf{U}_R = \boldsymbol{U} = \sum_k \mathbf{C}_{Pk}$, $\mathbf{U}_S = \mathbf{0}$, $\mathbf{V}_S = \mathbf{0}$, and

$$\mathbf{V}_R = \mathbf{V} = \begin{pmatrix} \mathbf{1}_J^t\mathbf{C}_{P1} \\ \vdots \\ \mathbf{1}_J^t\mathbf{C}_{PK} \end{pmatrix} = \begin{pmatrix} \boldsymbol{v}_{P1}^t \\ \vdots \\ \boldsymbol{v}_{PK}^t \end{pmatrix}.$$

The matrices $\mathbf{C}_{Pk}$ are blocks of the $\mathbf{C}_P$ matrix. The 441×7-matrix, $\mathbf{C}_P$, defined at the end of Section 8.1, is partitioned into 21 blocks, each of dimension 21 by 7.

Thus, the formula for the SEE for the SG Design is

$$\mathrm{SEE}_Y(x) = \frac{1}{G'}\left\|\frac{\partial F}{\partial \boldsymbol{r}}\mathbf{U} - \frac{\partial G}{\partial \boldsymbol{s}}\mathbf{V}\right\|. \tag{8.3}$$

Hence, the SE-vector for SG Design is

$$\frac{1}{G'}\left(\frac{\partial F}{\partial \boldsymbol{r}}\mathbf{U} - \frac{\partial G}{\partial \boldsymbol{s}}\mathbf{V}\right). \tag{8.4}$$

Table 8.7 displays the standard error of equating for the two equating functions, equating both $\boldsymbol{X}$ to $\boldsymbol{Y}$ and $\boldsymbol{Y}$ to $\boldsymbol{X}$, evaluated at each score

TABLE 8.7. Standard Error of Equating for Equating $\boldsymbol{Y}$ to $\boldsymbol{X}$ and for Equating $\boldsymbol{X}$ to $\boldsymbol{Y}$. Example 2, SG Design.

$\boldsymbol{Y}$-Score	$\mathrm{SEE}_X(y)$	$\boldsymbol{X}$-Score	$\mathrm{SEE}_Y(x)$
0	0.1617	0	0.1579
1	0.2208	1	0.2236
2	0.2208	2	0.2254
3	0.1931	3	0.1970
4	0.1593	4	0.1621
5	0.1284	5	0.1303
6	0.1044	6	0.1059
7	0.0886	7	0.0907
8	0.0805	8	0.0838
9	0.0776	9	0.0820
10	0.0770	10	0.0821
11	0.0768	11	0.0823
12	0.0766	12	0.0831
13	0.0779	13	0.0872
14	0.0831	14	0.0984
15	0.0951	15	0.1188
16	0.1147	16	0.1450
17	0.1404	17	0.1670
18	0.1674	18	0.1675
19	0.1854	19	0.1338
20	0.1581	20	0.0885

value. In this example, the SEE's range from 0.0766 to 0.2254 raw-score points.

Figure 8.10 shows the standard error of equating for the equating function $\hat{e}_Y(x)$.

8.6 Deciding Between $\hat{e}_Y(x)$ and $\widehat{\mathrm{Lin}}_Y(x)$

Combining (4.26) and the Theorem 1.1, when the bandwidths h_X and h_Y are both large, the KE equating function closely approximates the standard linear equating function because the shape difference function in Theorem 1.1 is then nearly zero. In this example, $\widehat{\mathrm{Lin}}_Y(x)$ was computed by choosing $h_X = h_Y = 20$.

In Figure 8.11 we plot $R(x)$, the difference

$$R(x) = e_Y(x) - \mathrm{Lin}_Y(x) \tag{8.5}$$

and

$$R(y) = e_X(y) - \mathrm{Lin}_X(y). \tag{8.6}$$

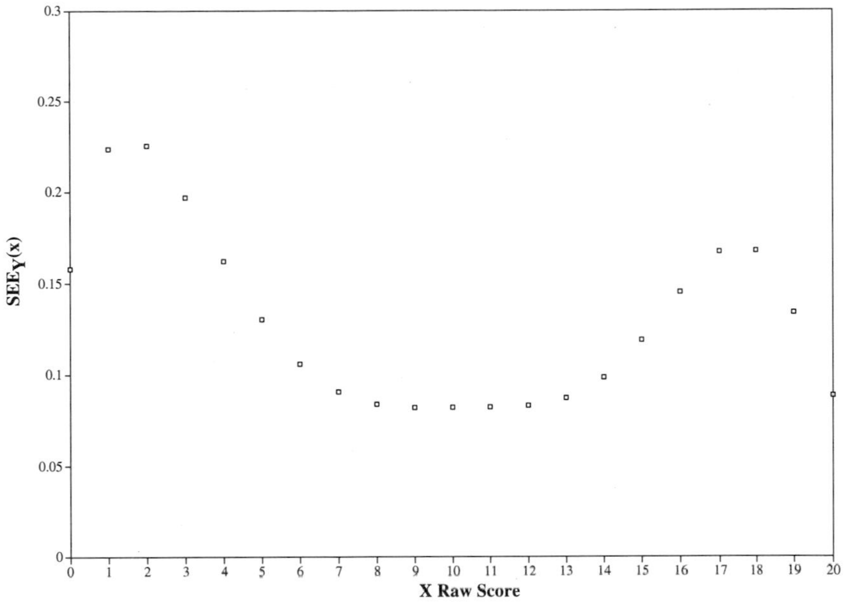

FIGURE 8.10. Standard error of equating for $\hat{e}_Y(x)$. Example 2, SG Design.

This shows how different the KE function is from the linear equating function.

To assess how this small difference compares to its uncertainty, we plot it along with $\pm 2\text{SEED}(x)$, the standard error of equating difference defined in Chapter 5 as

$$\begin{aligned} \text{SEED}^2(x) &= \text{Var}\left(\hat{e}_Y(x) - \widehat{\text{Lin}}_Y(x)\right) &(8.7)\\ &= \|\,\mathbf{J}_{e_Y}\mathbf{J}_{\text{DF}}\mathbf{C} - \mathbf{J}_{\text{Lin}_Y}\mathbf{J}_{\text{DF}}\mathbf{C}\,\|^2, &(8.8)\end{aligned}$$

where

$$\mathbf{J}_{e_Y}\mathbf{J}_{\text{DF}}\mathbf{C} = \frac{1}{G'}\left(\frac{\partial F}{\partial \boldsymbol{r}}\mathbf{U} - \frac{\partial G}{\partial \boldsymbol{s}}\mathbf{V}\right).$$

The formula for $\mathbf{J}_{\text{Lin}_Y}$ is the same as for $\mathbf{J}_{e_Y}$, with the difference that $h_X = h_Y = 20$. Formula (8.8) can be simplified in exactly the same way that we derived (8.3) in order to produce a useful computing formula for the SEED.

In this example $\hat{e}_Y(x)$ and $\widehat{\text{Lin}}_Y(x)$ are not far apart over the $\boldsymbol{X}$-raw score range, 0 to 20. For all but the highest raw-score, the linear equating function differs from the KE function by less than two standard deviations. This could be used to justify preferring $\widehat{\text{Lin}}_Y(x)$ to $\hat{e}_Y(x)$ in this example.

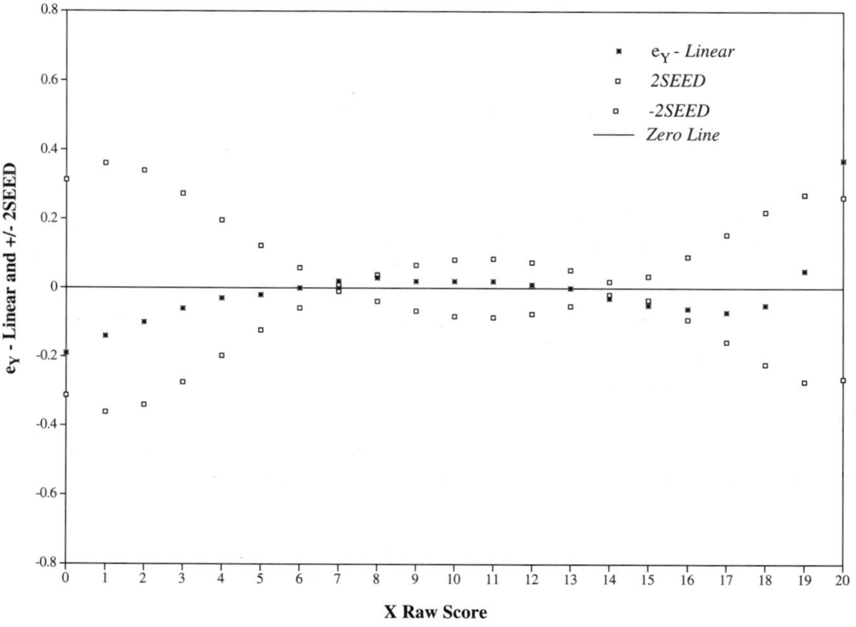

FIGURE 8.11. The difference between the KE and linear equating functions from $\boldsymbol{X}$ to $\boldsymbol{Y}$, and $\pm$2SEED. Example 2, SG Design.

9
The Counterbalanced Design

In the Counterbalanced (CB) Design, two independent, random samples of examinees from a single population P take both tests, $\boldsymbol{X}$ and $\boldsymbol{Y}$, in different orders. The first sample takes test $\boldsymbol{X}$ first (denoted in the following as $\boldsymbol{X}_1$) and test $\boldsymbol{Y}$ second (denoted $\boldsymbol{Y}_2$), as in a Single-Group Design. The other sample takes test $\boldsymbol{Y}$ first (denoted $\boldsymbol{Y}_1$) and test $\boldsymbol{X}$ second (denoted $\boldsymbol{X}_2$). Hence, the data consists of two SG Designs for $(\boldsymbol{X}_1, \boldsymbol{Y}_2)$ and $(\boldsymbol{X}_2, \boldsymbol{Y}_1)$.

This chapter illustrates how to carry out the five steps of the Kernel Equating (KE) method for the CB Design. As we mentioned in Section 2.3 we regard the "two independent SG approach to the CB Design" as the most accurate of the four alternatives described there in that it reflects the details of the sampling more faithfully and uses the data more completely than the three other approaches. This approach consists of pre-smoothing by fitting separate log-linear models to the two SG Designs, for $(\boldsymbol{X}_1, \boldsymbol{Y}_2)$ and $(\boldsymbol{X}_2, \boldsymbol{Y}_1)$, and then combining them by regarding $\boldsymbol{X}$ as a stochastic mixture of $\boldsymbol{X}_1$ and $\boldsymbol{X}_2$, and $\boldsymbol{Y}$ as a stochastic mixture of $\boldsymbol{Y}_1$ and $\boldsymbol{Y}_2$. The target population, T, is the common one, P, from which the two samples are drawn. In Section 2.3 we discussed the assumptions underlying this design and the population parameters which have to be estimated for computing the equating function.

We illustrate KE for the CB Design using an example from a small field study from an international testing program. Using these data, we will go through the details of the steps described in Chapters 3, 4 and 5 for the CB Design.

In this example X has 75 items and Y has 76 items. Both are scored by number-right. The two tables with the raw and fitted frequencies are too large to be given here. Instead, in an appendix at the end of this chapter, we give the observed values, $(\boldsymbol{X}_1, \boldsymbol{Y}_2)$, for each examinee from the first sample and the observed values, $(\boldsymbol{X}_2, \boldsymbol{Y}_1)$, for each examinee from the second sample, in Tables 9.7 and 9.8.

Tables 9.1 and 9.2 give summary statistics of the observed and fitted marginal frequencies for $\boldsymbol{X}_1$ and $\boldsymbol{Y}_2$, and $\boldsymbol{X}_2$ and $\boldsymbol{Y}_1$, respectively.

The two SG Designs within the CB Design result in data for two joint distributions. We denote the first by $\mathbf{P}_{(12)}$ for $(\boldsymbol{X}_1, \boldsymbol{Y}_2)$ from the first sample, and the second by $\mathbf{P}_{(21)}$ for $(\boldsymbol{X}_2, \boldsymbol{Y}_1)$ from the second sample. Both $\mathbf{P}_{(12)}$ and $\mathbf{P}_{(21)}$ are J by K matrices of the joint probabilities for $\boldsymbol{X}$ and $\boldsymbol{Y}$ (analogous to $\mathbf{P}$ in the SG Design).

Because each examinee in each of the two samples has two test scores, the sample data consists of two bivariate $(\boldsymbol{X}, \boldsymbol{Y})$-frequencies, i.e.,

$$n_{(12)jk} = \text{number of examinees with } \boldsymbol{X}_1 = \boldsymbol{x}_j \text{ and } \boldsymbol{Y}_2 = \boldsymbol{y}_k$$

and

$$n_{(21)jk} = \text{number of examinees with } \boldsymbol{X}_2 = \boldsymbol{x}_j \text{ and } \boldsymbol{Y}_1 = \boldsymbol{y}_k.$$

In this example, the x_j and y_k values are $x_1 = 0$, $x_2 = 1, \ldots, x_{76} = 75$ and $y_1 = 0$, $y_2 = 1, \ldots, y_{77} = 76$, respectively. The samples sizes are

$$N_{(12)} = \sum_j \sum_k n_{(12)jk} = 143$$

and

$$N_{(21)} = \sum_j \sum_k n_{(21)jk} = 140.$$

From the summary statistics in Tables 9.1 and 9.2 we can see that test Y_1, with a mean of 51.39 (± 1.0) is slightly harder than test X_1, which has a mean of 52.54 (± 1.0). As for order effects, we see that Y_2, has nearly the same mean, 51.29 (± 0.9), as Y_1, whereas X_2 has a mean of 50.64 (± 1.2) which is nearly two points smaller than X_1. Hence, it appears that the there is a small-order effect for the test X. For this example, the sample correlation between $\boldsymbol{X}_1$ and $\boldsymbol{Y}_2$ and between $\boldsymbol{X}_2$ and $\boldsymbol{Y}_1$ is 0.88.

In Tables 9.1 and 9.2 the fitted model is what we call (2, 2, 1) (see below in Section 9.1).

The raw sample proportions, $n_{(12)jk}/N_{(12)}$ and $n_{(21)jk}/N_{(21)}$, are unsmoothed estimates of the population score probabilities, $p_{(12)jk}$ and $p_{(21)jk}$, from (2.15), of the two joint distributions of $\boldsymbol{X}_1$ and $\boldsymbol{Y}_2$ and of $\boldsymbol{X}_2$ and $\boldsymbol{Y}_1$, respectively. With such small samples and so many score probabilities the raw sample proportions are very inaccurate estimates of these population parameters, and pre-smoothing is an essential step.

TABLE 9.1. Summary Statistics for the Observed and Fitted Distributions of $\boldsymbol{X}_1$ and $\boldsymbol{Y}_2$ for One Sample of Examinees. Example 3, CB Design.

	$\boldsymbol{X}_1$-Observed	$\boldsymbol{X}_1$-Fitted	$\boldsymbol{Y}_2$-Observed	$\boldsymbol{Y}_2$-Fitted
Mean	52.54	52.54	51.29	51.29
SD	12.40	12.40	11.0	11.0
Skewness	−0.48	−0.40	−0.34	−0.31
Kurtosis	2.77	2.76	2.32	2.78

TABLE 9.2. Summary Statistics for the Observed and Fitted Distributions of $\boldsymbol{X}_2$ and $\boldsymbol{Y}_1$ for One Sample of Examinees. Example 3, CB Design.

	$\boldsymbol{X}_2$-Observed	$\boldsymbol{X}_2$-Fitted	$\boldsymbol{Y}_1$-Observed	$\boldsymbol{Y}_1$-Fitted
Mean	50.64	50.64	51.39	51.39
SD	13.83	13.83	12.18	12.18
Skewness	−0.53	−0.44	−0.57	−0.37
Kurtosis	2.13	2.74	2.43	2.78

9.1 Pre-smoothing

The estimation procedure, using log-linear models, for each of the two bivariate distributions is exactly the same as that described in Chapter 8 for the SG Design. In this example the sample sizes are so small that the pre-smoothing is essential.

Using the "vectorizing notation" for arrays, that we describe carefully in Chapter 2, Section 2.2, the vectors of the $v(\mathbf{P}_{(12)})$ and $v(\mathbf{P}_{(21)})$ are assumed to follow log-linear models. The log-linear models for $v(\mathbf{P}_{(12)})$ and $v(\mathbf{P}_{(21)})$ have the form:

$$\log(p_{(12)jk}) = \alpha_{(12)} + \sum_{i=1}^{T_{X_1}} \beta_{X_1 i}(x_j)^i + \sum_{i=1}^{T_{Y_2}} \beta_{Y_2 i}(y_k)^i + \sum_{i=1}^{I_{(12)}} \sum_{l=1}^{L_{(12)}} \beta_{(12)il} x_j^i y_k^l \quad (9.1)$$

and

$$\log(p_{(21)jk}) = \alpha_{(21)} + \sum_{i=1}^{T_{X_2}} \beta_{X_2 i}(x_j)^i + \sum_{i=1}^{T_{Y_1}} \beta_{Y_1 i}(y_k)^i + \sum_{i=1}^{I_{(21)}} \sum_{l=1}^{L_{(21)}} \beta_{(21)il} x_j^i y_k^l, \quad (9.2)$$

where $p_{(12)jk}$ and $p_{(21)jk}$ are the probabilities from (2.15).

The data in this example are very sparse. There are about 140 observations for both $\mathbf{P}_{(12)}$ and $\mathbf{P}_{(21)}$ and in both cases they are spread over 76 times $77 = 5852$ combinations of XY-scores. Primarily for this reason we restricted our attention to very simple models for these two data arrays. In particular, we fit three different models to these data. They are described as follows.

Model (2, 2, 1). In (9.1), this log-linear model for $v(\mathbf{P}_{(12)})$ is specified by $T_{X_1} = T_{Y_2} = 2$, and $I_{(12)} = L_{(12)} = 1$. Model (2, 2, 1) has, as sufficient statistics, the first two moments of $\boldsymbol{X}_1$ and $\boldsymbol{Y}_2$, as well as the first cross-moment of $\boldsymbol{X}_1$ and $\boldsymbol{Y}_2$. This means that the fitted score probabilities for the joint distribution of $\boldsymbol{X}_1$ and $\boldsymbol{Y}_2$ will have the same means, same standard deviations and same correlation between $\boldsymbol{X}_1$ and $\boldsymbol{Y}_2$ as observed in the raw data. Model (2, 2, 1) is also used for $v(\mathbf{P}_{(21)})$, using (9.2) in the obvious way.

Model (3, 3, 1). In (9.1), this model is specified by $T_{X_1} = T_{Y_2} = 3$, and $I_{(12)} = L_{(12)} = 1$. It is similar to model (2, 2, 1), except that, in addition to the means and standard deviations, the fitted skewness values of $\boldsymbol{X}_1$ and of $\boldsymbol{Y}_2$ match those of the raw data as well.

Model (2, 2, 2). In (9.1) this model is specified by $T_{X_1} = T_{Y_2} = 2$, and $I_{(12)} = L_{(12)} = 2$. It is also similar to model (2, 2, 1) and in addition to matching the correlation of $\boldsymbol{X}_1$ and $\boldsymbol{Y}_2$ to their correlation in the raw data, three additional fitted cross-moments are also matched to their counterparts in the observed data. These three cross-moments are the ones between $\boldsymbol{X}_1$ and $(\boldsymbol{Y}_2)^2$, $(\boldsymbol{X}_1)^2$ and $\boldsymbol{Y}_2$, and between $(\boldsymbol{X}_1)^2$ and $(\boldsymbol{Y}_2)^2$.

Our interest in models (3, 3, 1) and (2, 2, 2) was to check on the adequacy of the simplest model, (2, 2, 1), to represent the very sparse data in this example. Tables 9.3 and 9.4 give the likelihood ratio (LR) chi-square statistics and their nominal degrees of freedom (*df*) for the three models for each data array. These statistics do not have chi-square distributions with these degrees of freedom when the data are this sparse, but their differences are usually better behaved in this regard. This means that changes in LR, as we add more parameters to the model, should be on the same order as the changes in the degrees of freedom, if the additional parameters of the log-linear model are not significantly different from zero.

For $\mathbf{P}_{(12)}$, the reduction in LR, as we increased the complexity of the model, was 592.53 to 592.09, for skewness (i.e., the model (3, 3, 1)) , and 592.53 to 590.04, for the cross-moments (i.e., model (2, 2, 2)). Both of these changes are on the order of the size of the corresponding changes in degrees of freedom (2 for skewness and 3 for the cross-moments). These results suggest that model (2, 2, 1) is adequate for these data.

The result for adding skewness, model (3, 3, 1), agrees with what we see in Table 9.1. There the fitted model is (2, 2, 1) and we see that the fitted

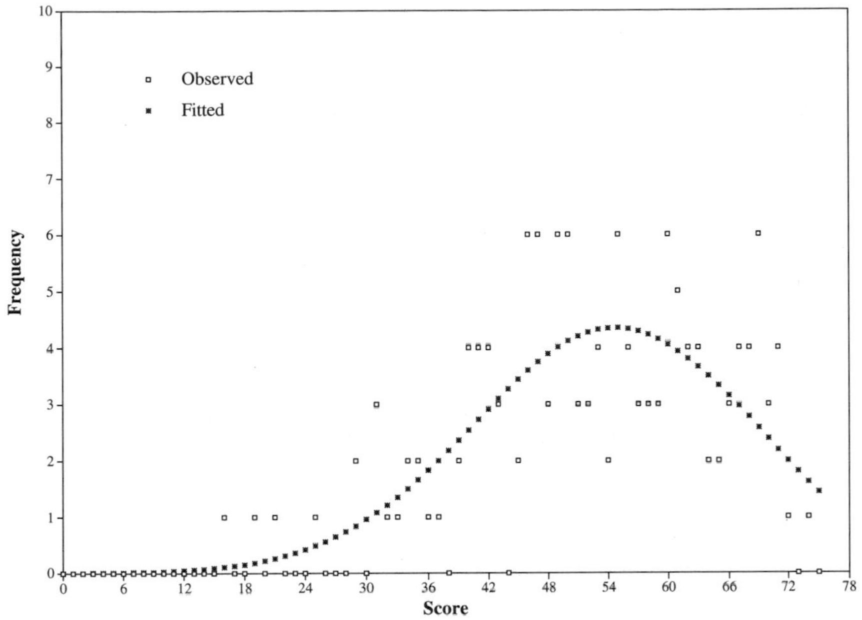

FIGURE 9.1. The observed and the fitted distributions of $\boldsymbol{X}_1$. Example 3, CB Design.

skewness values are nearly the same as the observed ones. The same is also true for the fitted kurtosis values, which are based on the fourth moments. Both the skewness and the kurtosis values of the data are well described by model (2, 2, 1). This means that the third and fourth marginal moments of $\mathbf{P}_{(12)}$ are nearly determined by the mean and variance and the form of log-linear model (2, 2, 1). From these results we decided that model (2, 2, 1) was adequate for the data from $\mathbf{P}_{(12)}$.

For $\mathbf{P}_{(21)}$, the results for adding skewness are similar to what we have just discussed for $\mathbf{P}_{(12)}$. The reduction in LR is from 647.92 to 646.47, a small change. This also agrees with what we see in Table 9.2, where the fitted distribution is model (2, 2, 1). The predicted skewness and kurtosis values are quite similar to their observed values. However, adding the cross moments had a larger reduction in LR than we saw for $\mathbf{P}_{(12)}$. The reduction was from 647.92 to 633.14, or a change of 14.78 but a change in *df* of only 3. This change value exceeds the 1% point on the chi-square distribution on 3 *df* so it would be considered statistically significant by many.

However, we decided to stay with model (2, 2, 1) for $\mathbf{P}_{(21)}$ even though model (2, 2, 2) might fit the data somewhat better. Our reason was that the primary difference between the two models is in the correlation structure of the bivariate distribution. While this difference might be important in the

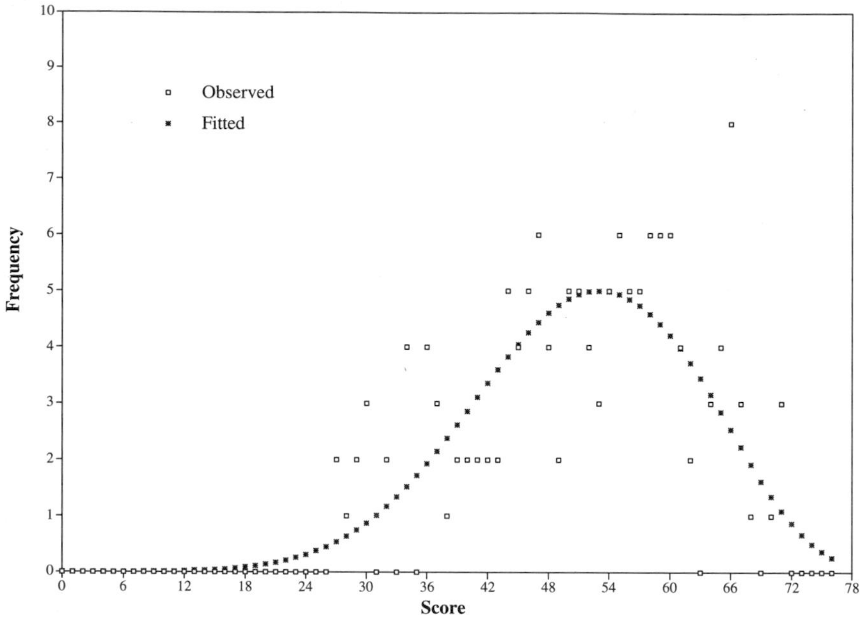

FIGURE 9.2. The observed and the fitted distributions of $\boldsymbol{Y}_2$. Example 3, CB Design.

TABLE 9.3. Likelihood Ratio Chi-Square and Degrees of Freedom for Three Models for $v(\mathbf{P}_{(12)})$. $N_{(12)} = 143$. Example 3, CB Design.

Model	LR	*df*
(2, 2, 1)	592.53	5846
(3, 3, 1)	592.20	5844
(2, 2, 2)	590.04	5843

NEAT Design, where post-stratification methods depend on the conditional distributions, in the CB Design, as in the SG Design, the equating function depends on the marginal $\boldsymbol{X}$- and $\boldsymbol{Y}$-distributions rather than on the full joint distribution of $\boldsymbol{X}$ and $\boldsymbol{Y}$. Model (2, 2, 1) seems to do an adequate job of fitting the marginal distributions, at least up to the first four moments, see Table 9.2, of $\mathbf{P}_{(21)}$.

The use of model (2, 2, 2) for $\mathbf{P}_{(21)}$ might have more of an effect on the SEE of the CB Design in this example, but we have not studied that possibility.

The observed and the fitted marginal frequencies of $\boldsymbol{X}_1$ and $\boldsymbol{Y}_2$ and of $\boldsymbol{X}_2$ and $\boldsymbol{Y}_1$ using model (2, 2, 1) for both data sets are plotted in Figure 9.1 to Figure 9.4. These plots show how sparse the data are and how important

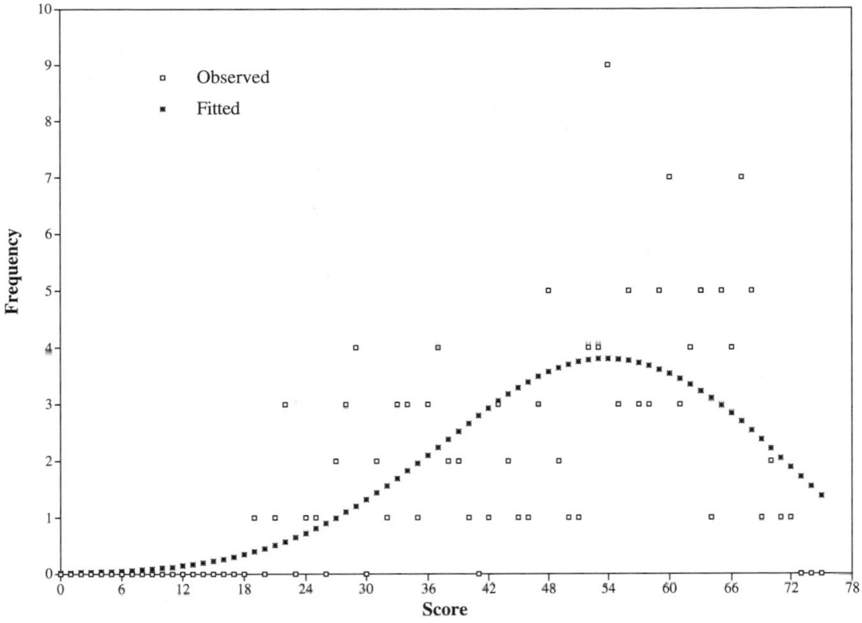

FIGURE 9.3. The observed and the fitted distributions of $\boldsymbol{X}_2$. Example 3, CB Design.

TABLE 9.4. Likelihood Ratio Chi-Square and Degrees of Freedom for Three Models for $v(\mathbf{P}_{(21)})$. $N_{(21)} = 140$. Example 3, CB Design.

Model	LR	*df*
(2, 2, 1)	647.92	5846
(3, 3, 1)	646.47	5844
(2, 2, 2)	633.14	5843

pre-smoothing is in this example. We note that the fitted frequencies pass through the scatter of the raw frequencies in a plausible manner.

In addition to Figures 9.1—9.4, we also include two graphs that give some information as to the ability of model (2, 2, 1) to describe the conditional distributions of $\boldsymbol{Y}_2$ given $\boldsymbol{X}_1$ from $\mathbf{P}_{(12)}$ and $\boldsymbol{Y}_1$ given $\boldsymbol{X}_2$ from $\mathbf{P}_{(21)}$. In Figure 9.5 we show the scatter plot of $\boldsymbol{Y}_2$ versus $\boldsymbol{X}_1$ from $\mathbf{P}_{(12)}$. In addition we plot the fitted conditional expectation, $\mathrm{E}(\boldsymbol{Y}_2 \,|\, \boldsymbol{X}_1 = x)$ along with the two "2-sigma curves" around it. The upper curve is the fitted curve $\mathrm{E}(\boldsymbol{Y}_2 \,|\, \boldsymbol{X}_1 = x) + 2SD(\boldsymbol{Y}_2 \,|\, \boldsymbol{X}_1 = x)$, while the lower one is $\mathrm{E}(\boldsymbol{Y}_2 \,|\, \boldsymbol{X}_1 = x) - 2SD(\boldsymbol{Y}_2 \,|\, \boldsymbol{X}_1 = x)$. From standard statistical analyses, we would expect that about 95% of the data points will lie between the two 2-sigma curves. Figure 9.6 shows the same plot for $\mathbf{P}_{(21)}$. In Figure 9.6

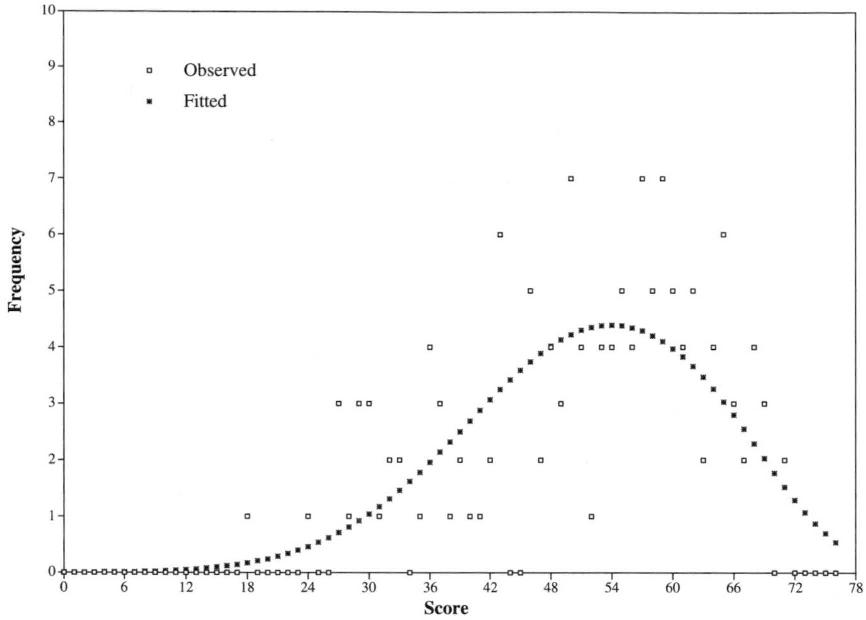

FIGURE 9.4. The observed and the fitted distributions of $\boldsymbol{Y}_1$. Example 3, CB Design.

the scatter is for $\boldsymbol{Y}_1$ versus $\boldsymbol{X}_2$ from $\mathbf{P}_{(21)}$ and the other curves are the conditional expectation and the two 2-sigma curves.

In fact, very close to 95% of the data lie between the two 2-sigma curves in both cases. These graphs support the use of model (2, 2, 1) for both $\mathbf{P}_{(12)}$ and $\mathbf{P}_{(21)}$.

In addition to the estimated joint probabilities, $\hat{p}_{(12)jk}$ and $\hat{p}_{(21)jk}$, the output of a satisfactory log-linear model program will include the "**C** matrices" that are the essential information needed to compute the standard errors of $\hat{p}_{(12)jk}$ and $\hat{p}_{(21)jk}$, and which are used to compute the SEE and the SEED described in Chapter 5.

In this example, there are two **C**-matrices, $\mathbf{C}_{(12)}$ and $\mathbf{C}_{(21)}$, because there are two bivariate distributions to be estimated although there is only one population, P, from which the samples are drawn. For model (2, 2, 1), $\mathbf{C}_{(12)}$ and $\mathbf{C}_{(21)}$, are both (5852×5)-arrays, and therefore they are not reported here.

The estimated covariance of $v(\hat{\mathbf{P}}_{(12)})$, i.e., $\boldsymbol{\Sigma}_{v(\hat{P}_{(12)})}$, is such that

$$\boldsymbol{\Sigma}_{v(\hat{P}_{(12)})} = \mathbf{C}_{(12)}\mathbf{C}_{(12)}^t.$$

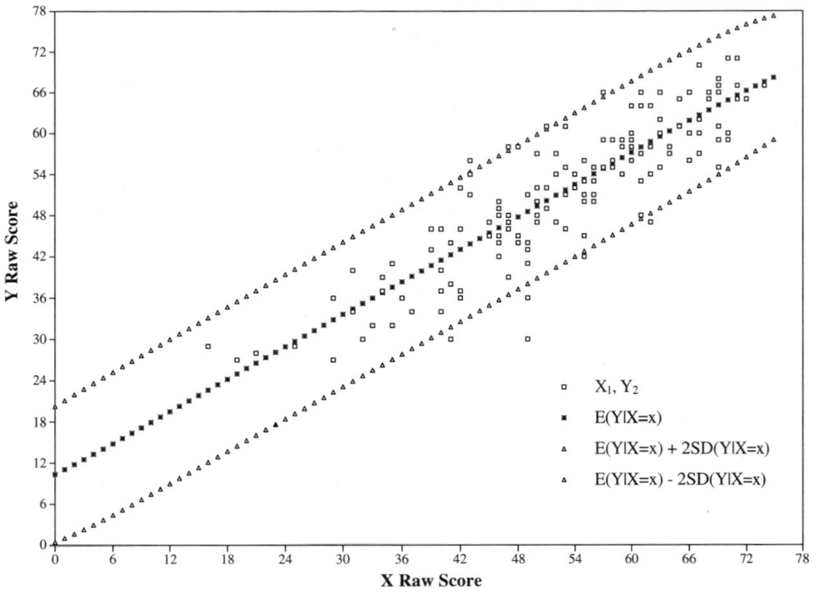

FIGURE 9.5. Scatter plot of $\boldsymbol{Y}_1$ vs. $\boldsymbol{X}_2$ from $\mathbf{P}_{(12)}$ along with the fitted conditional expectation, $\mathrm{E}(\boldsymbol{Y}_1 \mid \boldsymbol{X}_2 = x)$, and the two "2-sigma curves." Example 3, CB Design.

The estimated covariance of $v(\hat{\mathbf{P}}_{(21)})$, $\boldsymbol{\Sigma}_{v(\hat{P}_{(21)})}$, is such that

$$\boldsymbol{\Sigma}_{v(\hat{P}_{(21)})} = \mathbf{C}_{(21)}\mathbf{C}_{(21)}^t.$$

From Assumption 2.6, the covariance matrix between $v(\hat{\mathbf{P}}_{(12)})$ and $v(\hat{\mathbf{P}}_{(21)})$ is zero. Thus, the joint covariance matrix of $v(\hat{\mathbf{P}}_{(12)})$ and $v(\hat{\mathbf{P}}_{(21)})$ is

$$\boldsymbol{\Sigma}_{v(\hat{P}_{(12)}),\, v(\hat{P}_{(21)})} = \begin{pmatrix} \mathbf{C}_{(12)}\mathbf{C}_{(12)}^t & \mathbf{0} \\ \mathbf{0} & \mathbf{C}_{(21)}\mathbf{C}_{(21)}^t \end{pmatrix} = \mathbf{C}\mathbf{C}^t, \tag{9.3}$$

where

$$\mathbf{C} = \begin{pmatrix} \mathbf{C}_{(12)} & \mathbf{0} \\ \mathbf{0} & \mathbf{C}_{(21)} \end{pmatrix}. \tag{9.4}$$

9.2 Estimation of the Score Probabilities

As in the SG Design, for the CB Design we need to further transform the smoothed $\hat{p}_{(12)jk}$ and $\hat{p}_{(21)jk}$, to obtain $\hat{r}_j$ and $\hat{s}_k$. In particular, in the

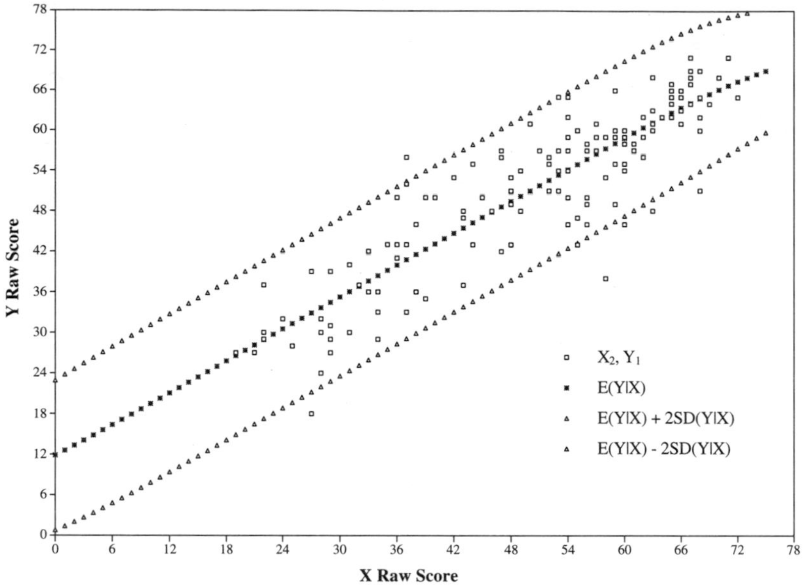

FIGURE 9.6. Scatter plot of $\boldsymbol{Y}_2$ vs. $\boldsymbol{X}_1$ from $\mathbf{P}_{(21)}$ along with the fitted conditional expectation, $\mathrm{E}(\boldsymbol{Y}_2 \mid \boldsymbol{X}_1 = x)$, and the two "2-sigma curves." Example 3, CB Design.

"two independent SG Designs approach," we use the *synthetic* $\boldsymbol{X}$-score probabilities, r_j, as defined in (2.20), and repeated here

$$\begin{aligned} r_j &= \mathrm{Prob}\{\boldsymbol{X} = x_j \mid T\} \\ &= w_X \mathrm{Prob}\{\boldsymbol{X}_1 = x_j \mid T\} + (1 - w_X)\mathrm{Prob}\{\boldsymbol{X}_2 = x_j \mid T\}, \end{aligned}$$

and the synthetic $\boldsymbol{Y}$-score probabilities, s_k,

$$\begin{aligned} s_k &= \mathrm{Prob}\{\boldsymbol{Y} = y_k \mid T\} \\ &= w_Y \mathrm{Prob}\{\boldsymbol{Y}_1 = y_k \mid T\} + (1 - w_Y)\mathrm{Prob}\{\boldsymbol{Y}_2 = y_k \mid T\}. \end{aligned}$$

The weights, w_X and w_Y, both lie in [0, 1], and need to be specified. These weights indicate the emphasis put on the data that is not subject to order effects.

We may express r_j and s_k in vector form as shown in (2.22) and (2.23) as follows:

$$\begin{aligned} \boldsymbol{r} &= w_X \boldsymbol{r}_1 + (1 - w_X)\boldsymbol{r}_2 \\ \boldsymbol{s} &= w_Y \boldsymbol{s}_1 + (1 - w_Y)\boldsymbol{s}_2. \end{aligned}$$

TABLE 9.5. Summary Statistics for the Fitted Average Score Frequencies That Correspond to $\boldsymbol{r}_{\frac{1}{2}}(\boldsymbol{X})$ and $\boldsymbol{s}_{\frac{1}{2}}(\boldsymbol{Y})$. Example 3, CB Design.

	$\boldsymbol{X}$-Fitted	$\boldsymbol{Y}$-Fitted
Mean	51.591	51.340
SD	13.122	11.559
Skewness	−0.448	−0.347
Kurtosis	2.846	2.852

Using this linear transformation, the CB Design Function, described by (2.27), is given by

$$\begin{pmatrix} \boldsymbol{r} \\ \boldsymbol{s} \end{pmatrix} = \mathrm{DF}\left(\mathbf{P}_{(12)}, \mathbf{P}_{(21)}\right) = \begin{pmatrix} w_X\mathbf{M} & (1-w_X)\mathbf{M} \\ (1-w_Y)\mathbf{N} & w_Y\mathbf{N} \end{pmatrix} \begin{pmatrix} v(\mathbf{P}_{(12)}) \\ v(\mathbf{P}_{(21)}) \end{pmatrix},$$

where $\mathbf{M}$ and $\mathbf{N}$ are the "row and column sum" matrices described in (2.9) and (2.10).

Our approach to the CB Design is to vary the weights, w_X and w_Y, over a reasonable range to see how sensitive to them are the resulting equating functions and their SEE's.

It is natural to regard $(w_X, w_Y) = (1, 1)$ as the default case because it is the most conservative use of the data in the CB Design. The case $(w_X, w_Y) = (\frac{1}{2}, \frac{1}{2})$ is the most generous in the use of the $(\boldsymbol{X}_2, \boldsymbol{Y}_2)$-data because it weights the two versions of $\boldsymbol{X}$ and $\boldsymbol{Y}$ equally. We can also consider intermediate cases of interest, i.e., $(w_X, w_Y) = (\frac{3}{4}, \frac{3}{4})$, where only one-fourth of the weight is put on the $(\boldsymbol{X}_2, \boldsymbol{Y}_2)$-data that is possibly subject to order effects. It is unlikely that we would ever allow w_X and w_Y to be less than $\frac{1}{2}$.

Table 9.5 gives the first four moments of the fitted average score frequencies, that correspond to $\boldsymbol{r}_{\frac{1}{2}} = \frac{1}{2}(\boldsymbol{r}_1 + \boldsymbol{r}_2)$ and $\boldsymbol{s}_{\frac{1}{2}} = \frac{1}{2}(\boldsymbol{s}_1 + \boldsymbol{s}_2)$. We see from Table 9.5 that these moments are similar to the corresponding moments given in Tables 9.1 and 9.2.

9.3 Continuization

The "stochastic mixtures," $\boldsymbol{X}$ and $\boldsymbol{Y}$, replace the actual scores, $\boldsymbol{X}_1$, $\boldsymbol{X}_2$, $\boldsymbol{Y}_1$ and $\boldsymbol{Y}_2$, in our approach to the CB Design. This is simply a device to give an interpretation to the way we will average the distributions of $\boldsymbol{X}_1$ and $\boldsymbol{X}_2$, and of $\boldsymbol{Y}_1$ and $\boldsymbol{Y}_2$. $\boldsymbol{X}$ and $\boldsymbol{Y}$ are simply tools for interpreting the averages that we propose for the four distributions that arise in the CB

Design. For example, the cdf of $\boldsymbol{X}$ is given by:

$$F(x) \quad = \quad w_X F_1(x) + (1 - w_X)F_2(x), \tag{9.5}$$

where $F_1(x)$ is the cdf of $\boldsymbol{X}_1$ on P, and $F_2(x)$ is the cdf of $\boldsymbol{X}_2$ on P. Similarly,

$$G(y) = w_Y G_1(y) + (1 - w_Y)G_2(y). \tag{9.6}$$

where $G_1(y)$ and $G_2(y)$ are the corresponding cdf's of $\boldsymbol{Y}_1$ and $\boldsymbol{Y}_2$ on P.

In using KE in the CB Design, we do not advocate continuizing the four cdf's, $F_1(x)$, $F_2(x)$, $G_1(y)$, and $G_2(y)$ first, and then averaging them as in (9.5) and in (9.6). Instead, we advocate using w_X and w_Y to average $\boldsymbol{r}_1$ and $\boldsymbol{r}_2$, and $\boldsymbol{s}_1$ and $\boldsymbol{s}_2$, first and then continuizing the two results. We denote these results by $\boldsymbol{r}_{w_X}$ and $\boldsymbol{s}_{w_Y}$. (In our example for this chapter, we computed $\boldsymbol{r}_{\frac{1}{2}}$ and $\boldsymbol{s}_{\frac{1}{2}}$ where w_X and w_Y both equal one-half.) Once $\boldsymbol{r}_{w_X}$ and $\boldsymbol{s}_{w_Y}$ are in hand, these two sets of score probabilities on the target population can be continuized to obtain $F_{w_X}(x;\, h_X)$, and $G_{w_Y}(y;\, h_Y)$. We note that h_X can depend on both w_X and the method of continuization. Similarly, h_Y can depend on both w_Y and the method of continuization. In our example, the two continuized cdf's are denoted $F_{\frac{1}{2}}$ and $G_{\frac{1}{2}}$, when $w_X = w_Y = \frac{1}{2}$, and by F_1 and G_1 when $w_X = w_Y = 1$. Note that this use of F_1 and G_1 is exactly the same as our usage in (9.5) and (9.6). Both usages refer to the cdf's of $\boldsymbol{X}_1$ and $\boldsymbol{Y}_1$.

Once these continuized cdf's, F_{w_X} and G_{w_Y}, are in hand, the equating function, $\hat{e}_{Y,\,w_X,\,w_Y}(x)$, is computed by

$$\hat{e}_{Y,\,w_X,\,w_Y}(x) = \hat{G}_{w_Y}^{-1}(\hat{F}_{w_X}(x;\, h_X);\, h_Y). \tag{9.7}$$

In our example, we wish to illustrate what happens for different choices of the weights, w_X and w_Y, and we use the two sets of choices mentioned above. The case where $w_X = w_Y = 1$ is the most conservative because with these weights the data for $\boldsymbol{X}_2$ and $\boldsymbol{Y}_2$ are ignored. This choice of weights could be appropriate if there were large order-effects of differing magnitude between $\boldsymbol{X}$ and $\boldsymbol{Y}$. The case where $w_X = w_Y = \frac{1}{2}$ is the most liberal because both sets of scores, $\boldsymbol{X}_1$ and $\boldsymbol{Y}_1$, and $\boldsymbol{X}_2$ and $\boldsymbol{Y}_2$, are given equal weight in the estimation of the equating function. This choice of weights could be appropriate if there were small order-effects or if they were of similar magnitude between $\boldsymbol{X}$ and $\boldsymbol{Y}$. In this and in the next section of this chapter we are concerned simply with estimating the two equating functions, $e_{Y,\,1,\,1}$ and $e_{Y,\,\frac{1}{2},\,\frac{1}{2}}$, which we will also denote more compactly by e_{Y1} and $e_{Y\frac{1}{2}}$.

Thus, in our example, we use the estimates of $\boldsymbol{r}_1$ and $\boldsymbol{s}_1$ (summarized in the second column ($\boldsymbol{X}_1$) of Table 9.1 and the fourth column ($\boldsymbol{Y}_1$) of Table 9.2. These estimated score probabilities are continuized to obtain $F_1(x;\, h_X)$ and $G_1(y;\, h_Y)$. Then we use the estimates of $\boldsymbol{r}_{\frac{1}{2}}$ and $\boldsymbol{s}_{\frac{1}{2}}$ (summarized in Table 9.5) to obtain the continuized cdf's $F_{\frac{1}{2}}(x;\, h_X)$ and

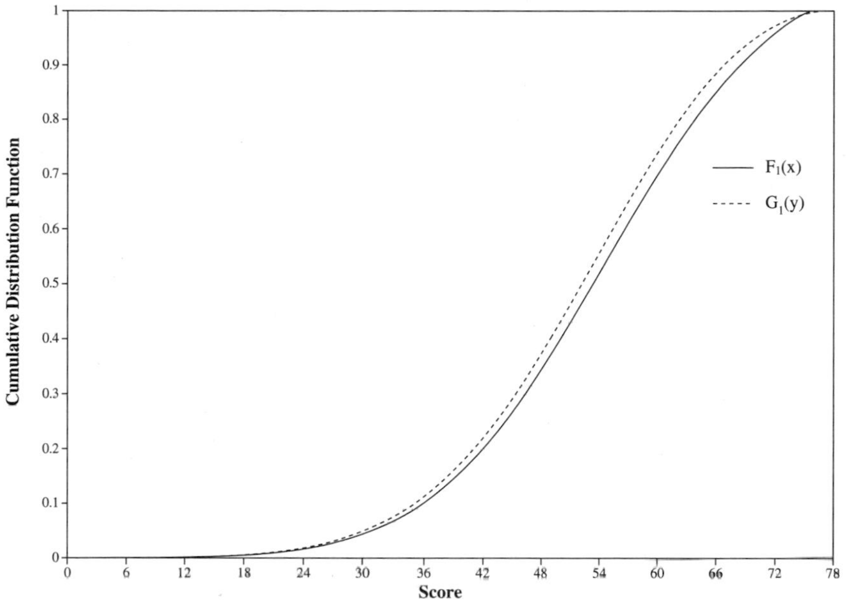

FIGURE 9.7. The continuized distributions, $\hat{F}_{1h_X}$ and $\hat{G}_{1h_Y}$. Example 3, CB Design.

$G_{\frac{1}{2}}(y;\, h_Y)$. Figures 9.7 and 9.8 show the four continuized cdf's. There is, in this example, very little difference between them.

As described in Section 4.2, h_X and h_Y are chosen to minimize the criterion

$$\text{PEN}_1(h)$$

where PEN_1 is defined in (4.27). We did not use PEN_2 because the fitted frequencies were very smooth (see Figures 9.1 to 9.4).

The resulting optimal values of h_X for $\hat{F}_1$ and h_Y for $\hat{G}_1$ were 0.5595 and 0.6099, respectively. The resulting optimal values of h_X for $\hat{F}_{\frac{1}{2}}$ and h_Y for $\hat{G}_{\frac{1}{2}}$ were 0.5587 and 0.6256, respectively.

9.4 Equating

In the example of this chapter we are considering two different equating functions that correspond to the choice of weights $(w_X,\, w_Y) = (1,\, 1)$, and $(w_X,\, w_Y) = (\frac{1}{2},\, \frac{1}{2})$, as discussed in Section 9.3. Equation (9.6) specializes to

$$\hat{e}_{Y1}(x) = \hat{e}_{Y,\,1,\,1}(x) = \hat{G}_1^{-1}(\hat{F}_1(x;\, h_X);\, h_Y) \tag{9.8}$$

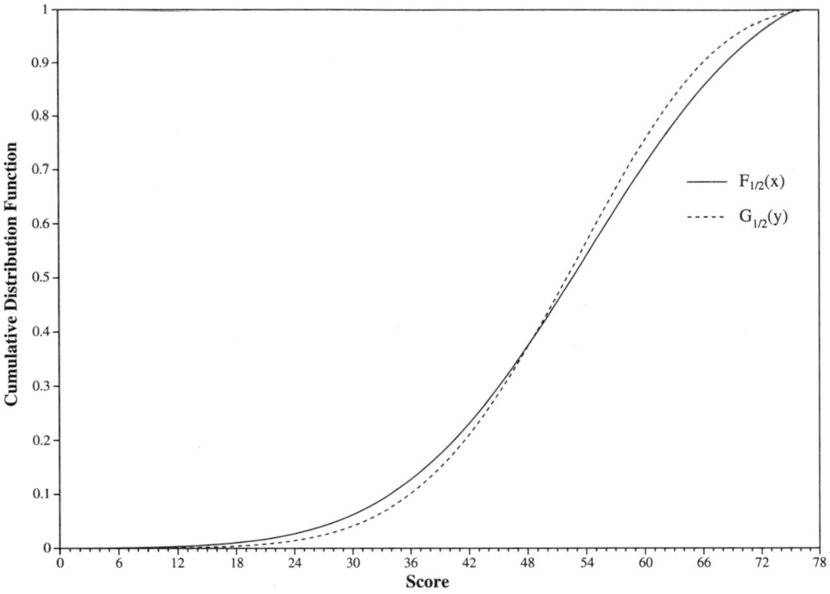

FIGURE 9.8. The continuized distributions, $\hat{F}_{\frac{1}{2}h_X}$ and $\hat{G}_{\frac{1}{2}h_Y}$. Example 3, CB Design.

and

$$\hat{e}_{Y\frac{1}{2}}(x) = \hat{e}_{Y,\frac{1}{2},\frac{1}{2}}(x) = \hat{G}_{\frac{1}{2}}^{-1}(\hat{F}_{\frac{1}{2}}(x;\, h_X);\, h_Y). \tag{9.9}$$

Inverting these two relationships, we obtain these two equating functions that go the other way to link $\boldsymbol{Y}$ to $\boldsymbol{X}$,

$$\hat{e}_{X1}(y) = \hat{e}_{X,1,1}(y) = \hat{F}_1^{-1}(\hat{G}_1(y;\, h_Y);\, h_X) \tag{9.10}$$

and

$$\hat{e}_{X\frac{1}{2}}(y) = \hat{e}_{X,\frac{1}{2},\frac{1}{2}}(y) = \hat{F}_{\frac{1}{2}}^{-1}(\hat{G}_{\frac{1}{2}}(y;\, h_Y); h_X). \tag{9.11}$$

As explained in both Chapters 7 and 8, we usually need the values of the equating function that equate $\boldsymbol{X}$ to $\boldsymbol{Y}$ only for each of the raw scores of $\boldsymbol{X}$, x_j. For example, we need to compute these values for the function in (9.8):

$$\hat{e}_{Y,1,1}(x_j) = \hat{G}_1^{-1}(u_{X_j};\, h_Y),$$

where

$$u_{X_j} = \hat{F}_1(x_j;\, h_X)$$

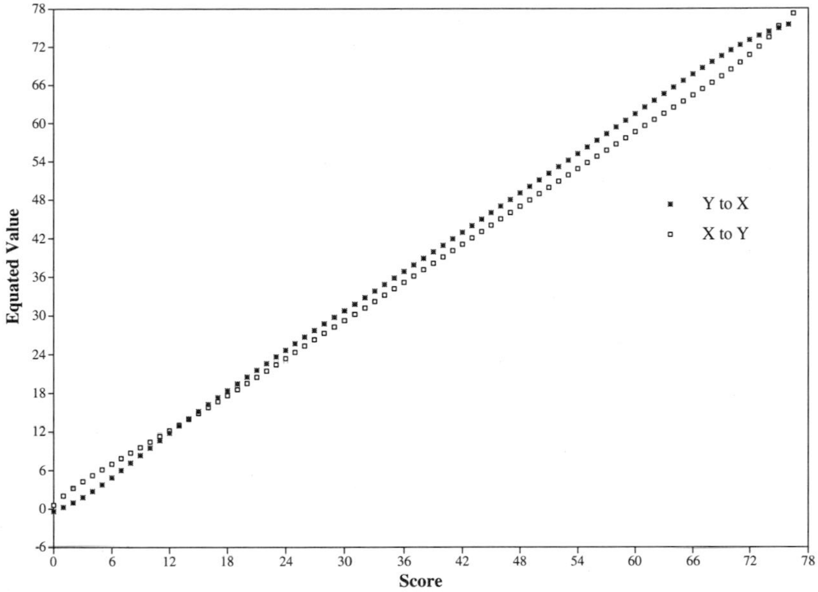

FIGURE 9.9. The equating functions, $\hat{e}_{X1}$ and $\hat{e}_{Y1}$. Example 3, CB Design.

Similar considerations hold for the computation of the other equating functions.

Figures 9.9 and 9.10 show $\hat{e}_1$ and $\hat{e}_{\frac{1}{2}}$ going in both directions, i.e. from $\boldsymbol{X}$ to $\boldsymbol{Y}$ and from $\boldsymbol{Y}$ to $\boldsymbol{X}$. The equating functions that ignore the $(\boldsymbol{X}_2, \boldsymbol{Y}_2)$-data, i.e., $\hat{e}_1$, are, in this example, more linear in their appearance than the ones that take the $(\boldsymbol{X}_2, \boldsymbol{Y}_2)$-data into account, i.e., $\hat{e}_{\frac{1}{2}}$. In Section 9.5 we will discuss tools that can help us decided which of these two equating functions is preferable.

9.5 Standard Error of Equating

In this section we address two related problems. The first is one that we have already considered in Chapters 7 and 8 for the EG and SG designs, namely, computing the SEE for the equating functions that we estimated for the example used in this chapter. What is different about the CB case is that there can be two equating functions, such as $\hat{e}_1$ and $\hat{e}_{\frac{1}{2}}$, instead of just one. We first show how to compute the SEE for these two functions and then compare them.

The second problem that we address in this section is how to choose between the two equating functions, $\hat{e}_1$ and $\hat{e}_{\frac{1}{2}}$. This is a new problem that arises in the CB Design due to the different types of data that can

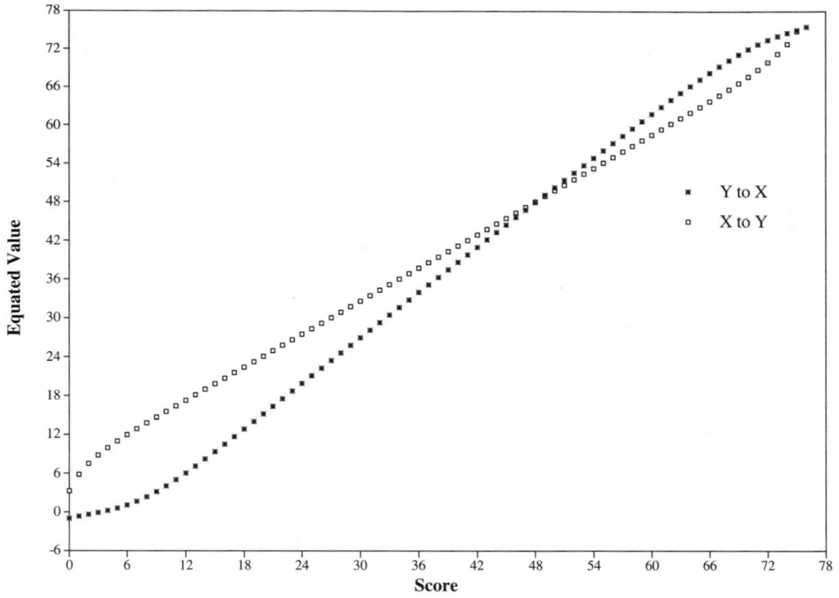

FIGURE 9.10. The equating functions, $\hat{e}_{X\frac{1}{2}}$ and $\hat{e}_{Y\frac{1}{2}}$. Example 3, CB Design.

be brought to bear on the estimation of the equating function in the CB Design.

To compute the SEE of the equating function, $\hat{e}_{Y, w_X, w_Y}(x)$, we apply Theorem 5.4 from Chapter 5.

The main result is equation (5.29), which we repeat here:

$$\mathrm{SEE}_Y(x) = \frac{1}{G'}\left[\left\|\frac{\partial F}{\partial \boldsymbol{r}}\mathbf{U}_R - \frac{\partial G}{\partial \boldsymbol{s}}\mathbf{V}_R\right\|^2 + \left\|\frac{\partial F}{\partial \boldsymbol{r}}\mathbf{U}_S - \frac{\partial G}{\partial \boldsymbol{s}}\mathbf{V}_S\right\|^2\right]^{\frac{1}{2}} \quad (9.12)$$

where $\mathbf{U}_R$, $\mathbf{U}_S$, $\mathbf{V}_R$, and $\mathbf{V}_S$ are the matrix-entries given in Table 5.5 and $||\boldsymbol{v}||^2 = \sum_i v_i^2$ is the squared Euclidian norm of the vector $\boldsymbol{v}$. For the CB Design

$$\mathbf{U}_R = w_X \mathbf{U}_{(12)} \quad \text{and} \quad \mathbf{U}_S = (1 - w_X)\mathbf{U}_{(21)}, \quad (9.13)$$

$$\mathbf{V}_S = w_Y \mathbf{V}_{(21)} \quad \text{and} \quad \mathbf{V}_R = (1 - w_Y)\mathbf{V}_{(12)}. \quad (9.14)$$

The four matrices $\mathbf{U}_{(12)}$, $\mathbf{U}_{(21)}$, $\mathbf{V}_{(12)}$, and $\mathbf{V}_{(21)}$ are given by

$$\mathbf{U}_{(12)} = \sum_k \mathbf{C}_{(12)k} \quad \text{and} \quad \mathbf{U}_{(21)} = \sum_k \mathbf{C}_{(21)k}, \quad (9.15)$$

and

$$\mathbf{V}_{(12)} = \begin{pmatrix} \mathbf{1}_J^t \mathbf{C}_{(12)1} \\ \vdots \\ \mathbf{1}_J^t \mathbf{C}_{(12)K} \end{pmatrix} = \begin{pmatrix} \boldsymbol{v}_{(12)1}^t \\ \vdots \\ \boldsymbol{v}_{(12)K}^t \end{pmatrix}, \tag{9.16}$$

$$\mathbf{V}_{(21)} = \begin{pmatrix} \mathbf{1}_J^t \mathbf{C}_{(21)1} \\ \vdots \\ \mathbf{1}_J^t \mathbf{C}_{(21)K} \end{pmatrix} = \begin{pmatrix} \boldsymbol{v}_{(21)1}^t \\ \vdots \\ \boldsymbol{v}_{(21)K}^t \end{pmatrix}. \tag{9.17}$$

$\mathbf{C}_{(12)k}$, and $\mathbf{C}_{(21)k}$ are the matrix-blocks in the partition of the matrices $\mathbf{C}_{(12)}$ and $\mathbf{C}_{(21)}$. Thus, the $(76)(77) \times 5$-matrices, $\mathbf{C}_{(12)}$ and $\mathbf{C}_{(21)}$, are partitioned into 77-matrix blocks, $\mathbf{C}_{(12)k}$ and $\mathbf{C}_{(21)k}$, each of dimension 76 by 5. They are too large to be included in this chapter.

The general formula (9.12) specializes to

$$\begin{aligned} \mathrm{SEE}_Y(x) &= \frac{1}{G'} \left[\left\| w_X \frac{\partial F}{\partial \boldsymbol{r}} \mathbf{U}_{(12)} - (1 - w_Y) \frac{\partial G}{\partial \boldsymbol{s}} \mathbf{V}_{(12)} \right\|^2 + \right. \\ &\quad \left. + \left\| (1 - w_X) \frac{\partial F}{\partial \boldsymbol{r}} \mathbf{U}_{(21)} - w_Y \frac{\partial G}{\partial \boldsymbol{s}} \mathbf{V}_{(12)} \right\|^2 \right]^{\frac{1}{2}}. \end{aligned} \tag{9.18}$$

In (9.18) we can see the dependence of the SEE on w_X and w_Y. For example, in the case where we "revert" to the EG part of the design, i.e., where we let $w_X = w_Y = 1$, (9.18) becomes:

$$\mathrm{SEE}_Y(x) = \frac{1}{G'} \left[\left\| \frac{\partial F}{\partial \boldsymbol{r}} \mathbf{U}_{(12)} \right\|^2 + \left\| \frac{\partial G}{\partial \boldsymbol{s}} \mathbf{V}_{(12)} \right\|^2 \right]^{\frac{1}{2}}. \tag{9.19}$$

The expression in (9.19) is similar to (7.5), where we give the SEE for the EG design. The difference between (9.19) and (7.5) is the replacement of $\mathbf{C}_r$ and $\mathbf{C}_s$ by $\mathbf{U}_{(12)}$ and $\mathbf{V}_{(21)}$, respectively. This replacement reflects the fact that in the CB design we do two bivariate pre-smoothings, whereas in the EG design we do two univariate pre-smoothings. Examining (9.18) we see that letting w_X and w_Y differ from 1, e.g., when they both equal $\frac{1}{2}$, allows the subtraction to take place within the two components of the SEE formula. It is this subtraction that causes the reduction in the SEE due to the correlations within each of the two samples.

Figure 9.11 gives the SEE for e_1 and $e_{\frac{1}{2}}$, respectively. In Figure 9.11 we see that the SEE for the case of $w_X = w_Y = 1$ is much larger than it is for $w_X = w_Y = \frac{1}{2}$. This shows the advantage of using all of the data in the CB Design when this is appropriate. The next question is how to decide when it is appropriate to use all of the data in the CB Design.

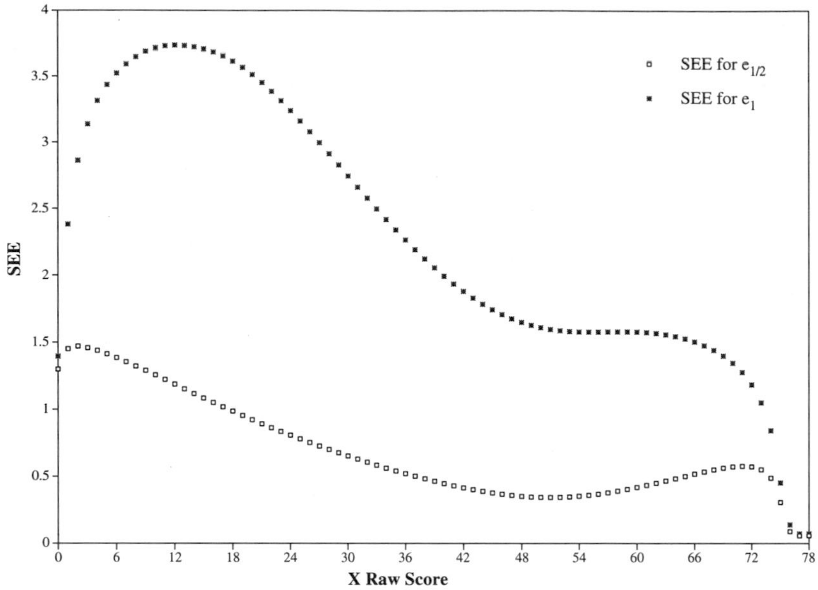

FIGURE 9.11. Standard error of equating for $\hat{e}_{\frac{1}{2}}$ and for $\hat{e}_1$. Example 3, CB Design.

9.6 Deciding Between $\hat{e}_{Y1}(x)$ and $\hat{e}_{Y\frac{1}{2}}(x)$

We address the problem of deciding between $\hat{e}_{Y1}(x)$ and $\hat{e}_{Y\frac{1}{2}}(x)$ in the following way. The equating function $\hat{e}_{Y1}(x)$ is always a possible choice since it is based on the simple EG design. However, as we see in Figure 9.11, it is based on less data and is, therefore, less accurate as an estimate of the population equating function. On the other hand, $\hat{e}_{Y\frac{1}{2}}(x)$ is based on data, some of which, $\boldsymbol{X}_2$ and $\boldsymbol{Y}_2$, is subject to possible order effects, that could cause a bias in estimating the desired population equating function. We form the difference, $\hat{e}_{Y1}(x) - \hat{e}_{Y\frac{1}{2}}(x)$, and compare it to its standard error, which we call the SEED, *the standard error of the equating difference.* If $\hat{e}_{Y1}(x)$ and $\hat{e}_{Y\frac{1}{2}}(x)$ differ by more than twice the SEED over important ranges of the raw scores of $\boldsymbol{X}$, then we regard this as evidence that the bias introduced by the use of the $\boldsymbol{X}_2$ and $\boldsymbol{Y}_2$ data is large enough to cause concern, and we would choose $\hat{e}_{Y1}(x)$. If, on the other hand, $\hat{e}_{Y1}(x)$ and $\hat{e}_{Y\frac{1}{2}}(x)$ do not differ by more than twice their SEED we regard this as evidence that the bias introduced by order effects is small enough to be ignored and we would choose $\hat{e}_{Y\frac{1}{2}}(x)$.

Of course, other considerations may enter into the choice between $\hat{e}_{Y1}(x)$ and $\hat{e}_{Y\frac{1}{2}}(x)$, but our use of the SEED can help clarify some of the issues that need to be addressed when making this choice. Another possibility is that we might not want to give equal weight to the two sets of data. This would be reflected by using $w_X = w_Y = \frac{3}{4}$ or some other value less than 1. We do not examine this issue in more detail in this book but it is an area worthy of further investigation that may be addressed using the ideas we present in this chapter.

To continue the example of this chapter, we compute the SEED using the results of Chapter 5. From Theorem 5.3 and (5.36) the SEED is given by

$$\begin{aligned} \mathrm{SEED}_Y^2(x) &= \mathrm{Var}\left(\hat{e}_{Y1}(x) - \hat{e}_{Y\frac{1}{2}}(x)\right) \\ &= \|\, \mathbf{J}_{e_{Y1}} \mathbf{J}_{\mathrm{DF}_1} \mathbf{C} - \mathbf{J}_{e_{Y\frac{1}{2}}} \mathbf{J}_{\mathrm{DF}_{\frac{1}{2}}} \mathbf{C} \,\|^2, \end{aligned} \tag{9.20}$$

where, setting $w = w_X = w_Y$, the SE-vector is

$$\begin{aligned} \mathbf{J}_{e_Y w} \mathbf{J}_{\mathrm{DF}_w} \mathbf{C} = \frac{1}{G'_w} \Bigg(& \frac{\partial F_w}{\partial \boldsymbol{r}} w \mathbf{U}_{(12)} - \frac{\partial G_w}{\partial \boldsymbol{s}} (1-w) \mathbf{V}_{(12)} \,, \\ & \frac{\partial F_w}{\partial \boldsymbol{r}} (1-w) \mathbf{U}_{(21)} - \frac{\partial G_w}{\partial \boldsymbol{s}} w \mathbf{V}_{(21)} \Bigg) . \end{aligned} \tag{9.21}$$

In Chapter 5 we discuss the Jacobian, $\mathbf{J}_{e_Y}$, for the Kernel Equating function (see in (5.19)). The expressions $\mathbf{J}_{e_{Y1}}$ and $\mathbf{J}_{e_{Y\frac{1}{2}}}$ are the corresponding Jacobians for the two equating function, $\hat{e}_{Y,1,1}(x) = \hat{G}_1^{-1}(\hat{F}_1(x;\, h_X);\, h_Y)$, and $\hat{e}_{Y,\frac{1}{2},\frac{1}{2}}(x) = \hat{G}_{\frac{1}{2}}^{-1}(\hat{F}_{\frac{1}{2}}(x;\, h_X);\, h_Y)$ from (9.8) and (9.9). Thus, there is nothing new about evaluating $\mathbf{J}_{e_{1Y}}$ and $\mathbf{J}_{e_{Y\frac{1}{2}}}$. The matrix-entries of $\mathbf{J}_{\mathrm{DF}_w}\mathbf{C}$ are $\mathbf{U}_R$, $\mathbf{U}_S$, $\mathbf{V}_R$, and $\mathbf{V}_S$, and are described above in more detail.

Formula (9.20) can be simplified in exactly the same way as we did for the SEE in (9.18).

Figure 9.12 shows both the difference between $\hat{e}_{Y1}(x)$ and $\hat{e}_{Y\frac{1}{2}}(x)$, and the curves for plus and minus two times the SEED. It is very clear from Figure 9.12 that the difference between $\hat{e}_{Y1}(x)$ and $\hat{e}_{Y\frac{1}{2}}(x)$ is small compared to the SEED and so we would decide to use $\hat{e}_{Y\frac{1}{2}}(x)$ in this example.

9.7 Diagnosis of the Equating Process

As we have done in the previous sections of Part II of this book, we now examine how well the equating functions do their job of matching the distribution of the transformed $\boldsymbol{X}$ to that of $\boldsymbol{Y}$. In this case, since we have examined two different equating functions, $\hat{e}_1$ and $\hat{e}_{\frac{1}{2}}$, we will examine how well they each match the first ten moments of the distribution of $\boldsymbol{Y}$. These are slightly different calculations because the distribution of both $\boldsymbol{X}$ and $\boldsymbol{Y}$ are different in the two cases.

For $\hat{e}_1$ we compare the moments of $\hat{e}_{Y1}(\boldsymbol{X}_1)$ with those of $\boldsymbol{Y}_1$. For $\hat{e}_{\frac{1}{2}}$ we compare the moments of $\hat{e}_{Y\frac{1}{2}}(\boldsymbol{X}_{\frac{1}{2}})$ to those of $\boldsymbol{Y}_{\frac{1}{2}}$, where the distribution

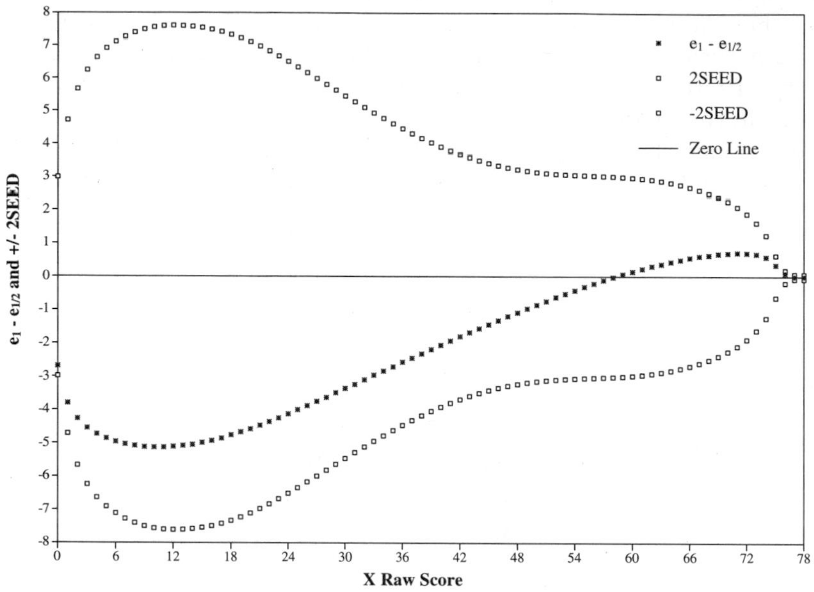

FIGURE 9.12. The difference between the $\hat{e}_{Y1}$ and $\hat{e}_{Y\frac{1}{2}}$ equating functions from $\boldsymbol{X}$ to $\boldsymbol{Y}$, and $\pm$2SEED. Example 3, CB Design.

of $\boldsymbol{X}_{\frac{1}{2}}$ is given by $\boldsymbol{r}_{\frac{1}{2}}$, and that of $\boldsymbol{Y}_{\frac{1}{2}}$ is given by $\boldsymbol{s}_{\frac{1}{2}}$. Table 9.6 gives these results. In this table we give the comparison of moments in terms of the Percent Relative Error, discussed in Chapter 4. The table shows that there is very little difference between the fit of these distributions in terms of their moments and that both distributions fit their targets very well. This is not surprising when we look at the graph of these equating functions. They are very similar, as supported by Figures 9.12.

9.8 Deciding Between $\hat{e}_{Y\frac{1}{2}}(x)$ and $\widehat{\mathrm{Lin}}_{Y\frac{1}{2}}(x)$

When the bandwidths, h_X and h_Y, are both large, the KE equating function closely approximates the standard linear equating function because the shape difference function in Theorem 1.1 is then nearly zero. In this example, $\widehat{\mathrm{Lin}}_{Y\frac{1}{2}}(x)$ is computed by choosing $h_X = h_Y = 120$ and $w_X = w_Y = \frac{1}{2}$.

In Figure 9.13 we plot the difference

$$\hat{e}_{Y\frac{1}{2}}(x) - \widehat{\mathrm{Lin}}_{Y\frac{1}{2}}(x). \tag{9.22}$$

This plot shows how the KE estimated equating function, $\hat{e}_{Y\frac{1}{2}}(x)$, differs from the KE linear equating function, $\widehat{\mathrm{Lin}}_{Y\frac{1}{2}}(x)$.

TABLE 9.6. Difference Between the Moments of the Equated Distribution and the Target Distribution Expressed as Percent Relative Error, PRE(p). Example 3, CB Design.

Moments	Percent Relative Error			
	$w_X = w_Y = 1$		$w_X = w_Y = \frac{1}{2}$	
	(X to Y)	(Y to X)	(X to Y)	(Y to X)
1	−0.0012	0.0004	−0.0024	0.0008
2	−0.0040	0.0015	−0.0064	0.0030
3	−0.0086	0.0032	−0.0142	0.0063
4	−0.0156	0.0057	−0.0253	0.0109
5	−0.0255	0.0093	−0.0412	0.0170
6	−0.0391	0.0142	−0.0631	0.0249
7	−0.0572	0.0205	−0.0922	0.0348
8	−0.0803	0.0287	−0.1295	0.0471
9	−0.1092	0.0387	−0.1763	0.0619
10	−1.1445	0.0510	−0.2334	0.0796

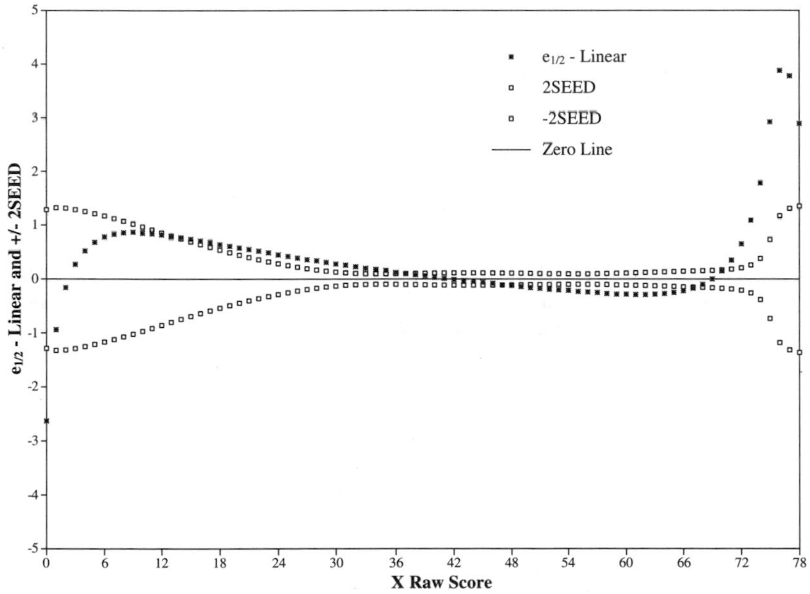

FIGURE 9.13. The difference between the equipercentile and linear equating functions (both with $w_X = w_Y = \frac{1}{2}$) from $\boldsymbol{X}$ to $\boldsymbol{Y}$, and ±2SEED. Example 3, CB Design.

To assess how this small difference compares to its uncertainty, we plot it along with $\pm 2\text{SEED}(x)$, the standard error of equating difference defined in Chapter 5 as

$$\begin{aligned} \text{SEED}^2(x) &= \text{Var}\left(\hat{e}_{Y\frac{1}{2}}(x) - \widehat{\text{Lin}}_{Y\frac{1}{2}}(x)\right) && (9.23) \\ &= \|\, \mathbf{J}_{e_{Y\frac{1}{2}}} \mathbf{J}_{\text{DF}_{\frac{1}{2}}} \mathbf{C} - \mathbf{J}_{\text{Lin}_{Y\frac{1}{2}}} \mathbf{J}_{\text{DF}_{\frac{1}{2}}} \mathbf{C} \,\|^2. && (9.24) \end{aligned}$$

The SE-vector for $e_{Y\frac{1}{2}}(x)$ is $\mathbf{J}_{e_{Y\frac{1}{2}}} \mathbf{J}_{\text{DF}_{\frac{1}{2}}} \mathbf{C}$ and for $\text{Lin}_{Y\frac{1}{2}}(x)$ the SE-vector is $\mathbf{J}_{\text{Lin}_{Y\frac{1}{2}}} \mathbf{J}_{\text{DF}_{\frac{1}{2}}} \mathbf{C}$.

The product, $\mathbf{J}_{\text{DF}_{\frac{1}{2}}} \mathbf{C}$, has appeared earlier in this chapter as the matrix with matrix components given by (9.13) and (9.14) with $w_X = w_Y = \frac{1}{2}$. $\mathbf{J}_{e_{Y\frac{1}{2}}}$ and $\mathbf{J}_{\text{Lin}_{Y\frac{1}{2}}}$ are both derived from the results from Chapter 5 in (5.19) with h_X and h_Y chosen by the use of a penalty function in the former and $h_X = h_Y = 120$ in the later. In both cases $w_X = w_Y = \frac{1}{2}$.

Figure 9.13 summarizes the results. It shows that in this example $\hat{e}_{Y\frac{1}{2}}(x)$ and $\widehat{\text{Lin}}_{Y\frac{1}{2}}(x)$ differ by less than one point over most of the score range. However, for a few $\boldsymbol{X}$-values at the upper end of the raw-score range they differ by as many as 4 raw-score points.

Our conclusion for this example is that the KE function,$\hat{e}_{Y\frac{1}{2}}(x)$ is preferable to the linear equating function because of the difference between them at the upper end of the score scale. In cases where this range is not important, as would occur in a test used to screen out low scoring examinees, the linear equating function would probably be satisfactory.

9.9 Appendix: The Data Used in This Chapter

The observed values of $(\boldsymbol{X}_1, \boldsymbol{Y}_2)$ for each examinee from the first sample and the observed values of $(\boldsymbol{X}_2, \boldsymbol{Y}_1)$ for each examinee from the second sample are given in Tables 9.7 and 9.8, respectively.

TABLE 9.7: ($\boldsymbol{X}_1$, $\boldsymbol{Y}_2$)-Observed Values. Example 3, EG Design.

Examinee	X_1	Y_2	Examinee	X_1	Y_2	Examinee	X_1	Y_2
1	55	53	50	62	64	99	56	50
2	48	58	51	59	54	100	46	42
3	56	55	52	40	34	101	52	47
4	67	60	53	72	65	102	68	66
5	42	52	54	51	61	103	19	27
6	53	51	55	61	48	104	32	30
7	48	45	56	59	59	105	60	60
8	43	51	57	63	55	106	62	54
9	63	66	58	59	58	107	50	50
10	45	45	59	65	61	108	57	59
11	47	39	60	53	61	109	67	62
12	46	49	61	67	57	110	55	56
13	71	65	62	56	53	111	41	30
14	63	60	63	51	49	112	68	66
15	47	48	64	39	43	113	58	55
16	21	28	65	60	56	114	60	59
17	49	41	66	46	50	115	41	44
18	50	52	67	56	51	116	63	62
19	71	67	68	40	46	117	53	55
20	69	67	69	31	34	118	70	59
21	53	46	70	41	38	119	71	71
22	50	48	71	16	29	120	57	66
23	34	39	72	51	52	121	60	58
24	33	32	73	49	44	122	47	47
25	69	55	74	50	47	123	50	57
26	54	52	75	64	58	124	36	36
27	55	45	76	49	36	125	62	47
28	43	54	77	43	56	126	58	59
29	69	66	78	61	64	127	41	44
30	61	53	79	57	55	128	45	47
31	52	57	80	39	46	129	55	50
32	61	66	81	42	46	130	68	66
33	48	44	82	42	37	131	65	65
34	70	71	83	70	60	132	71	71
35	46	48	84	69	61	133	49	43
36	55	42	85	69	68	134	68	65
37	49	30	86	50	50	135	31	34
38	35	41	87	54	54	136	37	34
39	66	66	88	47	58	137	58	56
40	52	54	89	46	44	138	64	57
41	29	36	90	60	64	139	55	51
42	74	67	91	29	27	140	67	70
43	62	58	92	42	36	141	47	46
44	66	56	93	34	37	142	35	32
45	49	51	94	31	40	143	60	60
46	47	47	95	40	37			
47	66	60	96	61	57			
48	25	29	97	40	40			
49	62	64	98	69	59			

TABLE 9.8: ($\boldsymbol{X}_2$, $\boldsymbol{Y}_1$)-Observed Values. Example 3, EG Design.

Examinee	X_2	Y_1	Examinee	X_2	Y_1	Examinee	X_2	Y_1
1	54	46	50	40	50	99	52	55
2	68	51	51	68	65	100	54	62
3	60	54	52	61	58	101	67	69
4	66	65	53	56	50	102	62	56
5	19	27	54	53	51	103	48	49
6	33	36	55	66	63	104	65	64
7	37	33	56	43	47	105	58	53
8	55	60	57	60	58	106	53	54
9	62	59	58	51	57	107	65	65
10	63	68	59	61	58	108	61	57
11	57	57	60	48	51	109	48	43
12	70	68	61	33	36	110	67	71
13	57	61	62	54	65	111	63	63
14	67	68	63	47	42	112	42	53
15	52	56	64	36	43	113	49	48
16	54	54	65	29	29	114	62	62
17	47	57	66	24	32	115	58	38
18	34	36	67	39	35	116	21	27
19	44	43	68	68	69	117	63	60
20	67	64	69	55	43	118	58	59
21	32	37	70	59	55	119	56	46
22	22	29	71	22	37	120	54	50
23	43	37	72	60	55	121	53	57
24	66	66	73	59	66	122	36	50
25	65	67	74	59	49	123	60	59
26	59	59	75	60	58	124	53	65
27	35	43	76	43	48	125	29	27
28	45	50	77	47	56	126	52	55
29	37	52	78	60	60	127	72	65
30	37	56	79	29	39	128	37	43
31	28	30	80	36	41	129	67	64
32	67	67	81	63	48	130	56	58
33	31	40	82	34	33	131	66	61
34	50	61	83	64	62	132	38	36
35	55	47	84	46	48	133	27	39
36	54	57	85	28	32	134	52	51
37	27	18	86	44	55	135	54	50
38	57	59	87	33	42	136	39	50
39	60	46	88	65	66	137	68	62
40	56	49	89	34	29	138	63	61
41	62	59	90	48	53	139	67	69
42	71	71	91	49	54	140	54	46
43	56	57	92	22	30			
44	29	31	93	38	46			
45	70	68	94	54	59			
46	31	30	95	68	60			
47	65	62	96	69	64			
48	25	28	97	28	24			
49	59	60	98	48	53			

10

The NEAT Design: Chain Equating

This chapter and the next deal with exactly the same data set and equating design. The difference between them is in the equating methods used. In this chapter we consider Chain Equating (CE) for the Non-Equivalent groups with Anchor Test (NEAT) Design. In the next chapter we consider its competitor for the NEAT Design, the method of Post-Stratification Equating (PSE).

The first step in the equating process, pre-smoothing (see Section 3.1) is exactly the same for the KE approach to both CE and PSE. Hence, we will give the details of the pre-smoothing step for our example data set in this chapter and will omit it in Chapter 11, where we discuss PSE. To avoid another repetition, we will postpone our comparison of the results of CE and PSE for this example until Chapter 11.

The NEAT Design involves two populations, P and Q, of test-takers and makes use of an anchor test A. A test X is administered to a sample of examinees from the population P, a test Y is administered to a sample of examinees from the population Q, and another set of items, A, is administered to both samples (see Assumption 2.7 and Table 2.4). The samples from the two populations are assumed to be independent (Assumption 2.8).

This chapter illustrates how to carry out the five steps of Kernel Equating (KE) for the Chain Equating approach to the NEAT Design. As mentioned in Section 2.4, the NEAT Designs are of two kinds, depending whether the set of common items is external or internal to the two tests, $\boldsymbol{X}$ and $\boldsymbol{Y}$. Our example for this and the next chapter has an external anchor. As we mentioned in Section 2.4.3, the NEAT Design with an internal anchor test introduces no new issues for Kernel Equating other than modeling the

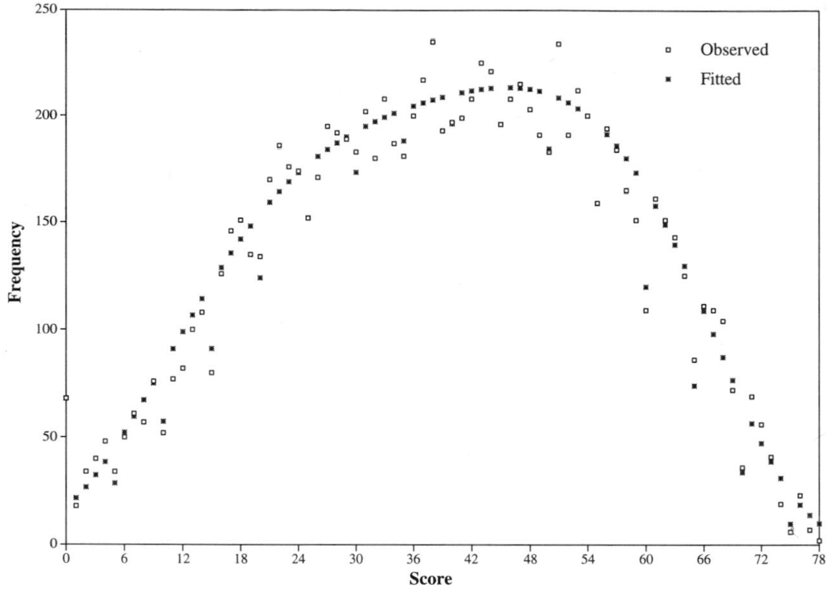

FIGURE 10.1. The observed and the fitted distributions of $\boldsymbol{X}$ on P. Example 4, the NEAT Design.

structural zeros that arise in that case during the pre-smoothing step. In every other respect, KE with an internal anchor test is exactly the same as KE with an external anchor test.

The example for this and the next chapter involves data from two national administrations of a high-volume testing program. The two testing administrations were in the Fall of 2001 (P) and in the Winter of 2000 (Q). We will go through the details of the steps described in Chapters 3, 4 and 5. In this example, samples of examinees are drawn from P and Q. Tests X and Y both have 78 items, and the anchor test, A, has 35 items.

Each examinee in each of the two samples has two test scores. Thus the sample data consists of two bivariate frequency tables. The entries in these tables are

$$n_{jl} = \text{number of examinees with } \boldsymbol{X} = x_j \text{ and } \boldsymbol{A} = a_l, \text{ in } P,$$

and

$$m_{kl} = \text{number of examinees with } \boldsymbol{Y} = y_k \text{ and } \boldsymbol{A} = a_l, \text{ in } Q,$$

with $j = 1, \ldots, 79$, $k = 1, \ldots, 79$, and $l = 1, \ldots, 36$.

In this example the x_j, y_k and a_l values are $x_1 = 0, \ldots, x_{79} = 78$, $y_1 = 0, \ldots, y_{79} = 78$, and $a_1 = 0, \ldots, a_{36} = 35$, respectively. The raw scores are all "rounded formula scores" in which the usual "right minus a quarter wrong" formula scores are rounded to integers. In addition, we also

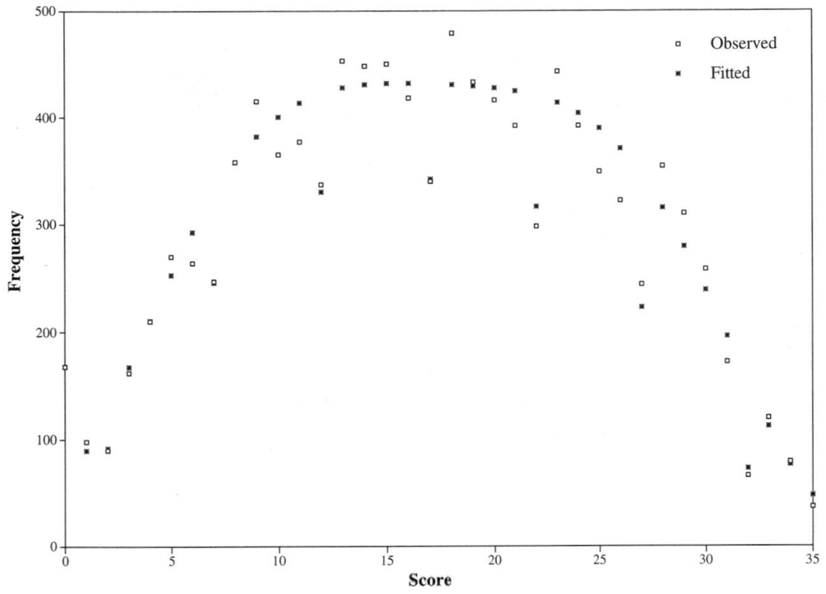

FIGURE 10.2. The observed and the fitted distributions of $\boldsymbol{A}$ on P. Example 4, the NEAT Design.

recoded all negative rounded formula scores to 0.0. We did this recoding for a practical reason. When we allowed all possible negative formula scores to be included in the values, x_j, y_k and a_l, we found that some of the log-linear models that we wanted to fit had singular $\mathbf{B}$-matrices due to the sparseness of the data for these very low scores. Recoding the negative rounded formula score as 0.0 removed this problem, but it gave each distribution a "lump" at 0 which we addressed in the log-linear models we selected.

The samples sizes are

$$N_P = \sum_j \sum_l n_{jl} = 10,634$$

and

$$N_Q = \sum_k \sum_l m_{kl} = 11,321.$$

The tables with the frequencies, $\{n_{jl}\}$ and $\{m_{kl}\}$, are too large to be given here, i.e., 79 by 36. Instead we give Tables 10.1 and 10.2 to describe the summary statistics of these two bivariate frequency tables.

From Tables 10.1 and 10.2 we see that the mean of the anchor test, $\boldsymbol{A}$, is 17.05 ($\pm$0.08) in population P, and 14.39 ($\pm$0.08) in Q. Thus, Q is a less proficient population than P, as measured by A. In terms of effect sizes, the difference between these two means is approximately 32% of the

TABLE 10.1. Summary Statistics for the Observed Frequencies of $\boldsymbol{X}$ and $\boldsymbol{A}$ for a Sample of Examinees from Population P. Example 4, NEAT Design.

	$\boldsymbol{X}$-Observed	$\boldsymbol{A}$-Observed
Mean	39.25	17.05
SD	17.23	8.33
Skewness	−0.11	−0.01
Kurtosis	2.23	2.15
Min	0	0
Max	78	35

TABLE 10.2. Summary Statistics for the Observed Frequencies of $\boldsymbol{Y}$ and $\boldsymbol{A}$ for a Sample of Examinees from Population Q. Example 4, NEAT Design.

	$\boldsymbol{Y}$-Observed	$\boldsymbol{A}$-Observed
Mean	32.69	14.39
SD	16.73	8.21
Skewness	0.24	0.26
Kurtosis	2.31	2.25
Min	0	0
Max	77	35

average standard deviation of 8.27. For this particular testing program, a mean difference of this magnitude on the anchor test indicates a fairly large difference between the two test administrations.

For this example, the sample correlation between $\boldsymbol{X}$ and $\boldsymbol{A}$ in P is 0.88, and the sample correlation between $\boldsymbol{Y}$ and $\boldsymbol{A}$ in Q is 0.87.

In Section 2.4 we discussed the target population, T, for the NEAT Design. T is a mixture of both P and Q where, in this example, the two populations refer to the populations of examinees from the two administrations. T is defined in (2.32) and is repeated here,

$$T = wP + (1 - w)Q,$$

where $0 \le w \le 1$ is the weight given to P. When $w = 1$ then $T = P$ and when $w = 0$ then $T = Q$. As we showed in Chapter 2, the specific choice of w is irrelevant for CE, but it can matter for PSE (see Chapter 11).

In Chapter 2 we pointed out that the NEAT Design also contains two independent SG Designs. Chain Equating exploits the two SG Designs within a NEAT Design and produces the equating function directly without first estimating $\{r_j\}$ and $\{s_k\}$. However, the cdf's of $\boldsymbol{X}$ and $\boldsymbol{Y}$ on the target population T, F_T *and* G_T, are implicitly defined through the assumptions that justify CE as an observed score equating method. We showed this in Section 2.4.1.

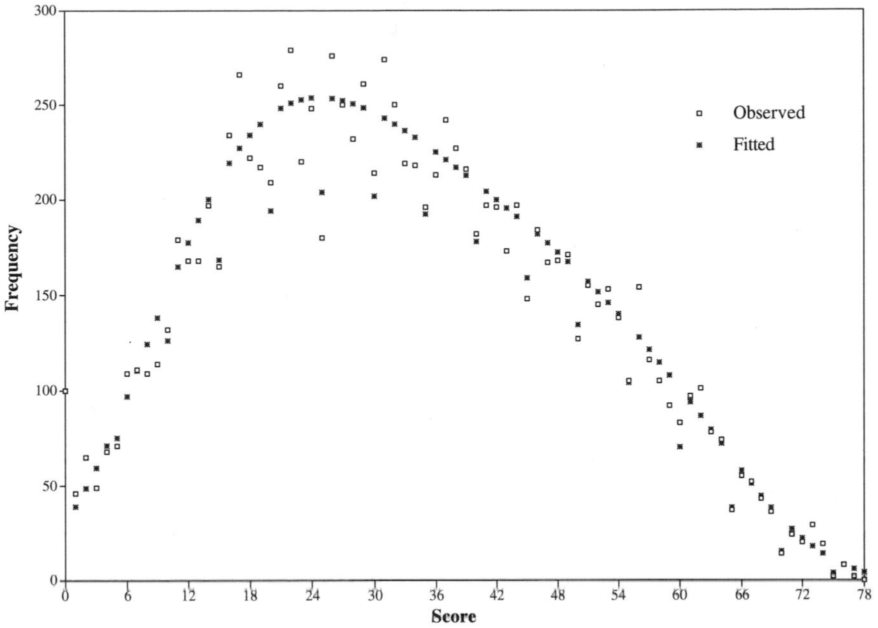

FIGURE 10.3. The observed and the fitted distributions of $\boldsymbol{Y}$ on Q. Example 4, the NEAT Design.

The two SG Designs within the NEAT Design result in data for two joint distributions. The first is denoted by $\mathbf{P} = (p_{jl})$, and the second by $\mathbf{Q} = (q_{kl})$. The probabilities of these bivariate distributions are defined by (2.30) and (2.31) and are repeated here

$$\begin{aligned} p_{jl} &= \text{Prob}\{\boldsymbol{X} = x_j,\, \boldsymbol{A} = a_l \,|\, P\}, \\ q_{kl} &= \text{Prob}\{\boldsymbol{Y} = y_k,\, \boldsymbol{A} = a_l \,|\, Q\}. \end{aligned}$$

The raw sample proportions, n_{jl}/N_P and m_{kl}/N_Q are unsmoothed estimates of the population parameters, p_{jl} and q_{kl}. We now turn to the problem of pre-smoothing the data to obtain better estimates of $\{p_{jl}\}$ and $\{q_{kl}\}$ than the raw sample proportions provide.

10.1 Pre-smoothing

In one sense, the estimation procedure, using log-linear models for the two bivariate distributions that arise in the NEAT Design, is the same as that used for the CB Design. However, in the CB Design there are often small samples that can only support simple log-linear models, whereas the NEAT Design data sets we examine here have samples nearly a hundred times

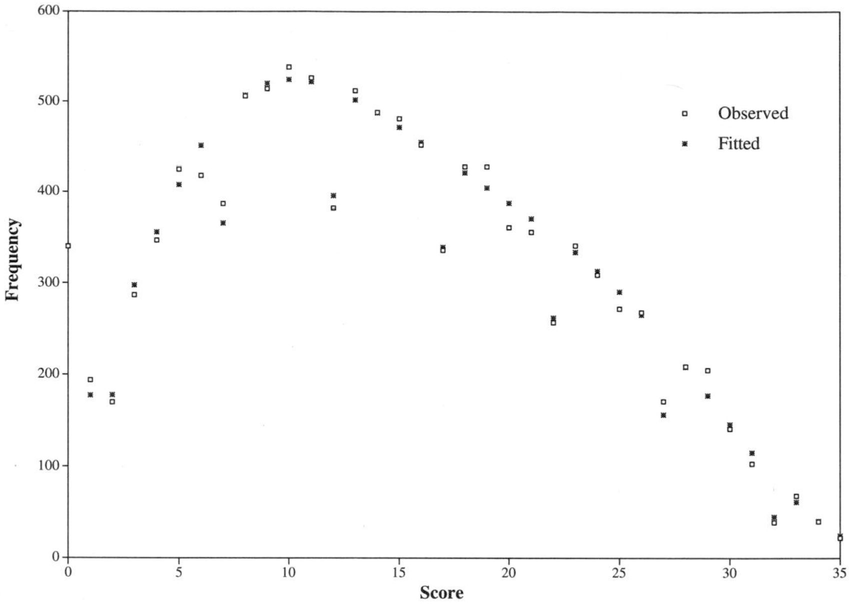

FIGURE 10.4. The observed and the fitted distributions of $\boldsymbol{A}$ on Q. Example 4, the NEAT Design.

larger than those of Chapter 9 and can support much more complicated models. Indeed, we chose this example because it illustrates some of the interesting complexities that can arise in real data when the samples are large. In particular, the models we selected for pre-smoothing $\{n_{jl}\}$ and $\{m_{kl}\}$ can exhibit these features.

1. "Teeth" or "gaps" in the frequencies that can occur at regular intervals when formula scores are rounded to integer values.

2. A "lump" at 0 in each of the marginal distributions. This is due to our recoding of negative rounded formula scores to 0.

3. A general unimodal but non-Normal shape both to: (a) the overall set of marginal frequencies for $\boldsymbol{X}$, $\boldsymbol{Y}$, and $\boldsymbol{A}$ in P and Q, and (b) to the frequencies of the regularly spaced "gaps" for each of these marginal distributions as well.

These phenomena are clearly visible in the observed frequencies displayed in Figures 10.1–10.4, and most easily seen in Figures 10.2 and 10.4.

Under the random sampling assumption, Assumption 2.8, the sample frequencies, $\{n_{jl}\}$, and $\{m_{kl}\}$, have independent, approximate multinomial distributions with population cell probabilities, $\{p_{jl}\}$ and $\{q_{kl}\}$, respectively. The log-linear models for $\{p_{jl}\}$ and $\{q_{kl}\}$, that we use in this chapter, are more complicated than we have used elsewhere in this book because the data have the interesting features just enumerated. We will describe each log-linear model in terms of seven components that we will discuss separately.

The two models have the following general form:

$$\begin{aligned}\log(p_{jl}) &= \alpha_P + L_P(x_j) + X_P(x_j) + A_P(a_l) \\ &\quad + XA_P(x_j, a_l) + GX_P(x_j) + GA_P(a_l),\end{aligned} \tag{10.1}$$

$$\begin{aligned}\log(q_{kl}) &= \alpha_Q + L_Q(y_k) + Y_Q(y_k) + A_Q(a_l) \\ &\quad + YA_Q(y_k, a_l) + GY_Q(y_k) + GA_Q(a_l).\end{aligned} \tag{10.2}$$

We will describe each component of the model for $\{p_{jl}\}$ in detail. The corresponding components for $\{q_{kl}\}$ are defined analogously.

First of all, α_P is just a normalizing constant to insure that the estimates of $\{p_{jl}\}$ sum to 1.0.

Next, the term $L_P(x_j)$ is designed to accommodate the "lump of probability" at $x_1 = 0$, caused by the recoding of negative values to 0, mentioned earlier. $L_P(x_j)$ has the form

$$L_P(x_j) = \beta_{P0} I_0(x_j), \tag{10.3}$$

where $I_0(x_j)$ is the (0/1)-indicator variable defined

$$I_0(x_j) = \begin{cases} 1 & \text{if} \quad x_j = 0, \\ 0 & \text{if} \quad \text{otherwise}, \end{cases} \tag{10.4}$$

and β_{P0} is the model parameter associated with this function of x_j.

Next, the term $X_P(x_j)$ is, like equation (7.1), designed to fit the first few power moments of the distribution of $\boldsymbol{X}$ in P. It has the form

$$X_P(x_j) = \sum_{i=1}^{T_{XP}} \beta_{XPi}(x_j)^i. \tag{10.5}$$

In $X_P(x_j)$, T_{XP} is the number of power moments fit to the marginal distribution of $\boldsymbol{X}$ in P, and β_{XPi} is the parameter associated with the ith power moment of $\boldsymbol{X}$.

The term, $A_P(a_l)$, serves the same purpose for $\boldsymbol{A}$ in P as $X_P(x_j)$ does for $\boldsymbol{X}$ in P. It has the form

$$A_P(a_l) = \sum_{i=1}^{T_{AP}} \beta_{APi}(a_l)^i. \tag{10.6}$$

The term $XA_P(x_j, a_l)$ is the interaction term designed to fit the correlation and other cross moments of $\boldsymbol{X}$ and $\boldsymbol{A}$ in P. It has the form

$$XA_P(x_j, a_l) = \sum_{i=1}^{I_{XP}} \sum_{i'=1}^{I_{AP}} \beta_{XAPii'}(x_j)^i (a_l)^{i'}. \tag{10.7}$$

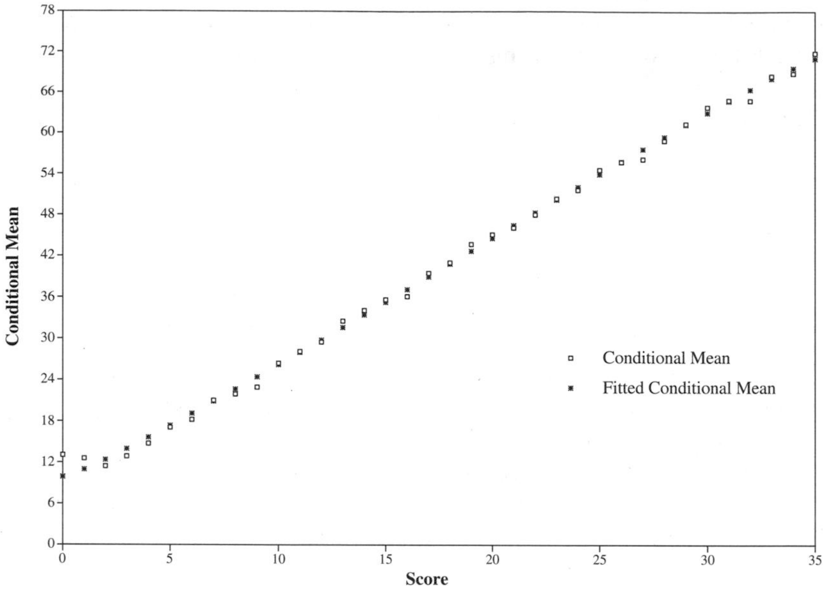

FIGURE 10.5. $\mathrm{E}(\boldsymbol{X} \mid \boldsymbol{A})$: observed and fitted values. Example 4, the NEAT Design.

In $XA_P(x_j, a_l)$, I_{XP} and I_{AP} define the number and type of cross moments fit to the joint distribution of $\boldsymbol{X}$ and $\boldsymbol{A}$ in P. When $I_{XP} = I_{AP} = 1$, the model will fit only the correlation between $\boldsymbol{X}$ and $\boldsymbol{A}$ in P. When $I_{XP} = I_{AP} = 2$, the model will, in addition, fit these cross moments of $\boldsymbol{X}$ and $\boldsymbol{A}$: $\mathrm{E}(\boldsymbol{X}^2\boldsymbol{A})$, $\mathrm{E}(\boldsymbol{X}\boldsymbol{A}^2)$, and $\mathrm{E}(\boldsymbol{X}^2\boldsymbol{A}^2)$. The parameter $\beta_{XAPii'}$ is associated with the $(\boldsymbol{X}^i, \boldsymbol{A}^{i'})$ cross-moment of $\boldsymbol{X}$ and $\boldsymbol{A}$.

The last two terms of the log-linear model for $\{p_{jl}\}$, $GX_P(x_j)$ and $GA_P(a_l)$ are designed to fit the "gaps" in the score frequencies that we see in Figures 10.1 (for X) and 10.2 (for A). $GX_P(x_j)$ has the form

$$GX_P(x_j) = \sum_{i=0}^{G_{XP}} \beta_{GXPi}(x_j)^i I_{S_X}(x_j). \tag{10.8}$$

In $GX_P(x_j)$, $I_{S_X}(x_j)$ is the (0/1)-indicator variable defined by

$$I_{S_X}(x_j) = \begin{cases} 1 & \text{if} \quad x_j \text{ in } S_X, \\ 0 & \text{if} \quad \text{otherwise}, \end{cases} \tag{10.9}$$

where S_X is the set of $\boldsymbol{X}$ scores that exhibit a "gap" in their frequencies, i.e., are lower than expected based on the frequencies of neighboring scores. Rounding the formula scores to integers causes the gaps in this example and they are fairly easy to see. For example, from Figure 10.1, starting with $x_j =$

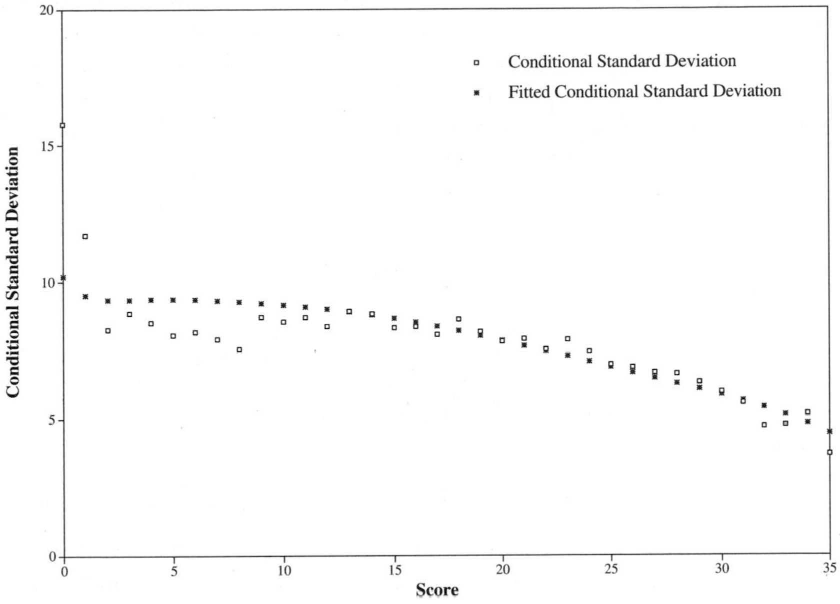

FIGURE 10.6. SD($\boldsymbol{X} \mid \boldsymbol{A}$) : observed and fitted values. Example 4, the NEAT Design.

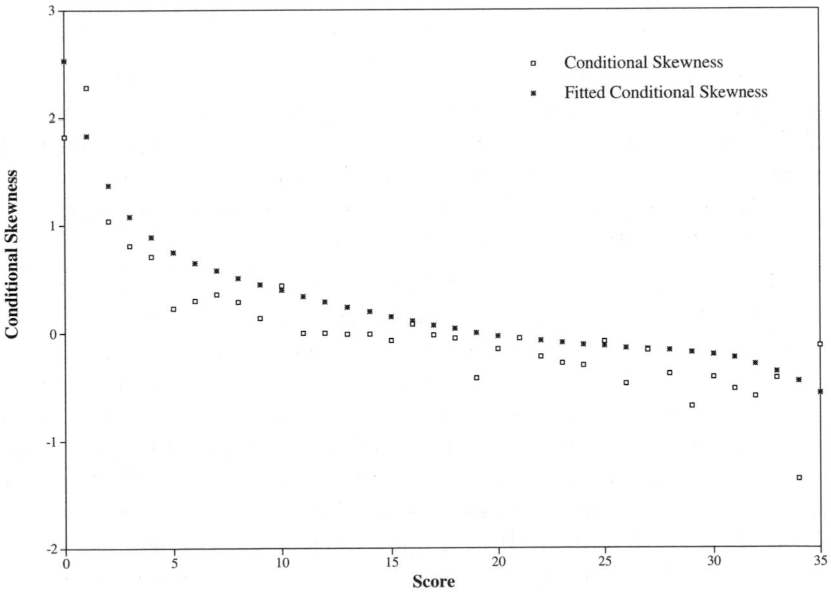

FIGURE 10.7. Skew($\boldsymbol{X} \mid \boldsymbol{A}$) : observed and fitted values. Example 4, the NEAT Design.

75, every fifth score frequency is lower than expected from its neighboring values. These are the "gaps" in the score frequencies. In this example, S_X is the set of scores $\{75, 70, 65, 60, \ldots\}$. The value of GX_P is the number of moments of these gap-frequencies that the model will fit. If $GX_P = 0$, only the total sum of the gap-frequencies is preserved by the model. The parameter β_{GXPi} is the parameter associated with $(x_j)^i I_{S_X}(x_j)$. $GA_P(a_l)$ is defined analogously and has the form

$$GA_P(a_l) = \sum_{i=0}^{G_{AP}} \beta_{GAPi}(a_l)^i I_{S_A}(a_l). \tag{10.10}$$

We can describe the class of models used in this example by the values of T_{XP}, T_{AP}, I_{XP}, I_{AP}, G_{XP}, and G_{AP}. For the example data set in this chapter we settled on the following log-linear model for both $\{n_{jl}\}$ and $\{m_{kl}\}$:

$$(T_{XP}, T_{AP}, I_{XP}, I_{AP}, G_{XP}, G_{AP}) = (4, 4, 2, 2, 3, 3). \tag{10.11}$$

Recall that there are two additional parameters, one for $\boldsymbol{X}$ and one for $\boldsymbol{A}$, for modelling the "lump" at 0. Also note that in (10.8) and (10.10) the summation starts at $i = 0$ and therefore, although $G_{XP} = 3$ there are actually four parameters in $GX_P(x_j)$. Similarly, for $GA_P(a_l)$.

Following the notation of Chapter 5 for this model for $\mathbf{P}$, the number of parameters fit is

$$T_P = 2 + T_{XP} + T_{AP} + I_{XP} + I_{AP} + G_{XP} + 1 + G_{AP} + 1 = 22.$$

The result is a 22-parameter model that describes the 79 by 36 matrix of bivariate score frequencies. Of these 22 parameters, 9 each are used to fit the two marginal distributions, and 4 more are used to account for the correlations and other cross-moments of the joint distribution.

The same type of model with the same number of parameters as indicated in (10.11) was fit to the $(\boldsymbol{Y}, \boldsymbol{A})$ frequencies, m_{kl}.

Assessing the fit of the models. As an overall assessment of the fit for the (4, 4, 2, 2, 3, 3) models, the likelihood ratio chi-square statistic are 1966.9 for the $\{n_{jl}\}$ and 1896.0 for the $\{m_{kl}\}$. These chi-square statistics have nominal degrees of freedom of 2821 each. It is unlikely that the chi-square distribution with these degrees of freedom is directly applicable to these two statistics due to the large number of relatively small frequencies that arise in the 79 by 36 matrices of score frequencies. As a check on the need for the higher cross moments we included in the model, we also fit models of the form (4, 4, 1, 1, 3, 3) that only include the correlation term. The change in likelihood ratio chi-square between these two models is 600 for $\{n_{jl}\}$, and 297.3 for $\{m_{kl}\}$. These likelihood ratio differences have 3 degrees of freedom each and give strong evidence for the need to improve the fit by adding the extra cross moments that we included.

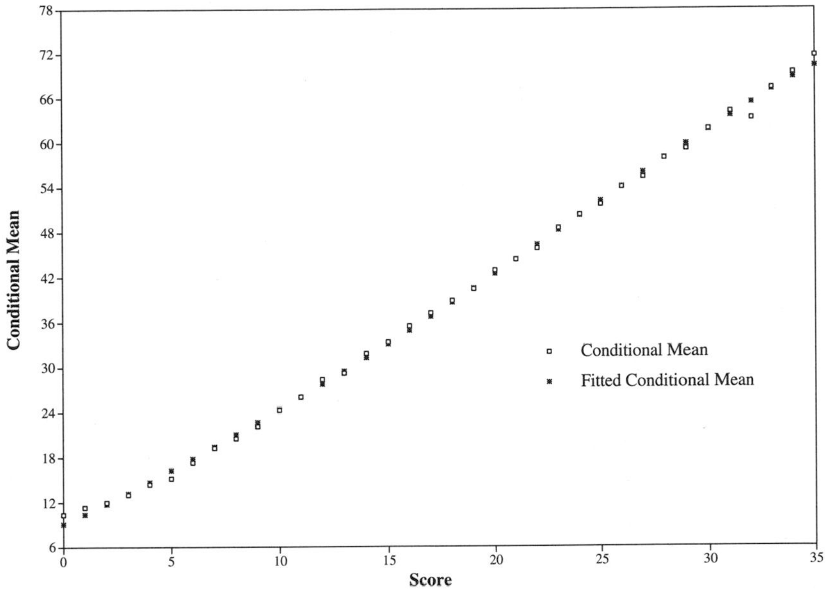

FIGURE 10.8. E($\boldsymbol{Y} \mid \boldsymbol{A}$) : observed and fitted values. Example 4, the NEAT Design.

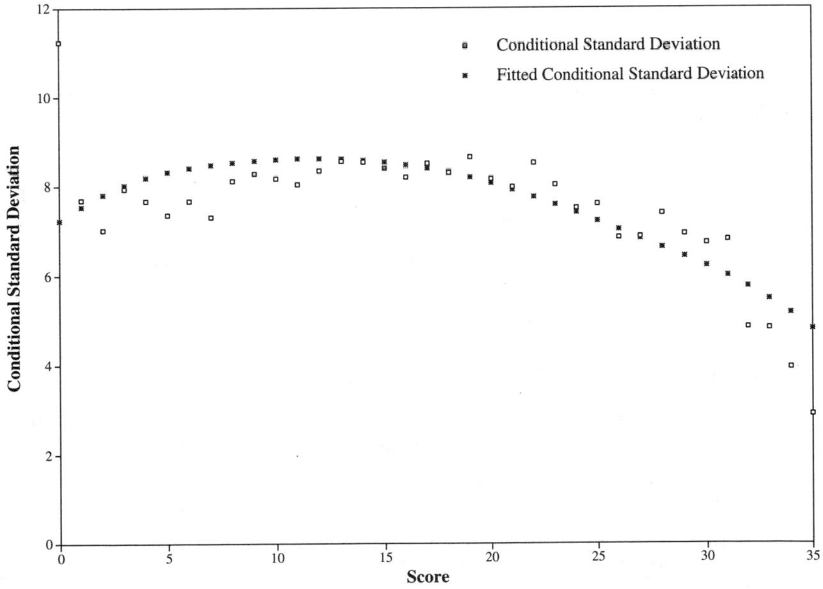

FIGURE 10.9. SD($\boldsymbol{Y} \mid \boldsymbol{A}$) : observed and fitted values. Example 4, the NEAT Design.

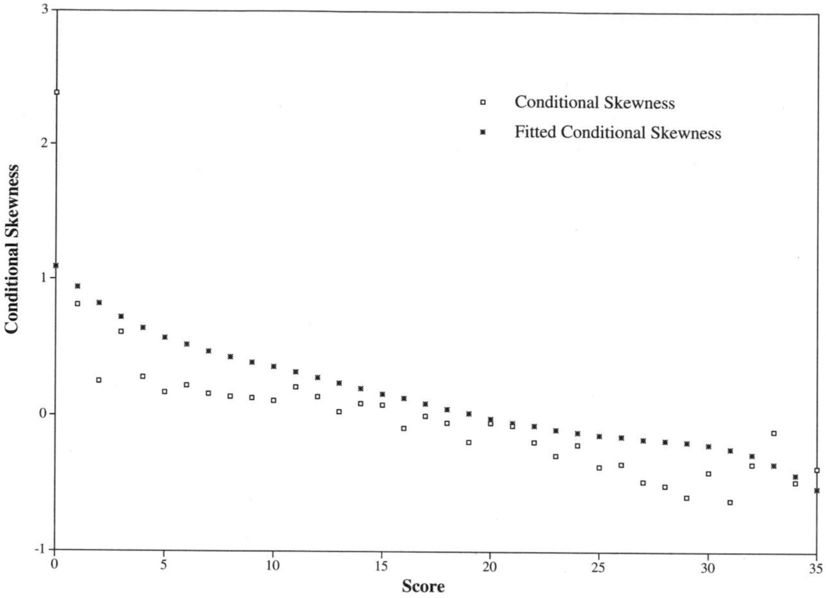

FIGURE 10.10. Skew($\boldsymbol{Y} \mid \boldsymbol{A}$) : observed and fitted values. Example 4, the NEAT Design.

The Freeman-Tukey (FT) deviates for investigating the fit in the marginal distributions of $\boldsymbol{X}$ and $\boldsymbol{A}$ in P has only one large, significant value of -3.24 at $\boldsymbol{X} = 78$.

Similarly, the FT deviates for investigating the fit in the marginal distributions of $\boldsymbol{Y}$ and $\boldsymbol{V}$ has also only one large, significant value of -3.19, also at $\boldsymbol{Y} = 78$.

The observed and the fitted marginal distributions of $\boldsymbol{X}$ and $\boldsymbol{A}$ and of $\boldsymbol{Y}$ and $\boldsymbol{A}$ are plotted in Figure 10.1—Figure 10.4. They show a remarkable degree of agreement between the observed and fitted frequencies.

For a more detailed examination of the fit of the bivariate distribution of $\boldsymbol{X}$ and $\boldsymbol{A}$ and of $\boldsymbol{Y}$ and $\boldsymbol{A}$ we examine the two sets of conditional distributions ($\boldsymbol{X}$ given $\boldsymbol{A}$, and $\boldsymbol{Y}$ given $\boldsymbol{A}$). We summarize the dependencies between $\boldsymbol{X}$ and $\boldsymbol{A}$ by calculating the conditional means, standard deviations, and measures of skewness of the fitted conditional distributions and comparing them to the corresponding values for the two observed conditional distributions. Similarly for the dependencies between $\boldsymbol{Y}$ and $\boldsymbol{A}$. Figures 10.5—10.10 plot these results.

The conditional means are nearly linear and very well reproduced by the fitted models. While there are more discrepancies between the observed and fitted conditional standard deviations and skewness measures, the models we selected reproduce the trends in these conditional moments to a remarkable degree.

In summary, we interpret this evidence as indicating a very close fit between the raw data and the fitted models used to pre-smooth them.

In addition to the estimated joint probabilities, $\hat{p}_{jl}$ and $\hat{q}_{kl}$, the output of a satisfactory log-linear model program will include the "**C**-matrices" that are the essential information needed to compute the standard errors of $\hat{p}_{jl}$ and $\hat{q}_{kl}$, and which are used to compute the SEE and the SEED described in Chapter 5.

In this example, there are two **C**-matrices, $\mathbf{C}_P$ and $\mathbf{C}_Q$, because there are two bivariate distributions to be estimated. $\mathbf{C}_P$ and $\mathbf{C}_Q$, are very large arrays (each is 2844×22), and therefore they will not be reported here.

The estimated covariance of $v(\hat{\mathbf{P}})$, $\boldsymbol{\Sigma}_{v(\hat{P})}$, is such that

$$\boldsymbol{\Sigma}_{v(\hat{P})} = \mathbf{C}_P \mathbf{C}_P^t,$$

and the estimated covariance of $v(\hat{\mathbf{Q}})$, $\boldsymbol{\Sigma}_{v(\hat{Q})}$, is such that

$$\boldsymbol{\Sigma}_{v(\hat{Q})} = \mathbf{C}_Q \mathbf{C}_Q^t.$$

Following Assumption 2.8, the covariance matrix between $v(\hat{\mathbf{P}})$ and $v(\hat{\mathbf{Q}})$ is zero. Thus the joint covariance matrix of $v(\hat{\mathbf{P}})$ and $v(\hat{\mathbf{Q}})$ is

$$\begin{aligned}
\boldsymbol{\Sigma}_{v(\hat{P}),\, v(\hat{Q})} &= \begin{pmatrix} \mathbf{C}_P \mathbf{C}_P^t & \mathbf{0} \\ \mathbf{0} & \mathbf{C}_Q \mathbf{C}_Q^t \end{pmatrix} \\
&= \begin{pmatrix} \mathbf{C}_P & \mathbf{0} \\ \mathbf{0} & \mathbf{C}_Q \end{pmatrix} \begin{pmatrix} \mathbf{C}_P & \mathbf{0} \\ \mathbf{0} & \mathbf{C}_Q \end{pmatrix}^t = \mathbf{C}\mathbf{C}^t, \qquad (10.12)
\end{aligned}$$

where

$$\mathbf{C} = \begin{pmatrix} \mathbf{C}_P & \mathbf{0} \\ \mathbf{0} & \mathbf{C}_Q \end{pmatrix} \qquad (10.13)$$

is a 5688×44 matrix.

10.2 Estimation of the Score Probabilities

Chain Equating (CE) uses a two-stage transformation of $\boldsymbol{X}$ scores into $\boldsymbol{Y}$ scores. First, it links $\boldsymbol{X}$ to $\boldsymbol{A}$ on P and then links $\boldsymbol{A}$ to $\boldsymbol{Y}$ on Q. We use "links" rather than "equates" because the test(s) and the anchor are not equally reliable, and, therefore, they violate requirement 2 mentioned in Chapter 1. These two linking functions are then functionally composed to equate $\boldsymbol{X}$ to $\boldsymbol{Y}$ using CE.

Chain equating does not involve any new ideas beyond those used in the Single-Group (SG) Design. It simply functionally composes or "chains together" the results from the two SG Designs.

The cdf's that are used in (2.43) to compute the Chain Equating function, i.e., F_P, H_P, G_Q, and H_Q, require estimates of four vectors of score probabilities: $\boldsymbol{r}_P = (r_{Pj})$, $\boldsymbol{t}_P = (t_{Pl})$, $\boldsymbol{t}_Q = (t_{Ql})$, and $\boldsymbol{s}_Q = (s_{Qk})$, for $j = 1, \ldots, J$, $k = 1, \ldots, K$, and $l = 1, \ldots, L$. These marginal probabilities for $\boldsymbol{X}$ and $\boldsymbol{A}$ in P, and $\boldsymbol{Y}$ and $\boldsymbol{A}$ in Q are given by (2.44) and are repeated here:

$$r_{Pj} = \text{Prob}\{\boldsymbol{X} = x_j \,|\, P\} = \sum_l p_{jl}, \qquad (10.14)$$

$$t_{Pl} = \text{Prob}\{\boldsymbol{A} = a_l \,|\, P\} = \sum_j p_{jl}, \qquad (10.15)$$

$$t_{Ql} = \text{Prob}\{\boldsymbol{A} = a_l \,|\, Q\} = \sum_k q_{kl}, \qquad (10.16)$$

$$s_{Qk} = \text{Prob}\{\boldsymbol{Y} = y_k \,|\, Q\} = \sum_l q_{kl}. \qquad (10.17)$$

10.3 Continuization

In Chain Equating we need to continuize not only the cdf's of $\boldsymbol{X}$ and $\boldsymbol{Y}$, F_P and G_Q, but also H_P and H_Q, the cdf's of the anchor test $\boldsymbol{A}$ in the two populations.

In the example of this chapter, the methods used to continuize the four cdf's are the same, so we will discuss only one of them in detail, i.e., $\hat{F}_{Ph_{XP}}(x)$, for $\boldsymbol{X}$ on P. Following the discussion in Section 4.1, we start with the vector of estimated score probabilities, $\hat{\boldsymbol{r}}_P$, and continuize it via formula,

$$\hat{F}_{Ph_{XP}}(x) = \sum_j \hat{r}_j \Phi\left(\hat{R}_{jXP}(x)\right), \qquad (10.18)$$

where

$$\hat{R}_{jXP}(x) = \frac{x - \hat{a}_{XP}x_j - (1 - \hat{a}_{XP})\hat{\mu}_{XP}}{\hat{a}_{XP}h_{XP}} \qquad (10.19)$$

and

$$\hat{a}^2_{XP} = \frac{\hat{\sigma}^2_{XP}}{\hat{\sigma}^2_{XP} + h^2_{XP}}. \qquad (10.20)$$

In this example we selected h_{XP} to minimize the criterion given in (4.30), i.e.,

$$\text{PEN}_1(h_{XP}) + K \times \text{PEN}_2(h_{XP}),$$

with PEN_1 and PEN_2 defined in (4.27) and (4.29), respectively. The weight K was set to 1.0 for all of the continuizations used in this chapter.

Figure 10.11 shows both the fitted score probabilities $\{\hat{r}_{Pj}\}$ and the density function of the continuized cdf, $\hat{F}_{Ph_{XP}}$. Had we used PEN_1 alone to

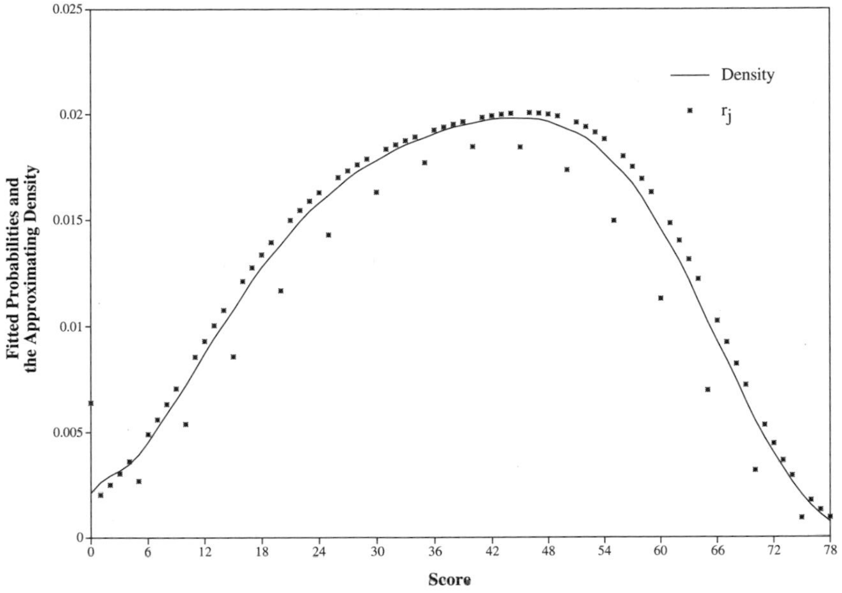

FIGURE 10.11. Fitted probabilities and the approximating density. Example 4, $\boldsymbol{X}$ on P, the NEAT Design.

determine h_{XP}, the approximating density function would have tracked the gaps and have exhibited rapid changes in its first derivative, as illustrated in Figure 4.2. Figure 10.11 illustrates what we mean by "grinding down the teeth" or "filling in the gaps" in the continuization phase of KE. The resulting density function passes between the two sets of smoothed score probabilities. The value of h_{XP} that minimizes the penalty function is $h_{XP} = 2.014$. Note that the density is not zero at $x = 0$ or $x = 78$ in Figure 10.11. This indicates that it places some probability outside the range of the raw scores of $\boldsymbol{X}$. The lump of probability at $x_1 = 0$ causes the density to be higher at $x = 0$ than it is at $x = 78$. Spreading the continuous distribution of probability beyond the range of the raw scores is an inevitable property of the use of the Gaussian kernel to continuize a discrete distribution. PEN_2 has smoothed the gaps away in the r_{Pj}. The same phenomenon occurs for t_{Pl}, t_{Ql}, and s_{Qk}, and we do not report them here.

We continuized H_P, H_Q, and G_Q in the same manner. The resulting h-values are: $h_{AP} = 2.040$, $h_{AQ} = 1.405$, and $h_{YQ} = 2.131$.

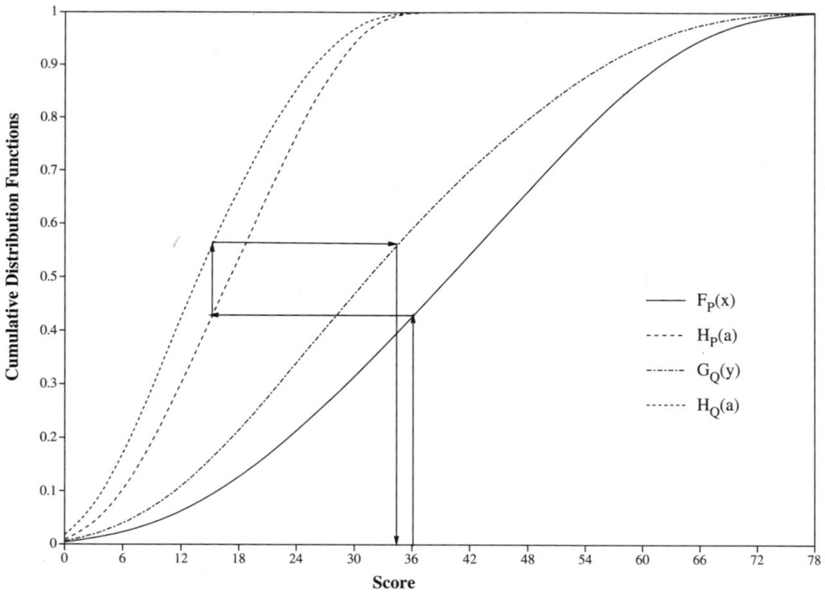

FIGURE 10.12. The smoothed cdf's, $\hat{F}_{Ph_{XP}}(x)$, $\hat{H}_{Qh_{AP}}$, $\hat{G}_{Qh_{YQ}}$, and $\hat{H}_{Qh_{AQ}}$ and the Chain Equating process. Example 4, CE for the NEAT Design. h-values found using criterion (4.30) with $K = 1$.

10.4 Equating

The Chain Equating function, $e_{Y(CE)}$, defined in (2.43) has the following form when we apply the four continuized cdf's to it:

$$\hat{e}_{Y(CE)}(x) = \hat{G}^{-1}_{Qh_{YQ}}\left(\hat{H}_{Qh_{AQ}}\left(\hat{H}^{-1}_{Ph_{AP}}\left(\hat{F}_{Ph_{XP}}(x)\right)\right)\right). \quad (10.21)$$

The equation for $\hat{e}_{Y(CE)}(x)$ can be expressed as the functional composition of the KE link from X to A on P, denoted by $\hat{e}_A(x)$, and the KE link from A to Y on Q, denoted by $\hat{e}_Y(a)$. In terms of the four continuized cdf's, $\hat{e}_A(x)$ and $\hat{e}_Y(a)$ are given by

$$\hat{e}_A(x) = \hat{H}^{-1}_{Ph_{AP}}\left(\hat{F}_{Ph_{XP}}(x)\right) \quad (10.22)$$

and

$$\hat{e}_Y(a) = \hat{G}^{-1}_{Qh_{YQ}}\left(\hat{H}_{Qh_{AQ}}(a)\right). \quad (10.23)$$

Then we have

$$\hat{e}_{Y(CE)}(x) = \hat{e}_Y\left(\hat{e}_A(x)\right). \quad (10.24)$$

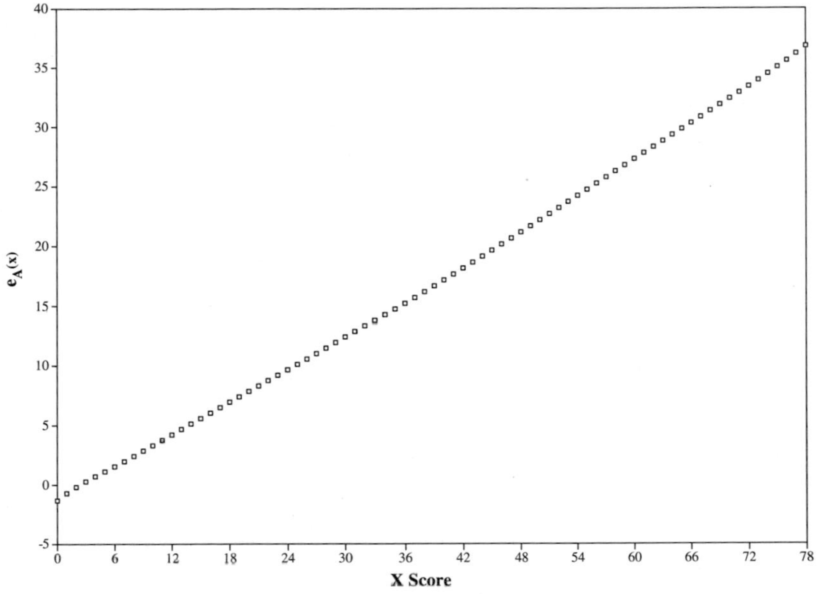

FIGURE 10.13. The linking function, $\hat{e}_A(x)$. Example 4, CE for the NEAT Design.

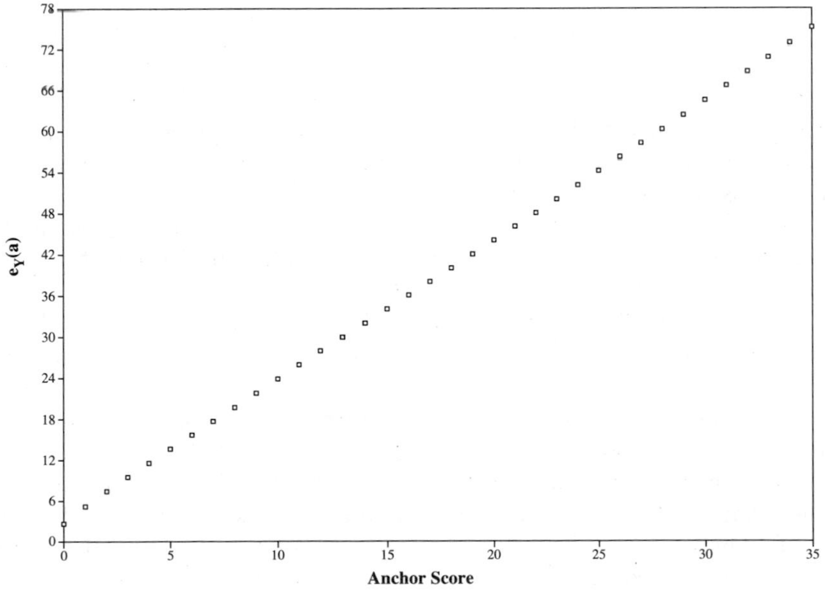

FIGURE 10.14. The linking function, $\hat{e}_Y(a)$. Example 4, CE for the NEAT Design.

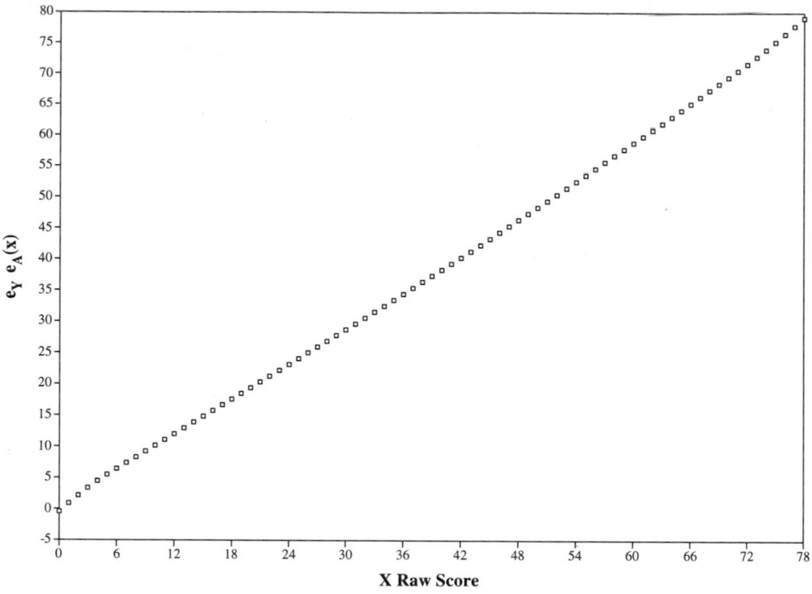

FIGURE 10.15. The CE function, $\hat{e}_{Y(CE)}(x)$. Example 4, CE for the NEAT Design.

Figure 10.12 gives a geometric view of how CE works. Starting at a particular X-score, go vertically up to the curve of $F_P(x)$, then move horizontally over to the curve of $H_P(a)$, from there go vertically to the curve $H_Q(a)$, then move horizontally over to the curve of $G_Q(y)$ and drop from there down to the horizontal axis to find the Y-score that the original X-score is equated to via CE.

For our example, $\hat{e}_A(x)$ is plotted in Figure 10.13. The second linking function, $\hat{e}_Y(a)$, is plotted in Figure 10.14. Finally, the CE equating function, $\hat{e}_{Y(CE)}(x)$, is plotted in Figure 10.15.

Figures 10.13–10.15 show that each link in the chain and their final composition is very linear in this example. We will investigate this in more detail using the SEED in Section 10.6.

To evaluate how well $\hat{e}_{Y(CE)}(x)$ transforms the discrete distribution of $\boldsymbol{X}$ on the target population T into the discrete distribution of $\boldsymbol{Y}$ on T, we would need estimates of $\{\hat{r}_j\}$ and $\{\hat{s}_k\}$. We were able to do this in the other chapters because in those cases $\boldsymbol{r}$ and $\boldsymbol{s}$ are explicitly estimated, but in CE they are not. This means that we cannot use the Percent Relative Error measure used in the other chapters to investigate how well CE transforms the discrete distribution of $\boldsymbol{X}$ into that of $\boldsymbol{Y}$ on a common target population, T. A useful area for future research is the development of such diagnostic tools for CE.

TABLE 10.3. Difference Between the Moments of the Linked Distribution and the Target Distribution Expressed as Percent Relative Error, PRE(p). Example 4, CE for the NEAT Design.

	Percent Relative Error	
Moments	(X to A)	(A to Y)
1	0.007	0.001
2	−0.009	−0.012
3	−0.037	0.020
4	0.074	0.014
5	0.357	−0.050
6	0.826	−0.182
7	1.482	−0.387
8	2.325	−0.666
9	3.354	−1.019
10	4.567	−1.447

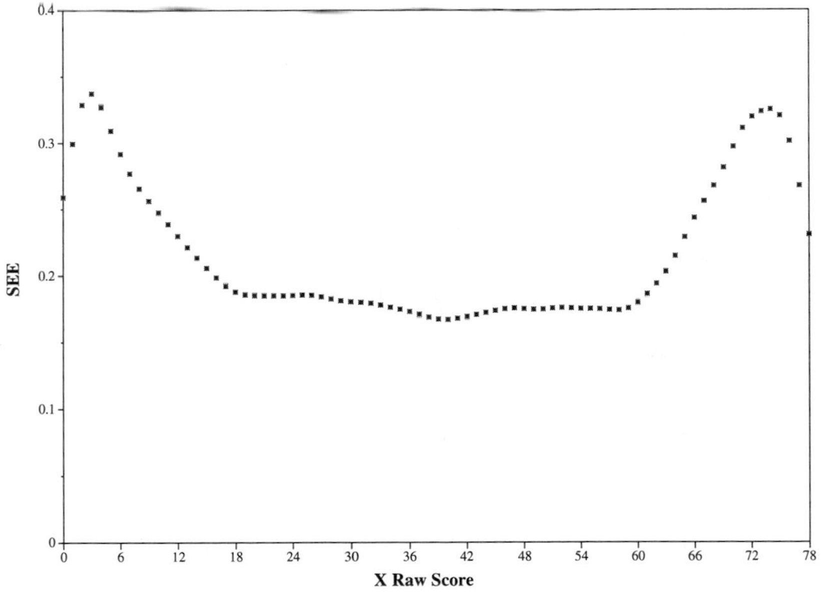

FIGURE 10.16. Standard Error of Equating, $\mathrm{SEE}_{Y(CE)}(x)$, for Equating $\boldsymbol{X}$ to $\boldsymbol{Y}$. Example 4, CE for the NEAT Design.

What we can do is to examine how well each link in the chain performs its transformation. Each of these links is a SG design so that we can apply the methods used in Chapter 8 to evaluate these linkings. Table 10.3 gives the results for linking X to A and for linking A to Y.

As we can see, the discrepancy between these moments ranges from -0.037% to $+4.567\%$ for the X to A linking on P and from -1.447% to $+0.02\%$ for the A to Y linking on Q. The values in Table 10.3 are somewhat larger than the corresponding value given in Chapters 7, 8, and 9. This is possibly due to the fact that A is less than half the length of X or Y.

10.5 Standard Error of Equating

In order to compute the SEE for Chain Equating we need to use the SEE's for the two SG Designs that are within the NEAT Design, and then combine them correctly to reflect the fact that the final equating function is a functional composition of the two links, X to A and A to Y. This is discussed more fully in Chapter 5. Here we simply summarize the computations.

Denote the SEE for the X-to-A link by $\text{SEE}_A(x)$ and for the A-to-Y link by $\text{SEE}_Y(a)$, continuing the notation developed in Section 10.4, where we denote the link from X to A by $e_A(x)$ and that from A to Y by $e_Y(a)$. $\text{SEE}_A(x)$ and $\text{SEE}_Y(a)$ may both be computed using appropriate translations of formula (8.3) for the SG Design. In addition, we also need the derivative of $e_Y(a)$ with respect to a, from the results of Section 5.3.4. We denote this derivative by $e'_Y(a)$. It is the slope of the linking function of A to Y at the value $A = a$. In the example of this chapter, from Figure 10.14 we see that this slope is nearly constant over the entire range of A values and is approximately 2.1 in value over this range.

The four components of the SEE for CE are $\text{SEE}_A(x)$, $\text{SEE}_Y(a)$, $e'_Y(a)$, and $e_A(x)$. They are combined as follows to give the SEE for CE, which we will denote by $\text{SEE}_{Y(CE)}(x)$,

$$[\text{SEE}_{Y(CE)}(x)]^2 = [\text{SEE}_Y(e_A(x))]^2 + [e'_Y(e_A(x))\text{SEE}_A(x)]^2. \qquad (10.25)$$

Figure 10.16 graphs the $\text{SEE}_{Y(CE)}(x)$ over the range of X raw-score values. It has some similarity to the trend in the SEE for the SG Design given in Table 8.7. The SEE in both cases is smaller in the middle of the score range, but at the either end of the range the SEE rises and then falls again near the extreme score values. This "dog-bone" shape is typical of the SEE for KE (although, it may take on some variations, such as we see in Figure 9.11 for the CB Design.) In Figure 10.16 it is clearly evident. In the middle of the score range, the $\text{SEE}_{Y(CE)}(x)$ for the example is about 0.2, near each end of the range it raises to a little over 0.3 and then starts to return to smaller values at the extreme ends of the raw-score range.

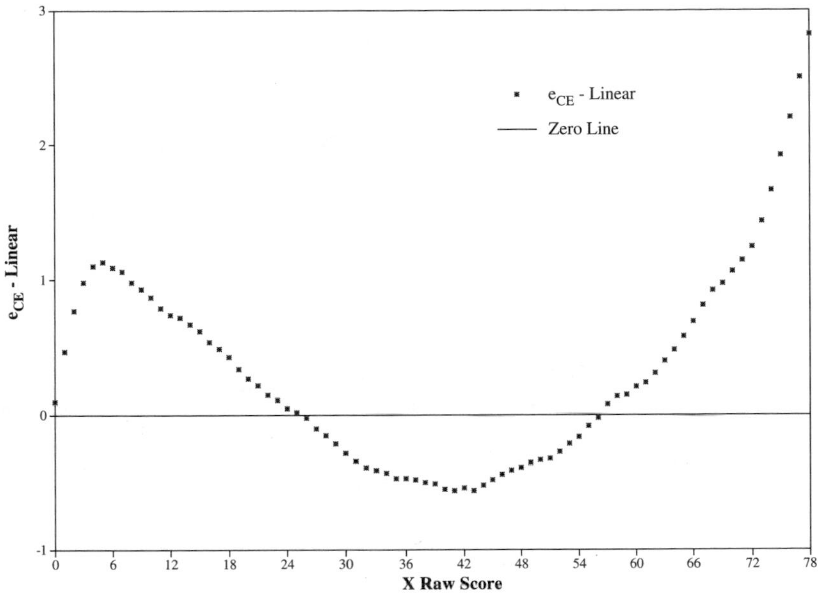

FIGURE 10.17. The difference between the equipercentile CE function, $e_{Y(CE)}(x)$, and linear equating function, $\widehat{\text{Lin}}_Y(x)$ for equating $\boldsymbol{X}$ to $\boldsymbol{Y}$. Example 4, CE for the NEAT Design.

10.6 Deciding Between $\hat{e}_{Y(CE)}(x)$ and $\widehat{\text{Lin}}_Y(x)$

We use the Standard Error of Equating Difference (SEED) to assist in making the decision between using a linear or nonlinear KE equating function in the Chain Equating case, as we do in the other chapters of Part II of this book. The CE case is somewhat different from the other cases because we do not directly estimate $\boldsymbol{r}$ and $\boldsymbol{s}$ for $\boldsymbol{X}$ and $\boldsymbol{Y}$ on the target population, T. Because the CE equating function, $e_{Y(CE)}(x)$, is a functional composition of two other linking functions, linearity of the final equating function can arise in two different ways. In the first case it is possible for each link to be nonlinear, but when they are functionally composed this nonlinearity cancels out and the final equating function is linear, or nearly so. In our example however, Figures 10.13–10.15 show that all three functions are nearly linear. This is the more usual case that leads to a final linear or near linear CE function.

In the CE case of KE, there are four bandwidth values that need to be specified. Up to now in this chapter, we have selected the bandwidths to minimize a penalty function (see Section 10.3). In order to obtain a KE function in the CE case that is guaranteed to be linear, we need to select all four bandwidths to be large. In this case we used $h = 10\sigma$ for all four

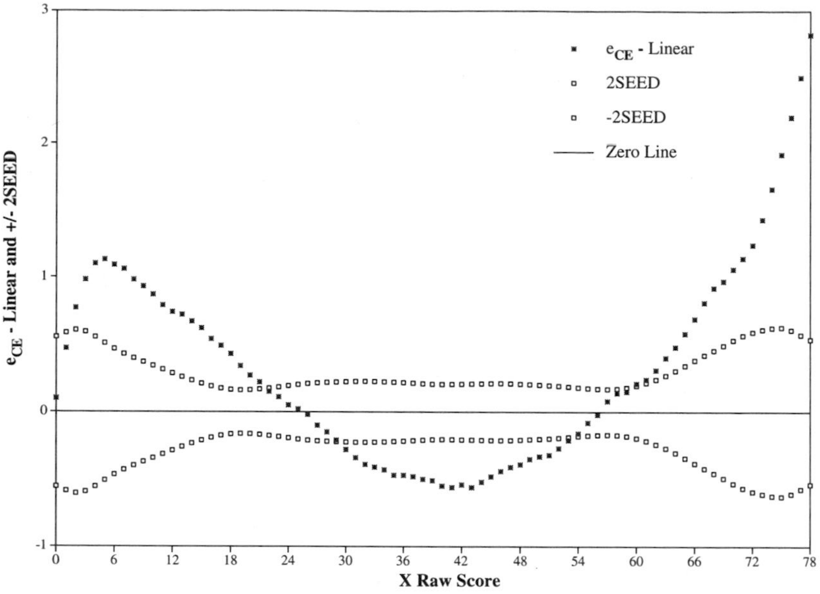

FIGURE 10.18. The difference between the equipercentile CE function, $e_{Y(CE)}(x)$, and linear equating function, $\widehat{\text{Lin}}_Y(x)$ for equating $\boldsymbol{X}$ to $\boldsymbol{Y}$, together with ±2SEED. Example 4, CE for the NEAT Design.

cases (see Tables 10.1 and 10.2 for the values of the standard deviations of the four distributions).

In Figure 10.17 we plot the difference

$$\hat{e}_{Y(CE)}(x) - \widehat{\text{Lin}}_Y(x). \tag{10.26}$$

This shows that $e_{Y(CE)}(x)$ differs for the linear equating function by less than a raw score point over most of the score range, but that at the extreme ends of the score scale this difference exceeds two points at the upper end of the raw-score scale and exceeds one point at the lower end of the scale.

To assess how this difference compares to its uncertainty, we plot it along with $\pm 2\text{SEED}(x)$, the standard error of equating difference defined in Chapter 5, i.e.,

$$\text{SEED}^2(x) \quad = \quad \text{Var}\left(\hat{e}_{Y(CE)}(x) - \widehat{\text{Lin}}_Y(x)\right). \tag{10.27}$$

Figure 10.18 graphs both the difference shown in Figure 10.17 along with ±2 times the SEED. Figure 10.18 shows that the difference between the equipercentile CE function, obtained using bandwidths chosen to fit the data well, and the linear CE function, obtained using bandwidths chosen to be large, is very large compared to the uncertainty in this difference that is due to the estimation of the score probabilities. The SEED is a measure of this uncertainty, and if the difference between the two CE functions was no larger than the noise level in the data it would have been smaller that twice the SEED in either direction. From Figure 10.18 we clearly see that this difference is only that small for a few of the possible $\boldsymbol{X}$ values. Hence, while the difference between the linear and equipercentile CE functions is relatively small except at the extremes, it is statistically significantly different from 0 for almost all of the $\boldsymbol{X}$ values. In addition, for the testing program from which these data come, such a difference would be considered large enough to have practical consequences for examinees scoring at the upper end of the scale. This combination of factors indicates that using the equipercentile CE function would be the better choice in practice. We do not mean to imply that the decision to choose between a linear or nonlinear equating function should be based on these criteria alone, but only that they are important considerations in making such decisions. More details are given in Section 5.4 of Chapter 5 regarding the calculation of the SEE and the SEED for CE.

11

The NEAT Design: Post-Stratification Equating

This chapter illustrates how to carry out the five steps of Kernel Equating (KE) for Post-Stratification Equating (PSE) in the NEAT Design. As mentioned in Chapter 2, PSE and Chain Equating (CE) share the same design and make the same basic assumptions about the design (Assumptions 2.7 and 2.8). Also the first step in Kernel Equating, pre-smoothing, is identical for PSE and CE.

To illustrate PSE we use the same data as in Chapter 10 for Chain Equating. This decision is motivated not only by the applicability of both PSE and CE to the same data but also by our intention to use the SEED from Chapter 5 to investigate the differences between the two resulting equating functions on the same data.

Hence, we refer the reader to Chapter 10, Section 10.1, for a description of the data and our use of special log-linear models to pre-smooth it in accordance with Step 1 from Section 3.1. We will use the same notation as we did in Chapter 10 to refer to the basic elements of the data and the equating design.

To summarize the NEAT Design and our notation for it, in this design there are two tests to be equated, X and Y, and an anchor test, A as well. There are two (non-equivalent) populations P and Q from which we have samples of examinees. X and A are both taken by the sample from P, while Y and A are both taken by a sample from Q. In our example for this and the last chapter, A is an external anchor test, as described in Chapter 2. In the NEAT Design there are two bivariate frequency distributions for the two samples. These are denoted by

$$n_{jl} = \text{number of examinees with } \boldsymbol{X} = x_j \text{ and } \boldsymbol{A} = a_l,$$

and

$$m_{kl} = \text{number of examinees with } \boldsymbol{Y} = y_k \text{ and } \boldsymbol{A} = a_l.$$

The bivariate score probabilities, p_{jl} and q_{kl}, are defined as

$$p_{jl} = \text{Prob}\{\boldsymbol{X} = x_j,\, \boldsymbol{A} = a_l \,|\, P\} \quad \text{and} \quad q_{kl} = \text{Prob}\{\boldsymbol{Y} = y_k,\, \boldsymbol{A} = a_l \,|\, Q\}.$$

The J by L matrix of bivariate score probabilities for P is denoted by $\mathbf{P}$, and the corresponding K by L matrix for Q is denoted by $\mathbf{Q}$. We will also use the vectorizing notation, $v(\mathbf{P})$ and $v(\mathbf{Q},)$ to denote the column vectors formed by stacking the columns of $\mathbf{P}$ and of $\mathbf{Q}$ (see Chapter 2).

There are two (potentially different) marginal distributions of $\boldsymbol{A}$, one from P and one from Q. We denote the corresponding score probabilities by

$$t_{Pl} = \text{Prob}\{\boldsymbol{A} = a_l \,|\, P\} \quad \text{and} \quad t_{Ql} = \text{Prob}\{\boldsymbol{A} = a_l \,|\, Q\},$$

and the vectors of these score probabilities by $\boldsymbol{t}_P$ and $\boldsymbol{t}_Q$. The target population is the mixture, $T = wP + (1-w)Q$, described in Chapter 2, and $\boldsymbol{r}$ and $\boldsymbol{s}$ are the vectors of score probabilities whose entries are defined by

$$r_j = \text{Prob}\{\boldsymbol{X} = x_j \,|\, T\} \quad \text{and} \quad s_k = \text{Prob}\{\boldsymbol{Y} = y_k \,|\, T\}.$$

By definition of T, r_j and s_k are defined as

$$r_j = w\text{Prob}\{\boldsymbol{X} = x_j \,|\, P\} + (1-w)\text{Prob}\{\boldsymbol{X} = x_j \,|\, Q\}, \tag{11.1}$$

$$s_k = w\text{Prob}\{\boldsymbol{Y} = y_k \,|\, P\} + (1-w)\text{Prob}\{\boldsymbol{Y} = y_k \,|\, Q\}, \tag{11.2}$$

and assumptions, PSE1 and PSE2, discussed in Chapter 2, are needed to allow $\text{Prob}\{\boldsymbol{X} = x_j \,|\, Q\}$ and $\text{Prob}\{\boldsymbol{Y} = y_k \,|\, P\}$ (and therefore $\boldsymbol{r}$ and $\boldsymbol{s}$) to be estimated from the data at hand.

In the next section we describe the estimation of the score probabilities exploiting the special PSE assumptions, (PSE1) and (PSE2), from Section 2.4.2. In Section 11.2 we describe continuization for PSE, and in Section 11.3 we show how to compute the equating function. Section 11.4 focuses on the SEE for PSE and Sections 11.5—11.7 describe how to apply the SEED to make decisions about the equating function. First, we will use the SEED to investigate the sensitivity of the PSE functions to the choice of w in $T = wP + (1-w)Q$. Second, we will compare the KE equipercentile function obtained through PSE to the KE linear function obtained through PSE. Third, we will compare the KE function obtained through PSE to the KE function obtained through CE that was derived in Chapter 10.

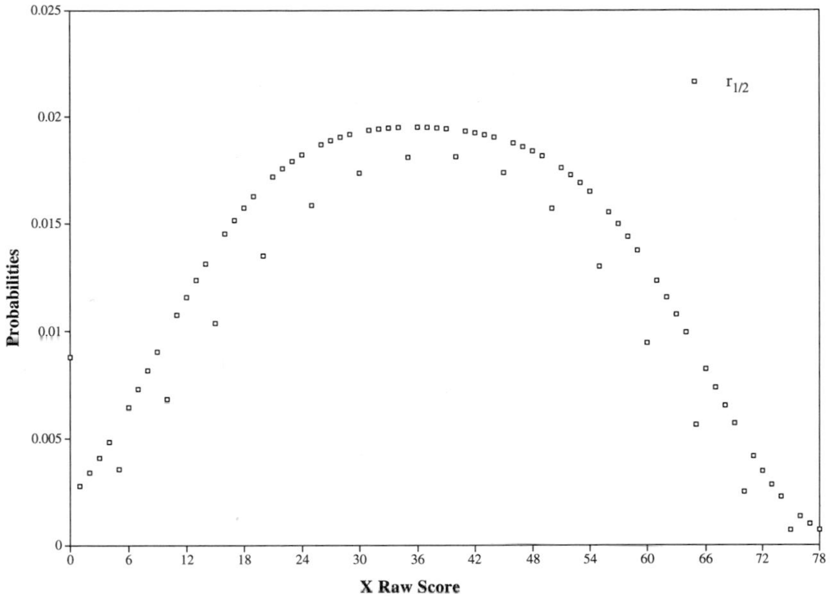

FIGURE 11.1. $\boldsymbol{r}_{1/2}$. Example 4, PSE in the NEAT Design.

11.1 Estimation of the Score Probabilities

In Post-Stratification Equating (PSE), after pre-smoothing, we estimate the marginal distributions, $\boldsymbol{r}$ and $\boldsymbol{s}$, of $\boldsymbol{X}$ and $\boldsymbol{Y}$ on the target population T, which is a specific mixture of P and Q in the form

$$T = wP + (1-w)Q,$$

where $0 \leq w \leq 1$ is the weight that defines T, see (2.32). Unlike Chain Equating, in PSE the choice of w, i.e., T, can affect the resulting equating function.

Under the assumptions, (PSE1) and (PSE2), given in Section 2.4.2, formulas (11.1) and (11.2) do define legitimate estimators of r_j and s_k over the target population, T. These are given by the Design Function for PSE that is specified by (2.60) and in (2.61), and are

$$\boldsymbol{r} = \boldsymbol{r}\left(v(\mathbf{P}),\, v(\mathbf{Q}),\, w\right) = \sum_l \left[w + \frac{(1-w)t_{Ql}}{t_{Pl}}\right] \boldsymbol{p}_l \tag{11.3}$$

and

$$\boldsymbol{s} = \boldsymbol{s}\left(v(\mathbf{P}),\, v(\mathbf{Q}),\, w\right) = \sum_l \left[(1-w) + \frac{wt_{Pl}}{t_{Ql}}\right] \boldsymbol{q}_l. \tag{11.4}$$

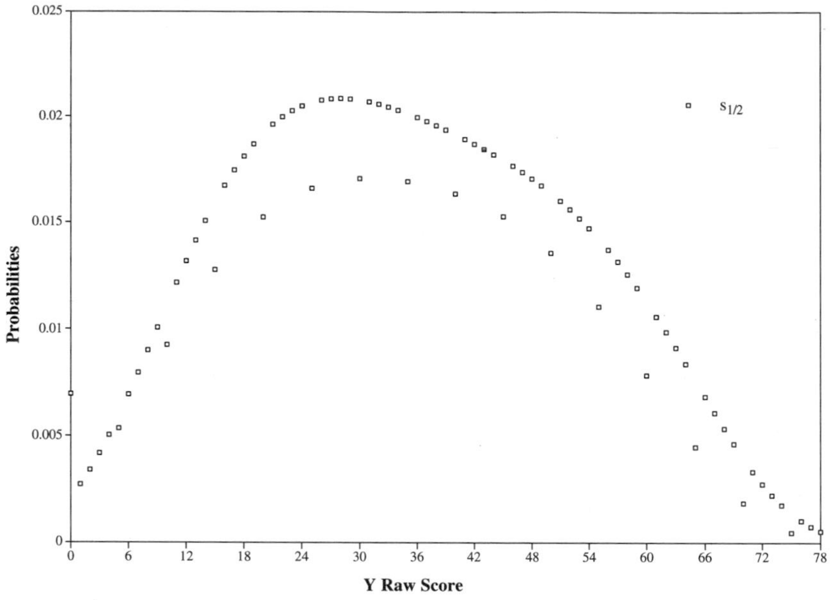

FIGURE 11.2. $\boldsymbol{s}_{1/2}$. Example 4, PSE in the NEAT Design.

In (11.3) and (11.4), the vectors, $\boldsymbol{p}_l$ and $\boldsymbol{q}_l$, are the lth-columns of $\mathbf{P}$ and $\mathbf{Q}$, respectively, i.e.,

$$\boldsymbol{p}_l = \begin{pmatrix} p_{1l} \\ \vdots \\ p_{Jl} \end{pmatrix} \quad \text{and} \quad \boldsymbol{q}_l = \begin{pmatrix} q_{1l} \\ \vdots \\ q_{Kl} \end{pmatrix}, \tag{11.5}$$

for $l = 1, \ldots, L$.

After obtaining $v(\hat{\mathbf{P}})$ and $v(\hat{\mathbf{Q}})$, $\hat{\boldsymbol{r}}$ and $\hat{\boldsymbol{s}}$ are computed from (11.3) and (11.4), respectively. The weight, w, that defines T, can play an essential role in PSE, in general. The choice of w is of a different nature than the choice of w_X and w_Y in the CB Design. In the NEAT Design, w reflects how much each population, P or Q, is relevant to the equating process.

In our example, we examined three choices of w ($w = 0$, $w = \frac{1}{2}$, and $w = 1$). This comparison can show how different these choices are in their effect on the equating function. However, in the example we chose for this chapter we will see that the effect of w is quite small.

The vectors, $\boldsymbol{r}$ and $\boldsymbol{s}$, each have 79 components so we will not table their values as we have done in the smaller examples of Chapters 7 and 8. However, we graph $\boldsymbol{r}_{\frac{1}{2}}$ and $\boldsymbol{s}_{\frac{1}{2}}$ (for $w = \frac{1}{2}$) in Figures 11.1 and 11.2. They show the pattern we see in Figures 10.1—10.4.

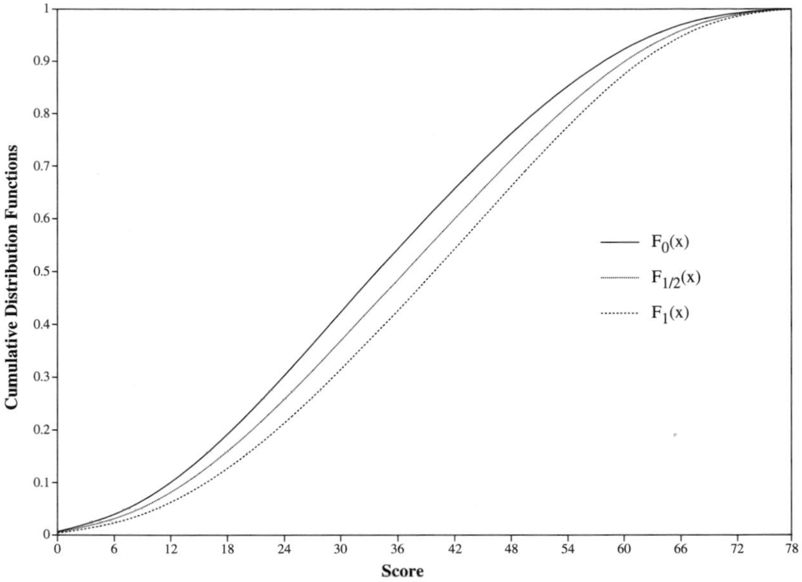

FIGURE 11.3. The cdf's of $\boldsymbol{X}$ for three values of w, $w = 0$, $w = 1/2$, and $w = 1$. Example 4, PSE in the NEAT Design.

11.2 Continuization

The cdf associated to the score probabilities defined for the test scores $\boldsymbol{X}$ and $\boldsymbol{Y}$ are

$$\hat{F}_w(x) = \text{Prob}\{\boldsymbol{X} \leq x_j\} = \sum_{x_j \leq x} \hat{r}_{wj} \tag{11.6}$$

and

$$\hat{G}_w(Y) = \text{Prob}\{\boldsymbol{Y} \leq y_k\} = \sum_{y_k \leq y} \hat{s}_{wk}, \tag{11.7}$$

with $\hat{r}_{wj}$ and $\hat{s}_{wk}$ from (11.3) and (11.4) with $w = 0, \frac{1}{2}, 1$.

Using the estimated values of $\boldsymbol{r}$ and $\boldsymbol{s}$ in the formulas from (4.5) and (4.8), the distribution functions from (11.6) and (11.7) will be approximated by the continuous $\hat{F}_{wh_X}(x)$ and $\hat{G}_{wh_Y}(y)$, with $w = 0, \frac{1}{2}, 1$.

As in the previous chapters, h_X and h_Y are chosen to minimize the criterion given in (4.30), with PEN_1 and PEN_2 defined in (4.27) and (4.29), respectively. The weight K was 1. The values of h_X and h_Y for each w are given in Table 11.1.

The resulting six cdf's, F_0, $F_{\frac{1}{2}}$, F_1, and G_0, $G_{\frac{1}{2}}$, G_1, are displayed in Figures 11.3 and 11.4. We point out that because population Q has lower

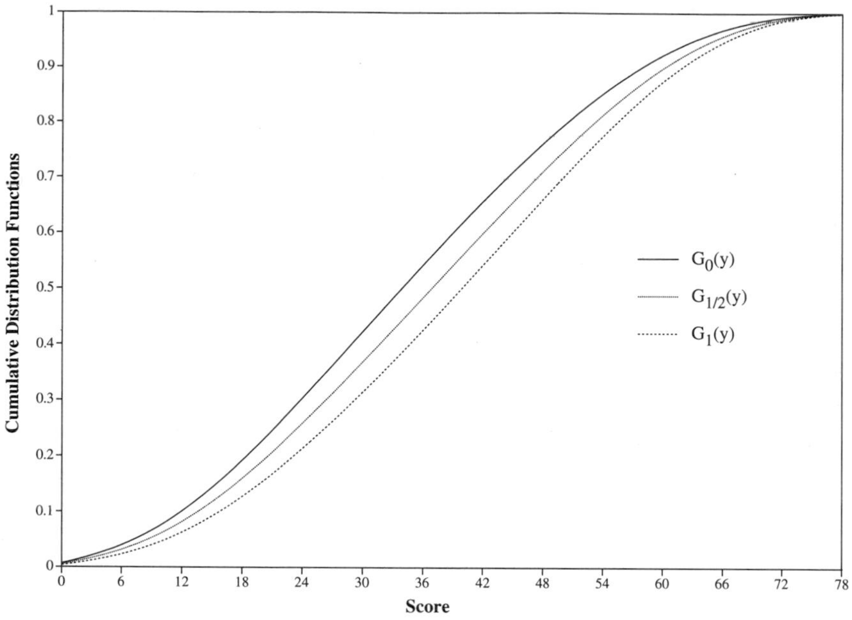

FIGURE 11.4. The cdf's of $\boldsymbol{Y}$ for three values of w, $w = 0$, $w = 1/2$, and $w = 1$. Example 4, PSE in the NEAT Design.

TABLE 11.1. The Values of h_X and h_Y for Each w. Example 4, NEAT Design.

h-Values	$w = 0$	$w = 1/2$	$w = 1$
$h_X(w)$	1.9527	1.9243	2.0137
$h_Y(w)$	2.1312	2.0056	2.2417

average scores than has population P, the cdf's move from left to right as w increases from 0 to 1 in these two figures. This is an indication that as w increases the cdf's are "stochastically ordered" from less proficient to more proficient, with respect to both $\boldsymbol{X}$ and $\boldsymbol{Y}$.

11.3 Equating

Once continuous approximations to $\hat{F}(x)$ and $\hat{G}(y)$ are available, we compute the equating functions via (4.31) and (4.32), i.e., the equating functions are

$$\hat{e}_{wY}(x) = \hat{G}^{-1}_{wh_Y}(\hat{F}_{wh_X}(x))$$

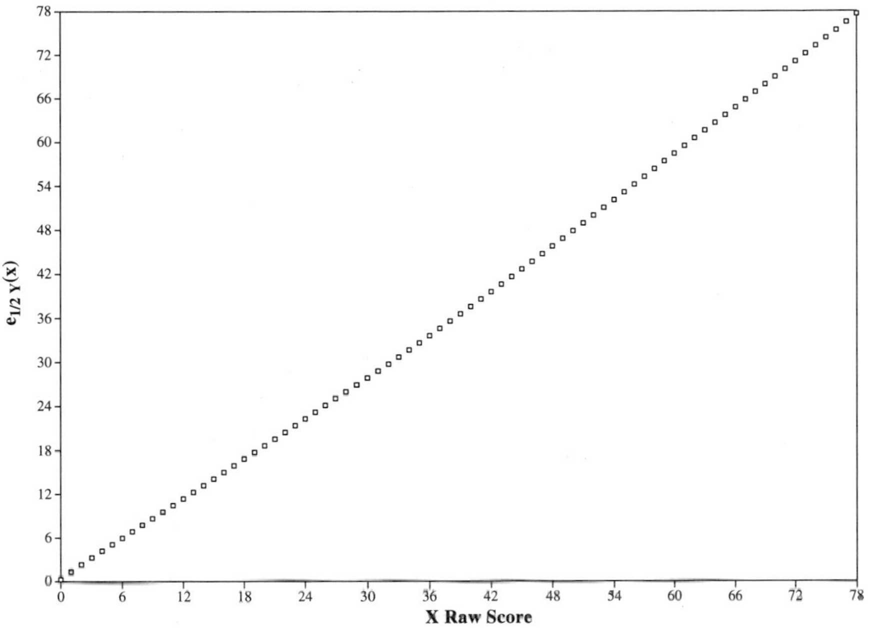

FIGURE 11.5. The equating function from $\boldsymbol{X}$ to $\boldsymbol{Y}$ for $w = 1/2$. Example 4, PSE in the NEAT Design.

and

$$\hat{e}_{wX}(y) = \hat{F}^{-1}_{wh_X}(\hat{G}_{wh_Y}(y)),$$

for each $w = 0, \frac{1}{2}, 1$.

As already explained in the previous chapters, we usually need the value of the equating function only for each raw score of $\boldsymbol{X}$. Hence, we need to compute

$$\hat{e}_{wY}(x_j) = \hat{G}^{-1}_{wh_Y}(u_{Xj}),$$

where $u_{Xj} = \hat{F}_{wh_X}(x_j)$ and

$$\hat{e}_{wX}(y_k) = \hat{F}^{-1}_{wh_X}(u_{Yk}),$$

where $u_{Yk} = \hat{G}_{wh_Y}(y_k)$.

As we alluded to earlier, in this example, the three equating functions are nearly identical. The biggest differences are less than 0.20 of a raw score point and these occur at the upper end of the raw score scale (see Section 11.5). For this reason, we will concentrate our attention on the case of $w = \frac{1}{2}$. (We examine the difference between $w = 0$ and $w = 1$ in terms

TABLE 11.2. Difference Between the Moments of the Equated Distribution and the Target Distribution Expressed as Percent Relative Error, PRE(p). Example 4, PSE with $w = \frac{1}{2}$ for NEAT Design.

	Percent Relative Error	
Moments	(X to Y)	(Y to X)
1	0.006	−0.004
2	0.005	−0.004
3	−0.020	0.017
4	−0.058	0.052
5	−0.104	0.095
6	−0.156	0.144
7	−0.212	0.200
8	−0.273	0.261
9	−0.337	0.327
10	−0.407	0.400

of the SEED in Section 11.5.) The equating function for $w = \frac{1}{2}$ is plotted in Figure 11.5. It is strongly linear, but has a slight bend.

Table 11.2 gives the percent relative error (PRE(p)) in the first 10 moments for the equating of X to Y and Y to X using PSE. The formula used for PRE(p) is given in (4.34) and (4.35). In this table, the PRE(p)'s are for $w = \frac{1}{2}$ and use the optimal h-values for that choice of w to compute the KE function. We see from Table 11.2 that the PRE(p) ranges from −0.407 percent to 0.400 percent over the two directions of the equatings. These are remarkably small values of PRE(p) if we compare them to the result of Chapters 7 and 8. We did somewhat better using KE for the CB Design (see Table 9.6), than we see in Table 11.2, but both examples give remarkably accurate results in terms of matching the estimated moments of the transformed distribution and its target.

If we compare the results of Table 11.2 to the results we obtained for CE in Table 10.3, we see that the PRE(p) values for CE are larger, overall, than those for PSE, indicating worse matching of the moments of the distributions. However, these values are not as comparable as we would like due to the fact that in CE we do not directly estimate values for $\boldsymbol{r}$ or $\boldsymbol{s}$ for the target population, as we do for PSE. Hence, all that is suggested by these results is that CE does somewhat worse in matching the moments relevant to it than PSE does for the moments relevant to it.

In order to give some comparison to Table 11.2 for CE, we offer Table 11.3. This gives the PRE(p)'s for CE where we use the CE function to compute the equated values and use $\boldsymbol{r}_{\frac{1}{2}}$ and $\boldsymbol{s}_{\frac{1}{2}}$ to compute the moments of the discrete distributions of $e_Y(\boldsymbol{X})$ and $\boldsymbol{Y}$ on $T = \frac{1}{2}P + \frac{1}{2}Q$. This is not an entirely fair calculation for CE because PSE is designed to match these moments very well. However, it is an interesting comparison to make and

TABLE 11.3. Difference Between the Moments of the Equated Distribution (computed via CE using the estimated score probabilities appropriate for PSE with $w = \frac{1}{2}$) and the Target Distribution Expressed as Percent Relative Error, PRE(p). Example 4, NEAT Design.

Moments	Percent Relative Error (X to Y)
1	1.904
2	2.997
3	3.706
4	4.296
5	4.882
6	5.518
7	6.232
8	7.037
9	7.939
10	8.939

for completeness we include these PRE(p) values for the X to Y transformation, only. In Table 11.3 we see that the PRE(p) values are larger than those of any that we have encountered in this book. Even the mean is not matched as well as it typically is. In Table 11.2 the mean is in error by almost 2%, whereas it is usually matched nearly perfectly. The higher moments are off by even more. The appropriate comparison that could favor CE is not entirely clear to us, and is a topic worth studying.

11.4 Standard Error of Equating

In order to compute the SEE of the equating function, $e_{\frac{1}{2}Y}(x)$, we will apply Theorem 5.4 from Chapter 5.

The main result is equation (5.29), which we repeat here,

$$\mathrm{SEE}_Y(x) = \frac{1}{G'}\left[\left\|\frac{\partial F}{\partial \boldsymbol{r}}\mathbf{U}_R - \frac{\partial G}{\partial \boldsymbol{s}}\mathbf{V}_R\right\|^2 + \left\|\frac{\partial F}{\partial \boldsymbol{r}}\mathbf{U}_S - \frac{\partial G}{\partial \boldsymbol{s}}\mathbf{V}_S\right\|^2\right]^{1/2},$$

where $\mathbf{U}_R$, $\mathbf{U}_S$, $\mathbf{V}_R$, and $\mathbf{V}_S$ are the matrix entries of $\mathbf{J}_{\mathrm{DF}}\mathbf{C}$ given in Table 5.6 and $||\boldsymbol{v}||^2 = \sum_i v_i^2$ is the squared Euclidian norm of the vector $\boldsymbol{v}$. From Table 5.6 it follows that, for PSE in the NEAT Design, the **U**'s and the **V**'s are given by

$$\mathbf{U}_R = w\mathbf{U}_P + (1-w)\mathbf{U}_P^* - (1-w)\sum_l (t_{Ql}/t_{Pl})t_{Pl}^{-1}\boldsymbol{p}_l\boldsymbol{v}_{Pl}^t, \quad (11.8)$$

$$\mathbf{V}_R = w\sum_l t_{Ql}^{-1}\boldsymbol{q}_l\boldsymbol{v}_{Pl}^t, \quad (11.9)$$

$$\mathbf{U}_S = (1-w)\sum_l t_{Pl}^{-1}\boldsymbol{p}_l\boldsymbol{v}_{Ql}^t, \quad (11.10)$$

$$\mathbf{V}_S = (1-w)\mathbf{U}_Q + w\mathbf{U}_Q^* - w\sum_l (t_{Pl}/t_{Ql})t_{Ql}^{-1}\boldsymbol{q}_l\boldsymbol{v}_{Ql}^t, \quad (11.11)$$

where

$$\mathbf{U}_P = \sum_l \mathbf{C}_{Pl};$$

$$\mathbf{U}_P^* = \sum_l (t_{Ql}/t_{Pl})\mathbf{C}_{Pl};$$

$$\mathbf{U}_Q = \sum_l \mathbf{C}_{Ql};$$

$$\mathbf{U}_Q^* = \sum_l (t_{Pl}/t_{Ql})\mathbf{C}_{Ql};$$

$$\boldsymbol{v}_{Pl}^t = \mathbf{1}_J^t\mathbf{C}_{Pl} \quad \text{and} \quad \boldsymbol{v}_{Ql}^t = \mathbf{1}_K^t\mathbf{C}_{Ql}.$$

$\mathbf{P} = (\boldsymbol{p}_1, \ldots, \boldsymbol{p}_L)$ and $\mathbf{Q} = (\boldsymbol{q}_1, \ldots, \boldsymbol{q}_L)$ are the matrices of the joint probabilities, p_{jl} and q_{kl}, defined in (2.30) and (2.31); $\mathbf{C}_{Pl}$ and $\mathbf{C}_{Ql}$ are the matrix blocks in the **C**-matrices, $\mathbf{C}_P$ and $\mathbf{C}_Q$.

The formulas for the vectors of the derivatives, $\frac{\partial F}{\partial r}$ and $\frac{\partial G}{\partial s}$, from (5.29) are given in Lemma 5.1 and Lemma 5.2.

Figure 11.6 displays the SEE, equating $\boldsymbol{X}$ to $\boldsymbol{Y}$. Figure 11.6 also includes the SEE for CE, copied from Figure 10.16. We see two obvious things from this comparison. First of all, the SEE's for PSE and CE are very similar over the entire score range and they both have the familiar KE "dog bone" shape. Second, PSE has a slight advantage over CE, but it is negligible over most of the score range.

11.5 The Choice of the Target Population

In the NEAT Design the target population is a weighted mixture of the two underlying populations, $T = wP + (1-w)Q$. The weight, w, determines how P and Q combine to determine T. In this chapter we used three values of $w : w = 0$ ($T = Q$), $w = \frac{1}{2}$ (P and Q weighted equally) and $w = 1$ ($T = P$). As we indicated in Section 11.3, while w does influence the three continuized pairs of cdf's in this example, it has very little effect on

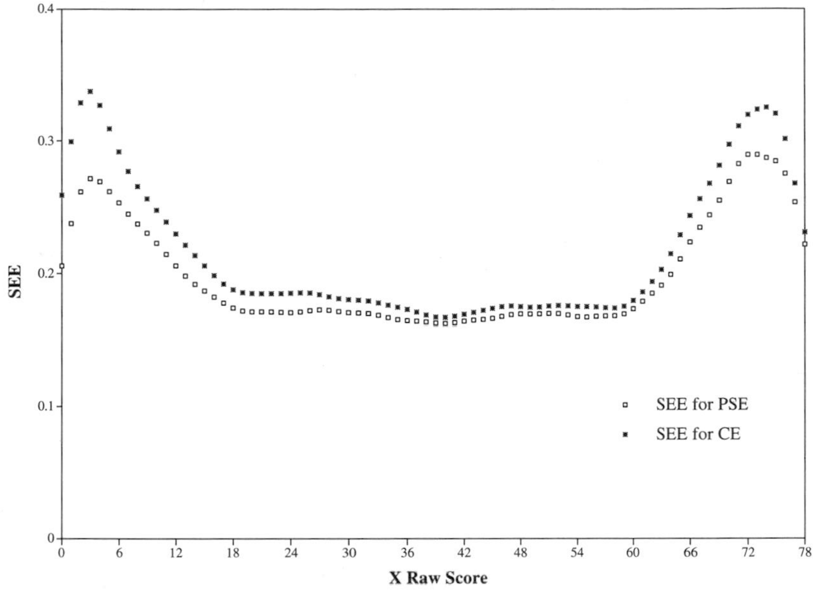

FIGURE 11.6. The SEE for PSE and CE in the NEAT Design. Example 4, PSE in the NEAT Design.

the resulting equating functions. To quantify this, in this section we will compare the difference between $e_{1Y}(x)$ and $e_{0Y}(x)$, defined in Section 11.3. These two equating functions correspond to $w = 1$ and 0, respectively, so they reflect the choices of $T = P$ versus $T = Q$.

We will use a version of the SEED to compare the difference between the two equating functions to the uncertainty in them due to statistical variation. The version of the SEED that we will use assumes that the equating functions being compared vary in the values of w and therefore in the values of $h_X(w)$ and $h_Y(w)$ as well. The different values of w affect the Jacobian matrix of the design function, $\mathbf{J}_{\mathrm{DF}_w}$ (see Table 5.4). The different values of $h_X(w)$ and $h_Y(w)$ affect the equating function, e_{wY}, and therefore affect its Jacobian, $\mathbf{J}_{e_{wY}}$. The $\mathbf{C}$-matrices, from the pre-smoothing, are not affected by w or the h's. Hence, the SEED for comparing $w = 1$ to $w = 0$ in the NEAT Design has the form:

$$\mathrm{SEED}_Y^2(x) = \mathrm{Var}\left(\hat{e}_{1Y}(x) - \hat{e}_{0Y}(x)\right) \quad (11.12)$$

$$= ||\, \mathbf{J}_{e_{1Y}} \mathbf{J}_{\mathrm{DF}_1} \mathbf{C} - \mathbf{J}_{e_{0Y}} \mathbf{J}_{\mathrm{DF}_0} \mathbf{C} \,||^2, \quad (11.13)$$

where $\mathbf{J}_{\mathrm{DF}_w}$, the Jacobian of the Design Function, and $\mathbf{C}$ are described in Theorem 5.1 of Chapter 5. $\mathbf{J}_{e_{wY}}$ was described in Chapter 5, in (5.19).

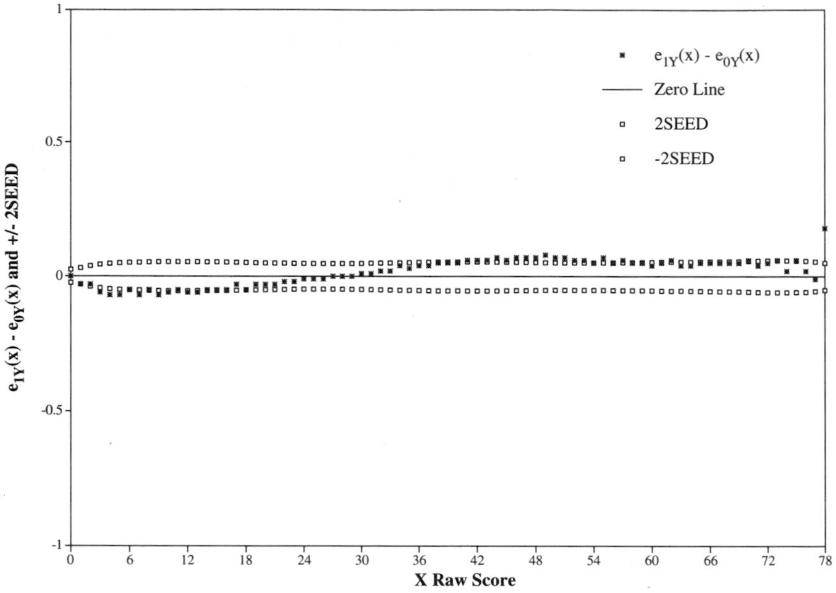

FIGURE 11.7. The difference between $e_{1Y}(x)$ and $e_{0Y}(x)$ as well as $\pm$2SEED(x). Example 4, PSE in the NEAT Design.

In Figure 11.7 we plot the difference between $e_{1Y}(x)$ and $e_{0Y}(x)$ as well as $\pm$2SEED(x) from (11.13). From this plot we see that the difference between the two equating functions is very small (as we mentioned earlier) and very close to the noise level in the data (as measured by the SEED). The difference between $e_{1Y}(x)$ and $e_{0Y}(x)$ is less than a tenth of a raw score point over most of the score range and well within the $\pm$2SEED band given in Figure 11.7. The one exception is the very highest raw score value where the difference is closes to two-tenths of a raw score point and exceeds the 2SEED band. Figure 11.7 gives clear quantitative support to our claim that, in this example, the effect of the choice of T is negligible.

11.6 Deciding Between $\hat{e}_{\frac{1}{2}Y}(x)$ and $\widehat{\text{Lin}}_{\frac{1}{2}Y}(x)$

Because of the small differences in the equating functions for the choices of w that we examined, we decided to concentrate on the case of $w = \frac{1}{2}$ for the rest of this chapter. In this section we examine how close the KE function displayed in Figure 11.5 is to the linear equating function using a version of the SEED, as we have in the other chapters of this part of the book.

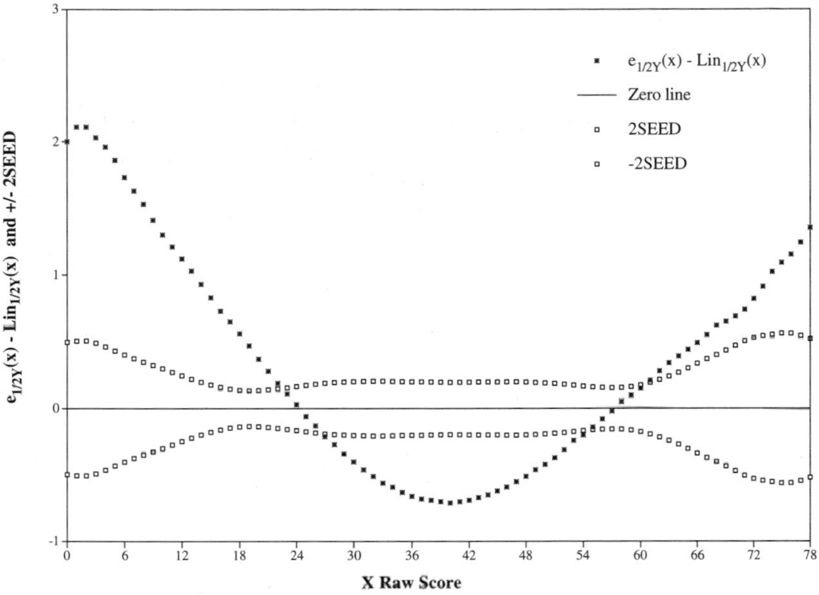

FIGURE 11.8. The difference between $e_{\frac{1}{2}Y}(x)$ and $\mathrm{Lin}_{\frac{1}{2}Y}(x)$ and $\pm 2\mathrm{SEED}_Y(x)$. Example 4, PSE in the NEAT Design.

Following the analysis we have used in previous chapters, we exploit the result that if the bandwidths are large enough, then the KE function will be linear. Hence, in this use of the SEED, $w = \frac{1}{2}$ but the two pairs of h values will be $h_X = 1.9243$, and $h_Y = 2.0056$ (see Table 11.1) versus $h_X = 170$, and $h_Y = 170$. These two pairs of bandwidths correspond to $e_{\frac{1}{2}Y}(x)$ and $\mathrm{Lin}_{\frac{1}{2}Y}(x)$, respectively. Thus, from the results of subsection 5.3.3 of Chapter 5, the SEED corresponding to the difference, $e_{\frac{1}{2}Y}(x) - \mathrm{Lin}_{\frac{1}{2}Y}(x)$, is given by

$$\mathrm{SEED}^2(x) = \mathrm{Var}\left(\hat{e}_{\frac{1}{2}Y}(x) - \widehat{\mathrm{Lin}}_{\frac{1}{2}Y}(x)\right) \tag{11.14}$$

$$= ||\, \mathbf{J}_{e_{\frac{1}{2}Y}} \mathbf{J}_{\mathrm{DF}_{\frac{1}{2}}} \mathbf{C} - \mathbf{J}_{\mathrm{Lin}_{\frac{1}{2}Y}} \mathbf{J}_{\mathrm{DF}_{\frac{1}{2}}} \mathbf{C} \,||^2. \tag{11.15}$$

Again, the SEED is the length of the difference between the two SE-vectors.

The Jacobian matrix of the Design function, $\mathbf{J}_{\mathrm{DF}_{\frac{1}{2}}}$, is similar to the Jacobians mentioned in the previous section, except with $w = \frac{1}{2}$. The Jacobians of the two equating functions, $e_{\frac{1}{2}Y}(x)$ and $\mathrm{Lin}_{\frac{1}{2}Y}(x)$, are the same except for the choices of the bandwidths, and their elements are given by (5.19) in Chapter 5. Thus, the SEED for this section is quite similar to the SEED for the last section, but the choices of w's and h's are different.

In Figure 11.8, we plot the difference $e_{\frac{1}{2}Y}(x) - \text{Lin}_{\frac{1}{2}Y}(x)$ and the band of $\pm 2\text{SEED}_Y(x)$, in order to compare the difference between the two equating functions to the uncertainty in their difference due to sampling. We see that the linear version of KE differs significantly from the KE function determined from the bandwidths selected to minimize the penalty function discussed in Section 11.2. The graph of the difference between the linear and curvilinear KE functions shown in Figure 11.8 is similar to the corresponding graph for CE (Figure 10.17). Both curves are quite linear but with a noticeable bend at about $\boldsymbol{X} = 40$. We turn to a direct comparison between CE and PSE in the next section.

11.7 Comparing the KE Functions for PSE and CE

While the assumptions of Chain Equating (CE) and Post-Stratification Equating (PSE) are different (see Section 2.4), it is possible for the results to be identical or very similar. In this section, we give another application of the SEED to compare the results of these two different methods of equating in the NEAT Design. In Chapter 10 we applied CE to the NEAT Design data that we also used in this chapter, where we used the PSE approach. Thus, Figures 10.15 and 11.5 are directly comparable and provide us with a choice between two equating functions that are the results of the different assumptions made in CE versus PSE.

For notation, we let $e_{Y(CE)}(x)$ and $e_{Y(PSE)}(x)$ denote the CE and PSE equating functions, respectively. In addition, because of the small effect of w on the results in this example, we use $w = \frac{1}{2}$ as we did in the previous section.

From the results of Chapter 5, the SEED corresponding to the difference, $e_{Y(CE)}(x) - e_{Y(PSE)}(x)$, is given by

$$\text{SEED}_Y^2(x) = \text{Var}\left(e_{Y(CE)}(x) - e_{Y(PSE)}(x)\right) \tag{11.16}$$

$$= ||\,\mathbf{J}_{e_{Y(CE)}}\mathbf{D} - \mathbf{J}_{e_{\frac{1}{2}Y}}\mathbf{J}_{\text{DF}_{\frac{1}{2}}}\mathbf{C}\,||^2. \tag{11.17}$$

In (11.17), $\mathbf{J}_{e_{Y(CE)}}$ is given by (5.42), $\mathbf{D}$ is the matrix defined in (5.49), and the SE-vector, $\mathbf{J}_{e_{Y(CE)}}\mathbf{D}$, is evaluated in (5.51). In addition, the components in the SE-vector, $\mathbf{J}_{e_{\frac{1}{2}Y}}\mathbf{J}_{\text{DF}_{\frac{1}{2}}}\mathbf{C}$, are exactly the same as those in the previous section.

In Figure 11.9 we plot the difference $e_{Y(CE)}(x) - e_{Y(PSE)}(x)$. From Figure 11.9 it is evident that there is a consistent difference between CE and PSE for this example. Over most of the raw-score range of X, CE produces higher equated values than PSE does. For most of the range this difference is less than a Y-raw-score point, but it exceeds half a Y-point over a large

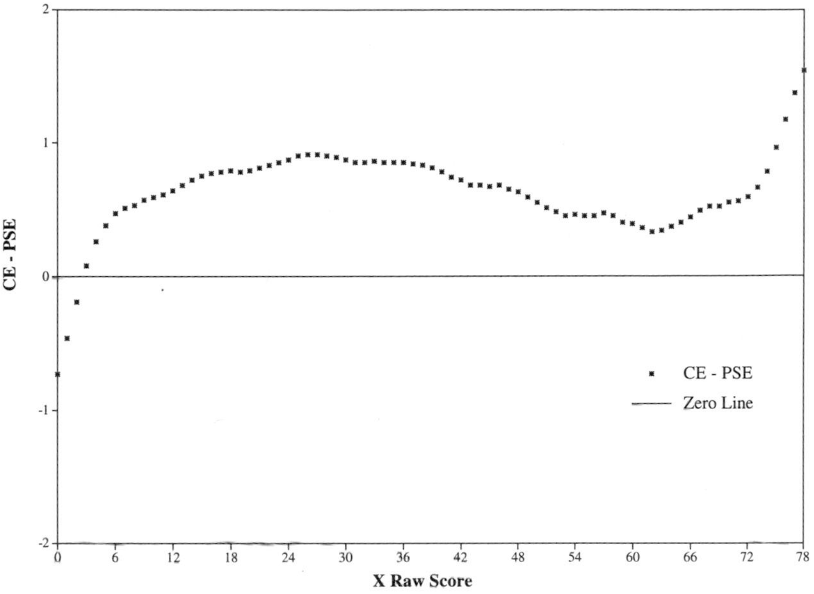

FIGURE 11.9. The difference between $e_{Y(CE)}(x)$ and $e_{Y(PSE)}(x)$. Example 4, PSE in the NEAT Design.

portion of the X-score range. For the four highest X values, the difference exceeds one Y-point. Such differences would be considered large enough to make a difference in the reported scores for this example and, from this point of view the differences, though small, are not negligible.

Another interpretation of the nearly consistent differences displayed in Figure 11.9 is that CE measures X as a "harder" test than PSE does. For all but the very lowest X-values, CE equates the scores of X to higher Y-scores than does PSE.

It is now of some interest to assess whether the apparent differences between CE and PSE are more than what we would expect from sampling variability. In Figure 11.10 we have overlaid Figure 11.9 with the band for $\pm$2SEED, where here the SEED is the standard error of the difference between CE and PSE, computed using (11.17). This comparison shows that sampling variability alone can not explain the differences between these two ways of computing equating functions for the NEAT Design. The difference curve lies outside the $\pm$2SEED band for most X-values. Hence, we would conclude that the differences that we see between CE and PSE, in this example, are reliably different from zero. In the next subsection, we will discuss the comparison between CE and PSE that this example illustrates.

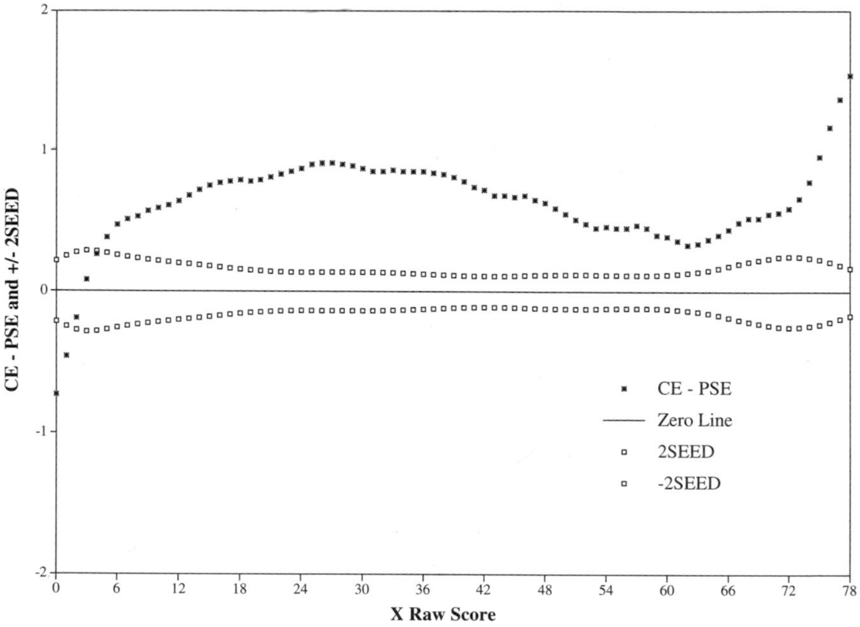

FIGURE 11.10. The difference between $e_{Y(CE)}(x)$ and $e_{Y(PSE)}(x)$ and ±2SEED. Example 4, PSE in the NEAT Design.

11.8 CE versus PSE: Which One to Choose?

Statisticians and psychometricians with test equating responsibilities for testing programs must choose a final equating function that will affect the scores of potentially thousands of test takers. This is often a very significant responsibility. These choices may involve decisions between linear or curvilinear functions and in the case of the NEAT Design between equating functions derived from the assumptions of both PSE and CE. As the example of this and the last chapter shows, choosing between PSE and CE can involve real differences that are not negligible relative to the final scores that will be reported. What can we expect such decisions to involve?

First of all, while the assumptions of CE and PSE (i.e., CE1 and CE2 and PSE1 and PSE2 from Section 2.4 of Chapter 2) are different, both sets of assumptions are not directly testable. Hence, we can not resolve the choice between CE and PSE by directly checking their assumptions against the data. Choosing between PSE and CE involves more than checking model fit.

Secondly, while the two sets of assumptions are different, there are circumstances where they can lead to exactly the same equating function. In von Davier et al. (2003) we show that when P and Q do not differ in terms of their distributions of the anchor test, $\boldsymbol{A}$, then CE and PSE give the same results regardless of how "good" the anchor test is (i.e., its correlation with $\boldsymbol{X}$ and $\boldsymbol{Y}$). Furthermore, we also give a case where the two tests to be equated, $\boldsymbol{X}$ and $\boldsymbol{Y}$, are perfectly correlated with $\boldsymbol{A}$ and, in that case, no matter how different P and Q are in terms of their distributions of $\boldsymbol{A}$, CE and PSE give identical results. From these two theoretical observations, we expect that the differences between CE and PSE will tend to be negligible when either (i) P and Q have very similar distributions of the anchor test, or (ii) when the anchor test correlates highly with both $\boldsymbol{X}$ and $\boldsymbol{Y}$.

However, in the example of this chapter and Chapter 10, the correlation between $\boldsymbol{X}$ and $\boldsymbol{A}$ is 0.88 and between $\boldsymbol{Y}$ and $\boldsymbol{A}$ it is 0.87. These are typical of "high" correlations between tests and anchor tests and they are certainly not "perfect." Furthermore, in this example, the difference between P and Q on $\boldsymbol{A}$ was about 32% of a standard deviation, which is quite large for this testing program. Thus, this real data example is not covered by the two theoretical cases just mentioned, and, in fact, in it we find a reliable difference between CE and PSE. The difference is small, but large enough to change the scores reported to examinees.

From Figure 11.6 we see that, in this example, PSE has a slight edge over CE in terms of its accuracy as measured by the SEE. However, the most striking thing about Figure 11.6 is how small these differences are. CE and PSE have very similar, small standard errors, so it not useful to choose between them based on their relative accuracy of estimation.

We are left with one idea for rationally choosing between CE and PSE in the NEAT design. However, because it is a relatively untried idea we will only briefly outline it here. We return to the five "requirements" of test equating mentioned in Section 1.1. The Population Invariance Requirement says that equating functions should not depend on the population on which they are computed. In fact, they always do depend on the population to some degree, (Dorans and Holland, 2000). However, if CE and PSE vary in their sensitivity to the choice of the target population, then we propose that choosing the equating method that is the less sensitive to T is a rational basis for choosing between CE and PSE in the NEAT Design. However, we can't use $T = wP + (1 - w)Q$ to measure this sensitivity because (a) CE gives the same result for any such T, and (b) as we saw in Section 11.5, w makes very little difference for PSE in this example. However, we can find corresponding subpopulations of both P and Q (e.g., males versus females, etc.) and use them. Thus, we may be able to partition P and Q into mutually exclusive and exhaustive subpopulation, $\{P_k\}$ and $\{Q_k\}$, and define $T_k = wP_k + (1 - w)Q_k$. In this notation, we mean to imply that P_k and Q_k are the same kind of examinees in P and Q (e.g., the males in P and the males in Q). We may then study the sensitivity of CE and PSE to the choice of T_k. This sensitivity could vary from example to example due to factors such as, (a) the correlation between the tests and $\boldsymbol{A}$, or, (b) the difference between P and Q in terms of the distributions of $\boldsymbol{A}$. We might have one example where CE is less sensitive and another where PSE is. In von Davier et al. (2003) we have begun to explore this idea using the measure of population sensitivity of observed score equating functions proposed in Dorans and Holland (2000). While we regard this work as promising, it is still very much an open research topic and an area ripe for additional research.

If it turns out that CE and PSE are not easily distinguished by their sensitivity to the choice of T_k, then we do not see an easy way to choose between CE and PSE in any example where they give reliably different results. One's belief in the plausibility of CE1 and CE2 versus PSE1 and PSE2 appears to be the sole basis left for making this important judgement. Improving on this "intuitive" approach is a topic well worth further research.

Appendix A
The δ-Method

The δ-method for computing large-sample approximations to the variance of statistics is based on the following theorem that we state without proof—see Rao (1973), Bishop et al. (1975), Lehmann (1999), or von Davier (2001), for more details.

Theorem A.1. *Suppose that there is given a sequence of statistical models indexed by $n \in \mathbb{N}$ (usually the sample size) with the same parameter space Θ which is a nonempty open subset of $\mathbb{R}^m$. Let $\widehat{\boldsymbol{\theta}}_n$ be a sequence of vector statistics, such that $\widehat{\boldsymbol{\theta}}_n$ is an asymptotically Normal estimator for $\boldsymbol{\theta}$, i.e.,*

$$\sqrt{n}\left(\widehat{\boldsymbol{\theta}}_n - \boldsymbol{\theta}\right) \xrightarrow{\mathcal{D}} \mathcal{N}\big(\mathbf{0}, \boldsymbol{\Sigma}(\boldsymbol{\theta})\big) \quad \forall \boldsymbol{\theta} \in \Theta\,,$$

where $\mathcal{N}\big(\mathbf{0}, \boldsymbol{\Sigma}(\boldsymbol{\theta})\big)$ denotes the multivariate Normal distribution with expectation zero and covariance matrix $\boldsymbol{\Sigma}(\boldsymbol{\theta})$. Consider a function R of $\boldsymbol{\theta}$

$$R : \Theta \longrightarrow \mathbb{R}^p,$$

with $p \leq m$ and assume that R is continuously differentiable on Θ. By $\mathbf{J}_R(\boldsymbol{\theta})$ we denote the Jacobian matrix of R at $\boldsymbol{\theta}$, which is a p by m matrix, i.e.,

$$\mathbf{J}_R(\boldsymbol{\theta}) = \left(\frac{\partial R_i}{\partial \theta_j}\right), \tag{A.1}$$

where $i = 1, \ldots, p$ and $j = 1, \ldots, m$. Then the distribution of $\sqrt{n}(R(\hat{\boldsymbol{\theta}}_n) - R(\boldsymbol{\theta}))$ converges to the $\mathcal{N}(0, (\mathbf{J}_R(\boldsymbol{\theta})\boldsymbol{\Sigma}(\boldsymbol{\theta})\mathbf{J}_R(\boldsymbol{\theta})^t)$ law, where $\mathbf{J}_R(\boldsymbol{\theta})$ is the Jacobian matrix in (A.1).

This result is often described by saying that if $\hat{\boldsymbol{\theta}}_n$ has an approximate $\mathcal{N}\ (0,\ \boldsymbol{\Sigma}(\boldsymbol{\theta}))$ distribution when $\boldsymbol{\Sigma}(\boldsymbol{\theta})$ is small then $R(\hat{\boldsymbol{\theta}}_n)$ has an approximate $\mathcal{N}\ \left(0, \partial R/\partial\boldsymbol{\theta}\boldsymbol{\Sigma}(\boldsymbol{\theta})\partial R/\partial\boldsymbol{\theta}^t\right)$ distribution.

Appendix B
Bivariate Smoothing

As we did for univariate smoothing, we will first describe the assumptions about the data and the model. We assume that the data were gather from a Single-Group Design to illustrate bivariate smoothing.

Sample level. The sample data consists of $(\boldsymbol{X}, \boldsymbol{Y})$-frequencies,

$$(n_{jk}) = \text{number of examinees with } \boldsymbol{X} = \boldsymbol{x}_j \text{ and } \boldsymbol{Y} = \boldsymbol{y}_k,$$

with $j = 1, \ldots, J$ and $k = 1, \ldots, K$. $\boldsymbol{n} = (n_{11}, \ldots, n_{JK})^t$ is the JK-column vector of the bivariate frequencies. The sample size is $N = \sum_j n_{jk}$. The raw sample frequencies could be used to estimate the bivariate probabilities, $p_{jk} = \text{Prob}(\boldsymbol{X} = x_j, \boldsymbol{Y} = y_k \mid T)$, in order to compute $\hat{r}_j$ and $\hat{s}_k$. However, rarely will these raw sample frequencies yield satisfactory estimates of all the probabilities involved except when N is very large.

Assumption B.1. *It is assumed that the vector* $\boldsymbol{n} = (n_{11}, \ldots, n_{JK})^t$*, has a multinomial distribution, i.e.,*

$$\text{Prob}(\boldsymbol{n}) \quad = \quad \frac{N!}{n_{11}! \ldots n_{JK}!} \prod p_{ij}^{n_{ij}} . \qquad \text{(B.1)}$$

The various (power) moments of this bivariate distribution can be expressed as linear combinations of the frequencies, e.g.,

$$\sum_{j,k} x_j^a y_k^b (n_{jk}/N). \qquad \text{(B.2)}$$

When $b = 0$, then this is the ath moment of the distribution of the row scores, and if $a = 0$, this is the bth moment of the distribution of the column scores. When a and b are both positive, these are the cross moments of the joint distribution of the row and column scores, e.g., if $a = b = 1$ then this is the cross moment related to the covariance and correlation between the two scores.

We recommend pre-smoothing the bivariate frequencies by fitting log-linear models in a way that is similar to Section 3.1. To put the bivariate case into the univariate framework, let

$$\mathbf{P} = (\boldsymbol{p}_1, \boldsymbol{p}_2, \ldots, \boldsymbol{p}_K) \tag{B.3}$$

where $\boldsymbol{p}_k$ denotes the kth column of $\mathbf{P}$. Then define the JK-dimensional vectorized version of $\mathbf{P}$ by

$$v(\mathbf{P}) = \begin{pmatrix} \boldsymbol{p}_1 \\ \vdots \\ \boldsymbol{p}_K \end{pmatrix}, \tag{B.4}$$

where $v(\mathbf{P})$ is composed by stacking the columns of $\mathbf{P}$ one on the top of the other.

Model level. In order to estimate the bivariate population parameters, $\mathbf{P} = (p_{jk})$, we first find satisfactory models for the two univariate marginal distributions of the bivariate distribution using the tools described for the univariate case (see Section 3.1). Once this is done, we fit a model to the bivariate distribution that has the sufficient statistics indicated by the two models for the marginal distributions, and then add parameters to these models that involve terms that contain both x_j and y_k—for example, such as the last term in the model specified by (B.6) below.

Assumption B.2. *The vectors $\boldsymbol{r}$, $\boldsymbol{s}$ and $v(\mathbf{P})$ satisfy log-linear models.*

The log-linear model for $\boldsymbol{r}$ and $\boldsymbol{s}$ will be of the form given in (3.4) or (3.5). The model for $v(\mathbf{P})$ is:

$$\log(v(\mathbf{P})) = \boldsymbol{\alpha} + \boldsymbol{u} + \mathbf{B}^t\boldsymbol{\beta}. \tag{B.5}$$

If we fit the first two moments for the two (univariate) marginal distributions and one moment for the interaction, then the log-linear model for $v(\mathbf{P})$ may be, for example, of the form

$$\log(p_{jk}) = \alpha + u_{jk} + x_j\beta_{x1} + (x_j)^2\beta_{x2} + y_k\beta_{y1} + (y_k)^2\beta_{y2} + x_jy_k\beta_{xy11}, \tag{B.6}$$

where p_{jk} are the probabilities from (2.5) associated with n_{jk}. If the subscript "jk" denotes the n_{jk} component of $\boldsymbol{n}$, then let $\boldsymbol{b}_{jk}$ denote the row of the matrix $\mathbf{B}$ corresponding to the jk. In the example of (B.6),

$$\boldsymbol{b}_{jk} = (x_j, x_j^2, y_k, y_k^2, x_jy_k). \tag{B.7}$$

If T_P denotes the column dimension of $\mathbf{B}$, then

$$T_P \leq JK - 1,$$

i.e., that the number of the parameter is less than the number of possible scores combinations for $\boldsymbol{X}$ and $\boldsymbol{Y}$. In the example in(B.6), $T_P = 5$.

The model from (B.6) is an analog of the bivariate normal distribution and it has the same sufficient statistics —the sample means, variances and covariance. Each choice of "null distribution" $\boldsymbol{u}$ in (B.6) results in a different model with these sufficient statistics.

Estimation level. These models are estimated by the maximum likelihood method using standard iterative techniques.

From Assumption 2 follows that the log-likelihood function is

$$L = \sum_{jk} n_{jk} \log(p_{jk}) \,. \tag{B.8}$$

The "moment matching" property of log-linear models also holds.

B.1 Assessing the Fit of the Log-Linear Models

For the bivariate case, Holland and Thayer (1987, 2000) recommend working from the "outside" (i.e., the two univariate margins) "in" to the full bivariate distribution. This means that we first find satisfactory models for the two univariate marginal distributions of the bivariate distribution using the tools described for the univariate case (see Holland & Thayer, 2000, p. 31). Once this is done, we fit a model to the bivariate distribution that has the sufficient statistics indicated by the two models for the marginal distributions, and then add parameters to these models that involve terms that contain both x_j and y_k. We recommend examining the two sets of conditional distributions (row given column and column given row) when diagnosing the fit of a bivariate distribution. Then we recommend investigating the dependencies between the two variables by calculating the conditional means, standard deviations and skewness measures of the two fitted conditional distributions and comparing them to the corresponding values for the two observed conditional distributions. More details are given in Holland and Thayer (1998, p. 34) and Chapter 10.

B.1.1 Covariance Matrix of the Parameters

In Section 5.2 it was shown how to derive computational formulas for the (asymptotic) covariance matrices $\hat{\boldsymbol{\Sigma}}_r$ and $\hat{\boldsymbol{\Sigma}}_s$ if the distributions of $\boldsymbol{r}$ and $\boldsymbol{s}$ are estimated separately (univariate estimation), without parameters sharing, from two independent random samples.

In the case of the bivariate estimation, let $\hat{p}_{jk}$ be the estimates of $\{p_{jk}\}$ based on the sample data $\{n_{jk}\}$. $v(\hat{\mathbf{P}})$ is the vector of $\hat{p}_{jk}$, which follows a log-linear model. From Chapter 2, we know that $\hat{\boldsymbol{r}}$ and $\hat{\boldsymbol{s}}$ are functions of $\hat{p}_{jk}$ and that these functions depend on each specific design through the Design Function (DF).

Hence, in order to obtain $\hat{\boldsymbol{\Sigma}}_r$ and $\hat{\boldsymbol{\Sigma}}_s$ we need the covariance matrix of $v(\hat{\mathbf{P}})$, i.e., $\hat{\boldsymbol{\Sigma}}_{v(P)}$. The estimated covariance matrix of $v(\hat{\mathbf{P}})$ is the analog of $\hat{\boldsymbol{\Sigma}}_r$. From (5.8) there is a matrix $\mathbf{C}$ such that

$$\hat{\boldsymbol{\Sigma}}_{v(P)} = \mathbf{C}\mathbf{C}^t\,, \tag{B.9}$$

where $\mathbf{C}$ is a JK by T_P matrix defined in Table 5.2.

In order to compute the covariance matrix of the parameters for each design that requires a bivariate estimation, we will make use of (B.9) and of the DF's given in Chapter 2, which link $\hat{\boldsymbol{r}}$ and $\hat{\boldsymbol{s}}$ to $v(\hat{\mathbf{P}})$.

Appendix C
Other Univariate Moments

As mentioned in Section 3.2.1, the power moments are not the only ones that have utility in fitting univariate distributions. A very useful class of alternative moments are the "subset moments" defined as follows. A subset, S, of scores is identified, and the indicator function for S, $I_S(x_j)$, is used to define the "subset moment for S,"

$$\sum_{x_j \in S} r_j = \sum_j I_S(x_j) r_j \,, \tag{C.1}$$

where $I_S(x_j) = 1$ if $x_j \in S$, and $I_S(x_j) = 0$, otherwise. Subset moments have several uses. For example, if the frequency for one score value of a histogram does not seem to follow the pattern of those for the other scores, then it is often useful to isolate that score so that it does not distort the fit for the remaining ones. Thus, if the score $x_j = 0$ is the problematic one, then $S = \{0\}$, and $I_{\{S\}}(x_j) = 0$ for all x_j except $x_j = 0$. In (3.4) this could be accomplished by using the model

$$\log r_j = \alpha + u_j + x_j\beta_1 + x_j^2\beta_2 + I_{\{0\}}(x_j)\beta_3 \,. \tag{C.2}$$

In this case, $\boldsymbol{b}_j = (x_j,\, x_j^2,\, I_{\{0\}}(x_j))$, $\boldsymbol{\beta}^t = (\beta_1,\, \beta_2,\, \beta_3)$ and u_j could be any one of several choices.

Another use for subset moments is to fit one set of power moments to one part of the data and another set of power moments to another part of the data. An example of such a model is one of the form

$$\log(r_j) = \alpha + u_j + x_j\beta_1 + x_j^2\beta_2 + I_S(x_j)\beta_3 + x_j I_S(x_j)\beta_4. \tag{C.3}$$

In this case, $\boldsymbol{b}_j = (x_j, x_j^2, I_S(x_j), x_j I_S(x_j))$, $\boldsymbol{\beta}^t = (\beta_1, \beta_2, \beta_3, \beta_4)$ and u_j could be one of several choices. This model will match the first two moments of the cell values for the entire distribution, the total frequency in the cells denoted by S, and the mean of the cell values for the cells in S. This is very useful when the cells indexed by S are different in systematic ways from the others. This can happen when the frequencies exhibit nonrandom features like "teeth" or gaps spaced at regular intervals along the score scale (see Chapter 10).

Appendix D

Review of the Use of Matrices in This Book

Matrices. A matrix is a rectangular array of numbers indexed by its rows and columns. If J is the number of rows and K the number of columns, then the matrix is said to be a "J by K matrix," and its shape is "J by K." One of the many types of matrices that arises in this book is a bivariate score probability matrix, $\mathbf{P}$. The number at the intersection of row j and column k of $\mathbf{P}$ is the probability, p_{jk}. The entry, p_{jk}, is also called an element of, or a coordinate of, $\mathbf{P}$; in particular, it is the $(j,\ k)$-element of $\mathbf{P}$. An example of a 3 by 4 matrix, $\mathbf{P}$, is

$$\mathbf{P} = \begin{pmatrix} .20 & .10 & .05 & .00 \\ .10 & .15 & .05 & .05 \\ .00 & .03 & .12 & .15 \end{pmatrix}.$$

In this example, the sum of all the entries is 1.00 because it is a bivariate probability distribution. The (2, 3)-element of $\mathbf{P}$ in this example is the number .05, whereas, the (3, 2)-element of $\mathbf{P}$ is .03.

Matrix Operations. We use matrix notation so that in algebraic expressions we can refer to the whole array, $\mathbf{P}$, without specifying the individual coordinates by using subscripts, i.e., p_{ij}. For example, if $\boldsymbol{A}$ and $\mathbf{B}$ are two J by K matrices, so that $\boldsymbol{A}$ and $\mathbf{B}$ have the same number of rows and the same number of columns, then their sum, $\boldsymbol{A} + \mathbf{B}$, is well defined and has as its $(j,\ k)$-element, the value $a_{jk} + b_{jk}$. Similarly, if c is a number (scalar) and $\boldsymbol{A}$ is a matrix, then the product $c\boldsymbol{A}$ is well defined, and has as its $(j,\ k)$-element the value, ca_{jk}. For example, $2\boldsymbol{A}$ is a matrix whose entries are two times the corresponding entries of $\boldsymbol{A}$.

The conventions for multiplying matrices introduce new complexities, but they provide convenient ways to describe important calculations in a compact way. At first, one might think that the product of $\boldsymbol{A}$ and $\mathbf{B}$ should be the coordinate-wise product, $a_{jk}b_{jk}$, in analogy with the matrix sum, $a_{jk} + b_{jk}$. However, while the coordinate-wise product does have some uses, we don't need it in this book. The *matrix product* of two matrices, $\boldsymbol{A}\mathbf{B}$, is defined in a special way that has its roots in the interpretation of a matrix as a linear operator on a vector space (however, linear operators play no direct role in this book). If $\mathbf{C} = \boldsymbol{A}\mathbf{B}$, then the $(j,\ k)$-element of $\mathbf{C}$ is defined as

$$c_{jk} = \sum_{l=1}^{L} a_{jl}b_{lk}. \tag{D.1}$$

In order for (D.1) to make sense, $\boldsymbol{A}$ has to be a J by L matrix and $\mathbf{B}$ must be an L by K matrix. Thus, the number of columns of $\boldsymbol{A}$ must equal the number of rows of $\mathbf{B}$. When this happens, $\boldsymbol{A}$ and $\mathbf{B}$ are said to be *conformable*, and their matrix product is well defined. Note that the result of a matrix product is a matrix whose shape may be different from the shape of either $\boldsymbol{A}$ or $\mathbf{B}$.

While the definition in (D.1) may be surprising at first, the "sum of products" rule describes many different calculations in mathematics and statistics.

An important property of this definition of matrix product, is that it does not have to be *commutative*, i.e., $\boldsymbol{A}\mathbf{B} = \mathbf{B}\boldsymbol{A}$. Ordinary numerical multiplication of numbers is commutative, but matrix multiplication need not be. It is even possible for $\boldsymbol{A}\mathbf{B}$ to be defined, but $\mathbf{B}\boldsymbol{A}$ not to be. For example, if $\boldsymbol{A}$ is 4 by 2 and $\mathbf{B}$ is 3 by 4, $\boldsymbol{A}\mathbf{B}$ is not well defined as a product according to (D.1), while the product $\mathbf{B}\boldsymbol{A}$ does make sense. Checking for the conformability of matrices in a complex product is a good way to see if the matrix algebra is correct.

Vectors. A vector is a matrix with either one row or one column. Thus, a *row* vector is a 1 by K matrix, and a *column* vector, is a J by 1 matrix. The *length* of a vector is the number of elements it has. A number or *scalar* is a 1 by 1 matrix, but in matrix multiplication we always treat a 1 by 1 matrix as a scalar rather than a matrix so that a scalar times a matrix is always a "conformable" product, i.e., $c(a_{ij}) = (ca_{ij})$, as indicated above.

We adopt the common convention that unless otherwise specified, a *vector* means a *column* vector. This means that whenever a vector is multiplied by a matrix, the vector, $\boldsymbol{v}$, appears to the right of the matrix, $\boldsymbol{A}$, i.e., $\boldsymbol{A}\boldsymbol{v}$. If a vector multiplies a matrix on the left, i.e., $\boldsymbol{w}\boldsymbol{A}$, then $\boldsymbol{w}$ has to be a row vector, or if $\boldsymbol{w}$ is a column vector, then $\boldsymbol{A}$ must be a row vector in order for $\boldsymbol{w}\boldsymbol{A}$ to be conformable. A *J-vector* refers to a row or column vector of length J.

Matrix Transpose. An important operation on a matrix is *transposition.* The *transpose* of $\boldsymbol{A}$, denoted by $\boldsymbol{A}^t$, has the same entries as $\boldsymbol{A}$ has except that the rows and columns are interchanged. The $(j,\, k)$ entry of $\boldsymbol{A}^t$ is a_{kj}. Hence, if $\boldsymbol{A}$ is J by K, then $\boldsymbol{A}^t$ is K by J. Taking the transpose of a transpose leads us back to the same matrix, $(\boldsymbol{A}^t)^t = \boldsymbol{A}$.

The other operations on matrices work in the following way with matrix transposition.

$$(c\boldsymbol{A})^t = c\boldsymbol{A}^t; \quad (\boldsymbol{A}+\mathbf{B})^t = (\boldsymbol{A}^t + \mathbf{B}^t); \quad \text{and} \quad (\boldsymbol{A}\mathbf{B})^t = \mathbf{B}^t\boldsymbol{A}^t. \tag{D.2}$$

Note that the last part of (D.2) insures that the product on the right-hand side of the equation is conformable if the one on the left-hand side is.

The transpose of a column vector is a row vector, and conversely. If $\boldsymbol{v}$ is J by 1 then $\boldsymbol{v}^t$ is 1 by J. The transpose of a scalar is itself.

The *inner product* of two vectors of the same length, $\boldsymbol{v}$ and $\boldsymbol{w}$, is the scalar, $\boldsymbol{v}^t\boldsymbol{w} = \boldsymbol{w}^t\boldsymbol{v}$. The inner product of a vector with itself, $\boldsymbol{v}^t\boldsymbol{v}$, is the sum of squares of its elements, or its *squared Euclidean length,* also denoted in this book by $||\boldsymbol{v}||^2$. Along these lines, it is sometimes convenient to denote the sum of the elements of a vector by $\mathbf{1}^t\boldsymbol{v}$, where $\mathbf{1}$ denotes a vector of all 1's. We use this trick in this book to denote the column sums of bivariate score probabilities, i.e., $\mathbf{1}^t\boldsymbol{p}_k$, where $\boldsymbol{p}_k$ denotes the kth column of $\mathbf{P}$. The *outer product,* $\boldsymbol{v}\boldsymbol{w}^t$, of a J-vector $\boldsymbol{v}$ and a K vector $\boldsymbol{w}$, is a J by K matrix, whose entries have the form $v_j w_k$. More generally, an outer product is the matrix product of column vector times a row vector, in that order.

Square Matrices. A *square matrix* is one that is J by J, with the same number of rows as columns. Examples of square matrices that arise in this book are the covariance matrices of vectors of score probabilities. If $\boldsymbol{r}$ is an estimated J-vector of score probabilities (and therefore a random vector with a distribution determined by the variability of sampling), its covariance matrix, $\boldsymbol{\Sigma}_{rr}$, is a J by J matrix of the covariances of the entries of $\boldsymbol{r}$. If $\boldsymbol{r}$ and $\boldsymbol{s}$ are two estimated score probability vectors, then their covariance matrix, $\boldsymbol{\Sigma}_{rs}$, need not be square, unless $\boldsymbol{r}$ and $\boldsymbol{s}$ are of the same length. Another important square matrix is the K by K *identity matrix,* $\mathbf{I}_K$, whose $(j,\, k)$-element is 0 unless $j = k$, when it is 1.

An important property of the identity matrix is that when it multiplies another conformable vector or matrix it does not change it, so that $\mathbf{I}_K\boldsymbol{v} = \boldsymbol{v}$, and $\boldsymbol{A}\mathbf{I}_K = \mathbf{I}_J\boldsymbol{A} = \boldsymbol{A}$, for any K-vector $\boldsymbol{v}$, or J by K matrix, $\boldsymbol{A}$.

Partitioned Matrices. When a given matrix can be viewed as having elements that are themselves matrices it is called a *partitioned* matrix. The component matrices are called the *matrix blocks* of the partitioned matrix. Partitioned matrices arise in several ways in this book. For example, any matrix may be viewed as partitioned by its column vectors. A bivariate J by K score probability matrix, $\mathbf{P}$, can be viewed as the partitioned matrix,

$$\mathbf{P} = (\boldsymbol{p}_1,\, \boldsymbol{p}_2,\, \ldots,\, \boldsymbol{p}_K), \tag{D.3}$$

where, $\boldsymbol{p}_k$ is the kth column of $\mathbf{P}$. $\boldsymbol{p}_k$ is a J-vector, and $\mathbf{P}$ has K of them.

We can combine two estimated score probability vectors, $\boldsymbol{r}$ and $\boldsymbol{s}$, into a single column vector, in the following way, as $\boldsymbol{v} = (\boldsymbol{r}^t, \boldsymbol{s}^t)^t$. In this representation, $\boldsymbol{r}$ and $\boldsymbol{s}$ are the matrix blocks of $\boldsymbol{v}$. It is a good exercise to check that $\boldsymbol{v}$ is a column vector, with $\boldsymbol{r}$ stacked over $\boldsymbol{s}$.

The joint covariance matrix of $\boldsymbol{v} = (\boldsymbol{r}^t, \boldsymbol{s}^t)^t$ inherits a partitioned form from the blocks that make up $\boldsymbol{v}$. It is

$$\boldsymbol{\Sigma}_v = \begin{pmatrix} \boldsymbol{\Sigma}_{rr} & \boldsymbol{\Sigma}_{rs} \\ \boldsymbol{\Sigma}_{sr} & \boldsymbol{\Sigma}_{ss} \end{pmatrix} = \begin{pmatrix} J \text{ by } J, & J \text{ by } K \\ K \text{ by } J, & K \text{ by } K \end{pmatrix}. \tag{D.4}$$

The two matrices $\mathbf{M}$ and $\mathbf{N}$, used for SG and CB Designs, are also examples of partitioned matrices (see (2.9) and (2.10). Another, reoccurring example of matrix partitioning in this book is the partitioning of the $\mathbf{C}$-matrix from a bivariate log-linear model used in pre-smoothing. The $\mathbf{C}$-matrix from such a pre-smoothing in the case of the NEAT Design, is a JL by T_P matrix, $\mathbf{C}_P$, where the bivariate smoothing is for a J by L matrix of bivariate score probabilities, $\mathbf{P}$, and T_P is the number of parameters fit in the log-linear model. In this case, $\mathbf{C}_P$ can be partitioned into a series of J by T_P matrix blocks, $\{\mathbf{C}_{Pl}\}$, in the form

$$\mathbf{C}_P = \begin{pmatrix} \mathbf{C}_{P1} \\ \vdots \\ \mathbf{C}_{PL} \end{pmatrix}. \tag{D.5}$$

Partitioned matrices that are *blockwise conformable* may be multiplied together treating the blocks as matrix entries, as for example,

$$\begin{pmatrix} \boldsymbol{A}_{11} & \boldsymbol{A}_{12} & \boldsymbol{A}_{13} \\ \boldsymbol{A}_{21} & \boldsymbol{A}_{22} & \boldsymbol{A}_{23} \end{pmatrix} \begin{pmatrix} \mathbf{B}_{11} \\ \mathbf{B}_{21} \\ \mathbf{B}_{31} \end{pmatrix} = \begin{pmatrix} \boldsymbol{A}_{11}\mathbf{B}_{11} + \boldsymbol{A}_{12}\mathbf{B}_{21} + \boldsymbol{A}_{13}\mathbf{B}_{31} \\ \boldsymbol{A}_{21}\mathbf{B}_{11} + \boldsymbol{A}_{22}\mathbf{B}_{21} + \boldsymbol{A}_{23}\mathbf{B}_{31} \end{pmatrix}. \tag{D.6}$$

Blockwise conformable means that $\boldsymbol{A}_{jl}$ and $\mathbf{B}_{lk}$ must be conformable for each j and k. This sort of notation can simplify formulas with several subscripts.

Vectorizing a Matrix. *Vectorizing* a matrix repositions its elements by stacking the *columns* of the matrix on top of each other to form a long column vector. In this book we denote vectorizing $\mathbf{P}$ by $v(\mathbf{P})$, another notation for this, used elsewhere, is vec($\mathbf{P}$) (see Searle, 1982, for example):

$$v(\mathbf{P}) = \begin{pmatrix} \boldsymbol{p}_1 \\ \vdots \\ \boldsymbol{p}_K \end{pmatrix}, \tag{D.7}$$

where $\boldsymbol{p}_k$ denotes the kth column of $\mathbf{P}$.

When we vectorize a matrix of bivariate score probabilities in this book, we do so in order to have the same matrix notation work for both univariate and bivariate log-linear models. A consequence of these vectorizings is that the $\mathbf{C}$-matrices may then be partitioned in the same way as indicated in (D.5).

Some Examples of Matrix Calculations. Interesting examples of matrix calculations arose in our development of the software needed to calculate the SEE's and SEED's for the various equating designs and equating methods described in this book. In developing software, it is very useful to have intermediate checks on the values of the quantities that are being computed, and in many circumstances there is no way to directly check calculations other than to show that they satisfied certain properties that can be derived for them. To illustrate what we mean, consider this example. The covariance matrix of an estimated probability vector, say, $\boldsymbol{r}$, must satisfy an interesting property that is easy to explain. The sum of the elements of $\boldsymbol{r}$ must be 1, because it is a probability vector. We can denote this as

$$\mathbf{1}^t\boldsymbol{r} = 1, \tag{D.8}$$

where $\mathbf{1}^t$ denotes a row vector of all 1's of the appropriate length. Thus, the variance of the sum of the elements of $\boldsymbol{r}$ must be zero because $\mathbf{1}^t\boldsymbol{r}$ is always the same value, 1. If the covariance matrix of $\boldsymbol{r}$ is $\boldsymbol{\Sigma}_{rr}$, then from (D.8) we can establish the following series of equations using what we have reviewed in the earlier sections of this appendix.

$$\begin{aligned} 0 &= \text{Var}(\mathbf{1}^t\boldsymbol{r}) = \mathbf{1}^t\boldsymbol{\Sigma}_{rr}\mathbf{1} \\ &= \mathbf{1}^t\mathbf{C}_r(\mathbf{C}_r)^t\mathbf{1} = \mathbf{1}^t\mathbf{C}_r(\mathbf{1}^t\mathbf{C}_r)^t = \|\, \mathbf{1}^t\mathbf{C}_r \,\|^2. \end{aligned} \tag{D.9}$$

In (D.9), we have used the basic rule for calculating the variance of a linear combination of random variables (i.e., $\mathbf{1}^t\boldsymbol{r}$) from the joint covariance matrix (i.e., $\boldsymbol{\Sigma}_{rr}$). We also use the "$\mathbf{C}$-matrix" factorization of the asymptotic covariance matrix of an estimated probability vector from a log-linear model, as discussed in Chapter 3. We conclude from (D.9) that the length of the vector, $\mathbf{1}^t\mathbf{C}_r$ is 0, and hence that $\mathbf{1}^t\mathbf{C}_r$ is the zero vector, i.e.,

$$\mathbf{1}^t\mathbf{C}_r = \mathbf{0}. \tag{D.10}$$

Equation (D.10) provides a very nice check on the results of programs that are designed to compute $\mathbf{C}$-matrices. It says that $\mathbf{C}$-matrices must have entries that sum to 0 down each of their columns.

Once we have the result in (D.10), we can apply it to a variety of other matrices that arise in the calculations of SEE's and SEED's. For example, all of the "$\mathbf{U}$ and $\mathbf{V}$" matrices that are given in Tables 5.5 and 5.6 in Chapter 5 also have the property that their column sums are always zero.

For example, from Table 5.5, consider the matrix

$$\mathbf{U} = \sum_k \mathbf{C}_{Pk}. \tag{D.11}$$

$\mathbf{U}$ arises in the analysis of the SG Design. It is a sum of the matrix blocks, $\mathbf{C}_{Pk}$, that come from the $\mathbf{C}$-matrix, $\mathbf{C}_P$, that is associated with the bivariate score probability matrix, $\mathbf{P}$ (see Section 2.2). Because $\mathbf{C}_P$ is a $\mathbf{C}$-matrix, its column sums are all 0 so that

$$\mathbf{1}^t\mathbf{U} = \mathbf{1}^t \sum_k \mathbf{C}_{Pk} = \sum_k \mathbf{1}^t\mathbf{C}_{Pk} = \mathbf{0}. \tag{D.12}$$

Similar equations hold for the other $\mathbf{U}$ and $\mathbf{V}$ matrices in Table 5.5, and we urge readers to check this by mimicking the calculations we did for (D.9) and (D.12).

As a final example of these types of matrix calculations, consider the matrix $\mathbf{U}_R$ defined in Table 5.6, for the NEAT Design. We will show that $\mathbf{1}^t\mathbf{U}_R = \mathbf{0}$, too. To do this, we write $\mathbf{U}_R$ as

$$\mathbf{U}_R = \sum_l (w+(1-w)(t_{Ql}/t_{Pl}))\mathbf{C}_{Pl} - (1-w)\sum_l (t_{Ql}/t_{Pl})t_{Pl}^{-1}\boldsymbol{p}_l\boldsymbol{v}_{Pl}^t, \tag{D.13}$$

where $\boldsymbol{v}_{Pl}^t = \mathbf{1}^t\mathbf{C}_{Pl}$ from the definitions of the entries in Table 5.6.

When we form $\mathbf{1}^t\mathbf{U}_R$ using(D.13) we get

$$\begin{aligned}\mathbf{1}^t\mathbf{U}_R = &\sum_l (w+(1-w)(t_{Ql}/t_{Pl}))\mathbf{1}^t\mathbf{C}_{Pl} \\ &-(1-w)\sum_l (t_{Ql}/t_{Pl})t_{Pl}^{-1}\mathbf{1}^t\boldsymbol{p}_l\boldsymbol{v}_{Pl}^t.\end{aligned} \tag{D.14}$$

However, $\mathbf{1}^t\boldsymbol{p}_l = t_{Pl}$ so that (D.14) becomes

$$\mathbf{1}^t\mathbf{U}_R = \sum_l (w+(1-w)(t_{Ql}/t_{Pl}))\mathbf{1}^t\mathbf{C}_{Pl} - (1-w)\sum_l (t_{Ql}/t_{Pl})\boldsymbol{v}_{Pl}^t. \tag{D.15}$$

Finally, we use the fact that $\mathbf{1}^t\mathbf{C}_{Pl} = \boldsymbol{v}_{Pl}^t$ using the definitions of the entries in Table 5.6. This is all we need, because (D.15) now becomes

$$\mathbf{1}^t\mathbf{U}_R = w\sum_l \mathbf{1}^t\mathbf{C}_{Pl}, \tag{D.16}$$

which we have already shown to be $\mathbf{0}$ in (D.12).

Vector-Functions. Vector-valued functions of vectors, and operations on them, are tools that we have found very useful in deriving the theory in Chapters 3, 4 and 5. Vector-valued functions of vectors (or, *vector-functions*, for short) are transformations that map vectors into other vectors. Design Functions (DF's, see Chapter 2) are vector-functions. The

Design Function for Post-Stratification Equating in the NEAT Design is the most complicated DF that appears in this book. It is discussed in Theorem 2.1 of Chapter 2, and has these two components:

$$\boldsymbol{r} = \boldsymbol{r}\,(\mathbf{P},\,\mathbf{Q},\,w) = \sum_l \left[w + \frac{(1-w)(t_{Ql})}{t_{Pl}} \right] \boldsymbol{p}_l, \tag{D.17}$$

and

$$\boldsymbol{s} = \boldsymbol{s}\,(\mathbf{P},\,\mathbf{Q},\,w) = \sum_l \left[(1-w) + \frac{w(t_{Pl})}{t_{Ql}} \right] \boldsymbol{q}_l, \tag{D.18}$$

where $t_{Pl} = \mathbf{1}^t\boldsymbol{p}_l$ is the sum of the elements in column l of $\mathbf{P}$, and $t_{Ql} = \mathbf{1}^t\boldsymbol{q}_l$ is the sum of the elements in column l of $\mathbf{Q}$.

In (D.17), $w + [(1-w)t_{Ql}/t_{Pl}]$ is a scalar, while $\boldsymbol{p}_l$ is a vector, so that their product is a vector that is the same shape as $\boldsymbol{p}_l$. Thus, $\boldsymbol{r}$ in (D.17) is a sum of L vectors of length J, so that the result is also a vector of length J. In (D.17) and (D.18) we regard w as fixed so that the functions, $\boldsymbol{r}\,(\mathbf{P},\,\mathbf{Q},\,w)$ and $\boldsymbol{s}\,(\mathbf{P},\,\mathbf{Q},\,w)$, are nonlinear functions of $v(\mathbf{P})$ and $v(\mathbf{Q})$. The quantities, $\boldsymbol{r}\,(\mathbf{P},\,\mathbf{Q},\,w)$ and $\boldsymbol{s}\,(\mathbf{P},\,\mathbf{Q},\,w)$, are both vector-functions, whose arguments are the vectors, $v(\mathbf{P})$ and $v(\mathbf{Q})$. Below, we use (D.17) in an extended example.

Matrix Differentiation. The most complicated thing we do with matrices in this book is to *differentiate* vector-functions by their vector arguments. This is required when finding the Jacobian matrices of these transformations, and we make consistent use of Jacobian matrices in our development. To introduce the notion of matrix differentiation we first discuss differentiating a scalar-valued function of a vector, and then generalize to the case of vector-functions. We assume the reader is familiar with the elements of differentiating a function of several variables, i.e., partial differentiation (see, e.g., Apostol, 1957).

Scalar-Functions:. If $f(\boldsymbol{x}) = f(x_1,\,x_2,\,\ldots,\,x_K)$ is a real-valued function of the K-vector, $\boldsymbol{x}$, then we let $\frac{\partial f}{\partial \boldsymbol{x}}$ denote the 1 by K *row* vector whose kth element is $\frac{\partial f}{\partial x_k}$, the partial derivative of f with respect to x_k. Thus, $\frac{\partial f}{\partial \boldsymbol{x}}$ always denotes a row vector, even though $\boldsymbol{x}$ may be a row or column vector.

An example of the derivative of a real-valued function of a vector that occurs in this book is the derivative of the continuized cdf, $F(x;\,\boldsymbol{r})$ with respect to the elements of the score probability vector, $\boldsymbol{r}$ (see Chapter 5, Lemma 5.2). While the derivative of $F(x;\,\boldsymbol{r})$ with respect to x, $\frac{\partial F}{\partial x}$, is just the familiar density function of the cdf, $\frac{\partial F}{\partial \boldsymbol{r}}$ is a row vector whose elements are given by Lemma 5.2.

Vector-Functions:. Generalizing, if $\boldsymbol{f}(\boldsymbol{x}) = \boldsymbol{f}(x_1,\,x_2,\,\ldots,\,x_K)$ denotes a J-vector-valued function of the K-vector, $\boldsymbol{x}$, then $\boldsymbol{f}$ transforms the K-vector,

$\boldsymbol{x}$, into a J-vector, $\boldsymbol{f}(\boldsymbol{x})$. We regard $\boldsymbol{f}(\boldsymbol{x})$ as a column vector with real-valued coordinates, $f_j(\boldsymbol{x})$. Thus, to differentiate $\boldsymbol{f}(\boldsymbol{x})$ with respect to $\boldsymbol{x}$, we first differentiate each coordinate, $f_j(\boldsymbol{x})$ with respect to $\boldsymbol{x}$ and then place these row vectors on top of each other to obtain the J by K matrix $\frac{\partial \boldsymbol{f}}{\partial \boldsymbol{x}}$. The $(j,\ k)$-element of $\frac{\partial \boldsymbol{f}}{\partial \boldsymbol{x}}$ is $\frac{\partial f_j}{\partial x_k}$.

In order to get some experience with derivatives of vector-functions, we suggest readers familiarize themselves with the details of the following important results. It is best to start from the definitions we have given above and do the coordinates one at a time.

1. If $\boldsymbol{f}(\boldsymbol{x}) = \boldsymbol{A}\boldsymbol{x}$, a linear function, then $\frac{\partial \boldsymbol{f}}{\partial \boldsymbol{x}} = \boldsymbol{A}$.
2. If $\boldsymbol{f}(\boldsymbol{x}) = \boldsymbol{x}$, the identity function, then
$$\frac{\partial \boldsymbol{f}}{\partial \boldsymbol{x}} = \mathbf{I}_K, \tag{D.19}$$
the K by K identity matrix.
3. If $\boldsymbol{f}(\boldsymbol{x}) = \boldsymbol{a}$, a constant J-vector, then $\frac{\partial \boldsymbol{f}}{\partial \boldsymbol{x}} = \mathbf{0}_{J\times K}$, the J by K matrix of 0's.
4. If c is a scalar constant, then $\frac{\partial c\boldsymbol{f}}{\partial \boldsymbol{x}} = c\frac{\partial \boldsymbol{f}}{\partial \boldsymbol{x}}$.
5. If $\boldsymbol{f}$ and $\boldsymbol{g}$ have the same shape, then $\frac{\partial(\boldsymbol{f}+\boldsymbol{g})}{\partial \boldsymbol{x}} = \frac{\partial \boldsymbol{f}}{\partial \boldsymbol{x}} + \frac{\partial \boldsymbol{g}}{\partial \boldsymbol{x}}$.
6. If $f(\boldsymbol{x})$ is a scalar-valued function of the vector $\boldsymbol{x}$, and $\boldsymbol{g}(\boldsymbol{x})$ is a vector-function of $\boldsymbol{x}$, then
$$\frac{\partial(f\boldsymbol{g})}{\partial \boldsymbol{x}} = f\frac{\partial \boldsymbol{g}}{\partial \boldsymbol{x}} + \boldsymbol{g}\frac{\partial f}{\partial \boldsymbol{x}}. \tag{D.20}$$
(Note that the second term is an outer product so that it is a matrix of the same shape as $\frac{\partial \boldsymbol{g}}{\partial \boldsymbol{x}}$.) The formula in (D.20) is a generalization of the usual "derivative of a product" rule from ordinary calculus.

An Application of Matrix Differentiation. As we have indicated earlier, Design Functions (DF's) are examples of vector-functions that occur throughout our theoretical analysis of KE. The Jacobian matrices of DF's lead us naturally to the derivatives of such functions. To end this appendix, we will show how the differentiation of the DF for PSE in the NEAT Design can be done using the tools developed in this appendix. This is mostly an exercise in keeping the ideas and notation clearly in mind, but the thought of doing this analysis using the subscripted elements of the various vectors and matrices instead of using matrix notation is far more daunting. We will use the notation of Chapters 5, 10 and 11 in this derivation.

The DF specified by the vector-functions given in (D.17) and (D.18) maps the $(JL + KL)$-vector, $(v(\mathbf{P})^t,\ v(\mathbf{Q})^t)^t$, into the $(J + K)$-vector, $(\boldsymbol{r}^t,\ \boldsymbol{s}^t)^t$, where we use the "transpose-transpose" notation used earlier—the reader should check that both $(v(\mathbf{P})^t, v(\mathbf{Q})^t)^t$ and $(\boldsymbol{r}^t, \boldsymbol{s}^t)^t$ are appropriate column vectors. Using the notation of partitioned matrices, the derivative matrix of the vector-function from $(v(\mathbf{P})^t, v(\mathbf{Q})^t)^t$ to $(\boldsymbol{r}^t, \boldsymbol{s}^t)^t$ implied by any DF can be expressed as

$$\begin{pmatrix} \dfrac{\partial \boldsymbol{r}}{\partial v(\mathbf{P})} & \dfrac{\partial \boldsymbol{r}}{\partial v(\mathbf{Q})} \\ \\ \dfrac{\partial \boldsymbol{s}}{\partial v(\mathbf{P})} & \dfrac{\partial \boldsymbol{s}}{\partial v(\mathbf{Q})} \end{pmatrix}. \tag{D.21}$$

Hence, we need to compute the four matrix blocks in (D.21). We will do $\frac{\partial \boldsymbol{r}}{\partial v(\mathbf{P})}$ and $\frac{\partial \boldsymbol{r}}{\partial v(\mathbf{Q})}$ in detail because the other two are similar. By definition, $\frac{\partial \boldsymbol{r}}{\partial v(\mathbf{P})}$ is a J by JL matrix which has the form

$$\left(\frac{\partial \boldsymbol{r}}{\partial \boldsymbol{p}_1} \cdots \frac{\partial \boldsymbol{r}}{\partial \boldsymbol{p}_L}\right), \quad \text{where} \quad \mathbf{P} = (\boldsymbol{p}_1, \ldots, \boldsymbol{p}_L), \tag{D.22}$$

and $\frac{\partial \boldsymbol{r}}{\partial v(\mathbf{Q})}$ is a J by KL matrix which has the form

$$\left(\frac{\partial \boldsymbol{r}}{\partial \boldsymbol{q}_1} \cdots \frac{\partial \boldsymbol{r}}{\partial \boldsymbol{q}_L}\right), \quad \text{where} \quad \mathbf{Q} = (\boldsymbol{p}_1, \ldots, \boldsymbol{p}_L). \tag{D.23}$$

Thus, we need to calculate $\frac{\partial \boldsymbol{r}}{\partial \boldsymbol{p}_l}$ and $\frac{\partial \boldsymbol{r}}{\partial \boldsymbol{q}_l}$, which are J by J and J by K, respectively. Referring to (D.17)), we let

$$w_{Pl} = w + (1 - w)(t_{Ql}/t_{Pl}).$$

Note that w_{Pl} is a scalar-valued function of the lth columns of $\mathbf{P}$ and $\mathbf{Q}$ because it depends on the column sums, t_{Pl} and t_{Ql}, i.e., $t_{Pl} = \mathbf{1}^t \boldsymbol{p}_l$, and $t_{Ql} = \mathbf{1}^t \boldsymbol{q}_l$. Next, we simplify (D.17) and express $\boldsymbol{r}$ as

$$\boldsymbol{r} = \sum_l w_{Pl} \boldsymbol{p}_l,$$

and remember that when we differentiate $\boldsymbol{r}$ with respect to the elements of $\boldsymbol{p}_l$ the result for each term of the sum is 0 except for the lth term. Thus, we need to find

$$\frac{\partial \boldsymbol{r}}{\partial \boldsymbol{p}_l} = \frac{\partial (w_{Pl} \boldsymbol{p}_l)}{\partial \boldsymbol{p}_l} = w_{Pl} \frac{\partial \boldsymbol{p}_l}{\partial \boldsymbol{p}_l} + \boldsymbol{p}_l \frac{\partial w_{Pl}}{\partial \boldsymbol{p}_l} \tag{D.24}$$

from the rule in (D.20). But, from (D.19) above,

$$\frac{\partial \boldsymbol{p}_l}{\partial \boldsymbol{p}_l} = \mathbf{I}_J, \tag{D.25}$$

and,

$$\frac{\partial w_{Pl}}{\partial \boldsymbol{p}_l} = \frac{\partial}{\partial \boldsymbol{p}_l}\left(w + (1-w)\frac{t_{Ql}}{t_{Pl}}\right) = (1-w)t_{Ql}\frac{\partial}{\partial \boldsymbol{p}_l}\left(\frac{1}{t_{Pl}}\right). \tag{D.26}$$

Hence, we need to find, $\frac{\partial}{\partial \boldsymbol{p}_l}\left(\frac{1}{t_{Pl}}\right)$. But, using the usual rules for differentiation,

$$\frac{\partial}{\partial \boldsymbol{p}_l}\left(\frac{1}{t_{Pl}}\right) = -\left(\frac{1}{t_{Pl}}\right)^2 \frac{\partial t_{Pl}}{\partial \boldsymbol{p}_l}. \tag{D.27}$$

It is easy to see that for any $j = 1, \ldots, J$,

$$\frac{\partial t_{Pl}}{\partial p_{jl}} = 1. \tag{D.28}$$

From (D.28) it follows that

$$\frac{\partial t_{Pl}}{\partial \boldsymbol{p}_l} = (\mathbf{1}_J)^t. \tag{D.29}$$

If we put the above results together we find that

$$\frac{\partial \boldsymbol{r}}{\partial \boldsymbol{p}_l} = w_{Pl}\mathbf{I}_J - (1-w)(t_{Ql}/t_{Pl})(t_{Pl})^{-1}\boldsymbol{p}_l(\mathbf{1}_J)^t. \tag{D.30}$$

The right-hand-side of (D.30) is the difference between two J by J matrices, a useful check that we have kept track of the matrix dimensions correctly.

Next we turn to

$$\frac{\partial \boldsymbol{r}}{\partial \boldsymbol{q}_l} = \frac{\partial (w_{Pl}\boldsymbol{p}_l)}{\partial \boldsymbol{q}_l} = \boldsymbol{p}_l \frac{\partial w_{Pl}}{\partial \boldsymbol{q}_l}. \tag{D.31}$$

But

$$\frac{\partial w_{Pl}}{\partial \boldsymbol{q}_l} = (1-w)\left(\frac{1}{t_{Pl}}\right)\frac{\partial t_{Ql}}{\partial \boldsymbol{q}_l}. \tag{D.32}$$

And, $\frac{\partial t_{Ql}}{\partial \boldsymbol{q}_l} = (\mathbf{1}_K)^t$, as in (D.29), so that

$$\boldsymbol{p}_l\frac{\partial w_{Pl}}{\partial \boldsymbol{q}_l} = \boldsymbol{p}_l(1-w)\left(\frac{1}{t_{Pl}}\right)(\mathbf{1}_K)^t = (1-w)\left(\frac{1}{t_{Pl}}\right)\boldsymbol{p}_l(\mathbf{1}_K)^t, \tag{D.33}$$

which is a J by K matrix.

Hence, we may indicate the entries in the top "row" of (D.21) by

$$\left(\ldots, w_{Pl}\mathbf{I}_J - (1-w)\frac{t_{Ql}}{t_{Pl}}\frac{1}{t_{Pl}}\boldsymbol{p}_l(\mathbf{1}_J)^t, \ldots; \ldots, (1-w)\frac{1}{t_{Pl}}\boldsymbol{p}_l(\mathbf{1}_K)^t, \ldots\right).$$

Similar calculations (that the reader should supply) show that the "bottom" row of (D.21) is

$$\left(\ldots, w\frac{1}{t_{Ql}}\boldsymbol{q}_l(\mathbf{1}_J)^t, \ldots, ; \ldots, w_{Ql}\mathbf{I}_K - w\left(\frac{t_{Pl}}{t_{Ql}}\right)\frac{1}{t_{Ql}}\boldsymbol{q}_l(\mathbf{1}_K)^t, \ldots\right).$$

Putting these two pieces together finishes the job.

The matrix in (D.21) can be quite large. In the example of Chapters 10 and 11, it is a 158 by 5688 matrix. It is difficult to keep track of all these matrix entries without using the matrix notation illustrated here to simplify the bookkeeping. Computing all of the entries in (D.21), one coordinate at a time, is an exercise we gladly leave to others.

Bibliography

Agresti, A. (1990). *Categorical Data Analysis.* New York: Wiley.

Angoff, W.H. (1971). Scales, norms, and equivalent scores. In R.L. Thorndike (Ed.), *Educational Measurement* (2nd ed., pp. 508–600). Washington, DC: American Council on Education. (Reprinted as W.H. Angoff, *Scales, Norms, and Equivalent Scores.* Princeton, NJ: Educational Testing Service, 1984).

Angoff, W.H. (1987). Technical and practical issues in equating: A discussion of four papers. *Applied Psychological Measurement*, 11, 291–300.

Apostol, T.M. (1957). *Mathematical analysis. A Modern Approach to Advanced Calculus* Reading, MA: Addison Wesley.

Barndorff-Nielsen, O. (1978). *Information and Exponential Families in Statistical Theory.* New York: Wiley.

Bishop, Y.M.M., Fienberg, S.E., & Holland, P.W. (1975). *Discrete Multivariate Analysis: Theory and Practice.* Cambridge, MA: MIT Press.

Braun, H.I. & Holland, P.W. (1982). Observed score test equating: a mathematical analysis of some ETS equating procedures. In Holland, P.W. & Rubin, D.B. (Eds.), *Test Equating* (pp. 9–49). New York: Academic Press.

Brennan, R.L. & Kolen, M.J. (1987a). Some practical issues in equating. *Applied Psychological Measurement, 11*, 279–290.

Brennan, R.L. & Kolen, M.J. (1987b). Reply to Angoff. *Applied Psychological Measurement, 11*, 301–306.

von Davier, A.A. (2001). *Testing Unconfoundedness in Regression Models with Normally Distributed Variables.* Aachen: Shaker Verlag.

von Davier, A.A., Holland, P.W. & Thayer, D.T (2003). Population invariance. Paper submitted for publication.

Dongarra, J.J., Moler, C.B., Bunch, J.R., & Stewart, G.W. (1979). *LINPAK User's Guide.* Philadelphia: SIAM.

Dorans, N.J. (2000). Scaling and equating. In H. Wainer (Ed.), *Computerized Adaptive Testing: A Primer* (2nd ed., pp. 135–158). Hillsdale, NJ: Erlbaum.

Dorans, N.J. (2002). Recentering and realigning the SAT score distributions: how and why. *Journal of Educational Measurement, 39*, 59–84.

Dorans, N.J. & Holland, P.W. (2000). Population invariance and equitability of tests: Basic theory and the linear case. *Journal of Educational Measurement*, 37, 281–306.

Epperson, J.F. (2002). *An Introduction to Numerical Methods and Analysis.* New York: Wiley.

Fairbank, B.A. (1987). The use of presmoothing and postsmoothing to increase the precision of equipercentile equating. *Applied Psychological Measurement, 11*, 245–262.

Feldt, L.S. & Brennan, R.L. (1989). Reliability. In R.L. Linn (Ed.), *Educational Measurement* (3rd ed., pp. 105-146). New York: Macmillan.

Feuer, M.J., Holland, P.W., Green, B.F., Bertenthal, M.W., and Hemphill, F.C. (1999). *Uncommon Measures: Equivalence and Linkage Among Educational Tests.* Washington DC: National Academy Press.

Fienberg, S.E. (1980). *The Analysis of Cross-Classified Categorical Data* (2nd ed.). Cambridge MA: MIT Press.

Flanagan, J.C. (1939). *The cooperative achievement tests: A bulletin reporting the basic principles and procedures used in the development of their system of scaled scores.* New York: American Council on Education Cooperative Test Service.

Gulliksen, H. (1950). *Theory of Mental Tests.* New York: Wiley.

Haberman, S.J. (1979). *Analysis of Qualitative Data, Vol. 2, New Developments.* New York: Academic Press.

Hambleton, R.K., Swaminathan, H., & Rogers, H.J. (1991). *Fundamentals of Item Response Theory*. Newbury Park, CA: Sage.

Hanson, B.A. (1996). Testing for differences in test score distributions using log-linear models. *Applied Measurement in Education, 9*, 305–321.

Holland, P.W., King, B.F., & Thayer, D.T. (1989). *The standard error of equating for the kernel method of equating score distributions* (Technical Report 89–83). Princeton, NJ: Educational Testing Service.

Holland, P.W. & Rubin, D.B. (1982). *Test Equating*. New York: Academic Press.

Holland, P.W. & Thayer, D.T. (1981). *Section pre-equating: the Graduate Record Examination*. Program Statistics Research Technical Report No. 81-13, Princeton, NJ: Educational Testing Service.

Holland, P.W. & Thayer, D.T. (1987). *Notes on the use of log-linear models for fitting discrete probability distributions* (Technical Report 87–79). Princeton, NJ: Educational Testing Service.

Holland, P.W. & Thayer, D.T. (1989). *The kernel method of equating score distributions* (Technical Report No. 89–84). Princeton, NJ: Educational Testing Service.

Holland, P.W. & Thayer, D.T. (2000). Univariate and bivariate loglinear models for discrete test score distributions. *Journal of Educational and Behavioral Statistics, 25*, 133–183.

Holland, P.W. & Wainer, H. (1993). *Differential Item Functioning*. Hillsdale, NJ: Erlbaum.

Hull, C.L (1922). The conversion of test scores into series which shall have any assigned mean and dispersion. *Journal of Applied Psychology, 6*, 298–300.

Jarjoura, D. & Kolen, M.J. (1985). Standard errors of equipercentile equating for the common item nonequivalent populations design. *Journal of Educational Statistics, 10*, 143–160.

Keats, J.A. & Lord, F.M. (1962). A theoretical distribution for mental test scores. *Psychometrika, 27*, 59–72.

Kelley, T.L. (1923).*Statistical method*. New York: Macmillan

Kendall, M.G. & Stuart, A. (1977). The Advanced Theory of Statistics. Vol. I, 4th ed. New York: Macmillan.

Kennedy, W.J. & Gentle, G.E. (1980). Statistical Computing. New York and Basel: Marcel Dekker.

Kolen, M.J. (1984). Effectiveness of analytic smoothing in equipercentile equating. *Journal of Educational Statistics, 9*, 25–44.

Kolen, M.J. (1985). Standard errors of Tucker equating. *Applied Psychological Measurement, 9*, 209–223.

Kolen & Brennan (1987). Linear equating models for the common item nonequivalent populations design. *Applied Psychological Measurement, 11*, 263–277.

Kolen, M.J. & Brennan, R.J. (1995). *Test Equating: Methods and Practices*. New York: Springer-Verlag.

Kolen, M.J. & Jarjoura, D. (1987). Analytic smoothing for equipercentile equating under the common item nonequivalent populations design. *Psychometrika, 52*, 43–59.

Lehmann, E.L. (1999). *Elements of Large-Sample Theory*. New York: Springer-Verlag.

Linn, R.L. (1993). Linking results of distinct assessments. *Applied Measurement in Education, 6*, 83–102.

Liou, M. & Cheng, P.E. (1995). Asymptotic standard error of equipercentile equating. *Journal of Educational and Behavioral Statistics, 20*, 259–286.

Liou, M., Cheng, P.E., & Johnson, E.G. (1997). Standard errors of the kernel equating methods under the common-item design. *Applied Psychological Measurement, 21*, 349–369.

Livingston, S.A. (1993a). Small-sample equatings with log-linear smoothing. *Journal of Educational Measurement, 30*, 23–39.

Livingston, S.A. (1993b). *An empirical tryout of kernel equating ETS*. (Research Report 93–33). Princeton, NJ: Educational Testing Service.

Livingston, S.A., Dorans, N.J., & Wright, N.K. (1990). What combination of sampling and equating methods works best? *Applied Measurement in Education, 3(1)*, 73–95.

Lord, F.M. (1950). *Notes on comparable scales for test scores* (Research Bulletin 50–48). Princeton, NJ: Educational Testing Service.

Lord, F.M. (1955a). Equating test scores: a maximum likelihood solution. *Psychometrika, 20*, 193–200.

Lord, F.M. (1955b). A survey of observed test-score distributions with respect to skewness and kurtosis. *Educational and Psychological Measurement, 20*, 383–389.

Lord, F.M. (1980). *Applications of Item Response Theory to Practical Testing Problems.* Hillsdale, NJ: Erlbaum.

Lord, F.M. (1982). The standard error of equipercentile equating. *Journal of Educational Statistics, 7*, 165–174.

Lord, F.M. & Novick, M.R. (1968). *Statistical Theories of Mental Test Scores.* Reading, MA: Addison Wesley.

Marco, G.L., Petersen, N.S., & Stewart, E.E. (1983). A test of the adequacy of curvilinear score equating models. In Weiss, D.J. (Ed.), *New Horizons in Testing* (pp. 147–176). New York: Academic Press.

McAllister, P.H. (1993) Testing, DIF and public policy. In Holland, P.W. and Wainer, H. (Eds.) *Differential Item Functioning*(pp. 389-396). Hillsdale, NJ: Erlbaum.

Mislevy, R.J. (1992). *Linking Educational Assessments: Concepts, Issues, Methods, and Prospects.* Princeton, NJ: Educational Testing Service.

Morris, C.N. (1982). On the foundations of testing equating. In P.W. Holland & D.B. Rubin (Eds.), *Test Equating* (pp. 169–191). New York: Academic Press.

Otis, A.S. (1922). The method for finding the correspondence between sores in two tests. *Journal of Educational Psychology, 13*, 529–545.

Petersen, N.S., Marco, G.L., & Stewart, E.E. (1982). A test of the adequacy of linear score equating models. In P.W. Holland & D.B. Rubin (Eds.), *Test Equating* (pp. 71–135). New York: Academic Press.

Petersen, N.S. Kolen, M.J., & Hoover, H.D. (1989). Scaling, norming, and equating. In R.L. Linn (Ed.), *Educational Measurement* (3rd ed., pp. 221–262). New York: Macmillan.

Rao, C.R. (1973). *Linear Statistical Inference and Applications* (2nd ed.). New York: Wiley.

Rosenbaum, P.R., & Thayer, D.T. (1987). Smoothing the joint and marginal distributions of scored two-way contingency tables in test equating. *British Journal of Mathematical and Statistical Psychology, 40*, 43–49.

Rubin, D.B. (1980). Using empirical Bayes techniques in the Law School validity studies. *Journal of the American Statistical Association, 75*, 801–827.

Searle, S.R. (1982). *Matrix Algebra Useful for Statistics.* New York: Wiley.

Silverman, B.W. (1986). *Density Estimation for Statistics and Data Analysis.* London: Chapman and Hall.

Tapia, R.A. & Thompson, J.R. (1978). *Non-parametric probability density estimation.* Baltimore: Johns Hopkins University Press.

Thissen, D. & Wainer, H. (2001). *Test Scoring.* Mahwah, NJ: Erlbaum.

Thorndike, E.L. (1922). On finding equivalent scores in tests of intelligence. *Journal of Applied Psychology, 6*, 29–33.

Wilks, S.S. (1961). *Scaling and Equating College Board Tests.* Princeton, NJ: Educational Testing Service.

Author Index

Subject Index

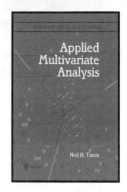

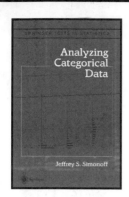

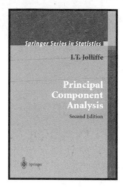